Educational Psychology
and Children

Educational Psychology and Children

K. LOVELL
B.Sc., M.A., Ph.D.

FOREWORD BY

P. E. VERNON
M.A., Ph.D., D.Sc.

HODDER AND STOUGHTON
LONDON SYDNEY AUCKLAND TORONTO

ISBN 0 340 17674 1 Boards
ISBN 0 340 17675 x Unibook

First published 1958
Eleventh edition 1973: fifth impression 1980
Copyright © 1973 K. Lovell

Printed and bound in Hong Kong for
Hodder and Stoughton Educational,
a division of Hodder and Stoughton Ltd,
Mill Road, Dunton Green, Sevenoaks, Kent,
by Colorcraft Ltd., Hong Kong.

FOREWORD

MANY is the time that I have been asked by a teacher, or a student in
training, to recommend a good general textbook of educational psychology,
and been unable to give an answer. There are of course plenty of excellent
American books. However, not only are these very expensive and—to
British readers—unnecessarily prolix, but also the American approach to
education differs in so many respects from our own that the books seem
quite unrealistic in relation to the children and the schools with which we
have to deal. In this country, educational psychology owes a tremendous
debt to William McDougall and Charles Spearman for their fundamental
writings on motives (instincts and sentiments) and abilities, respectively.
Possibly, however, their prestige has been so great that we have found it
difficult to progress much beyond the position to which they brought us
in the 1920's. The teacher who is interested in psychology is indeed aware
of some of the contributions of Burt, Thomson, Valentine and Schonell,
but it is doubtful if he or she has ever heard of Hull, Tolman, Lewin,
Thurstone, or Allport. The staffs of our Training Colleges were mostly
brought up on the textbooks of the 1920 vintage, and they tend to pass on
the same doctrine to their students, almost regardless of the vast amount
of investigation that has been carried out in the United States and elsewhere in recent years. True, these older textbooks show an admirable
sympathy with the English school-child and the English school-teacher's
problems; true also that a large proportion of American educational
writings and researches seem to yield nugatory rewards. Yet there is a very
real need for a more up-to-date book, which tries to give a balanced
picture of recent as well as of classical contributions; and this Dr. Lovell
has tried to supply.

Quite rightly, in my opinion, he has aimed primarily at students in
University Departments of Education and has credited them with the
inclination and the capacity to study fundamental theories and important
experimental findings. He does not gloss over controversies among psychologists, nor gaps in our knowledge. But though there is plenty of 'meat' in
the book, the topics that it covers have been chosen for their relevance to
children's development and to classroom learning. The book will be
valuable also to the more enterprising Training College students and
lecturers, and to practising teachers who wish to extend their acquaintance

with psychology. Dr. Lovell has used this material for several years in a Training College course, and is by no means unaware of what interests students, and what they can absorb. I hope that his book will do much to raise the standards of psychological knowledge among English educationists generally.

P. E. VERNON

PREFACE TO THE ELEVENTH EDITION

FURTHER fresh material and new references have been incorporated into the text. This continues the policy of keeping the book as up-to-date as possible.

K.L.

PREFACE TO THE FIRST EDITION

THIS book has been written to help teachers to have a better understanding of their pupils and of some of the problems which both of them face in school life. It is hoped that it will provide a comprehensive and up-to-date textbook for students preparing for the various Teachers' Certificate and Postgraduate Certificate Examinations; and for those commencing a course leading to a diploma or higher degree in Education in which Educational Psychology is included. To cater for the needs of these varying groups of students is a difficult task. It is also anticipated that it will serve as a source of reference to keen parents, to some members of the medical and nursing professions, social workers and all who are interested in educational psychology and children.

It is not pretended that any new material is presented in this book, but every effort has been made to encourage readers to study original publications by providing many references in the footnotes.

The author's thanks are due to his former tutor Professor P. E. Vernon, who kindly read the whole of the manuscript and made many valuable suggestions. He also saved the writer from many obscurities and repetitions, and whatever remains of these faults are the writer's sole responsibility. Thanks are also due to Dr. H. B. Cardwell for his advice on sentence structure and punctuation, and to Mr. H. S. Foster, of the University of London Press, for his interest and help in seeing this book through all the stages of its production. Finally, the author acknowledges the inspiration that he has received from Professor Sir Cyril Burt, Professor C. W. Valentine, and the late Professor Sir Godfrey H. Thomson—all very distinguished British psychologists of this century.

K.L.

CONTENTS

To
ANNE

Chapter One

INTRODUCTION

A definition of psychology. Before one can appreciate the value of educational psychology, it is first necessary to understand what is meant by the word 'psychology' itself. Aristotle, who lived over 2000 years ago, is generally regarded as the founder of the subject for his treatise *De Anima* (Concerning the Soul) marks the beginning of psychology as a separate study. Since his time, however, psychology has changed from being a study of the soul to being a study of the mind, then to being a study of consciousness, and finally it has become part of the study of human and animal activity. Today, psychology includes a study of the individual's behaviour and thinking from the time before birth, through maturity, to the declining years; it compares and contrasts the normal and abnormal, the human and animal. It interests itself in knowledge-getting activities like seeing, thinking and remembering, while it is equally concerned with emotional activities like laughing, crying, feeling happy and sad. Again, psychology is concerned with the study of the problem of creating and maintaining good relationships between management and labour in industry, the selection of personnel for various trades in H.M. Forces, the diagnosis and treatment of certain nervous conditions in children and adults, the giving of educational and vocational guidance to children, the intellectual and emotional changes which follow surgery or injury to different parts of the brain, the way in which human beings and animals learn, and with many other vital issues. Indeed, it is the application of psychology to practical problems of everyday life that has brought the subject so much to the notice of the general public.

Furthermore, whereas psychology in the past was mainly in the hands of philosophers, it is today in process of becoming a science. This means that it is increasingly using the methods, materials and apparatus of the physical sciences, and basing its theories not on opinion, but on experiment and careful observation. Psychology can thus be defined as a branch of that science which studies the activities of the organism (human or animal). The term 'activity' is used rather than the word 'behaviour', for the former has a wider meaning embracing both thought and behaviour. Other important branches of this science are physiology, which investigates the organs and cells which do the work of the organism, and sociology which, for human beings, studies the social behaviour of the many and varied groups of mankind.

Physiology, psychology and sociology are thus linked, and each gives its own picture of the activity of the individual. Strictly speaking, the term 'psychology' also includes a study of lower animals, but in practice when the word is used by the general public it always refers to the study of the activities of human beings.

The Divisions of Psychological Studies. It is important for those studying educational psychology to realise that they are studying only one division of psychology. In order to stress this, some of the branches of psychology are now briefly described:

(*a*) Normal Psychology is a study of the activities of normal individuals. It is true that normal individuals exhibit variations, but these must not be so great as to be classed as abnormal.

(*b*) Abnormal Psychology deals with the activities of abnormal individuals. It is especially interested in the mentally sub-normal, the insane, and those suffering from neuroses and behaviour disorders. The work in this field is undertaken by medical psychologists, who are called psychiatrists, or clinical psychologists who are psychologists without a medical qualification.

(*c*) Child Psychology studies the development of young children. The scientific study of the pre-school child has given a great impetus to this branch of the subject.

(*d*) Animal Psychology describes the behaviour of animals. It is a purely experimental branch and the experiments that have been carried out in connection with learning in animals have thrown some light on the way in which human beings learn. Some of our knowledge of the functions of different parts of the brain and the central nervous system has been gained through experiments with animals.

(*e*) Social Psychology is concerned with the way in which the thought and behaviour of the individual are influenced by the structure, customs and institutions of the group or society of which he forms a part. This term must not be confused with sociology, which is the study of human institutions and groups of all kinds.

(*f*) Applied Psychology is the application of the findings of psychology to the practical situations of life, e.g. to the grading of children in some school subject or to the design and layout of equipment in an aircraft cockpit.

These divisions are not the only ones that could be made, but they are the most important from the point of view of this book. Some branches of the subject, such as experimental or physiological psychology are really methods of studying psychology rather than divisions of the subject matter.

The scientific method in psychology. It was not until the middle of the last century that the scholars who had studied psychology realised the need for carefully observed facts. They relied on their own general impressions and felt, as many do today, that having observed people for years they must, of necessity, understand human nature and know the right answers to any questions likely to be asked. Then there followed the anecdotal period, when the need for definite facts was recognised but no systematic investigations were made. For example, in animal psychology or in the study of infants, the older study of psychology relied largely upon anecdotal method, that is on casual observations. These observations were sometimes made by untrained observers and reported secondhand. Anecdotes and general impressions derived from past experience are more than likely to give a distorted view of the facts in any controversial issue.

Again, in the days when psychology was regarded as a study of consciousness, introspection was the chief source of information about the mind. Psychologists mean by introspection, not morbid self-analysis but the observation of one's own mental states, as in joy or anger, or in reasoning. However, it soon became clear that introspection does not always yield consistent or verifiable results, and some psychologists today would exclude introspections altogether, believing them to be untrustworthy. This is taking an extreme view, for while more complex forms of introspection tend to be unreliable, better results are obtained if the circumstances are of a comparatively simple nature. For instance, most people will agree that when an illuminated electric light bulb is looked at for a short time and the eyes are then turned to a dark background, an 'after image' appears against the background. Furthermore, in conversation we accept a person's introspection if he says, 'I do not understand what you say'. Indeed, we cannot dispense with introspection in everyday life and there is no reason to exclude it completely in psychology.[1]

Generally, however, psychologists have decided that their subject must follow the lead of the physical scientists and make psychology an experimental science. Essentially this consists of deliberately setting up an experiment, or carefully noting phenomena which occur naturally, to get the facts concerning a process or activity that they are studying. From the observed facts, generalisations are made, which are then tested by experiments to see how well they will predict facts as yet unobserved. The experiment itself, and the testing of the generalisation, may take place in a psychological laboratory, a classroom or in a mental hospital. The following techniques are thus used in psychology today:

(a) The Designed Experiment.

In order to illustrate this approach, let us suppose that we wish to compare the value of two particular methods of teaching a certain topic. It might, for example, be posited that method A was better than method B. Let us also suppose that the investigator had decided to measure the efficiency of the methods by the amount of knowledge retained afterwards

---

[1] Introspective data is necessarily private, while objective data is public. For example, all, given sufficiently good eyesight, can examine a germ under a microscope.

by the pupils. First, it would be necessary to get two classes of children comparable in age range and in general ability. The teacher would then teach the first class using method A and the second class using method B, it being assumed that he is capable of teaching by both methods equally well. It would then be necessary to compare the improvement of both these classes with another group of children of the same age and general ability which, during the given period, was given no instruction at all in the topic. This third group is called a 'control group', for we have to make sure that the increase in knowledge in the two classes is, in fact, a real increase due to teaching and not a natural increase that would have occurred anyhow. Such control groups are very important in psychological and much other research. If, after these precautions, it was found that the class taught by method A had retained more knowledge than the class taught by method B, and it was found that the difference in the amount of knowledge retained was mathematically significant, then it could be taken that our hypothesis regarding the value of method A was correct.[2]

(b) The Developmental Method.

One of the tasks of the psychologist is to trace the development of thought and behaviour of the individual from babyhood to old age, and to note the effects which changing environments have on such development. Psychologists cannot, of course, give a child inadequate food or allow a child insufficient sleep to see how mental growth will suffer. He could do such things to animals, but with children he must find examples already occurring in the community and study them. The results obtained will not be as clear-cut as those obtained by experiment, but they will be the best obtainable in the circumstances. Thus, in the developmental method we observe and record the activities of children at various ages. This must be done carefully, for such records will not necessarily prove or disprove anything unless the observer makes his observations accurately, asks specific questions, and has clear theories to be checked by observation. Thus, if we wish, we can prove or disprove the hypothesis that most children stand erect for the first time without support at twelve months by carefully watching a large number of children passing through this stage of development. The work of tracing the activities of children is difficult but it has been undertaken by many skilled and scientifically-minded observers.

(c) The Case History Method.

In the true developmental method the psychologist actually observes the individual as the latter passes through various stages. Unfortunately, psychologists have to spend a good deal of their time studying children who are delinquent, or who display behaviour difficulties such as over-

---

[2] In practice, the design of the experiment would be much more complicated than that indicated. See Lindquist, E. F., *Design and Analysis of Experiments in Psychology and Education*. Boston: Houghton Miffin, 1953. Williams, J. D., 'Some Problems involved in the Experimental Comparison of Teaching Methods,' *Educ. Res.*, 1965, 8, 26–41. Lewis, D. G., *Experimental Design in Education*. London: University of London Press Ltd., 1968.

aggressiveness or intense shyness. Here an effort is made to get information concerning the child's heredity, family environment and early upbringing, as these may have a bearing on present behaviour. Often the case history is obtained at the Child Guidance Clinic, usually by a psychiatrist or a clinical psychologist aided by a social worker. It is possible that careful use of the method might reveal a relationship between certain conditions in childhood and specific types of behaviour in later life. It is regrettable that this method has been used a great deal with children and adults who are in some sort of trouble, and that it has been used but little with distinguished people and with ordinary folk who have lived useful and successful lives. We need to know more about the early upbringing of the latter. The method has disadvantages, of course, much like those of the anecdotal method; for when questioning a child or adult about the past, one is asking him to recall events which were not systematically observed in the first place. Nevertheless, the method seems to be the only one available at certain times, and has to be used, just as the doctor has frequently to use it in coming to a decision about a case of bodily illness.

These are the three main approaches used today in the study of the activities of individuals in relation to their environment. Now, since psychology is becoming a science and is using the scientific approach, it is necessary to point out certain limitations of science. There is no doubt that science has greatly improved the material conditions of mankind, and that biologists and psychologists have extended the scope of science and brought about a greater understanding of living things and of mental life. In consequence, many people believe that science will answer all our questions as well as bring about a material paradise. This former belief is certainly untrue, even if the latter is not.

Science is a positive study and not a normative one. That is to say, it is the study of facts as they are, and not as they ought to be. Science will not tell us which of several courses is the 'right' one from the moral point of view. Thus psychology concerns itself with the activities of an individual as they are, and is not concerned with judging qualities, values, or standards of behaviour from an ethical point of view. Again, science employs the inductive method, in that a number of generalisations or laws are derived from a limited number of observations and experiments. In psychology, for instance, the proper way to study the effects of physiological conditions on temperament is by the method of observation, interpretation and generalisation.[3]

The nature of Educational Psychology and its relevance to all concerned with the education of children. Educational psychology is an important branch of applied psychology. In this branch the laws and principles learned in

[3] For a clear and fairly easy treatment of problems associated with educational research see Lovell, K. and Lawson, K. S., *Understanding Research in Education.* London: University of London Press, 1970.

general psychology are applied to all manner of problems in the education and upbringing of children. A good deal of educational psychology, too, is concerned with getting a better understanding of the intellectual, emotional, social (and even the physical) growth of children—phenomena in which parents and teachers should be vitally interested. Educational psychology cannot, of course, solve all our problems about children, partly because no branch of psychology has yet become an exact science, and partly because science does not deal with values and judgments.

Teachers, especially, cannot afford to overlook this branch of psychology, as such knowledge will help to increase their efficiency. To be a successful teacher one is forced to be a successful psychologist, and a study of educational psychology involves an attempt to add the experience of research workers in the field of education to that obtained by personal experience. Such a study does not necessarily change a person not already interested in children, but it can greatly assist in making the teacher aware of some of his problems and help him to solve them. It can, for example, suggest to him methods, other than those that occur to him as a result of his own acumen, which will save time and effort in learning on the part of his pupils, and suggest ways of dealing with backward children. The study of educational psychology has brought about the recognition that people have differing abilities, contradicting the assumption of individual similarity which was the basis of 'payment by results' in the last century.

Most of this book will deal with normal children. Some aspects of abnormal behaviour must be mentioned, but it must be clearly stated that, although it is the duty of teachers and parents to be able to recognise unusual behaviour, it is not their job to attempt to treat such conditions other than in their strict capacity as teacher or parent. Further, many people acquire from the press and the commercial psychological magazines, a lot of information on the more sensational aspects of psychology. Some mention, therefore, must be made of abnormal behaviour and of unconscious processes, in order that these topics may be placed in their proper perspective.

Teachers should know something of the uses, and especially the limitations of the commoner psychological tests devised for assessing capacity or attainment in school work. This should include a study of the assessment of general intelligence (perhaps better termed academic aptitude) and of personality traits. They ought to know enough about the reliability, validity, and standardisation of examination marks to be able to give assessments which are satisfactory in these respects. Again, since teachers are required to play some part in the allocation of children to different courses within secondary education, they should have clear ideas regarding the relationship of general and special abilities and the dangers which accompany any attempt to divide pupils rigidly into types. Other important topics on which the reader should be informed include:

(a) The value of motivation in learning,
(b) A study of the most effective methods of learning,
(c) The possibilities and limitations of the transfer of training,
(d) Conditions associated with juvenile delinquency,
(e) Emotional disturbance in children,
(f) Vocational guidance for school leavers.

This list mentions only a few of the problems in which our subject can be of help.

Today a knowledge of the meaning of the term Correlation Coefficient and of the mechanism of Heredity is necessary in order to understand many of the problems which arise in educational psychology. Accordingly the term Correlation Coefficient and the mechanism of Heredity are now discussed in order that the material which follows may be meaningful to the reader.

The meaning of the term Correlation Coefficient. An indispensable tool of the modern psychologist is a branch of mathematics known as statistics. It is often very important to know the significance of some result which has been obtained in an experimental investigation. For example, if an investigator found that girls scored less than boys on a mathematics test, he would use an appropriate statistical technique to see if the result was mathematically significant, i.e. whether it represents a genuine difference between boys and girls, or whether it might be an accidental characteristic of the particular groups investigated.

Probably one of the statistical techniques most frequently used in educational psychology is one known as correlation. In Chapter Twenty we shall show how a correlation coefficient may be calculated, but as these coefficients will be frequently used throughout the book, a simple explanation of the meaning of the term will be given here. The correlation coefficient, denoted by r, tells us the degree of agreement between two sets of scores or orders. It will range from $+1 \cdot 0$ if there is perfect agreement between the two sets of scores or orders, through nought if there is no agreement, to $-1 \cdot 0$ if there is complete disagreement. Thus, if we measure the lengths of the two legs of a number of men or women, it is found that the correlation coefficient between them is $\cdot 97$. In other words, for most people the lengths of their two legs are almost the same. On the other hand, the correlation coefficient between the intelligence test scores of the children, and the number of children in the family, is between $-\cdot 2$ and $-\cdot 3$, telling us that the more children there are in a family, the lower are likely to be their scores in an intelligence test.

If the coefficient of correlation is greater than about $\cdot 8$, the agreement between the two sets of marks or other variables is said to be rather high, whereas if the figure is between $\cdot 4$ and $\cdot 7$ the relationship may be called moderate. It is very important, however, to note carefully the following two points. First, one must make sure that the correlation coefficient obtained is significant in the sense that it denotes a real relationship and is not the result of a chance happening due to the particular group of children studied. Second, one must be extremely careful in interpreting the term. If it is found, for instance, that there is a positive and significant correlation between broken homes and delinquency among the children of such homes it would be quite wrong to assume, on that evidence alone, that broken homes cause delinquency. It might well be that a third agent causes both broken homes and delinquency in the children of such homes. A significant correlation coefficient certainly indicates that there is a connection between the two variables, but it does not in any way prove that one caused the other.

The mechanism of Heredity. Much has been said about the part played by heredity, as distinct from environment, in determining human thought and behaviour. If a child is stubborn and the same characteristic is present in one parent, is the trait in the child's personality due to his having inherited this trait, or is it due to the fact that he was brought up in a home where he saw many acts of stubbornness? The confusion and emotion which has surrounded the general question is not confined to laymen alone, but extends to scientists. A good deal of the literature in educational psychology between 1920 and 1935 was taken up with this heredity-environment quarrel. The problem had, naturally, some connection with politics. Those who maintained that heredity was all-important in deciding human activities were supposed to have the support of the 'right wing groups', while the environmentalists found more favour among the more 'liberal' or 'leftish' groups.

It is now generally recognised that in actual life neither heredity nor environment can be ignored, and that an organism is the product of both forces. In the chapters which follow, reference will be made to experiments which have been helpful in enabling scientists to estimate the parts played by heredity and environment in determining certain human characteristics. The general plan of these experiments is as follows. We can have several groups which differ in heredity but which differ but little in environment, and in this case we can estimate the effect of heredity with environment held constant. On the other hand, we can have groups which differ in environment but which differ but little in heredity, and from such groups we can work out the effect of environment. However, the problem of heredity is of such importance that we turn to the biological science of genetics in order to understand something of its mechanism.

Human Heredity. The human being begins as a single cell formed by the fusion of two separate cells, the ovum from the mother's ovary and the spermatozoon from the father's testes. This cell, the fertilised ovum as it may be described, is about 1/200th inch in diameter, and divides into two cells, then into four, then into eight and so on up to billions of cells which go to make up the body. These cells develop differently, some becoming nerve cells, some muscle cells, while others form bone and supporting tissue. All these cells contain a *nucleus* derived by division from the nucleus of the fertilised egg, and they are all equivalent one to another in carrying hereditary factors bequeathed by the mother and father to the first nucleus of the fertilised egg. Thus, a child's heredity or genetic content pervades his whole being, since it is present in the nucleus of every cell, and is determined at the moment of fertilisation equally from both parents.

Each cell nucleus contains twenty-three pairs of thread-like structures called chromosomes, apart from the sex cells (female ovum, male spermatozoon) whose nuclei each contain twenty-three single chromosomes. The ordinary cells in each parent, from which these sex cells are formed, contain twenty-three pairs of chromosomes, and during the formation of the sex cells, members of pairs of chromosomes separate one from the other into the resultant nuclei independently of the separation of the members of other pairs. Thus the sex cells contain a random collection of twenty-three chromosomes of an original set of twenty-three pairs. It can be seen, therefore, that when an ovum is fertilised by a spermatozoon from another individual, the random collection of twenty-three pairs formed is unique to the individual that results from that particular conception. Thus, except in the instance of identical twins (to be discussed later) an individual is unique in his complement of hereditary factors.

Each chromosome carries lengthwise, groups of complex molecules of deoxyribonucleic acid (DNA) called genes. The latter are associated with the way in which information is coded for genetic purposes, that is, for the purpose of influencing, say, growth, intelligence, temperament and so forth. Some human characteristics seem to be more influenced by heredity than others, although the environment in which the child is reared usually interacts with heredity to yield the traits which we see the individual display. Thus within a given environment a certain percentage of the variability in 'intelligence' or 'temperament', etc., is due to heredity (genotype), some other percentage due to environment, and a third percentage due to genotype-environment interaction.[4] The more uniform the environmental conditions are, the greater is the percentage in the variability of human traits due to the genotype. Traits which are of interest to teachers such as emotional stability or intelligence, can be considered as due, in part, to many pairs of genes (polygenes) producing effects which are cumulative. Such traits are present in the child to a lesser or greater degree rather than being absent or present. It is also important to note that a parent may possess and transmit to his child genes which influence traits which he himself does not display.

The chromosome number in man is forty-six as stated above. Recent work has shown, however, that sufferers from a number of serious

[4] See also Lovell, K., *An Introduction to Human Development*. London: Macmillan, 1968, Ch. 1.

defects such as mongolism and leukaemia have an irregular number of chromosomes ranging from forty-five to forty-eight.

Identical and Fraternal Twins. Identical twins are exceptional in that each twin usually receives an assortment of genes exactly like that of the other. It happens in this way. The first two cells formed from the fertilised ovum part, and each forms an independent embryo. In other twins, two separate egg cells are fertilised each by a different spermatozoon at almost the same time. Such twins are called fraternal twins and as far as heredity is concerned they have no more in common than brothers and sisters.

Later in this book mention will be made of experiments in which heredity was thought to have been held constant, and an attempt made to establish the influence of environment in the case of intelligence, neuroticism, and in other studies of children. For such purposes identical twins have been studied. More recent work, however, has shown that the genes alone are not the only agents responsible for heredity, and it cannot now be assumed that heredity is completely held constant in the case of identical twins.

The inheritance of acquired characteristics. A question which greatly interests scientists is whether characteristics which have been acquired by parents during their lifetime can be passed on, genetically, to their children. For example, suppose a man has acquired special facility in speaking a foreign language, or in weaving, or in draughtsmanship, are such traits passed on to his children by the mechanism of heredity? As far as we can judge, the answer is no. Many attempts have been made to find evidence supporting the hypothesis that acquired characteristics are thus transmitted, but no clear confirmation has yet been found. With our present knowledge it would be difficult to see how such characteristics could be passed on by the genes, but one must not be over dogmatic in saying that such transference never takes place.[5] When some skill or trait is first noted in a parent and later in a child, what probably happens is this. The potentiality to do well in the skill was there in the parent all the time, and this potentiality was normally transmitted to the child so that he, too, does well in that skill, given the opportunity. Or, it may be that the child acquires the skill through watching his parent performing, or listening to his parents' conversation. Thus a parent can pass on knowledge and skill, also good and bad habits, by example and not by heredity.

The limitations of Psychology. It has already been clearly stated that psychology cannot answer many of the questions we would like to ask about human thought and behaviour, partly because it is not an exact science, and partly because it cannot deal with value judgments. Indeed,

[5] See Kushner, K., 'Environment and Heredity—1: The Soviet View,' *New Scientist*, 18th April 1962, 142–144; Waddington, C. H., 'Environment and Heredity —2: A Western View,' *New Scientist*, 18th April 1963, 45–147.

it is impossible to say at present if psychology will ever become an exact science. From time to time throughout this book different theories or models will be invoked to explain the same fundamental aspects of human thought and behaviour. Readers should, perhaps, be warned at the outset that more than one system or model can often be devised to explain some fundamental issue equally well (or equally poorly!). For example, it is likely that other theoretical systems could be erected which would cover the same ground as, say, the systems of Freud or Piaget,[6] and explain the relevant observations just as well. In other words, psychology often does no more at present than provide us with a useful set of concepts with which we can discuss major problems. At the same time, however, it can sometimes suggest possible solutions to our day-to-day problems. Moreover, it can often help us to discuss more objectively, such controversial questions as: What is the best age for starting school? Is it better to use more active, or verbal methods in teaching?[7]

[6] See McLaughlin, G. H., 'Psycho-Logic: A Possible Alternative to Piaget's Formulation,' *Brit. J. Educ. Psychol*, 1963, **33**, 61–67. He suggests that the level at which a child can reason can be inferred from his digit span, presuming this is equivalent to his memory span for concepts.

[7] See Rusk, R. R., *An Outline of Experimental Education*. London: Macmillan, 1960, Chapters 7 and 8.

Chapter Two

MOTIVATION

THE first main topic to be discussed in this book is that of human motivation. By this we mean the drive, energy, or degree of activity that an individual displays.[1] Psychologists used to concern themselves mainly with subjects like sensation and memory, all of which are involved in the process of obtaining and using knowledge. But in this century they have become increasingly interested in the motivation of human behaviour. In straightforward practical terms, we may say that today psychologists are not only concerned with differences in intellectual abilities (in learning capacity, for example), but are also vitally interested in why it is that one child works hard at many different tasks and persists in face of difficulty, while another is rather lazy at school, has few interests, and tends to quit in the face of frustration. Of course, it is not only among children that we find individuals who are poorly motivated; the problem of the motivation of students in colleges and universities and of workers in industry is also of considerable practical consequence. Indeed, a study of the basic motives which underlie human behaviour is of the greatest importance. However, there are no really satisfactory answers, as yet, to many of the questions that can be raised in this field.[2]

Contemporary theories of motivation.
Instinct theory. Probably the most popular theory about human motivation is that known as instinct theory. Burt[3] broadly defines an instinct as a complex inherited tendency, common to all members of a species, compelling each individual (i) to perceive and pay attention to certain objects and situations, (ii) to become pleasurably or unpleasurably excited about those objects when they are perceived, and (iii) thereupon to act in a way likely in the long run to preserve the individual. Many distinguished British psychologists have held the view that human behaviour is largely instinctive in origin and this view has been transmitted to many teachers and others interested in children by Burt, Nunn, Hughes and Hughes, Ross

[1] Motivation may be defined more formally as a psycho-physiological or internal process, initiated by some need, which leads to activity which will satisfy that need. We also have *incentives*, which are administered by external causes, and which often determine the nature and direction of human activity.
[2] A more advanced treatment has been provided by Hebron, M. E., *Motivated Learning.* London: Methuen, 1966.
[3] Burt, C., 'Is the Doctrine of Instincts Dead? A symposium, I—The Case for Human Instincts,' *Brit. J. Educ. Psychol.*, 1941, 11, 155-172.

and Valentine. Instinct theory has been, however, most closely linked with the name of McDougall (1871–1938) ever since he first published his book *An Introduction to Social Psychology* in 1908. In later editions he finally concludes that 'The human mind has certain innate or inherited tendencies which are the essential springs or motive powers of all thought and action . . .'[4] and lists the main instincts as parental instinct, escape, pugnacity, repulsion, gregariousness, self assertion and submission, mating, acquisitiveness, and a number of minor ones. He further argues that under the influence of intelligence and experience, the emotional[5] disposition linked with each specific instinctive tendency (e.g. fear with escape, disgust with repulsion, and so on) becomes organised into attachments to persons, objects or principles. These attachments are called sentiments of which the chief, according to McDougall, is the self-regarding sentiment. This may be defined as the concept or ideal of the self that often determines moral behaviour and will. It is these sentiments which bring order into our emotional life and tend to make our behaviour relatively consistent and predictable.

Instinct theory has been attacked by many American psychologists while in this country Vernon[6] has been among its critics. One of the general objections levelled against it is that many of the so-called instincts are not innate but are learnt by children soon after birth. Again, social psychologists have brought forward evidence suggesting that some behaviour regarded as instinctive can be accounted for by the influence of the customs and values of the group in which the child is reared. Yet another criticism is that made by Allport[7] who denies the possibility of deriving all motives from a list of inherited tendencies. He argues that during one's lifetime new motives arise and become self motivating,[8] although the given activity may remain the same. For example, a young person may begin to smoke cigarettes because he sees his contemporaries smoking; later he may continue to smoke because he has come to like it.

Supporters of instinct theory have, in return, replied to these and other criticisms, and there has been a revival of interest in it both in America and here. Thus some recent writers on personality refer to dispositional tendencies in much the same way as McDougall did. Further, the work of Tinbergen,[9] Lorenz and others in zoology, suggests that there are inborn

[4] McDougall, W., *An Introduction to Social Psychology*. London: Methuen, 30th Edition, 1950.

[5] Emotion is a 'moved' or 'stirred up' state of feeling in the individual linked with some tendency. There are physiological changes associated with each emotion, frequently of a muscular or glandular nature.

[6] Vernon, P. E., 'Is the Doctrine of Instincts Dead? A Symposium, II,' *Brit. J. Educ. Psychol.*, 1942, **12**, 1–10.

[7] Allport, G. W., *Personality. A Psychological Interpretation*. London: Constable, 1937.

[8] Allport uses the term *functionally autonomous* to describe these motives.

[9] Tinbergen, N., *The Study of Instinct*. London: Oxford University Press, 1951. See especially Chapters 2, 3, 4, 5 and 6. Also Lorenz, K. Z., *King Solomon's Ring*. London: Methuen, 1953.

patterns of behaviour in animals which appear before learning in any form occurs, and are triggered off by certain stimuli. Thus a specific 'sign stimulus' in the environment arouses an 'innate releasing mechanism' (I.R.M.). Or, the I.R.M. may be set off by internal conditions such as maturation of the central nervous system or hormones. But there is also evidence to suggest that the vicissitudes of the early environment may have a greater effect upon instinctive behaviour than has been supposed. For example, many birds do not appear to recognise their species instinctively, although they appear to have an innate predisposition to acquire this capacity. This learning takes place during a well-defined but very short period of time after the bird is hatched from the egg.[10] But if the bird is kept from other members of its species from birth, and sees only men during this critical period, then Man as a species becomes its 'object-fixation', and it behaves towards Man as it would normally do towards other members of its species. This phenomenon is termed *imprinting* and may be irreversible.[11] In human beings the problem of instinct seems to be even more complicated because of the remarkable plasticity of their behaviour.

Other psychologists do not claim as specifically as McDougall that certain tendencies are necessarily unlearnt. Thus F. H. Allport[12] talks of *prepotent reflexes*, Cattell of *ergs*,[13] Murray[14] and Maslow[15] speak of *needs*, Tolman[16] of *drives*, and Dunlap[17] of *primary desires*, and each puts forward his own list of suggested basic motives.

From the point of view of those responsible for the upbringing of young children the following conclusions should be borne in mind:

(*a*) There are many reflexes[18] present in the baby at birth, while other behaviour patterns emerge at fairly definite intervals (e.g. walking).

(*b*) Many instinctive tendencies subserve appetites of the body.

(*c*) All human beings have strong drives to self and race preservation—as do animals.

[10] Work by Thorpe suggests that some birds have their song patterns determined completely by heredity, while other birds (e.g. chaffinches) have their song patterns modified somewhat as a result of early upbringing in groups. See 'Learning in Man and Animals,' *Nature*, June 23, 1956.

[11] As far as the *following* response is concerned, it seems that in some birds the strength at which the response is maintained is related to anxiety. See Moltz, H., 'Imprinting: Empirical Basis and Theoretical Significance,' *Psychological Bulletin*, 1960 57, 219–314.

[12] Allport, F. H., *Social Psychology*. Boston: Houghton Mifflin, 1924.

[13] Cattell, R. B., *General Psychology*. Cambridge, Mass., Sci-Art Publishers, 1941.

[14] Murray, H. A., *Explorations in Personality*. New York: Oxford University Press, 1938.

[15] Maslow, A. H., 'A Theory of Human Motivation,' *Psychol. Rev.*, 1943, 50, 370–396.

[16] Tolman, E. C., 'Motivation, Learning and Adjustment,' *Proceedings of the American Philosophical Society*, 1941, 84, 543–653.

[17] Dunlap, K., *Civilised Life*. London: Allen and Unwin, 1934.

[18] A reflex action is an involuntary one, as for example, when the individual blinks at the sudden flashing of a bright light.

(d) That there are behaviour patterns in which these drives are expressed (e.g. various forms of aggressive behaviour or flight).

Psychoanalytic theory. Most readers will have heard some of the popular talk about psychoanalysts, especially of the work of such eminent investigators in the field as Freud (1856–1939), Adler (1870–1937) and Jung (1875–1961). Certain theories which they and other psychoanalysts have proposed are illuminating and plausible although many still remain unproven. True, a very welcome development in psychoanalysis has been the attempt to verify some theories experimentally.[19] To understand in a very simple and restricted way how psychoanalytic theory is said to explain human motivation, two terms, *unconscious mind* and *repression*, must first be explained. For some, the former implies mental tendencies and traces of past experiences which once acted in full consciousness. These affect our behaviour without entering consciousness although how they function is not clear; they may also come back into consciousness again, given the appropriate stimulus. But, for Freud, the unconscious mind consists mainly of repressed sentiments and has its foundation firmly laid in infancy. By repression is meant the exclusion of painful and unpleasant material from consciousness. Repression is thus a defensive mechanism; it is also an unconscious one, for the subject does not realise that he is repressing certain sentiments. As the infant grows up he soon realises that certain of his actions and feelings evoke disapproval in adults, and these forbidden impulses tend to be pushed out of consciousness by the mechanism known as repression. Adler and Jung also have their own slightly different views on the nature of the unconscious mind, but all agree that our behaviour is frequently influenced by motives and attitudes of which we are quite unaware, although such influences are said to be brought into consciousness by psychoanalytic techniques. Psychoanalysts have also made valuable suggestions concerning other defence mechanisms and some of these will be described in Chapter Four. Some think that all defence mechanisms, although they appear to be irrational, depend for their existence upon the fact that they reduce anxiety. Thus Symonds[20] has suggested that repression may be expressed in such behaviour as laziness, social withdrawal, secretiveness and indecision, all of which are of value to the individual in reducing anxiety.

Freud maintained that all unconscious impulses could be reduced to sex and aggression. Today this view is doubted. It is well realised that in most civilisations, impulses connected with sex and aggression are those which most frequently involve social restrictions and taboos, but today it seems doubtful whether aggression is a primary impulse or a reaction to frustra-

[19] See Farrell, B. A., 'Some Hypotheses of Psychoanalysis,' in *Experimental Psychology.* Oxford: Basil Blackwell, 1955.
[20] Symonds, P. M., *Dynamics of Human Adjustment.* New York: Appleton-Century, 1931.

tion, and it is now thought that there are additional unconscious motives which affect our behaviour.

Social theory. Social theory is of two kinds, the first of which may be called culture-pattern theory. Social anthropologists such as Mead, Gorer and Benedict have described correspondence between different methods of child-rearing and later behaviour patterns. For example, it is claimed that in a tribe where the children are shown much affection, where weaning is late, where there is no rigid discipline and where no high standards are maintained, they grow up into co-operative and generous adults lacking in aggression. In contrast, it is claimed that when children are denied attention, and are frequently thwarted and rebuffed, they grow up to be sly, or apathetic, or evasive, or bad-tempered individuals. Those who hold to this kind of social theory do not deny individual differences in personality necessarily, because (a) some personality characteristics are innate, and (b) each individual infant will be handled by a unique mother, different from all other mothers, and play with other children who have their own specific personalities. Thus each child will have a unique experience of upbringing but the general pattern will be the same.

This type of social theory, then, suggests that the behaviour of children brought up in different cultures will be affected by the differences in methods of upbringing practised by the different cultures. But, as some sociologists and social psychologists point out, there are always sub-cultural patterns within the total culture pattern connected, for example, with the type of work one is engaged in, or the social class to which one belongs, and so on. Thus the motivation and behaviour of an individual are likely to be shaped to some extent by his 'status' as boy or girl, husband or wife, farm labourer or lawyer, manager or employee. Generally, it is rather easier to accept social theory when considering tribal societies (although even here the thesis is not proven, as many have pointed out), than it is in a more complicated society such as ours, where there is a greater number of sub-cultural groups and where there is considerable social mobility. In the latter type of society, motivation and behaviour depend to some extent upon the actual social group in which we find ourselves at a particular time and upon the declared aims and accepted standards within that group. For example, it is trite to say that young men do not behave in a barrack room as they would in their own home, nor do girls having a midnight feast in a boarding school conduct themselves as they would when having tea at a friend's home.

This leads us at once to the second kind of social theory, which is termed *field theory*. The founder of psychological field theory was Kurt Lewin.[21] The fundamental notion is that the behaviour of an individual in a given situation is due to all the forces (i.e. the demands, attitudes,

[21] Lewin, K., *Principles of Topological Psychology*. New York: McGraw Hill, 1936.

sanctions, attractions, etc., of other individuals and groups) acting between the person and his environment, rather than to the properties of the individual as such. This theory is acceptable to some, although it must be remembered that the present condition of the person is one force influencing his motivation and behaviour, and this condition was brought about by all his previous experiences from birth affecting the inherited constitution.

Thus both kinds of social theory maintain that motivation is determined by the interaction of the organism with the environment. Culture-pattern theory stresses the effect of early upbringing, and field theory the total effect of all forces acting on the individual in the current situation.

Learning or Behaviour theory. Clark Hull[22] of Yale University and his associates proposed that, generally, all behaviour is dependent upon the needs[23] of the individual and that learning depends upon whether the individual's needs are satisfied and tension thereby reduced. If the behaviour of a person is such that his needs are not met, then the responses associated with that behaviour are not retained and the individual does not learn. Hull's theory has been criticised by many psychologists mainly on the grounds that learning does sometimes take place even when the individual is not rewarded, and that all behaviour is not necessarily motivated.

As far as the more social needs of children are concerned, that is, their need for attention, social approval and so forth, Hull was of the opinion that these are brought about by experience. His argument is that when the child is being fed and having his organic needs satisfied, he learns to associate certain social conditions with these physiological or primary needs. These social conditions are thus associated with the reduction of needs in the first place and ultimately become needs themselves.

Summarising the different points of view which have· been expressed, we may suggest:

(a) Some motives are widely recognised to be the result of physiological process. Thus Tolman when dividing his drives speaks of appetites (maternal drive, thirst, hunger, sex, general activity, exploration, rest, urination and defaecation, play) depending upon the chemistry of the body. Cattell when discussing ergs, talks of organic needs (air, water, avoiding pain, heat, cold, to urinate and defaecate) and tendencies which are organic (rest, food-seeking, mating, protecting young). Some of McDougall's tendencies, too (e.g. food-seeking), must rest on a physiological basis and it seems likely that tendencies having such a basis are innate.

(b) All theories of motivation admit an interaction between the organism

[22] Hull, C. L., *Principles of Behaviour*. New York: Appleton-Century, 1943.
[23] A need may be a primary one, e.g. food, or a necessary or acquired one, e.g. a liking for the theatre.

and the environment. McDougall specifically recognised that basic motives do not appear in crude instinctive form, but in the form of sentiments brought about by experience.

(c) There has been great argument as to whether the more social tendencies (e.g. assertion) are unlearnt or are brought about by training and experience. As yet this problem cannot be resolved in a satisfactory manner. Even if some of these social tendencies were inherited, it is certain that they would be markedly affected by the environment. The inherited constitution is being constantly modified by the environment from the moment of conception, and it is certain that training and experience will affect the social tendencies as it does the more organic ones. For example, cultural customs clearly affect the pattern of sexual behaviour.

(d) Most, if not all psychologists would agree that much of our behaviour is brought about by unconscious motives, but there would be less agreement about the validity of various defence mechanisms proposed by psychoanalysts.

It is also necessary to mention a physiological view of motivation. There is a group of ceaselessly active nerve cells in the brain stem which acts as an 'arousal system' and makes activity in the cerebral cortex possible. This group of cells is known as the reticular formation and there are different areas within it for different functions in respect of arousal. It seems that the 'arousal system' can be equated to the general 'drive' state of the organism; it controls the signals entering and leaving the cerebral cortex. The spontaneous activity of the reticular formation requires no external rewards because this motivation makes activity on the part of the organism 'self rewarding', i.e. it seeks activity for its own sake. This 'neurogenic activity motive' is likely to be the most important source of motivation in children under school age. They are thereby forced into active interaction with their environment.[24]

The concept of Competence. R. W. White[25] has proposed the concept of 'competence' to indicate the nature of the motivation when the child is active but not under the influence of tension reduction or discomfort. When the child is free of conflict but active in exploring, looking, running, imitating and so forth, White contends that the child is impelled by the need to establish his competence in handling his environment. The satisfaction for this comes from being able to bend the environment to one's will rather than from social approval or escape from discomfort.

[24] Hebb, D. O., 'Drives and the C.N.S. (Conceptual Nervous System),' *Psychol. Rev.*, 1955, **62**, 243–254. Madsen, K. B., 'Modern Theories of Motivation and Their Educational Consequences,' *Child and Education*. Copenhagen: Munksgaard, 1962.

[25] White, R. W., 'Motivation Reconsidered: the Concept of Competence,' *Psychol. Rev.*, 1959, **66**, 297–333.

Stott[26] proposes a rather similar notion. He suggests that much behaviour in young children can be accounted for by the hypothesis that the
child is attempting to demonstrate his effectiveness in controlling his
environment. The child constantly seeks new modes of effective action and
abandons any mode of handling his environment once it has been achieved
at the point of full mastery. Educational psychology may well have to pay
more attention to the neglected notions of White and Stott.

The motivation of children. In this section we want to outline some general
principles which will help to motivate children in school and in other day-
to-day situations. There has already been some discussion of the organic
needs of human beings, such as air and food. In school these organic needs
are rarely involved when we try to spur our pupils to make greater efforts.[27]
For example, a teacher never motivates children by means of hunger, and
rarely now by inflicting pain. Occasionally he makes use of organic motives
indirectly, as when he encourages an adolescent to work harder in order
to be in a favourable economic position to secure and support a mate. The
child himself is, of course, motivated (though not as a result of any effort
on the part of the teacher or other adult) in everyday situations by his
organic needs if he goes, say, to the pantry when hungry, or withdraws his
hand from a hot poker. It is rather to the child's social and intellectual
needs that teachers and parents usually appeal. Now there is no completely
satisfactory explanation of the origin of many of our needs, as we have
already said, nor is there any clear-cut list of what human needs actually
are. Nevertheless all children appear to need the approval of parents,
teachers and equals; to be loved; to achieve some success; to experience
stability of social relationships; to have some attention paid to them; to
be able to manipulate things and ideas; and to think well of themselves
(self-regarding sentiment). In addition there are certain other sources of
motivation more directly due to opportunity and environment, such as
the day-to-day interests of children and their long term interests and
hobbies. These are very powerful motives at times. Hence we suggest:

(a) Children will work harder at tasks when they feel the result is important to them, or that in some way the task measures their real worth as
persons. Thus, since academic aptitude is greatly valued in our culture,
most children try hard when they work at an intelligence test. Again, if
pupils are allowed to make suggestions and to contribute ideas, they will
generally feel more responsible in their attitude towards the task and think
that the outcome is dependent upon their efforts. Obviously such tactics
bring into play a certain amount of self or ego-involvement. While ego-
involvement acts as a powerful motive, it must be insisted that one must

[26] Stott, D. H., 'An Empirical Approach to Motivation,' *J. Child Psychol.
Psychiat.*, 1961, **2**, 87–113.
[27] Such primary needs as food, sleep and air must, of course, be met before good
school work can be expected from pupils.

be sure that it is used with discretion so that pupils will not meet continual failure or suffer undue anxiety.

(b) Children tend to exert themselves more when a standard of attainment has been set. In all probability, the child who cannot reach the standard feels a reduction in his own sense of worth, and feels that he is losing the approval of his teachers and equals. It is important that the target be set within the capacity of the children, providing they work hard.[28]

(c) Moderate competition among children seems generally to increase their output of work. Too much competition can bring about an unhealthy state of mind, but situations where each student is asked to compete against himself and increase his own score are very useful and generally harmless.

(d) Telling older pupils that a certain task is likely to contribute to success in life is likely to stimulate them. Success, of course, must be interpreted widely and must include both social and occupational life. Such success is likely to increase the degree to which others think well of one, to increase the chances of stability in social relationships, to attract the attention of others, to increase the chances of material rewards, to give greater opportunities to manipulate things and ideas, and to increase one's own sense of worth. Indirect use of organic needs can sometimes be made, as in the example that has already been given.

(e) Under the influence of basic motives and opportunities, experience and training, pupils develop strong interests (at certain ages) in, say, stamp collecting, dramatics, athletics and flying. These interests can act as very powerful motives and should be enlisted whenever possible.

Attention is also drawn to the following:

(a) Investigations into the relative effects of praise and blame, and of deterrents and incentives on children, have not produced clear findings. Sometimes one, and sometimes the other produces the better results depending, it seems, on the respective personalities of the pupil and adult, and on the adult-child relationships. The work of Johannesson[29] is important in this respect. He studied the effects of praise and blame on performance in mechanical and problem arithmetic among a large number of 10–11-year-old children drawn from forty-one classes in Stockholm. In respect of mechanical arithmetic he found that the praise of the teacher seemed to be of great importance to highly anxious pupils, to pupils with low self-reliance, and to pupils with negative attitudes towards the teacher. Repeated blame seemed to affect, adversely, the performance of the high scoring pupils, those who were highly anxious in the test situation and those with negative attitudes to the teacher. Pupils with low levels of

---

[28] If the goal is too remote, or cannot be clearly seen, activity ceases unless a substitute goal is found.

[29] Johannesson, I., 'Effects of Praise and Blame upon Achievement and Attitudes of Schoolchildren,' *Child and Education*. Copenhagen: Munksgaard, 1962.

anxiety were less affected by both praise and blame. In respect of problem arithmetic, however, praise and blame had no effect. This confirms Thurstone's view put forward in 1937 that motivation cannot—in a decisive manner—affect the individual's ability to solve problems. Praise cannot help the pupil to solve a problem if he does not know how to do it, whereas motivation does affect the number of correct answers obtained when the exercise is within his understanding or within his power to work by rote.

(b) Some claim that children should be taught to work for work's sake. This does act as a motive for a few in that by doing so a minority of children feel virtuous, and their worth in their own eyes is increased. But for the majority it appears that ego-involvement must be brought about by other means.

(c) One important experiment conducted by Abel[30] studied the effects of various incentives and goals on children's learning. The general conclusion was that it is the goal rather than the attainment of the goal which stimulates learning, for the former creates in the individual the restlessness and energy which brings about activity while the latter brings inactivity and a cessation of striving. This suggests that we should constantly present to children challenges which they are likely to accept. Our challenge will set in motion the striving, while failure resulting from giving up the struggle means some loss of self respect for the individual and some loss of face in the eyes of his peers. The child or adolescent tends to protect the self against threat or humiliation. When challenged he is, therefore, likely to strive harder, or to adopt various defence mechanisms that we shall discuss in the next chapter, in order to defend the self.

Motivation has been dealt with before abilities, for the latter may be of little use if the child is poorly motivated.[31, 32, 33]

[30] Abel, L. B., 'The Effects of Shift in Motivation upon·the Learning of a Sensori-motor Task,' *Arch. Psychol.*, 1936, **29**, No. 205.

[31] For some suggestions regarding the ways in which differences in upbringing between working-class and middle-class families are likely to affect motivation in relation to learning, see Cohen, A. K., *Delinquent Boys*. London: Routledge and Kegan Paul, 1955.

[32] The problem of children's motivation is discussed by Wall, W. D., 'The Wish to Learn—Research into Motivation,' *Educational Research*, 1958, **1**, 23–37. See also Vernon, M. D., *Human Motivation*. London: Cambridge University Press, 1969.

[33] For a treatment of the theories of motivation, see Madsen, K. B., *Theories of Motivation*. Copenhagen: Munksgaard, 1961, Second Edition.

Chapter Three

HUMAN ABILITIES AND THEIR MEASUREMENT

The Nature of Intelligence.[1,2] Since the beginning of this century psychologists have been measuring intelligence with some success, and yet they are unable to agree completely as to its nature. One should not be too dismayed at this, for we can measure electricity and predict how it will behave, and yet we are unable to say precisely what it is. The many definitions of intelligence that have been suggested can be classified into several groups.

One group of definitions placed the emphasis upon the adjustment or adaptation of the individual to his environment or to limited aspects of it. Thus intelligent people would more appropriately and extensively vary their behaviour as changing conditions demanded, and be able to deal with novel situations. Another definition of intelligence stressed the ability to learn, or the extent to which a person could be educated in the broadest sense. A third group of definitions maintained that the intelligence is the ability to carry on abstract thinking. This implies the effective use of ideas and symbols in dealing with situations, especially verbal and numerical symbols. However, there is much overlapping of these viewpoints.

Later in this chapter we shall see that in Great Britain psychologists have reached a measure of agreement that a good working definition of intelligence (although not necessarily a complete one) is:

1. The ability to see relevant relationships between objects or ideas; and

2. The ability to apply these relationships to new but similar situations.

In order to work out an arithmetical problem, say, the pupil has to grasp the relationships between the data presented, and then deduce something new to reach an answer which bears the correct relationship to the data. But if he is asked to multiply 147 by 18 no new relationships are involved. Hence the problem is more dependent upon intelligence than the mechanical exercise. Moreover, if we define and measure intelligence in this way, there is no doubt that intelligence is largely involved in academic aptitude and general all-round ability at work.

Eysenck[3] in a stimulating but critical analysis of the various approaches

---

[1] For a thorough study of the whole problem see, Vernon, P. E., *Intelligence and Attainment Tests*. London: University of London Press Ltd., 1960.

[2] Butcher, H. J., *Human Intelligence: Its Nature and Assessment*. London: Methuen, 1968.

[3] Eysenck, H. J., 'Intelligence Assessment: a Theoretical and Experimental Approach,' *Brit. J. Educ. Psychol.*, 1967, **37**, 81–98.

to intelligence assessment, supports the view of Furneaux that the solution of mental test items depends upon three issues. These are: speed of working, persistence in efforts to solve problems the solution to which is not immediately apparent, and a mental set which predisposes the individual to check his solution against the problem before writing it down immediately. This suggests that at least as far as test items are concerned, speed of working coupled with other aspects of personality determined the degree of the intelligence which is displayed. Readers should bear in mind Eysenck's views when reflecting upon the criticism that intelligence tests are unfair because those who cannot think quickly are penalised (see page 49).

Here, however, we propose to leave the discussion on the nature of intelligence, since for the moment we shall not be able to go much further towards finding out what intelligence is. It is now known that the whole position is less simple than was once supposed. Later it will be argued that there are probably three meanings of the term 'intelligence'. First, there is intelligence A which is innate potentiality (neither observable nor measurable), for acquiring intelligence B, which is all-round ability in daily life, at school or work. Thus intelligence B will closely accord with what we call, in everyday life, understanding, insight, quickness of thought, and practical judgment. Third, there is intelligence C, which in our culture, is represented by the score on a recognised intelligence test, devised in such a way as to measure intelligence in terms of the definition given at the beginning of the previous paragraph. Moreover, there is no doubt that the score gives a useful indication of the extent of intelligence B. (See also p. 54.)

Spearman's two-factor theory and extensions. As long ago as 1904, Professor Spearman, produced strong evidence,[4] based on his own researches which involved tests and estimates of intelligence, that there was one fundamental ability underlying all cognitive activities. By cognitive activities we mean those that have to do with thinking or intellectual aspects of the mind, and not with feeling or desiring. Furthermore, he maintained that entering into each test was another ability, specific to that test alone. He and his students concluded, therefore, in the above-mentioned and later researches, that every task involving intellectual activity depended upon a general ability, which he called 'g', and a separate ability specific to each task involved. Thus, performance in tests of handwriting, vocabulary, or mechanical arithmetic, would be explained by Spearman as due to the general ability or factor, and a specific ability in each of the tests. His view became known as the theory of Two Factors. For all practical purposes, the word 'factor' means the same as 'ability', but it may be defined more formally as a group or category of performances which correlate highly with one

[4] Spearman, C., ' "General Intelligence", Objectively Determined and Measured,' *Amer. J. Psychol.*, 1904, 15, 201–293.

another, and are relatively distinct from other categories of performances. Spearman refused at first to identify 'g' with intelligence, but suggested that it was the general mental energy with which each individual is endowed.

By studying the types of test which had the highest correlations with the general factor, 'g' (or had the highest 'g' 'saturation'), Spearman showed that a task involved the general factor in so far as it necessitated the discovery of relations and the education of correlates. Indeed, he later came to believe that intelligence comprised three abilities. These were: (1) the ability to observe one's own mental processes; (2) the ability to discover essential relationships between items of knowledge; (3) the ability to educe correlates. Thus the definition of intelligence suggested on page 32 is really a simplified version of the views put forward by him.

The chief criticism that would be levelled, nowadays, against Spearman is that he failed to allow sufficiently for abilities which, while less general than 'g', are not specific to one test. By 1917, Burt[5] had provided clear evidence, through examining children in school subjects, that there were verbal, numerical, and practical group abilities, in addition to a general ability. These group abilities were linked to a group of subjects and were not specific to just one subject. Thus Burt found that performance in Handwork, Drawing and Writing Quality depended on the general factor, 'g', and on a separate practical factor common to all three. In 1931 Stephenson[6] showed the presence of a verbal ability ('v') over and above the general ability in tests which he applied to a large group of schoolgirls. Again, in 1935, El Koussy[7] first showed the presence of a spatial factor

Table I

	Spearman			Group Factors		
	g	S	g	verbal	numerical	spatial
1	+	S¹	+	+		
2	+	S²	+	+		
3	+	S³	+	+		
4	+	S⁴	+		+	
5	+	S⁵	+		+	
6	+	S⁶	+		+	
7	+	S⁷	+			+
8	+	S⁸	+			+
9	+	S⁹	+			+

[5] Burt, C., *The Distribution and Relations of Educational Abilities*. London: King, 1917.

[6] Stephenson, W., 'Tetrad-Differences for Non-Verbal Subtests; Tetrad-Differences for Verbal Subtests; Tetrad-Differences for Verbal Subtests relative to Non-Verbal Subtests,' *J. Educ. Psychol.*, 1931, 22, 167–185, 255–267, 334–350.

[7] El Koussy, A. A. H., 'The Visual Perception of Space,' *Brit. J. Psychol, Monogr. Suppl.*, 20, 1935.

('k') in tests which he applied to boys aged 11–14 years; the essence of this ability being the capacity to manipulate shapes imaginatively.

The crosses indicate, in each case, the correlation between the test and the factor or factors. A blank space indicates that there is a zero or negligible correlation between the test and the factor.

Table I compares Spearman's Theory of Two Factors with the modern viewpoint which insists on group factors. To illustrate this table, let us suppose that we give nine tests to 200 children aged about 13 years. Tests 1–3 inclusive involve words and the meaning of words; tests 4, 5 and 6 contain exercises in mechanical arithmetic while tests 7–9 inclusive involve the imaginative manipulation of shapes. According to Spearman, each test would depend on the general factor but all the S's would be specific to each test. A situation now acceptable to British Psychologists would show the general factor as before, but in addition it would reveal group factors. Thus in addition to general ability, performance in tests 1–3 inclusive is dependent on verbal ability, tests 4, 5 and 6 on numerical ability, and tests 7–9 inclusive on spatial ability.

Intelligence Tests. We have already seen that the size of the correlation coefficient between a test and the general factor, shows the extent to which the test involves the discovery of relations and the education of correlates. Burt confirmed this using a different approach. He gave a number of varied tests to school children at Oxford and Liverpool and got the teachers to make careful estimates of the children's intelligence. After working out the correlation between the test scores and the teacher ratings, he found that tests which demanded the discovery of relevant relationships and the application of the relationships to new but similar situations, gave the highest agreement with the estimates of general ability. In the paragraphs which immediately follow, there will be some discussion of what are known as Binet-Simon Scales for measuring intelligence. Some of the items in these scales depend largely on information and knowledge, whereas modern group tests emphasise more the discovery of essential relationships. Note, however, that group verbal intelligence tests are increasingly being described as Verbal Reasoning Tests, reflecting the current view that performance on these is partly dependent on education.

Individual Tests of Intelligence or Reasoning. In 1905 Binet[8] constructed his first test to measure children's intelligence levels. It became known as the 1905 Binet-Simon Scale and was devised for the express purpose of picking out mentally subnormal children in the schools of Paris who were unable to profit from a normal education. Such children were to be taught in a special school, but it was first necessary to devise some objective means of selecting them. In this scale we find an idea which has been very useful when measuring the intellectual abilities of children. It is the principle

[8] Alfred Binet, 1857–1911.

that, if we know the scores of typical children at each age, we can determine, in the case of a particular child, the extent to which his intellectual development is above or below average, or normal for his age.

The scale was composed of thirty items in increasing order of difficulty, and all the questions were put individually to the child by the examiner. Five typical items are given below:

(a) Execution of simple directions; imitation of simple gestures.

(b) Definition of familiar objects such as house, horse, fork.

(c) Drawing from memory two different geometrical designs which had been shown simultaneously for 10 seconds.

(d) Giving rhymes to selected words.

(e) Giving the definition of, and distinction between, paired abstract terms; e.g. sad and bored.

Judged against intelligence tests in use today this was rather a crude effort, but it did enable mentally sub-normal children to be classified in a more objective manner than had been possible before.

A second scale known as the 1908 Binet-Simon Scale appeared three years later. This remedied many of the defects in the earlier scale. There were separate tests for children of from 3 to 13 years inclusive, and the scale was tried out on typical children, and standards of performance for each group obtained. One important principle introduced was that each test was placed at the year-level where it was passed satisfactorily by seventy-five per cent of the age-group. Binet also introduced the concept Mental Age (see page 44), which was the first device for expressing intelligence in objective numerical units. A few typical tests in this scale are listed:

Age 3.   Repeat two digits.

Age 7.   Describe presented pictures.

Age 10. Name the months of the year in their correct order.

Age 13. Draw the design made by cutting a triangular piece from the once-folded edge of a quarto-size piece of paper.

Altogether there were fifty-nine tests in the eleven age levels, Once again it should be noted that the test was given individually to the child. Moreover, Binet was interested not only in the number of questions correctly answered, but in the quality of judgment and reasoning shown by the child. Thus, in some measure, he used the test situation as an opportunity for a clinical interview.

This scale caused great interest among psychologists in many countries, and many revisions and improvements soon appeared. Binet himself brought out another scale in 1911, while in 1916, L. M. Terman[9] published in America what was known as the Stanford revision of the Binet-Simon Intelligence Scale. This revision was constructed for the purpose of providing an instrument which was properly standardised and adapted for

[9] Terman, L. M., *The Measurement of Intelligence*. Boston: Houghton Mifflin Co., 1916

use in the U.S.A. It was based upon results obtained from about 1,000 native-born children in California. Each of the children came from an unselected group of average social status and was within two months of his birthday. This scale contained 90 items covering an age range from 3 to 14 years (excluding 11 and 13 years) together with a group of tests at the 'average adult level', and another at the 'superior adult' level.

The version of the Binet Scales that has been widely used in English-speaking countries is the Terman-Merrill New Stanford Revision published in 1937.[10] The principle modifications in this scale, as compared with the 1916 scale, were as follows:

(a) There were two equivalent or parallel forms (L. & M.) of the scale, each of which contained 129 items.

(b) The scoring standards and instructions for administering the test were improved.

(c) The items extended the range that can be examined from 2 years of age upwards, through three grades of 'superior adult'. Between 2 and 5 years there are tests timed for six-monthly intervals, yielding greater differentiation during those early years. There were also tests for the 11 and 13 year age levels.

(d) Some of the questions depending largely upon information were left out and some non-verbal practical problems were introduced.

(e) It was standardised (see page 41) on a more carefully chosen and much larger group of subjects.

On the other hand a number of criticisms have been made of this most popular scale. Some of these are listed:

(a) It tends to exaggerate the higher mental ages and IQ's. This may be due to the varying spread or range of IQ's at different ages, but Vernon suggests that the standardisation is inaccurate in Britain: for example, a mental age of 15 as indicated by this scale should really be 13·9.

(b) Some of the items are misplaced. A child may fail all the items at one year and yet do two or three items in a higher year.

(c) The typical responses quoted in the scoring instructions sometimes need amending in Great Britain as they represent the thoughts and expressions of American children.

(d) The items are so varied that the test is not always measuring the same ability. Spatial, numerical, and verbal abilities are involved, as well as 'g'.

Meanwhile Burt[11] in 1921 published his version of the 1908 Binet-Simon Scale. However, a new version of the Binet Scale was published in America in 1960 and became available in this country in 1962.[12] Suitable items from both Forms L and M of the 1937 Revision were taken to form one test. One advantage of this test is that it gives the intelligence quotient

[10] Terman, L. M., and Merrill, M. A., *Measuring Intelligence*. Boston: Houghton Mifflin Co., 1937. London: Harrap, 1937.
[11] Burt, C., *Mental and Scholastic Tests*. London: Staples Press, 1921.
[12] London: Harrap, 1962.

as a 'deviation IQ' instead of calculating it through the mental age (see Chapter 20). But one study[13] has confirmed that this Revision, like the 1937 Revision, exaggerates the higher mental ages and IQ's.

An entirely new individual test, in the sense that it is not a revision of the Binet Scales, is the Wechsler-Bellevue Intelligence Test.[14] It is intended to measure the intelligence of adolescents and adults between the ages of 10 and 60 years and is increasingly being used. It, too, depends on verbal and spatial abilities as well as general intelligence. A similar test, the Wechsler Intelligence Scale for Children[15] (WISC), constructed for the 5–15 year age range, is now often used instead of the Terman-Merrill test (see also p. 305), while the Wechsler Pre-School and Primary Scale of Intelligence[16] (WPPSI) can be used between 4 and 6½ years of age.

Individual tests are not normally used by teachers. They are mainly applied by clinical psychologists and psychiatrists in testing young children, in the diagnosis of mental sub-normality, in the examination of children backward in their school work, or in the case of those suffering from some forms of nervous or behaviour disorders. Readers who want further information regarding the scales themselves, their construction and the scoring techniques, must refer to the appropriate handbooks listed in the footnotes. The use of individual tests is a skilled job and must not be undertaken without training. It is absolutely essential that good rapport with the examinee be established. Moreover, the application of individual tests may take a long time.

Group Tests of Intelligence or Reasoning. Teachers and others concerned with testing older, normal children, use group intelligence tests. The questions are usually printed in a booklet, so that by giving out a booklet to each examinee large numbers of children or adults can be tested at the same time. Such tests were first used by the American Army authorities in World War I to examine the intelligence of their recruits and so select those with enough ability for commissioned and non-commissioned officer rank, and eliminate those whose low intelligence made them unfit for military service.

Group tests are of two kinds, verbal or non-verbal. The former usually

[13] Estes, B. W. *et al.* 'Relationships between 1960 S-B, 1937 S-B, WISC, Raven and Draw a Man,' *J. consult. Psychol.*, 1961, 25, 388–391.
[14] Wechsler, D., *The Measurement of Adult Intelligence.* Baltimore: Williams & Wilkins Co., 1944. A revised version, the Wechsler Adult Intelligence Scale (WAIS) appeared in 1955.
[15] Seashore, H., Wesman, A., and Doppelt, J., 'The Standardization of the Wechsler Intelligence Scale for Children,' *J. consult. Psychol.*, 1950, 14, 99–110. Wechsler, D., *Wechsler Intelligence Scale for Children.* New York: Psychol. Corp., 1949. A Scottish standardisation of WISC was published in 1965.
[16] Wechsler, D., *Wechsler Pre-School and Primary Scale of Intelligence.* New York: Psychological Corporation, 1967.

demand the intelligent manipulation of words, or rather of ideas expressed in words, and the items set out below are among those frequently set in such a test. When the subject has to select the correct answer from a number of possible answers, the item is known as a selective-response or multiple-choice item. But when the candidate has to supply the correct answer it is known as a creative-response item. The following are typical items:

1. *Sentence Completion.* An incomplete sentence is given and the subject has to supply the word or words that best complete it. e.g. There are .... months in a year.

2. *Classification.* A number of words are given, and the subject has to underline a given number of words that belong together, or are alike in some way.
   e.g.   Apple, turnip, bicycle, cabbage, letter, carrot.

3. *Synonyms and Antonyms.* A word is given and the subject has to underline the word in brackets which is the same or opposite in meaning.
   e.g.   Tall (Heavy, quick, short, thin).
   Frequently (Never, always, hurriedly, often).

4. *Number or Letter Series.* A series of numbers or letters is given and the subject must supply two numbers or letters that continue it.
   e.g.   10 13 16 19 ( ) ( )
   BA DC FE HG ( ) ( ).

5. *Ordering.* A series of words or numbers are given and the subject has to underline the smallest and largest units indicated.
   e.g.   Week, second, day, hour, minute.
   2158 8521 5218 1528 5182.

6. *Codes.* A statement is given and the subject has to put it in code according to a given principle. Or, a code word is given together with its meaning, and the subject has to find the meaning of another code word.
   An example of the second type:
   If QTF means rug, what does GDM mean?

7. *Analogies.* The subject has to select a fourth word, which is to a third word, as a second word is to a first word.
   e.g.   Thermometer is to temperature as clock is to
   (hour, strike, day, time, hands).

8. *Inferences.* A problem is given which demands reasoning for its solution. The subject has to supply or select the correct solution.
   e.g.   John is three years younger than Mary. She is eight years older than Tom and ten years older than Susan. How many years older than Susan is John?

These types of items do not exhaust all those that involve relational thinking, nor are they always presented in the way they are in the text.

The selective type answer is preferred to the inventive as it makes the marking easier and more objective. Occasionally the items of various types are grouped in 'omnibus' fashion; that is, they are grouped in short sub-tests and occur in regular or irregular order. This ensures that the candidates attempt every kind of item even if they cannot complete more than half of the test in the time allowed. Generally group verbal tests provide a good measure of general intelligence but they also depend to some extent on verbal ability. Such tests are worked with greater facility by children coming from a background which has encouraged good language development.[17]

Non-verbal tests of intelligence or reasoning. Many of the items used in non-verbal intelligence tests can be obtained by taking the same types of items as are used in group verbal tests, and adapting them for use with non-verbal material. Thus the subject may be required to do any or all of the following operations:

(*a*) Arrange figures of similar shape in order of size, and underline the largest and smallest of the figures.

(*b*) Underline one figure out of, say, five which is most unlike the other four.

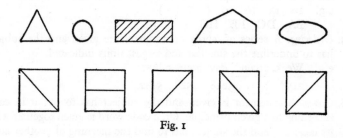

Fig. 1

(*c*) Study, say, five figures, note the four which have something in common, and cross out the extra one.

(*d*) Work an analogies test which has been devised using shapes. For example, the subject might see the picture of a small triangle and of a large triangle; also of a small square. He then has to select a large square from three or four alternatives given.

In one very famous non-verbal test of intelligence, the Progressive Matrices Test,[18] the candidate has, in some items, to study a pattern, part of which is missing. The subject has to perceive relationships, and then

---

[17] For a study of the errors made by children in intelligence-test type questions, see Donaldson, M., *A Study of Children's Thinking.* London: Tavistock Pubs., 1963.
[18] Prepared by Raven, J. C., 1938 and 1947. There is a shortened version of the 1947 (Advanced) Matrices test (1962). A Matrices test for children is also available.

select a piece of pattern from a number of pieces of pattern to complete the diagram. This test thus utilises a logical method of reasoning with non-verbal materials.

A pictorial test of intelligence is sometimes given to children between the ages of about 5 and 8 years. Such a test is given as a group test. In one type of item often set, the child has to examine, say, six small pictures representing articles or activities, and underline the picture which does 'not belong' to the other five.

A well constructed non-verbal test of intelligence does not involve much spatial ability. Such a test gives a better indication of intelligence for those whose language development has been retarded, but it does not usually give such a good forecast of scholastic success. It is now often called a Non-Verbal Reasoning Test.

The Construction and Standardisation of a Psychological Test. A psychological test may be defined as a standardised task which elicits a sample of the subject's behaviour, which can be objectively scored and compared with standards of performance. Such a test has been shown to be predictive of future behaviour. An intelligence test is just one example of such a test; other examples being, say, vocabulary and arithmetic tests. Two main types may be distinguished. In a power test, ample or unlimited time is given, but the level of difficulty of the harder items is such that few can complete all the tasks. In a speed test, the score is determined by the number of operations carried out correctly in a given time.

The main characteristics of a psychological test are:

(*a*) There is a series of tasks or questions graded in difficulty.

(*b*) The acceptable response to an item must be independent of the opinion of the examiner. Thus in an intelligence test the child usually selects and underlines the correct response from a number of possible responses. In a problem arithmetic test the child supplies the answer because there is only one correct reply.

(*c*) The test has to be suited to the average, and range, of the ability (or knowledge) of the candidates. Thus the test must be devised for a specific age group or a limited range of groups.

Objective measures of many human traits, e.g. height, tend to conform to the *normal* or Gaussian curve. It is symmetrical, bell or cocked-hat shape (Figure 2). It shows that in a group of a hundred or more persons, most obtain measures round about the average and few obtain extreme measures either very high or very low. In a smaller group the distribution of traits is likely to be more irregular, merely on account of the size of the group.

We do not, however, always require a normal distribution of test scores. For example, if we wish to set a test to differentiate between the ablest, or dullest, children only, then a skewed or asymmetrical distribution may be better. Thus Figure 3 shows the results of a test which has

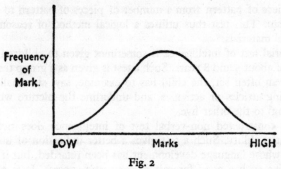

Fig. 2

spread out the marks of the ablest children, and Figure 4 the results of a test which has differentiated between the scores of the least able.

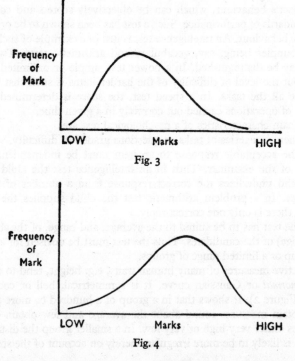

Fig. 3

Fig. 4

(*d*) Norms or standards have to be obtained for the test so that a particular score can be compared with the scores of an age, or other well-defined group. Thus if a child aged 9 years 6 months obtained a score of 54, we may wish to compare his score with those of other children of the same age. Again, if a young man training to be an aircraft pilot obtained a score of 82 in a test, we may want to know how this score compares with those obtained by young men in general who are training to be pilots. The norms of psychological tests for use with children are usually obtained for monthly or three-monthly intervals. This process is known as standardisation. To get these age-norms the test must be given to a truly representative population. Such a population can be obtained either by taking children from all types of school (e.g. city, urban, and rural state schools; also independent schools), or by taking the children of parents in certain occupations.

(e) If a test is applied a second time under similar conditions, and the candidates' scores differ widely from those obtained previously, the test is obviously a poor one. It is said to be a reliable test only if the two sets of scores correlate highly with one another. Two ways of studying the reliability of a test are listed below:

(i) The test may be given again sometime later and the two sets of scores correlated thus giving a reliability coefficient. This technique may give an unfair picture of the reliability of the test since some subjects may remember a few responses. If, however, the second test is given after a long interval, the children's abilities may have altered considerably.

(ii) The test can be supplied in two parallel forms, so that when the re-test is given, the different questions in the second form yield much the same scores as those in the first form. To obtain the reliability of the test the scores on the parallel forms are correlated. This is a preferable method, though even here, the first test may influence the second.

There are other methods of obtaining the reliability of a test but these are too technical for inclusion in this book. For a psychological test to be of value (other than for research purposes) it must have a reliability coefficient of at least 0·90 whatever method is used. If the reliability falls below this figure, the scores are too unstable to be trusted.

(f) The test must be a valid one. This means that it must measure whatever it is supposed to measure. Readers will often meet the terms construct validity, concurrent validity, predictive validity, content validity, factorial validity, face validity, etc. These different types overlap to some extent. Teachers are mainly concerned with concurrent validity and predictive validity. The former is estimated by calculating the correlation between scores obtained on the given test and other criterion measures (e.g. school marks), while the latter is found by correlating the scores obtained on the test with *later* measures of performance.

To find out whether a test measures what it purports to measure we usually proceed as follows:

(i) By inspection to see what the test involves. This in itself is rarely enough but it is a necessary preliminary step.

   (ii) By correlating the test results with some external criterion such as teacher-estimates or educational success.

   (iii) By using a mathematical technique known as factor analysis we can find out to what extent our new test correlates with general intelligence, 'g', and with other group abilities. Thus we can find out what our test measures.

Teachers are strongly advised not to make up their own tests apart from objective tests (*see* Chapter 11) which are used for normal school examinations. It is easy to devise items similar to those in published intelligence or other psychological tests, but many technical features enter into the selection and standardisation of suitable items in addition to those described here.[19]

Mental Age (MA). We have seen that by giving intelligence tests to fairly large and representative groups of children at different ages, it is possible to get averages or norms of performance at monthly or three-monthly intervals. By this means we can assign a child a Mental Age by comparing his score with the norm for the test being used. Thus if he obtained a score equal to the norm of a $10\frac{1}{2}$-year-old population, his Mental Age is said to be $10\frac{1}{2}$ years regardless of his chronological age. Hence Mental Age is the level of a person's mental ability, as expressed in terms of the chronological age, of average persons having the same level of mental ability. Similarly a person's attainment age in arithmetic, or reading, or spelling, is the level of his performance, as expressed in terms of the chronological age, of average persons having the same level of attainment.

Intelligence Quotient (IQ). Mental Age indicates the level of a child's intellectual development but it does not say whether he is bright or dull for his chronological age. Accordingly the term Intelligence Quotient, or IQ, was introduced to give an index of brightness. Thus:

$$\text{IQ} = \frac{\text{Mental Age}}{\text{Chronological Age}} \times 100$$

If a child, then, has a mental age of 8 years 0 months and a chronological age of 10 years 0 months, he has an IQ of 80; while a child having a chronological age of 9 years 0 months and a mental age of 11 years 3 months has an intelligence quotient of 125. Obviously the child of average mental ability has an IQ of 100.

   The terms MA and IQ are now passing from use and a person's standing on a test is expressed either in terms of percentiles (page 45) or in standardised scores (Chapter 20). The distribution of intelligence seems to follow a curve which is almost the normal probability curve, and so we find that

[19] An advanced treatment of the problem of constructing such tests and of assessing their results has been provided by Anstey, E., *Psychological Tests.* London: Nelson, 1966.

IQs are similarly distributed.[20] Note, however, that the mean IQ as revealed by an intelligence test must be 100 and the Standard Deviation (*see* Chapter 20), or spread of IQ's should be 15. If the standard deviation of the test is less or greater than 15, the distribution of IQ's will be less or more spread out respectively. This is one reason why a child can get slightly different IQ's on different intelligence tests. The distribution of IQ's among a representative sample of white American children is given by Merrill[21] as approximately:

IQ	Per cent of Population
Greater than 129	4
120–129	8
110–119	18
100–109	23
90–99	23
80–89	15
70–79	6
Less than 70	3

The examination of children in Great Britain gives much the same results, so that for the two populations in question, we may say that 46 per cent of children have IQ's between 90 and 109, and that an IQ of 130 is equalled or surpassed by only 4 per cent of children. At the other end of the scale, only 3 per cent of children have an IQ lower than 70. There are, of course, no distinct classes of children: there is a slow gradation from very bright to very dull individuals.

It will be shown later in this chapter that there is no appreciable growth of intelligence for some children after about 15 years of age. If MA then becomes constant and the chronological age goes on increasing, the calculated IQ's of these adolescents and adults would rapidly decline. This difficulty is now met by using percentiles or standardised scores (Chapter 20) after the age of 10–11 years.[22]

Percentiles. Suppose in an intelligence or attainment test 55 per cent of a representative group of 10-year-olds obtain a mark of less than 70. This mark is said to be the '55th percentile' and is, of course, reached or exceeded by 45 per cent of the group. Again, if a person obtains a mark at the

[20] See Lewis, D. G., 'The Normal Distribution of Intelligence: a Critique,' *Brit. J. Psychol.*, 1957, **48**, 98–104. Burt, C., 'Is Intelligence Normally Distributed?' *Brit. J. Stat. Psychol.*, 1963, **16**, 175–90. This paper suggests that there are both more very high, and very low, scorers than the normal curve would allow.
[21] In the 1937 Terman-Merrill revision of the Stanford-Binet test the standard deviation is 16. The data is based upon information supplied by Merrill, M. A., 'The Significance of the IQ's on the Revised Stanford-Binet Scales,' *J. Educ. Psychol.*, 1938, **29**, 641–651.
[22] For a discussion on the ambiguity of IQ units see: Vernon, P. E., *The Measurement of Abilities*. London: University of London Press Ltd., 1956, 2nd Edition, Chapter 4.

75th percentile for college students, and at the 99th percentile for adults generally, we can immediately assess its level relative to the scores of other students or adults, for a percentile always designates the percentage of cases or scores lying below it. Percentiles always bear a relation to specific age, or other groups. The idea of percentile is a most useful one for there is no underlying assumption as to the way intelligence or other trait, varies with age, or indeed with any variable. Thus if a girl aged 17 years at a grammar school obtained a score in a test that was at the 99th percentile for grammar school pupils, age 16–18 years, it means that her score exceeded those of 99 per cent in her age and educational group. A method for finding percentiles will be given in Chapter 20.

The Effects of Practice and Coaching on Intelligence Test Scores. In the 1950's there was considerable interest in the question of the effects of practice and/or coaching on intelligence test scores. Experiments were devised to measure these effects. It is quite true that some researches into the problem had been carried out in the middle 1920's, but, in general, British psychologists tended to ignore these earlier findings. The later work has shown beyond doubt that both coaching and practice can affect test scores. This is a serious matter, for when pupils sit for a competitive examination children who have not been coached or practised are at a disadvantage. Most of the relevant investigations have been carried out with children aged 10–11 years.

It is necessary at the beginning to point out the difference between practice and coaching. In the former, the child merely works tests which are fairly similar to those that he will take in the future examination. But he is given no hints or tips, and the test papers are not marked in front of him so that he does not know which items he has worked incorrectly. It is not difficult to get hold of material similar to that set in intelligence tests, since some publishers issue books of questions based on those in standard tests. Coaching, however, usually involves going through the instructions to each item carefully; explaining additional items on the blackboard and getting the pupils to suggest new items; getting the pupils to work quickly but carefully, and inducing a spirit of competition and the desire to improve on one's previous performance.

Unfortunately it is extremely difficult to summarise the work in this field since the investigations did not always yield the same results. Thus Vernon,[23] Watts *et al.*,[24] Dempster,[25] and Wiseman[26] agreed on some

[23] Vernon, P. E., 'Intelligence Testing,' London: *Times Educational Supplement*, 25th January and 1st February, 1952.

[24] Watts, A. F., Pidgeon, D. A., and Yates, A., *Secondary School Entrance Examinations.* London: Newnes Educational Publishing Co., 1952.

[25] Dempster, J. J. B., 'Symposium on the Effects of Coaching and Practice in Intelligence Tests,' *Brit. J. Educ. Psychol.*, 1954, 24, 1–4.

[26] Wiseman, S., and Wrigley, J., 'The Comparative Effects of Coaching and Practice on the Results of Verbal Intelligence Tests,' *Brit. J. Psychol.*, 1953, 44, 83–92.

points but not on others. Among the issues on which there was agreement were the following:

(a) Practice and/or coaching make sufficient difference to intelligence test scores to affect the fate of a proportion of children at the borderline between those accepted for the grammar schools and those rejected.

(b) After three or four hours of practice or coaching the maximum average gain is obtained. Further practice or coaching seems to be of no avail.

(c) In both practice and coaching there are large individual differences in gains, and great irregularities in progress at successive steps. This seems to be a fairly firm finding quite apart from any argument concerning the average gain brought about by the various forms of practice and coaching. These irregularities may be due to emotional factors affecting the subject's performance. Test results seem likely to be most reliable and valid when they are obtained from two or more tests, and after all children have had some experience of the tests.

(d) Some types of test items are more susceptible to improvement by practice and coaching than others. Creative-response opposites, and familiar multi-choice questions, show little gains, whereas unfamiliar multiple-choice questions show greater rises. Likewise, non-verbal material tends to show greater practice and coaching effects than verbal tests or the Stanford-Binet test.

(e) The effects of coaching fade more rapidly than those of practice. Gains due to the latter appear to be roughly halved by the end of one year.

(f) The type of practice and coaching seems important. Coaching done either by parents or teachers, without complete tests under examination conditions, is surprisingly ineffective.

(g) There is little transfer effect from one type of material to another. Hence children must be practised and coached with similar material and similar conditions of testing, to those obtaining in the final test.

We now turn to discuss the points on which there was a difference of opinion among investigators:[27]

(a) There was fair agreement in the older literature that coaching on parallel test material leads to rises in test scores equivalent to 15 IQ units or more. But in more recent researches, smaller rises in test scores were claimed. Vernon maintained that after three or four hours of coaching the figure was 11 points. Against this, Wiseman, also Watts *et al.* found gains of only five to six points after coaching; no more, in fact, than that of matched groups who receive extensive practice without coaching and little more than that of the control groups who took only the initial test (i.e. one practice test). On the other hand, Dempster in his 1951 and 1953 experiments obtained a rise of 8–9 points after coaching which is closer to Vernon's figure.

[27] See, Vernon, P. E., 'Symposium on the Effects of Coaching and Practice in Intelligence Tests,' *Brit. J. Educ. Psychol.*, 1954, 24, 57–63.

(b) The investigations conducted by Watts *et al.* suggested that teachers differ in their effectiveness as coaches. Vernon did not deny such differences, but maintained that their existence is difficult to prove when random variations between classes were so large.

(c) The evidence seemed to show that usually, although not always, dull children benefit less than bright children from uninstructed practice; but they are helped relatively, even if not absolutely, more by coaching.

(d) There was no clear evidence whether boys or girls obtained the greater gains after practice or coaching.

The point of disagreement which has caused most controversy revolved around the size of the gains due to practice and coaching. Some of the difference in opinion on this issue was no doubt due to defects and difficulties connected with the methods used in studying the whole problem, although these cannot be discussed here because of the many technicalities involved. But part was due to the suitability of the coaching employed, and part due to the degree of test-sophistication of the pupils before the experiments began. Generally, the work conducted under Vernon's direction involved children who had had much less experience of intelligence tests than those in other experiments. This problem of test-sophistication is important. For example, the Scottish Counctil for Educational Research found a rise of 4 points among 11-year-olds between 1932 and 1947 in areas where the children were likely to be familiar with intelligence tests by 1947. On the other hand, there was no increase in score in remote areas where group tests were novel, and no gain anywhere on Binet Tests.

So long as there was competition to get into Grammar Schools, and tests were used as the chief instrument of selection, there was bound to be practice and coaching by teachers or parents. Various suggestions were put forward regarding the amount of practice and/or coaching which should be carried out in primary schools in order that all children might sit the entrance examination on an equal footing. Some workers in this field were strongly against authorised coaching, but would admit practice. Vernon suggested that in places where competition for grammar school places was severe, it was necessary to give two parallel trials of the whole selection procedure (not just the intelligence test) before the actual examination. These papers should be marked in front of the children and the teachers should give further guidance for a few periods after each trial. But in areas where competition was less severe, and where adequate use was made of primary teachers' estimates, a single trial plus coaching might be sufficient to smooth out differences between individuals who had had different amounts of experience of the tests.

Although the overall problem was studied mainly in relation to educational selection at about 11 years of age, the effects of practice and coaching[28]

---

[28] These effects must be clearly distinguished from a real rise in IQ due to genuine environmental stimulation.

cannot be ignored in either vocational guidance or in selection procedures such as those in use by the Defence and Civil Services.

Criticisms of Intelligence Tests. Intelligence tests, in spite of their usefulness, are not popular with some people. Many criticisms have been made of such tests and a few of these are now examined briefly:

(a) *The tests are not reliable tests of innate intelligence in that the ability to work them is affected by education and environment generally.* Evidence has certainly accumulated which shows that the ability to do such tests does depend to some extent on the culture pattern, education, and intellectual stimulation which the child has received from his environment. If these tests are regarded as tests of academic aptitude, or ability to profit from an academic type of education, then the usefulness of the test score is not lessened although the criticism has less point. Clearly, the child who has had good intellectual stimulation from home and school is likely to get a higher test score, to do better in his academic subjects at school, and to do work of a more intellectual character in later life. On the other hand, verbal intelligence tests do to some extent give a fairer chance to those pupils from poor environments or with inadequate schooling, than do school examinations or teachers' estimates.

(b) *Intelligence tests are unfair because those who cannot think quickly are penalised.* Speeded tests correlate ·90 or more with scores obtained on the same tests without time limit. However, there is now good evidence to suggest that among adults of wide age range the time allowance should be generous, or the test completely untimed, for speed of work does fall off with age. Again, Yates[29] showed that among a group of university students, the score obtained on Progressive Matrices (1947) after 40 minutes, underestimates the level the subject would have reached if given longer time. There may also be some effect in the case of children. Moreton and Butcher[30] studied the effect of speeded tests on selection procedures at eleven among rural children. Although these workers did not come to any clear conclusions, Armstrong[31] provided evidence that pupils in a rural environment were to some extent handicapped by an assessment in an 11 plus examination weighted in favour of speeded tests. Again Yates[32] has shown that among 9-year-olds, children can be identified who are slow but accurate workers whose ability can be seriously underestimated by imposed time limits on intelligence tests.

[29] Yates, A. J., 'A Further Study of Progressive Matrices,' *Brit. J. Educ. Psychol.*, 1963, **33**, 306–311.

[30] Moreton, C. A. and Butcher, H. J., 'Are Rural Children handicapped by the use of Speeded Tests on Selection Procedures?' *Brit. J. Educ. Psychol.*, 1963, **33**, 22–30.

[31] Armstrong, H. G., 'A Comparison of Rural Schools' Performance in a Test-Controlled and Test-Free Selection Procedure at Eleven,' *Brit. J. Educ. Psychol.*, 1964, **34**, 237–246.

[32] Yates, A. J., 'Level Speed and Personality Factors in the Intelligence Performance of Young Children,' *Brit. J. Educ. Psychol.*, 1966, **36**, 312–316.

(c) *It is possible to give practice and coach for intelligence tests.* This possibility is now well recognised and the whole problem has already been dealt with earlier in this chapter.

(d) *Intelligence tests measure abilities other than general intelligence or 'g'.* This is generally true. A verbal group test is to some extent dependent on verbal ability, while a well-constructed non-verbal test of intelligence is dependent, although even to a smaller extent, on spatial ability. Both kinds of tests bring in specific abilities, of course. Note, however, that if a test measures a little 'v' and 'k' ability as well as 'g', its predictive power is increased somewhat from the educational point of view, since most school tasks depend on 'g' plus 'v', or 'g' plus 'k', abilities, rather than on 'g' alone. On the other hand it seems likely that the form of the test introduces what is known as a formal factor. For example, all objective tests of the selective-response type appear to embody a formal factor (or specific ability to do that type of test) which detracts from their educational value.

(e) *Performance in an intelligence test is dependent upon the emotional mood of the subject.* Available evidence suggests that most children or adults of nervous temperament are not handicapped in the usual short intelligence test. There are, however, three points to note. First, there are a few individuals who always get 'nerves' in any test or school examination and do not do themselves justice. Such people are likely to react similarly in any real life situation when a little stress is placed upon them. Second, a child, whether normally nervous or not, is unlikely to do his best in any test if he has recently suffered some severe emotional experience, e.g. death of a parent. Third, emotionally maladjusted children who have difficulty in absorbing the ordinary concepts of the culture over the years will do less well in an intelligence test than will normal children. Their condition is such that it is equivalent to their having received a poorer education. By and large, however, most children and adults are not handicapped by their emotional attitude provided that the intelligence tests are short and interesting.

(f) *There is a mistaken notion among some people concerning what an intelligence test is supposed to measure, and to belittle it when it fails to predict traits and abilities it was never intended to.* An intelligence test does not measure attainment, or special abilities, such as capacity for music or art; nor is its purpose to estimate temperament, morals or good manners. A child can be ill-mannered, and possess little musical ability, and yet be highly intelligent. Provided we keep clearly in mind the purpose of our test, we shall not make undue claims for it.

(g) *Some people have decried the use of intelligence tests on the grounds that they do not accurately predict performance in school work, employment, or other real life situations.* These critics have forgotten that success in school work or in an occupation, depends upon special abilities and temperament, as well as intelligence.

Summing up, we may say that most of the criticisms levelled against intelligence tests can be countered, if the limitations of the tests are understood. Such tests do, in spite of their limitations, forecast future academic aptitude better than ordinary school examinations.

Validity of Intelligence Tests. Inconstancy of IQ yet its high predictive value.
Tests for measuring the intellectual growth of children under two years of age have been devised by Gesell, Bühler, Griffiths and others. Generally, research evidence shows that estimates of intelligence made by means of such scales are useless for predicting IQ's of normal children after that age. Honzik *et al.*[33] gave mental tests to 252 children at regular age intervals between 21 months and 18 years. It was found that the correlation between mental test scores secured at 21 months and those obtained at 18 years was about ·08. Again, Anderson[34] has shown that mental test items of the Gesell and Bühler type given to infants under 2 years of age are of little value even in predicting intellectual status at 5. But from 2 years of age onwards, there is a gradual increase in relationship between test scores with decrease in time interval between tests. Thus Anderson[35] quotes the following figures for the correlation coefficients between intelligence test scores obtained at different age levels:

Between 2 and 7 years	·46
Between 6 and 7 years	·81
Between 11 and 16 years	·74
Between 15 and 16 years	·90

More recently Hindley[36] gave details of children tested at 6 months and 18 months on the Griffiths Scale, and again at 3 and 5 years of age on the Stanford-Binet Scale. The intercorrelations of scores ranged from ·32 (6 months vs. 5 years) to ·78 (3 years vs. 5 years). Moreover, highly significant differences between social classes appeared by 3 years of age.

Thus the younger the child when first tested, and the longer the period of time between the tests, the greater is the error in predicting the second score from the first. Hence the IQ, although fairly constant for most children, can no longer be thought of as completely fixed in value. Indeed, some children suffer considerable changes in IQ as we shall see. For example, when children were tested within one week on the two parallel forms of the 1937 Terman-Merrill Revision of the Stanford-Binet Test,

[33] Honzik, M. P., Macfarlane, J. W., and Allen, L., 'The Stability of Mental Test Performance between Two and Eighteen Years,' *J. Exp. Educ.*, 1948, **17**, 309–324

[34] Anderson, L. D., 'The Predictive Value of Infancy Tests in Relation to Intelligence at Five Years,' *Child Development*, 1939, **10**, 203–212. The Cattell test at 20 months has given better predictions. See Werner, E. E., Honzik, M. P. and Smith, R. S., 'Prediction of Intelligence and Achievement at Ten Years from Twenty Months,' *Child Developm.*, 1968, **39**, 1063–76.

[35] Anderson, J. E., 'The Limitations of Infant and Pre-school Tests in the Measurement of Intelligence,' *J. Psychol.*, 1939, **8**, 351–379.

[36] Hindley, C. B., 'Stability and Change up to Five Years. Group Trends,' *J. of Child Psychol. and Psychiat.*, 1965, **6**, 85–99.

it was found that children with high IQ's went up or down, on the average, by about 6 points of IQ, the middle ones about 5 points and those of lower IQ's about 2½ points.[37] Studies of individual children, however, can be selected to give the impression of either constancy or inconstancy of IQ. It would be quite easy to find a child who would not vary more than 5 points of IQ, between the highest and lowest scores obtained, after being tested six times over as many years. It is also possible to find a child who would vary as much as 20 points of IQ, between the highest and lowest scores obtained, when similarly tested. Generally speaking, though, the re-test results of hundreds of children over long periods of time, show on the average, a shift of up to 10 points of IQ up or down, with a few changes as large as 30 points.

The dull child thus usually grows up to be the dull adult, the bright child the bright adult and so on. Hence the IQ obtained in childhood has considerable predictive value, for among other things it has been shown to be of great use in:

(a) Predicting academic aptitude in school.

(b) Placing school leavers in suitable employment.

Intelligence tests have also shown themselves to be of value with older subjects when selection is being made for industry or the Defence and Civil Services. Another interesting piece of work is that of Terman,[38] who followed the progress of 1,000 intellectually gifted children (Stanford-Binet IQ's above 140) from 1921–1955. At the latter date their vocational achievement was well above that of college graduates in general, showing that these people had maintained their intellectual superiority over a quarter of a century.

Why is it that the IQ is not constant and yet remains relatively so? First, no intelligence test is completely reliable and some change of score is bound to take place on re-testing. Second, it is possible that a test has been properly standardised at one age level but not at another, although it must be stated that there is no evidence that Terman and Merrill failed to get representative groups at all ages. Third, the degree of intellectual stimulation received from the environment will vary from child to child, but for a particular child it usually, but not always, remains fairly constant. If a child starts with a good home it often remains good; if he begins with the advantages of a stimulating school he often retains this advantage during the school years. Expressing these facts rather differently, we may say that the IQ is of considerable predictive value in dealing with the children of this country, or white children of the U.S.A., where the degree of intellectual stimulation received by such children usually, but not

[37] Terman, L. M., and Merrill, M. A., *Measuring Intelligence*. London: Harrap, 1937.
[38] Terman, L. M., and Oden, M. H., *Genetic Studies of Genius. V. The Gifted Group at Mid-Life*. London: Oxford University Press, 1959. Oden, M. H., 'The Fulfilment of Promise: 40-year Follow-up of the Terman Gifted Group,' *Genet. Psychol. Monogr.*, 1968, 77, 3–93.

always, remains fairly constant for a particular child. Fourth, the Fels[39] study suggests that children who show the greatest need of achievement, who strive in competitive fashion, and who are curious about nature, show the greatest upward changes in IQ, since these activities may facilitate the acquisition of skills assessed by IQ. Fifth, emotional maladjustment may affect intellectual development. Thus feelings of insecurity, social withdrawal, and other psychological difficulties may bring about changes in IQ. Sixth, changes in physiological development may bring about changes in IQ (see p. 261).[40]

Uses of Intelligence Tests.

1. *Grading.* It was the policy in many schools to have classes which contained pupils of roughly the same ability and attainment and of approximately the same age. This grading was sometimes performed on the basis of scores obtained on group verbal intelligence tests, but more often scores obtained on tests of attainment, were added to, or taken into consideration with, the scores obtained on the intelligence test.

2. *In selection for different types of secondary education.* Many Education Authorities used to set a group verbal intelligence test, along with tests of attainment, in the examination taken at 10/11 or 13 years of age, to select children for different types of secondary education. With the coming of comprehensive schools this practice has declined somewhat.

3. *In Educational Guidance within a school.* Within school, cumulative and continuous educational guidance is necessary for pupils. An intelligence test can be one instrument among many others which will help the staff in advising a pupil whether or not to take a particular course or subject. See also page 167.

4. *In Vocational Guidance and Selection.* Although intelligence is not the only attribute which determines one's degree of success in an occupation, it is important that an individual should possess intelligence of the same order as that required by his work. If he has too little intelligence he will be incompetent, if too much for his work he will feel frustrated. Thus when giving vocational guidance to young men and women the scores obtained on verbal or non-verbal intelligence tests are nearly always taken into account. Likewise many firms use such tests when selecting new employees. The Civil Service Commissioners have introduced intelligence tests in their selection procedures for many classes of Civil Servants while most entrants into the armed forces must sit an intelligence test before they are allocated to their trade, or before they are considered for a commission.

5. *Diagnosis of Mental Sub-normality.* An individual test, e.g. the 1937

[39] Kagan, J., Sontag, L. W., Baker, C. T., Nelson, V. L., 'Personality and IQ Change,' *J. abn. soc. Psychol.*, 1958, 56, 261–266.
[40] Compare Clarke, A. D. B. and Clarke A. M., 'Consistency and Variability in the Growth of Human Characteristics'. In *Advances in Educational Psychology*, 1 (Eds. Wall, W. D. and Varma, V. P.). London: University of London Press, 1972.

or 1960 Revision of the Stanford-Binet Scale, or WISC, is used in the detection of mental sub-normality. Whereas many instances of severe sub-normality are easily recognisable, a more refined technique such as we have in the individual intelligence test is necessary in borderline cases. An IQ of 75/80 is usually the level of intelligence below which children in Great Britain are sent to a special school for educationally sub-normal children (see Chapter 12).

6. *In the case of emotionally maladjusted children.* When children exhibiting psychological difficulties are examined at the Child Guidance clinics, it is frequently found that their attainment in school subjects is much lower than would be expected for their age and intelligence level. Thus children sent to the clinics are examined in order to get an assessment of the level of their intelligence, and for this purpose an individual test is always used.

Intelligence and attainment. As we say on page 33, intelligence is reflected in a person's all-round ability in daily life. The thinking skills involved give powers of insight, understanding, conceptualization, quickness of thought and practical judgment. These skills are dependent to some extent on the environmental stimulation received since birth. Again, although attainment is clearly related to intelligence in the case of the more academic school subjects, it is more dependent upon teaching, attitudes and temperament than is intelligence. Thus measured intelligence (intelligence C) and measured attainment differ in the degree to which they depend on environmental stimulation. They are not essentially different in kind.

The relative contribution of heredity and environment to intellectual growth. Many attempts have been made to estimate the relative contributions of heredity and environment to children's intellectual growth. Before some of these are discussed it will be helpful to note some suggestions regarding the nature of intelligence put forward by Hebb.[41] He maintains that 'intelligence' has two meanings and both of these are important. Intelligence A is innate potential and cannot be observed or measured. This may have a neurophysiological basis and be wholly determined genetically. Intelligence B relates to the functioning of the brain after development has occurred; it reflects the all-round performance of the individual in daily life including school or work. A high innate potential does not guarantee that development will occur to the full extent of the potentiality. Thus although intelligence A sets the upper limit to intelligence B, the latter is going to be affected by early learning and its transfer effects. Intelligence B, however, can only be measured by a test appropriate to the culture. Thus we may also distinguish intelligence C, which is the observed

[41] Hebb, D. O., *The Organisation of Behaviour*. London: Chapman & Hall, 1949.

intelligence in IQ or other units as estimated by the intelligence test. It must be remembered, then, that in our investigations, it is changes in intelligence C that we record. Sometimes it is possible to make judgments on changes in intelligence B although these cannot be made as objectively as can the changes in intelligence C. It is never possible, however, to note changes in intelligence A.

The hereditary background of our children cannot, at present, be improved by selective breeding, so those interested in the education of children should be concerned with the limits within which environmental stimulation can bring about changes in intellectual growth.

In an early experiment Burks[42] worked out correlations between children's IQ's and certain environmental and/or hereditary conditions within two populations; children living in foster homes, and children living with their natural parents. She concluded that some 75 per cent of the variability of the IQ's of these children was due to hereditary causes. Another interesting study was conducted by Newman, Freeman and Holzinger.[43] They collected data from 50 pairs of like-sexed fraternal twins, 50 pairs of identical twins reared together, and 19 pairs of identical twins most of whom were separated from one another before two years of age. A large number of psychological and physical tests were administered to these children. The average differences for identical twins reared apart were much greater than for identical twins reared together in respect of intelligence, weight and school achievement. Certain of the identical twins who had been reared in very different environmental circumstances differed by as much as 24 points of IQ. In spite of the criticisms that have been made of this investigation, it does show that substantial environmental differences produce different rates of mental growth in children with equal hereditary endowment.

A third investigation of importance is that of Schmidt.[44,45] Between 1935 and 1942, she studied 320 Chicago children all of whom had been diagnosed as feeble-minded (all had IQ's below 70) when aged 12–14 years. Of these, 252 were educated for three years at special experimental schools where appropriate training was given in academic subjects and manipulative skills, and where the curriculum was designed to increase emotional and social adjustment. The remaining 68 cases went to more conventional schools. All the young people were followed up for between one and a half and four and a half years after the end of this schooling.

[42] Burks, B. S., 'On the Relative Contributions of Nature and Nurture to Average Group Differences in Intelligence,' Proc. nat. Acad. Sci., 1938, 24, 276–282.

[43] Newman, H. F., Freeman, F. N., and Holzinger, K. J., Twins: A Study of Heredity and Environment. Chicago: University of Chicago Press, 1937.

[44] Schmidt, B. G., 'Changes in Personal, Social and Intellectual Behaviour of Children originally Classified as Feeble Minded,' Psychol. Monogr., 1946, 60, No. 5.

[45] As a contrast to Schmidt's work see that of Honzik, M. P., 'Developmental Studies of Parent-Child Resemblance in Intelligence,' Child Developm., 1957, 28, 215–228. It suggests that individual differences are largely genetically determined.

Certain educational tests, the Stanford-Binet tests, and tests of personality adjustment were applied at eighteen-month intervals throughout. The IQ's of the children in the experimental schools continued to rise during the three years' schooling and increased thereafter. The personality tests also showed these children to be better adjusted. Half the pupils from the experimental schools went on to ordinary American High School courses, and 27 per cent graduated from such schools. When last surveyed 83 per cent of the children from the progressive schools were in regular employment, and nearly two-thirds of these were in clerical or skilled work. The controls, however, showed a very poor educational and employment record. Many criticisms have, however, been made of the large increases in IQ which Schmidt claimed. Some of these criticisms are undoubtedly justified, and it seems likely that the IQ rises are less than she suggested. On the other hand, it is impossible to dismiss the finding that, when steps are taken to improve emotional adjustment and to provide a suitable and stimulating environment, a large proportion of children once diagnosed as feeble-minded are turned into reasonably capable adults.

Vernon[46] concludes that the following inferences may be drawn from the many investigations that have been carried out in this field:

(a) Within the primary school population of Great Britain or the U.S.A. (white children only), which are fairly homogeneous from a cultural point of view, something like 75 per cent of the variability in intelligence test scores can be attributed to hereditary factors. Care must be taken, of course, to ensure a uniform degree of familiarity with the tests employed, for when practice and coaching varies between different sections of these populations, no worthwhile conclusions can be drawn.

(b) This large hereditary influence is manifested only because the intellectual stimulation received from the environment is fairly uniform for all children. They all receive more or less the same kind of education which employs the same language, concepts, and pictorial or other symbols. Further, they are all trained to study printed questions and write down their answers quickly. These factors vary, of course, between schools, between social classes, and between families within such classes, though not enough to account for more than 25–30 per cent of the IQ variability.

(c) When children are separated into different types of secondary education and so receive different degrees of intellectual stimulation, the environment probably accounts for more of the IQ variability. Different occupations into which young people go when they leave school also provide differing degrees of intellectual stimulation.

(d) The factors listed under (b) probably vary more widely among emotionally maladjusted and dull children. The former have difficulty in absorbing the normal concepts of the culture, while the latter sometimes fall so far behind their fellows, that the education which stimulates the

[46] Vernon, P. E., 'Recent Investigations of Intelligence and its Measurements,' *Eugenics Rev.*, 1951, 43, 125–137.

intellectual growth of the ordinary child becomes too advanced for them.

The upshot of more recent investigations bearing on the issue suggests that we cannot regard intelligence as fixed and its development completely determined by the genes (cf. Hunt[47]). Intelligence depends in part on the degree of intellectual stimulation the child has experienced from his earliest days. Moreover, it does not seem possible to give a general answer to the question as to what proportion of the variation in intelligence between individuals is due to heredity and what due to environment, since the proportions differ between individuals. There is an interaction between level of intelligence and experience. For example, adults are likely to give a different range of experiences to a bright than to a dull child: again, the brighter the child the more likely that he can build on a wider range of experiences compared with the dull child. It is also worth noting a controversial article by Jensen[48] on the extent to which IQ and scholastic achievement can be boosted. He argues that environmental factors are not nearly as important as genetic factors, and that prenatal influence may well constitute the largest environmental factor on IQ. However, in the same volume of the journal there is a critical discussion of Jensen's paper by other well-known psychologists, and their contributions should also be read. But it does appear clear that the early years (perhaps the first four or five) are extremely important in the development of intelligence.[49] In these years intellectual growth is likely to be affected by encouragement to explore the environment and to interact with problems, and by the presence of an adult who is able and willing to help a child to appreciate the significance of his own actions.

General Educational and Occupational Abilities. Up to the 1930's the predominant view among American psychologists was that all abilities and personality characteristics were highly specific. But in Great Britain the importance of the general intellectual factor, 'g', was demonstrated by Spearman, and the existence of additional sub-types of ability (group factors) gradually emerged from the work of Burt, Stephenson, El Koussy and others as we have seen. The main abilities in educational and vocational achievement as suggested by Vernon are indicated in Figure 5.

The main ability is 'g' together with two group abilities. One of the latter is the verbal-numerical-educational ability (called the v:ed ability) and the other practical-mechanical-spatial-physical ability (called the k:m ability). The former indicates the ability to understand and handle words both written and spoken, to manipulate number, and to profit generally from a verbal type of education. The latter ability seems to divide into (a) spatial ability—the ability to perceive, interpret and mentally rearrange

[47] Hunt, J. McV., *Intelligence and Experience*, New York: Ronald Press, 1961.

[48] Jensen, A. R., 'How much can we Boost IQ and Scholastic Achievement,' *Harvard Educational Review*, 1969, 39, 1–123.

[49] Bloom, B. S., *Stability and Change in Human Characteristics*. New York: Wiley, 1964.

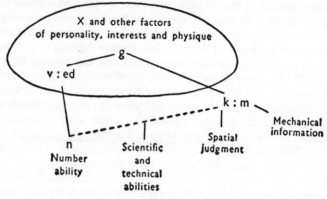

Fig. 5

objects spatially related,[50] and, (b) mechanical ability which depends to some extent upon knowledge and experience. While both the v:ed and k:m abilities seem to depend on inborn potential, they are also affected by temperament and cultural opportunities. Thus the k:m ability is less well marked in girls than in boys, and this is no doubt due in part to the different kinds of activities in which the sexes indulge.[51] If, in the case of girls, tests of domestic or social abilities were given, it is possible that a practical ability would emerge which would overlap to some extent with our k:m ability, but not be identical with it.

In a group which showed a considerable range of ability, 'g' would usually account for some 40 per cent, and v:ed and k:m together, for some 15–20 per cent of the variability in test scores. Hence we are justified in attempting to estimate a person's score on these abilities when giving educational and vocational guidance.

When school marks are analysed, as distinct from the marks obtained on psychological tests, we find an industriousness factor (named the X factor by Alexander). This 'drive' factor is a complex of personality traits, interests and background influences, and it, together with the g and v:ed abilities, form the major influences in educational and occupational success. Note also that the v:ed ability can be broken down into minor group factors. One of these is the *n* ability, which underlies our capacity to do arithmetic and elementary mathematics. But at more advanced levels of mathematics (say above the 'O' level in the General Certificate of Education), spatial and non-verbal tests of intelligence forecast mathematical success better than g plus v:ed tests. Probably this is due to the influence

[50] For a detailed study of the nature of the ability see: Macfarlane Smith, I., *Spatial Ability*. London: University of London Press, Ltd., 1964.

[51] A biochemical theory has also been proposed to explain some of the sex difference. See Macfarlane Smith, I., 'The Use of Diagnostic Tests for Assessing the Abilities of Overseas Students attending Institutions of Further Education,' *The Vocation Aspects of Education*, 1971, **54**, 39–48.

of science training on both spatial-mechanical and mathematical abilities.

Numerous other factors are claimed, especially by American psychologists, such as reasoning, attention, rote memory, and fluency, but as far as is known these are of little relevance in academic or occupational success. Lovell[52] has produced strong evidence that there is an ability to group ideas or objects to a given criterion, or in a given way, and to switch from one criterion to another. This ability is over and above the g, v:ed, and k:m abilities. Moreover, there is a good deal of evidence in the literature dealing with mental deterioration in clinical cases which supports this finding. But how far this ability will be of help when giving educational or vocational guidance, or in the examination of mental patients is not precisely known.

Psychologists when giving educational or vocational guidance are justified in making the fullest possible use of g, v:ed and k:m tests. Thereafter their success is likely to depend chiefly on the extent to which they can gauge each candidate's previous attainment and relevant experience, determine his interests, and judge his more general motivation, or X; and his specific attitudes to the type of education or to the job under consideration.

Mangan[53] has shown that g, v and k abilities cannot, as it were, ever be measured in isolation. They always seem to be conditioned by work-attitude factors of which the chief ones are persistence, and speed versus accuracy. The former affects all test results when the test material is difficult, and the latter when it is easy. Thus in power tests with ample or unlimited time, our measurement of g, v and k abilities depends considerably upon a work habit of persistence. If, however, we use highly-speeded tests involving a large number of easy questions, the other general attitude enters. Thus the g, v and k abilities which underlie performance on the rather highly-speeded Arithmetic, English and Intelligence Tests, and which were commonly used at 10–11 years of age when selecting children for different types of secondary education, differ from the abilities measured by the power type of test, despite great overlapping between the two sets.

The conceptual framework for the structure of abilities as illustrated in Figure 5 is widely held among British psychologists. But Eysenck and White[54] have indicated that work involving 15–16-year-olds suggests that in emotionally labile adolescents, abilities are less clearly structured. Great emotional stability and ability, respectively, may go with greater degrees of organisation of ability and stability. If this is confirmed it will be an important finding.

[52] Lovell, K., 'A Study of the Problem of Intellectual Deterioration in Adolescents and Young Adults,' *Brit. J. Psychol.*, 1955, **46**, 199–210.
[53] Mangan, G. L., 'A Factorial Study of Speed, Power and Related Variables,' *Brit. J. Educ. Psychol.*, 1959, **29**, 144–154.
[54] Eysenck, H. J. and White, P. O., 'Personality and the Measurement of Intelligence,' *Brit. J. Educ. Psychol.*, 1964, **34**, 197–201.

Before concluding this section it must be stressed that the g, v:ed and k:m abilities are not identical with the degree and speed of learning new skills, although there is a positive correlation with these abilities in complex learning tasks. In fact there is little evidence that there is a general learning ability[55] common to a wide variety of tasks—psychomotor, mechanical, verbal and non-verbal, rote and meaningful—whether such a general factor appears seems determined by the complexity of the task. Measures of learning tend to be grouped under a number of ill-defined factors which depend upon such influences as type of material, or conditions of learning and recall. But some of these group abilities do correlate with educational and occupational abilities, so that verbal learning relates more highly to verbal abilities.

Thurstone's Group Abilities. Some American psychologists prefer a number of independent abilities, rather than a general ability and a number of important group abilities. Thurstone[56] identifies the following aspects of intelligence all of which he considers to be correlated with one another to some extent:

Space factor (S): the ability to visualise flat or solid objects; it is linked with mechanical ability.

Number ability (N): the ability to carry out rather simple numerical exercises.

Verbal comprehension factor (V): the ability to deal with ideas expressed in words.

Word fluency factor (W): the ability to think of isolated words at a rapid rate.

Rote memory factor (M).

Induction factor: the facility in discovering the principle that applies to a series of problems.

Deduction factor: the ability to apply a given principle to a series of specific problems. (There is only a small amount of evidence for this.)

Flexibility and speed of closure: the ability to interpret instructions, and to size up a problem situation, quickly. In essence this is the ability to abandon a configuration in favour of a more promising one.

Thurstone has termed these *primary mental abilities* and claims that they are found both in very young children and in adults; in other words the abilities maintain their identity throughout life. He further concludes that the primary abilities are more useful than the notion of general intelligence, or 'g'. A child's level of intelligence, he maintains, can best be represented as a profile of mental abilities, and this will provide better prediction of his abilities along various lines than will a single score of intelligence.

[55] Mackay, G. W. S. and Vernon, P. E., 'The Measurement of Learning Ability,' *Brit. J. Educ. Psychol.*, 1963, 33, 177–186.
[56] Thurstone, L. L., 'Theories of Intelligence,' *Scient. Monthly*, 1949, 62, 101–112.

Convergent and Divergent Thinking. Guilford[57] distinguishes between *convergent* and *divergent* thinking. The former calls for one right answer which can be determined closely, if not exactly, from the data given. The ordinary intelligence test tends to measure this type of thought. On the other hand, divergent thinking goes off in different directions. With given data, such thinking leads to a diversity of answers. Thus in creative people one might expect to find more divergent thinking than in non-creative people. Guildford claims that among able adults, creative individuals are more flexible in their thinking, and that they show more fluency and originality compared with those of less creativity. Getzels and Jackson[58] also claim to have demonstrated a low correlation between creativity and IQ in able 12–18-year-olds even when pupils were matched for chronological age and sex, although Sultan[59] in a study of English grammar school children did not find such clear-cut results. Vernon[60] surveying the position in 1964 concluded that while there is a need to continue with tests of the Getzels-Guilford type,[61] there is doubt about their reliability, and whether they indicate abilities which have much bearing on performance in real life situations. To check on this would require a follow-up study of some 10–20 years.

There remains much discussion about the value of the so-called tests of creativity, and it is helpful to bear in mind some of the more recent studies in this field. These are briefly mentioned below.

(I) Cropley[62] using the Wallach-Kogan tests of creativity among university men found a large general intellective factor with substantial correlations with both creativity and intelligence tests, suggesting a good deal of overlapping between the abilities involved in the two kinds of test.

(II) Ginsburg and Whittemore[63] used Mednick's Remote Associates Test to measure 'creative potential' among both American students and Australian boys. They concluded that tests of creativity and intelligence measure somewhat different, albeit overlapping, abilities and warn that the case for creative thinking independent of other facets of the intellect should not be overstated.

[57] Guilford, J. P., *The Nature of Human Intelligence.* New York: McGraw Hill, 1967. Guilford, J. P. and Hoepfner, R., *The Analysis of Intelligence.* New York: McGraw Hill, 1972.

[58] Getzels, J. W. and Jackson, P. W., *Creativity and Intelligence.* London: Wiley, 1961.

[59] Sultan, E. E., 'A Factorial Study in the Domain of Creative Thinking,' *Brit. J. Educ. Psychol.*, 1962, **32**, 78–82.

[60] Vernon, P. E., 'Creativity and Intelligence,' *Educational Research*, 1964, **6**, 163–169.

[61] See also Goldman, R. J., 'The Minnesota Tests of Creative Thinking,' *Educational Research*, 1964, **7**, 3–14.

[62] Cropley, A. J., 'A Note on the Wallach-Kogan Tests of Creativity,' *Brit. J. Educ. Psychol.*, 1968, **38**, 197–201.

[63] Ginsburg, G. P. and Whittemore, R. G., 'Creativity and Verbal Ability: A Direct Examination of the Relationship,' *Brit. J. Educ. Psychol.*, 1968, **38**, 133–139.

(III) Lovell and Shields[64] have shown that among children with WISC Verbal Scores of 140 or more and aged 8 years 5 months to 11 years 7 months, the evidence indicates that after a large general factor has been extracted from an appropriate battery of intelligence and attainment tests, and tests of logical thinking, only a moderate amount of the variability in the creativity test performance was left over for distribution among a number of further small factors.

(IV) Performance on the so-called tests of creativity depend upon the atmosphere in which they are administered. In a study involving some 400 Canadian boys and girls of median age 13 years 11 months, Vernon[65] gave a battery of divergent thinking tests to two sets of seven classes. The first set was given the tests under ordinary test-like conditions, while the second set worked the tests in an informal and relaxed atmosphere with generous time allowance. Under the relaxed conditions more high scores were obtained, and correlations with other variables such as intelligence measures, and tasks said by the teachers to be creative ones, were somewhat higher. Yet the mean intercorrelation of the tests were only ·287 and ·346 in the formal and relaxed groups respectively.

(V) Vernon[66] (1967) concludes that there is little evidence to show how validly creativity tests can discriminate potentially creative persons in arts or sciences from the non-creatives. Such programmes as have been designed in the U.S.A. to train creative thinking may contain useful educational ideas, but in Vernon's view they are irrelevant to the development of outstanding thought in real-life situations.[67]

The Decline of Abilities with age. Vernon and Parry[68] have summarised the position as it was up to about 1947 in relation to the effects of age on intelligence test score. Many of the relevant researches, although often on a small scale, had established the following facts. Thus according to the authors:

(a) Up to about 12 years of age general intelligence increases, on the average, at a steady rate in most children. The rate of increase then slows and for most adolescents a maximum intelligence test score is reached at about 15 years. On some tests, though, there is no improvement after 13 years, while on others (largely verbal in character) rises have been reported after 20 years of age.

[64] Lovell, K. and Shields, J. B., 'Some Aspects of a Study of the Gifted Child,' *Brit. J. Educ. Psychol.*, 1967, 37, 201–208.

[65] Vernon, P. E., 'Effects of Administration and scoring on Divergent Thinking Tests,' *Brit. J. Educ. Psychol.*, 1971, 41, 245–257.

[66] Vernon, P. E., 'Psychological Studies of Creativity,' *J. Child Psychol. and Psychiat.*, 1967, 8, 153–164.

[67] Vernon, P. E. (Ed.), *Creativity*. Harmondsworth: Penguin 1970. For another recent review see Butcher, H. J., 'Divergent Thinking and Creativity'. In *Advances in Educational Psychology*, 1 (Eds. Wall, W. D. and Varma, V. P.). London: University of London Press, 1972.

[68] Vernon, P. E. and Parry, J. B., *Personnel Selection in the British Forces.* London: University of London Press Ltd., 1949.

(*b*) From 20–60 years of age there is a steady decline on 'g' tests which involve abstract reasoning and speed of mental manipulation; but scores on tests of vocabulary and information decline more slowly with age.

(*c*) A particular child may show great irregularities in mental growth. This is partly due to the stimulating or inhibiting effects of the child's environment (both home and school), and partly due to unreliability, or change in content, of the tests used.

Ever since large scale intelligence testing began in the American Army in 1917, two apparently conflicting results have been obtained. The average mental age of representative adult groups is about 13½ years, but when students in high schools or colleges are given intelligence tests of proper difficulty, they usually continue to show rises in test scores from 15 to 20 years of age or more. Vernon[69] reconciles these findings by suggesting that the growth of intelligence continues only so long as education or other intellectual stimulus continues. Thereafter a decline sets in. In Great Britain most adolescents leave school at 15, hence the growth and decline of their intelligence may be represented by the lines A and B in Figure 6.[70]

Curves of Mental Growth and Decline

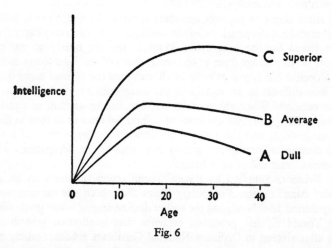

Fig. 6

These lines reach their maximum height at about 15 years. But a percentage of pupils stay on at secondary school, or have college or university education up to 18, 22 years of age, or later, and they then enter jobs where there is still a certain amount of intellectual stimulation. These may be represented by the line C which shows an increase in intelligence up to

[69] Vernon, P. E., 'Recent Investigation of Intelligences and its Measurement,' *Eugenics Rev.*, 1951, **43**, 125–137.
[70] Reproduced with permission of the Eugenics Society.

about 25 years of age and then a slow decline. But since these are relatively few in number, the mean mental age of the population at 20 years of age is lower than the maximum that the average pupils reach at 15.

Five pieces of evidence are adduced supporting Vernon's hypothesis:

(a) Lorge[71] re-tested a number of adults at the age of 34 whose test results at 14 years of age were known. Those adults who had received a university education were, on the average, two years superior in mental age to those who had received no further schooling but whose intellectual level had been the same at 14 years.

(b) Vernon and Parry[72] quote results for an intelligence test (which measured almost wholly 'g' and very little 'v'), a spelling test, and arithmetic test and for a spatial test involving the building of patterns from coloured blocks. The average standards reached on these tests by 18-year-old entrants into the Forces were reached by children of 13, 12½, 13 and 15½ years respectively. Analysis of the results revealed, however, that the best ten per cent of adult recruits did as well as the best ten per cent of the normal 14-year-olds, but that there was a progressive decline at the lower end. Thus the bottom ten per cent of entrants to the Forces appeared to lose 1½ years on intelligence, 2 years on arithmetic and 3 years on spelling. Hence, as the authors suggest, there is a differential decline in abilities between different groups.

(c) After about 18 years of age there is no doubt that there is both an absolute and a differential decline in intelligence. Vernon and Parry[73] give mean scores for the Progressive Matrices test for nearly 90,000 naval recruits varying in age from 17 to over 40 years of age. The scores indicate that a decline has begun as early as 18, although the authors make it clear that it is difficult to be certain of the comparability of the various age group samples. When the recruits are classified by civilian occupations, however, there is definite evidence of differential rates of decline in different occupations, and the authors put forward the hypothesis of a more rapid decline in intelligence among men who are in occupations where they make 'least use of their brains'.

(d) Evidence supplied by Raven[74] from scores obtained on his Progressive Matrices and Vocabulary Tests show both the fanning out of ability during adulthood, and the earlier decline among lower grade adults.

(e) Venables[75] has produced evidence that intellectual growth takes place after sixteen in Ordinary National Certificate students taking part-time day release courses in engineering at technical colleges.

[71] Lorge, I., 'Schooling Makes a Difference,' *Teach. Coll. Rec.*, 1945, 46, 483–492.
[72] Vernon, P. E., and Parry, J. B., *Personnel Selection in the British Forces.* London: University of London Press Ltd., 1949.
[73] Vernon, P. E., and Parry, J. B., *ibid.*
[74] Raven, J. C., 'The Comparative Assessment of Intellectual Ability,' *Brit. J. Psychol.*, 1948, 39, 12–19.
[75] Venables, E. C., 'Changes in Intelligence Test Scores of Engineering Apprentices between the First and Third Years of Attendance at College,' *Brit. J. Educ. Psychol.*, 1961, 32, 257–264.

Current studies show that when longitudinal studies of the same people are made over a number of years, intelligence test scores continue to rise. This is not surprising if the test used has a strong verbal component (see below).

The available evidence suggests, therefore, that for most people, intelligence as measured by tests containing little 'v', reaches its peak at 15 or soon after at present. Conditions are similar in the case of the very dull child too, so that we find some extremely backward children learning to read a little at 15, while some mental subnormals are trainable in adolescence. Unfortunately dull children often go to jobs where there is little intellectual stimulation. For able people, however, who receive further education, the maximum test scores may be reached anytime up to 25— and much later if the test has a strong verbal component.

Next there is the question of what happens to the v:ed abilities during adolescence. It seems likely that reading ability increases between 15 and 18 years[76]; also size of vocabulary increases from 15 years for about another 10 years in the dullest, and 20 years in the brighter, individuals. Arithmetical ability, however, remains stationary for a few years after 15 or declines somewhat, unless stimulated by further schooling or work. Norris[77] in an extensive investigation, found that educational attainments tend to be forgotten rapidly after leaving school except in so far as they are used in daily life. For example, he showed that scores on tests of language may rise until about 40 years of age, but arithmetic attainment declines in most people other than clerks who practise arithmetic in their jobs.

There is not much evidence to suggest what happens to the k:m abilities during adolescence. Bradford[78] has shown that spatial ability (k) sometimes increases in males between 14 and 16 years of age, and declines after 20/25 years of age. Again, Vernon and Parry,[79] by comparing scores obtained by Glasgow school leavers and Glasgow Naval recruits, suggest that k:m abilities increase between the ages of 14 and 18 years with or without much schooling. On balance it seems likely that in young men at least, there is some increase in k:m abilities up to the late teens and a decline after the early twenties.

More recently Bayley has given details of changes in scores on the Verbal and Performance Scales of the Wechsler Intelligence Test over the age range 16 to 36 in American subjects. The data relate to 28 males and 30 females—born in the period 1928-30 and representing a broad range of full-time healthy babies born in Berkeley, California, hospitals—who have been studied since birth. They were tested at 16, 18, 21, 26 and 36 years of age. From this longitudinal study it was found that scores increased with age up to 36 years (although the rate of increase was then

[76] Ministry of Education, *Reading Ability*. London: H.M.S.O., 1950.
[77] Norris, K. E., *The Three R's and the Adult Worker*. McGill University, 1940.
[78] Bradford, E. J. G., 'Performance Tests in the Diagnosis of Mental Deficiency,' *Brit. J. Med. Psychol.*, 1943, **19**, 394-414.
[79] Vernon, P. E., and Parry, J. B., *op. cit.*

decreasing) on the Verbal Scale, whereas on the Performance Scale there was either no increase in score or a slight deline after 26 years.[80]

It is possible that raising the full-time school leaving age to sixteen and instituting compulsory part-time education from sixteen to eighteen might alter the pattern of adolescent abilities somewhat. The government has indicated that the former change will be carried out in the year 1972–73, but there is no indication that the latter change will come about although the Crowther Report (1959) recommended it.

Intelligence of children and size of the family. Since about 1920 many investigations have shown that there is a negative correlation of about — ·2 to — ·3 between children's intelligence test scores and the size of the family to which they belong. Nisbet[81] reported a number of researches undertaken between 1922 and 1952, and of the forty-four correlation coefficients reported for the relationship between intelligence and family size, thirty-eight are negative. Among the more recent investigations three are worthy of special mention. First, in the 1947 Scottish Mental survey some 70,200 children aged 11 years (almost the whole of the 11-year-old age group in Scotland) were examined by a Moray House Intelligence Test—a group test of a verbal nature. There was a steady decline in mean standard scores from 105·3 among only children, to 95·8 among families of 5 children, and to 86·5 in families of 13–18 children. Second, Vernon[82] published the scores which he obtained from giving six mental tests to about 10,000 male National Service recruits, mostly aged 18 years, and called up in 1947. Their height, and their physical and eyesight gradings, were also available. He found that as the size of the family increased, so the scores on the intelligence and some educational tests declined and both clearly paralleled the results obtained in the Scottish Mental survey. On the tests which involved mechanical ability the decline was less marked, and was smaller still on physical measures. Third, Nisbet and Entwistle[83] gave data on 2,868 pupils at ages 11 and 12 years of whom 2,734 had also been tested at ages 7 and 9. There was again the inverse relationship between test score and family size, the magnitude of the relationship being greater in the case of tests involving verbal items than in the case of non-verbal ones. Moreover, the familiar relationship between test score and family size was found in all social classes both in respect of English and non-verbal tests, thus confirming the view of Douglas.[84] It is true that the effect of family size on test score was least in social classes I and II, this finding

[80] Bayley, N., 'Learning in Adulthood: The Role of Intelligence.' In *Analyses of Concept Learning.* New York: Academic Press, 1966.

[81] Nisbet, J. D., *Family Environment.* London: Cassell & Co., 1953.

[82] Vernon, P. E., 'Recent Investigation of Intelligence and its Measurements,' *Eugenics Rev.,* 1951, **43**, 125–137.

[83] Nisbet, J. D. and Entwistle, N. J., 'Intelligence and Family Size 1949–1965,' *Brit. J. Educ. Psychol.,* 1967, **37**, 188–193.

[84] Douglas, J. W. B., *The Home and the School.* London: McGibbon and Kee, 1964.

being consonant with small amounts of evidence provided by other workers that at the uppermost socio-economic levels there might be a slight positive correlation between the intelligence of a *pair* of parents and size of completed family.

This evidence suggests that children who have many brothers and sisters tend to make lower scores in intelligence tests than do children who belong to smaller families. There are, of course, many exceptions. But it is the cause that is the matter of controversy. If it is due to the less intelligent parents having more children, there might be a steady fall in the level of the average national intelligence. Alternatively it could be that the findings can be explained in part by better opportunities for language development in smaller families which provide, on the average, more child–adult contacts and more reading material per child (cf. Nisbet, *op. cit.*). Other environmental influences could also play a part in large families such as deficiencies in parental care, or that those who have smaller families also give greater support and encouragement to the children they have. On the other hand,[85] Higgins *et al.* give some evidence suggesting that the higher reproductive rate of low IQ parents is offset by a larger proportion of their siblings who fail to reproduce at all. When non-reproducing siblings of parents are included, these workers claim that the negative relationship between IQ and mean number of offspring per person disappears. This suggestion might explain the findings of the Scottish Mental Survey which, among other aims, attempted to establish if there was a decline in the intelligence level of successive generations by testing all the 11-year-olds in Scotland in 1932 and 1947. No evidence of such a decline in intelligence as between 1932 and 1947 was shown. It was, however, impossible to make the testing conditions identical on both occasions, and by the latter date it seems likely that many of the children had become somewhat sophisticated as far as intelligence testing was concerned.

Summing up we may say that we do not yet fully understand why children from large families make smaller scores on intelligence tests than children from smaller ones. Part of the negative correlation can probably be explained by environmental effects such as a lower degree of language experience with adults, and a greater lack of parental forethought and support.

The problem of inter-racial differences in intelligence.[86] In the past, many attempts have been made to compare the intelligence levels of different races, which have entirely different cultures, using the same intelligence

[85] Higgins, J. V., Reed, E. W. and Reed, S. C., 'Intelligence and Family Size. A Paradox Resolved,' *Eugen. Quart.*, 1962, 9, 84–90. See also Goodhart, C. B., 'World Population Growth and its Regulation by Natural Means,' *Nature*, September 15, 1956, 561–565.

[86] In connection with this section see Vernon, P. E., *Intelligence and Cultural Environment*. London: Methuen, 1969.

tests. Today it is realised that the problem of inter-racial differences in intelligence is a complicated one, although there is still controversy among psychologists as to whether certain races are intellectually inferior to others or not, and lack of clear thinking remains.[87]

According to contemporary opinion among anthropologists the notion of race is doubtful. It seems that all races are to some extent mixed, those of purest descent being those that have had least mixing. Thus most anthropologists today admit only four broad groups; the Caucasian, Mongol, Negro and Australasian.

During the First World War, soldiers in the U.S.A. were classified according to their country of origin. The rank order for intelligence seemed to be, English, Scottish, Dutch, Danish and German all of the same level; then Irish, Austrian and Belgian; and Turkish, Greek and Russian in the lowest group. The following points, however, must be carefully watched when studying these and similar findings:

(a) The range of scores within any group is always much greater than the average differences between groups. Thus although the average score of American Negroes may be 85, ten per cent will score higher than the average American white.

(b) The groups examined must be really representative of the country of origin.

(c) The rank order given above corresponds closely to educational opportunities available in those countries then.

(d) The closer the culture of the race to that of the race for which the intelligence test was devised, the more likely the average scores for the two races will be the same. Or again, the longer the migrants have been within the new culture, the more likely it is that their scores will be equal to those of the native peoples. For example, in one investigation two comparable groups of American Negroes, who had migrated from the southern part of the U.S.A. to New York varying lengths of time previously were studied. For those who had been in New York 1–2 years the average IQ was 72, but for those who had been there 9 years or more the average was 94.

When tests of spatial ability are given (these often involve the building of patterns or shapes from blocks or similar material) there are also differences between the scores obtained by different racial groups. Strange results are sometimes given, in that the test scores are not always in the same rank order as one would expect from the cultural advancement of the races concerned. But there is increasing evidence that if, say, spatial ability is poorly developed under certain cultural conditions, the ability may be increased under appropriate educational methods.[88] Again, when

---

[87] There may, of course, be real differences in the levels of intelligence between varying races or groups due, say, to diet or vitamin deficiency.

[88] McFie, J., 'The Effect of Education on African Performance on a Group of Intelligence Tests,' *Brit. J. Educ. Psychol.*, 1961, **31**, 232–240.

intelligence or other tests are given, one cannot be sure that the motivation, or the willingness to work quickly, is the same among other races as it is among the people of Europe or among the white population of the U.S.A. Children in Great Britain tend to work at speed when completing tests as such behaviour fits into our way of life both inside and outside the school.

Most psychologists are now agreed that no material can be used in intelligence tests which is culturally neutral. In our society intelligence appears as an ability to deal primarily with verbal and other symbolic relationships, and with spatial relationships which are common to our culture pattern, but in other societies it might appear as an ability to deal with problems of the desert or jungle. Irvine[89] suggests that some of the influences affecting the testing of abilities and attainments in Africa are: content of the test; form and style of test; the transfer that takes place between practice and actual test items when the material is unfamiliar; the particular cultural or educational bias of the test scores; local school standards; and the motivational influence of the tester. Two points emerge:

(a) When designing an intelligence test for children of another culture, one must set about the problem by trial and error, adapting the test items to the new culture. An excellent example of this approach is provided by the work of Scott[90] who was concerned with the selection of Sudanese children for intermediate and secondary schools. He found that a mere translation of a group verbal test into their language was unsatisfactory, and that a non-verbal test was of little use in forecasting educability. As a result of his experiments he was forced to the conclusion that one cannot predict how a test item will work in a new cultural setting, and that the only way to proceed is by trial and error, thereby finding which items will give a reliable and valid test.

(b) It is possible to study how intelligence develops within a culture. Thus we can analyse the growth of intelligence among a given group of, say, African children, but it is less easy to compare that growth with the growth of intelligence among European children. At the same time, it must be realised that there are very great differences between the peoples of Africa in respect of language, tribal structure, educational support given to, and the educational expectations for, their children, so that it is also difficult at times to compare African groups one with another.

All that we have said in this section really amounts to this. If we could

[89] Irvine, S. H., 'Towards a Rationale for Testing Attainments and Abilities in Africa,' *Brit. J. Educ. Psychol.*, 1966, **36**, 24-32. Compare Lloyd, F. and Pidgeon, D. A., 'An Investigation into the Effects of Coaching on Non-Verbal Test Material with European, Indian and African Children,' *Brit. J. Educ. Psychol.*, 1961, **31**, 145-151.
[90] Scott, G. C., 'Measuring Sudanese Intelligence,' *Brit. J. Educ. Psychol.*, 1950, **20**, 43-54.

observe and measure our intelligence A it might be possible to compare the intelligence levels of different races. But since we can only observe intelligence B and intelligence C, we cannot compare the intelligence of peoples of widely differing cultures since these intelligences are only manifest through the cultures.

Chapter Four

PERSONALITY AND ITS MEASUREMENT

IN everyday speech the term 'personality' refers to the extent to which a person impresses or attracts other people, but in psychology it means the whole of a person's outstanding characteristics, his abilities, his emotional and social traits, his interests and attitudes. There are two other terms, temperament and character, frequently used in connection with the term 'personality' which we must also describe. The former is now taken to refer to the innate bases of personality, such as natural tendencies and organic drives, the effects of glandular balance on the emotions, or other physiological causes which affect a person's behaviour. Character, however, is personality evaluated against the current standards of the culture pattern. Thus it refers to traits such as honest, reliable, truthful or their opposites, which are either approved or disapproved of by the society. Personality results from the interplay of the inherited constitution with all the forces of the environment from the moment of conception. Until birth, the environmental forces acting within the uterus help to shape the future personality; thereafter the forces range from the physical conditions of up-bringing to the ideas and attitudes of the parents and others with whom the child comes in contact.

Some theories of Personality Organisation. Attempts to build theories of personality organisation began more than 2,000 years ago when the Greeks proposed that there were four types of temperament, the sanguine, choleric, melancholic and phlegmatic, depending upon the relative prominence of blood, yellow bile, black bile and phlegm respectively. In this century a large number of theories have been proposed, and it is quite impossible to discuss more than a few of them. No theory has yet been put forward that includes all the known facts and is generally acceptable. Notcutt[1] has usefully classified these many hypotheses into three main types or systems. First, there are systems which describe a person in terms of basic traits; for example, introvert, athletic. Second, there are systems which describe a person in terms of the external forces acting on him; for example, descriptions of personality made in terms of culture pattern and social role (see Chapter 2). Third, there are systems which describe the interaction of a person and his environment; for example, instinct theory, or psycho-analytic theory which stresses the use of defence mechanisms. More

[1] Notcutt, B., *The Psychology of Personality*. London: Methuen, 1953.

recently Mischel[2] divided personality theories into five groups. First, Type and Trait theories. Second, Psychodynamic theories such as those of Freud and his later followers. These emphasise, in varying degrees, the role of instincts, the growth of psycho-sexual stages, and the social milieu. Third, Psychodynamic Behaviour theories which try to combine psychoanalytic concepts and learning theory. Fourth, Social Behaviour theories which search for causes in the current conditions that control the person's present behaviours. Fifth, Phenomenological theories which minimise all concepts of motivation, and stress the person's immediate experiences, perceptions, encounters, and his striving for growth and self-actualisation.

We shall have space only to discuss three[3] theories of personality organisation:

(a) *Personality Types.* Several attempts have been mâde to divide people into types based on psychological or physical characteristics which they exhibit. Jung distinguishes between extraverts and introverts, the former being people who are socially co-operative, and have a liking for others, and the latter the rather unsociable. Kretschmer divides normal personalities into schizothymes (inflexible, suspicious, secretive people) and cyclothymes (easy going, adaptable, generous individuals), and associates these with an asthenic body form (tall and thin) and pyknic[4] body build (short and fat) respectively. Again Sheldon links three types of body-build with three personality types, viz. those who are sociable and love comfort (rather fat), the energetic and assertive with a liking for muscular activity (exceptional bone and muscle growth), and the withdrawn who have a liking for mental activity (rather thin).[5] Many other types have been proposed, but in spite of the great efforts that have been made in the study of personality types, this system of classification has been of limited value. Readers who are particularly interested in the relationship between personality and body-build, and the possible implications for education, should consult Parnell.[6]

(b) *Personality factors.* In the previous chapter we discussed some of the main factors found in the study of human abilities. The technique of factor-analysis has also been applied to personality in order to see if we

[2] Mischel, W., *Introduction to Personality.* New York: Holt, Rinehart & Winston, 1971.
[3] Another recent concept of personality structure is briefly noted at the end of Chapter 14.
[4] Eysenck suggests a body-build index of $\dfrac{\text{Height} \times 100}{6 \times \text{Chest Diameter}}.$
The average adult male gets an index of about 100, asthenics range up to about 130 and pyknics down to about 70.
[5] These three body types are known respectively as Endomorphic, Mesomorphic and Ectomorphic. For a somatotype study among young children see, Davidson, M. A., McInnes, R. G., Parnell, R. W. 'The Distribution of Personality Traits in Seven-Year-Old Children: A Combined Psychological, Psychiatric and Somatotype Study,' *Brit. J. Educ. Psychol.*, 1957, **27**, 49–62.
[6] Parnell, R. W., *Behaviour and Physique.* London: Arnold, 1958.

can get clear-cut dimensions in this wider field. Unfortunately the results which have been obtained by Cattell, Eysenck and others do not show the degree of agreement that one would like. However, two dimensions (other than that of general intelligence) have been isolated with some certainty. The first of these Vernon[7] calls dependability versus undependability, characterised by the presence or absence of such traits as persistence, purposiveness, stability and good character. This may also be called a factor of emotional stability versus neuroticism. The second dimension, almost but not quite independent of the first, may be labelled extraversion versus introversion. Later, Hallworth,[8] also Hallworth and Morrison,[9] have shown that teachers' personality ratings of secondary school pupils yield two main dimensions supporting Vernon's earlier suggestion. Hallworth calls the first dimension 'reliability and conscientiousness' or 'emotional stability'; and the other 'sociability' or 'social extraversion'. Morrison et al.[10] have also shown that Scottish primary school teachers consistently rate 11–12-year-old pupils along three dimensions. The positive aspects of these dimensions are good behaviour, high attainment, and sociability and social leadership. Other dimensions have been suggested but as yet these must be regarded as being very tentative. Factor analysis is not yet in a position to supply a complete map of the personality but this approach has one advantage over types, namely that a slow gradation from one extreme of the dimension to the other is permitted.

(c) *Freud's Personality Theory*. This theory has caused much controversy and stimulated research. The account given here is very brief and over-simplified, but some mention must be made of his suggestions. He recognises three main components of the human personality—the *id*, *ego*, and *super-ego* which are in constant interaction with the outside world. The *id*, almost wholly within the unconscious mind, consists of man's instinctive drives and natural tendencies; it is amoral, infantile, non-rational, and demanding immediate satisfaction. The *ego* is what we call consciousness, will, reason, wisdom, sanity. It is in contact with both the id and the external world and its function is to hold a balance between the constant strivings of the id for satisfaction, the censure of the super-ego (see below) and the demands of the outside world. The *super-ego*, like the id, is an unconscious survival from infancy and is akin to what most people call conscience, ideals, training, or what McDougal calls the self-regarding sentiment. As the young child develops he assimilates and incorporates (this process is called introjection) the values and standards of his parents,

[7] Vernon, P. E., *Personality Tests and Assessments*. London: Methuen, 1953.
[8] Hallworth, H. J., 'Personality Ratings of Adolescents: a Study in a Comprehensive School,' *Brit. J. Educ. Psychol.*, 1964, **34**, 171–177.
[9] Hallworth, H. J. and Morrison A., 'A Comparison of Peer and Teacher Personality Ratings in a Secondary Modern School,' *Brit. J. Educ. Psychol.*, 1964, **34**, 285–291.
[10] Morrison, A., McIntyre, D. and Sutherland, J., 'Teachers' Personality Ratings of Pupils in Scottish Primary Schools,' *Brit. J. Educ. Psychol.*, 1965, **35**, 306–319.

grandparents and other children of his own age. Thus the child takes unto himself or internalises the demands of others (this usually means the demands of the culture) and so develops his conscience or super-ego. The job of the super-ego seems to be to criticise the ego and make it conform by bringing about feelings of guilt.

Freud claims that the way in which the ego resolves the conflicting demands of the id, super-ego and the external world, brings about the individual personality. To overcome the conflicts, the ego may employ repression (see Chapter 2) or one or more of the other chief defence mechanisms listed below:

Projection. The thrusting forth, on the external world and other persons, unconscious wishes and ideas which would be painful if accepted as part of the self. This is said to happen frequently in children's play, as, for example, when the child in playing with dolls often expresses his underlying needs, purposes and conflicts.

Rationalisation. The unconscious manipulation of our opinions to evade the recognition of the unpleasant or the forbidden. Thus a child who has found difficulty with school work might proclaim that he did not know what he had to do.

Reaction-formation. This is the mechanism whereby one tendency is hidden from awareness by its opposite. As a result of certain infantile, unsocialised tendencies, an individual may be inclined to behave in a manner repugnant to society. But he unconsciously responds by doing the opposite. One writer claims to have demonstrated that women who do not particularly want to be pregnant often become over-anxious about their babies after they are born.

Conversion. The individual unconsciously develops certain physiological symptoms which express symbolically both repressed wishes and the defence set up against them. Thus functional blindness or paralysis which are sometimes seen in the conversion hysteric enables the individual to escape the recurrent source of frustration without loss of face.

There are other defence mechanisms and those who are interested should consult the work of Hall.[11] Moreover, there are a large number of ways in which all these mechanisms may be employed, so that there are almost an infinite number of personality structures.

In addition, Freud posits a theory of psycho-sexual development. In infancy there is first the *Oral Stage* where the manner of obtaining pleasure is through sucking, swallowing, biting; then the *Anal Stage*

[11] Hall, C. S., *A Primer of Freudian Psychology.* New York: The World Publishing Co., 1954.

where pleasure is obtained by expelling or retaining; and finally the *Phallic Stage*[12] where pleasure is obtained by touching, and looking at genitalia, by comparing, investigating and questioning. According to Freud, if the infant experiences certain kinds of treatment such as over-indulgence or severe frustration at any of these stages, the growth of the ego is likely to be adversely affected, yielding, in turn, distorted personality characteristics later on. It is this part of his theory of personality development that has been most severely criticised.

Some difficulties in personality measurement. Personality assessment, although very important, is one of the most difficult problems in psychology. Thus Vernon,[13] in a survey of personality tests and methods of assessing personality, thinks that while the outlook in certain fields, as in the measurement of interests and attitudes, is hopeful, it is better to be very cautious regarding personality testing in general. A number of the difficulties experienced in this field are:

(*a*) Many links of the personality are not to be found in the conscious mind. This is one reason why one can never be sure that the motives ascribed to another are correct.

(*b*) From the work of G. W. Allport it seems that fresh interests, attitudes and motives develop with time and become self-supporting.

(*c*) The work of Lewin and others suggests that personality structure is linked with environment and is capable of being restructured to some extent in new surroundings. As was mentioned in Chapter 2, the behaviour of a person varies to some extent according to the nature of the social group in which he finds himself and the aims and activities of that group. A teacher, for example, may show one set of traits in a classroom and rather different characteristics at a parents' meeting. It is important to stress this since some theories of personality assume the existence of highly general-ised traits (i.e. habits, behaviour tendencies) which the individual possesses independent of environmental stimulus and situation. More recently Mischel[14] has reviewed much evidence which suggests that, with the exception of intelligence, the idea of highly-generalised behaviour traits is untenable. However, while behaviour is largely specific to the situations and types of stimuli encountered, there may well be considerable consis-tency in a person's behaviour under well-defined conditions; for example, in a history group with teacher A and fellow pupils B and C, or on a golf course with friends X and Y.

(*d*) Objective measurements can be made of height, spelling, attainment and so forth. But it is much more difficult to get observers to agree on the extent to which a person is aggressive or introverted.

---

[12] These three stages together occupy the first five years of life.

[13] Vernon, P. E., *op. cit.* For a more recent and very thorough study of personality assessment, including the difficulties involved, see Vernon, P. E., *Personality Assessment.* London: Methuen, 1964.

[14] Mischel, W., *Personality and Assessment.* New York: Wiley, 1968.

(e) Since personality measurements are to some extent subjective, the personality of the observer will influence what he notices in others, and his interpretation of the traits which he thinks must cause the behaviour.

(f) Changes in personality can be brought about by physiological changes in the organism. Thus vitamin deficiency, lack of balance in the endocrine glands, and brain lesions, can all bring about changes in personality.

Methods of Measuring personality.[15] Many of the techniques about to be described cannot be applied by teachers in assessing their pupils. Nevertheless they should know something of the methods now in use. The main approaches are grouped under six headings:

(a) *Physiological Signs.* In spite of the popular interest in palmistry, phrenology and physiognomy, physiological signs in general give very little indication of personality. Mention has already been made of a slight relationship between body-build and temperament; there is also a correlation of about 0·15 between height or weight and intelligence test score. Note, however, that this does not prove that a large physical frame implies a large brain nor that this in turn indicates higher intelligence. Children with good physical development might have had more intelligent parents who passed on their ability genetically, and provided better nutrition and a more favourable environment for their offspring. There is also a small positive relationship between body size and leadership.

Slightly better estimates of personality are made from a study of expressive movements.[16] The way we walk, dress, write, speak and so forth, depend both on the customs and conventions in which we were brought up, also on inner traits and wishes.

There is certainly a relationship between the physical and the emotional. For example, some peptic ulcer patients have a typical drawn and anxious look, and it seems that excessive drive, worry and nervous tension are often linked with this clinical condition. Alexander[17] has brought forward some evidence supporting the view that those who crave for love, sympathy and support, often become hardworking and ambitious, and develop an ulcer. This is an example of a mind-body or psychosomatic disturbance (emotional overdependence leading to peptic ulcer. Here the bodily state gives rise to definite external physiological signs, but usually the connection between emotion and external physiology is not clear at all.

In conclusion, it might be said that any assessment of personality made on external physiology is most likely to be wrong.

---

[15] See Warburton, F. W., 'The Measurement of Personality,' *Educ. Research*, 1961, 4, 2–17; 1962, 4, 115–132, 193–206. Vernon, P. E., *Personality Assessment*. London: Methuen, 1964, Part 4.

[16] See Allport, G. W., and Vernon, P. E., *Studies in Expressive Movement*. New York: The Macmillan Co., 1932.

[17] Alexander, F. and others. In *Personality and the Behaviour Disorders, Vol. I.* Ed. by Hunt, J. McV. New York: Ronald Press Co., 1944.

(b) *Objective tests.* A great deal of work has been done by Eysenck, Cattell and others in attempting to devise objective tests which assess a person's placing on such personality dimensions as stability-neuroticism, or extraversion-introversion. Some process has been made but as yet no single test has the reliability and validity of a good intelligence test. One of the most promising approaches to the assessment of the degree of neuroticism involved the measurement of the body control of the subject. In one test of this type the subject was told to stand still and relax, with eyes closed, hands hanging down the side and feet close together. With neurotics and those with a tendency to neuroticism there was greater body sway than with normals. However, results from these tests tend to be variable, and more recent work has not always supported earlier findings.

Other physiological measures such as pulse rate, blood pressure and some biochemical functions, all of which can be measured objectively, have not been helpful as yet. These quantities vary from day to day, and with emotional mood, and their actual significance in personality assessment is not known with certainty. The electro-encephalograph, which records the electrical activity in the brain of a living organism, has been of great help in the diagnosis of epilepsy and brain lesions and it also reveals abnormalities in some types of delinquents; otherwise it has been of little use so far in the study of personality.

(c) *Ratings of past behaviour.* Vernon regards ratings not so much as summaries of directly observed behaviour, but as rationalisations abstracted from the rater's overall picture of the subject. Nevertheless, this method is of particular value to teachers; they thereby arrive at many of their judgments which they enter on Cumulative Record Cards. But a special word of warning is needed to put readers on their guard against 'Halo Effect'. When we form a favourable impression about a child or adult because he exhibits some trait which we admire (e.g. we think him to be tidy or good-looking) we are inclined to award him high marks on all traits which we think are desirable. Thus if a child is clean and tidy we are likely to upgrade him for intelligence, emotional stability and other desirable traits as well, so that we find that traits which *a priori* had nothing to do with each other now correlate highly. On the other hand if we dislike a person we tend to undermark him on traits which we think of value. It is unlikely (although occasionally possible) to find a child with an A rating for intelligence, A for sociability, B for persistence, and A for fearlessness. It would be more likely that he would have A for intelligence, C for sociability, B for persistence and perhaps D for fearlessness. Experience shows that ratings are improved once the rater is aware of a possible halo effect. It is important that those doing the ratings should have had the opportunity to observe their subjects over a long period, but too close an acquaintance tends to give more bias than accuracy. In other words, as soon as the rater becomes personally involved with those he is assessing, his judgment is likely to become distorted. Having a number of raters who see the subject from varying angles is better than having one opinion. A number of methods for obtaining the actual ratings are now given:

(i) If the group is a small one, say of up to 15 children, first put them in rank order for the trait (i.e. in order 1 to 15). Individual children can then be rated as indicated in (iii) below.

(ii) Grades. With more than about 15 cases ranking becomes difficult and this step should be omitted. Use a five point scale A, B, C, D, E, where A stands for, say, the top 5 per cent rated on a given trait, B the next 25 per cent, C the middle 40 per cent, D the next 25 per cent, and E the bottom 5 per cent. With 100 or more children, one should get numbers of pupils corresponding fairly closely to the given percentages, but in a group of, say, 30 children, an irregular distribution will often be found; for example:

	A	B	C	D	E
	1	10	13	4	2
or	2	5	12	9	2

(iii) Written Scale. Before the rating is made, lay down in writing a clearly defined scale for each trait. This helps tremendously in assigning a child to the right category. Suppose, for example, we wish to make ratings on sociability. Our scale might read:

A	B	C	D	E
Very sociable and companionable. Extraverted.	Socially active, happy and easy in company.	Normally sociable. Withdraws occasionally.	Unsociable. Retiring.	Unsociable by choice. Unfriendly. Markedly introverted.

The rater considers each child and writes down the letter most appropriate to him. When choosing traits take those that can be defined in concrete terms and avoid using terms which imply approval or disapproval. Rate all children on one trait before rating any on a second.

Children cannot rate one another, but by about 9 plus years of age they are able to pick out the two or three children in a class who are highest or lowest in certain traits. This technique is known as *Nominations*. Thus each child in a class might be asked to answer a paper:

Which boy is a thief?
Which girl is a flirt?
Which three children work hardest at their lessons?
Which children are always happy and enjoying themselves?

A pupil's score for honesty or happiness is obtained from the number of times a trait is assigned to him. This technique has good statistical reliability although pupils' judgments are sometimes biased.

If the teacher's opinion differs from that of the classmates it does not necessarily follow that the former is right. Many experiments have shown that ratings made by equals have a better validity than those made by superiors.[18]

(d) *Self-inventories*. In America great use has been made of questionnaires in the assessment of personality. In these there are a large number of questions said to measure neurotic tendency, introversion-extraversion, dominance-submissiveness and many other traits. The subject often has merely to underline 'Yes' or 'No' in answer to questions of which the following are typical:

Are you sometimes troubled by feelings of guilt or remorse over comparatively unimportant trifles?

Do you avoid meeting people in the street because you are not in the mood for conversation?

In this country some use has been made of questionnaires. Only a few have been employed to any extent: the Maudsley Personality Inventory,[19] Cattell's Sixteen Personality Factor Inventory, and the Minnesota Multiphasic Personality Inventory[20] used in mental hospitals. However, the following questionnaires, specially designed for use with children, may be used more often in the future: the Junior Maudsley Personality Inventory; the Junior Eysenck Personality Inventory; also Cattell's High School Personality Questionnaire, and his Children's Personality Questionnaire.

The results obtained by this approach must be treated with great caution. First, many subjects are not prepared to answer truthfully, although this can be overcome to some extent by not having names put on the form. But the answers do depend upon the subjects' interpretation of the object of the questions and on how much they are prepared to reveal. Second, although a subject might be willing to co-operate, his responses may be affected by unconscious motives. Third, the better educated turn out to be more neurotic and introverted than the less cultured when these tests are used alone. Since there is no other evidence to support this, it seems likely that the better educated are more able to put their emotional experiences into words.[21] It should also be noted that Nunnally[22] quotes evidence suggesting that the emotional-stability factor found in self-

[18] For a fuller account, see Vernon, P. E., *Personality Assessment*. London: Methuen, 1964.

[19] Eysenck, H. J., *Manual of the Maudsley Personality Inventory*. London: University of London Press Ltd., 1959.

[20] Hathaway, S. R., and McKinley, J. C., 'A Multiphasic Personality Schedule (Minnesota). I. Construction of the Schedule,' *J. Psychol.*, 1940, 10, 249–254. Inventory published by Psychological Corporation, New York, 1942.

[21] See Vernon, P. E., *op. cit.*, for a fair and thorough summing up of the value of Personality Questionnaires. One study suggests that questionnaires can be virtually useless with children. See Thorpe, J. G., and James, D. P., 'Neuroticism in Children,' *Brit. J. Psychol.*, 1957, 48, 26–34.

[22] Nunnally, J. C., *Introduction to Psychological Measurement*. London: McGraw Hill, 1970.

inventories can also be interpreted as the tendency to say good rather than bad things about oneself, or as a dimension of social desirability. People high on this trait mark 'yes' on socially desirable traits, and 'no' to socially undesirable traits, and vice versa for persons low on this factor. Nunnally even goes so far as to say that the assumption that the former person is adjusted and the latter neurotic is unproven as yet.

(e) *Attitudes and Interests.*[23] *Attitudes.* Although there are many conflicting definitions of the term attitude, we may for present purposes regard it as the sum total of a person's inclinations towards a certain type of object, institution or idea; for example, towards a school subject, the Church, or pacifism. Tests of attitude are usually in questionnaire form, but are more reliable and valid instruments than questionnaire tests of temperament. At the same time the attitudes that we express in public are sometimes different from our private feelings so that occasionally answers given in attitude tests will be untruthful. Furthermore, the causes of behaviour are many and complex, and attitudes play only a small role in affecting it.[24]

Answers to single questions about some topic are of little use since one single instance may give an inaccurate picture of a person's more general attitude. Moreover, the answer given to a single question is more likely to be influenced by what the subject regards as being socially acceptable. Thus in an attitude test a number of statements are presented to the candidate bearing on diverse aspects of the issue, and as far as possible describing concrete behaviour. Thus in a test devised to measure attitude towards Geography as a school subject, we might include:

I listen to as many travel talks as possible on the wireless since I think they improve my knowledge of other lands and people.

I rarely read any Geography books other than those I have to read at school.

Our attitudes to many issues are complex and show qualitative differences as well as being 'for' or 'against' the issue. Other topics are more 'unidimensional' and we can place people on a continuum ranging from strongly 'pro' to strongly 'con'. It is better to select such topics for study if possible. It is also most important to choose an issue which is of real interest and significance to the subjects, and about which they have definite views. In the typical attitude test some twenty to thirty items are presented to the candidate and he has to tick the statements with which he agrees, or which are true in his case. The construction of such a test involves the use of statistical techniques which have not yet been discussed and we leave the details of construction and further information regarding the selection and scoring of items, until Chapter 20. Attitude tests with

[23] See Evans, K. M., *Attitudes and Interests in Education.* London: Routledge and Kegan Paul, 1965.

[24] And sometimes attitudes held merely reflect intellectually or socially conditioned beliefs or opinions and do not necessarily predict behaviour. See Belbin, E., 'The Effects of Propaganda on Recall, Recognition, and Behaviour. I,' *Brit. J. Psychol.*, 1956, 47, 163–174.

children should be used with care; one cannot get results which are likely to be of much value until they have reached an educational and mental age of twelve years.

Some of the best known tests of attitude were produced by Thurstone[25] and his colleagues. These scales covered attitude to the Church, war, capital punishment, etc. Since about 1930 there have been many investigations into the attitudes of children towards various educational and social questions.[26]

Interests. Interests, like attitudes, are difficult to define. In essence, interest consists of a set of subjective feelings about some rather concrete matter such as cricket, stamp collecting or needlework, and a tendency to behave towards the topic in certain ways. But in psychology an interest may be defined as an individual's behaviour tendency to be attracted towards a certain class or classes of activities. Obviously, both the everyday and scientific usage of the term places it in the area of general motivation. Interest tests are also often of the paper and pencil type. Here again, single questions of the kind: 'Are you interested. . . .?' are of little value. Rather the test should include perhaps a number of occupations, school subjects, types of people and so on, and the candidate has to underline those he likes, dislikes or is indifferent to.[27] In other tests the subject is forced to express his interests by sets of questions of the kind indicated below, which show preferences for physical, literary, more practical, or musical activity, respectively.

As a member of a school community do you prefer,
(*a*) To be an active member of a sports team,
(*b*) To be Secretary of the Debating Society,
(*c*) To play a major role in the life of the Craft Club.
(*d*) To spend a good deal of time with the Music Club.

The subject then ticks the item in each set which he prefers,[28] or arranges them in order of likeness.

In all paper and pencil tests candidates can be untruthful if they wish, so that it is possible to raise or lower scores and thus appear to be interested or disinterested if one chooses. Tests of interests cannot, of course, be used with young children, but from about 9 years of age useful results can

[25] Thurstone, L. L., *Scales for the Measurement of Social Attitudes.* Chicago: University of Chicago Press, 1930.

[26] A typical example is: Jordan, D., 'The Attitude of Central School Pupils to Certain School Subjects, and the correlation between Attitude and Attainment,' *Brit. J. Educ. Psychol.*, 1941, 11, 28–44.

[27] See for example, Strong, E. K., *Vocational Interest Blank for Men.* Stanford, Cal.: Stanford University Press, 1951.

[28] See Kuder, G. F., *Kuder Preference Record.* Chicago: Science Research Associates, 1942. Later there was a revision and downward extension of the Record using simpler language and making it suitable for Grades 6 to 12. See Kuder, G. F., *Kuder General Interest Survey General Manual.* Chicago: Science Research Associates, 1966.

be obtained provided one remembers that interests are likely to be unstable up to and during adolescence, and that they are affected by changes in social outlook, and environmental circumstances such as economic depression, war, and so forth. Furthermore, the less able children have a smaller span and less variety of interests than the bright, while the correlation coefficients between reported interests and ability are very low since children of differing abilities can show such qualitative differences in the same topics.

(f) *Projection tests.*[29] Another approach to the assessment of personality is through the projection test. In this case the subject does not realise what is being measured, hence he is less likely to falsify his responses deliberately. We have already seen that 'projection' implies thrusting forth on to the external world and other persons, unconscious wishes and ideas. Thus when a projection test is used, it is assumed that the individual organises events, apparatus, toys and so forth in terms of his motivation, attitudes, emotions and other aspects of his personality. Note that this type of test, usually but not always, assesses overall or 'global' personality and does not generally measure personality dimensions such as introversion-extraversion. It is well known that writers, poets, musicians and painters express their personalities in the style and content of their work, as ordinary folk do in everyday conversations. But creative works and day-to-day speech are too complex to provide a scientific approach to personality study.

One type of projection test involves *word connection*. A series of key words are presented on paper to the subject, and against each of these are two other words. The one which is associated with the key word in the subject's mind has to be underlined. Thus in Crown's[30] list, one item is:

SINK   wash   drown.

It is claimed that neurotics tend to underline one word and normals the other. Another test of similar nature is Sentence Completion, where the candidate is given a number of phrases which he has to complete; for example,

I failed ....
As a child he ....

Tests of sentence completion have been used with children from about 9 years of age upward.

It is claimed that Raven's Controlled Projection Test[31] can be used with children from 6 years of age. In the individual form of the test which is suitable for young children, the subject makes a free drawing and is told a story about a child like himself. He then has to answer, orally, questions

---

[29] See Vernon, P. E., *Personality Assessment.* London: Methuen, 1964, Ch. 10.
[30] Crown, S., 'The Word Connection List as a Diagnostic Test. Norms & Validation,' *Brit. J. Psychol.*, 1952, **43**, 103–112.
[31] Raven, J. C., *Controlled Projection Test.* London: Lewis, 1952.

like, 'What did he do next?' With older children a group form of the test can be given in which they are shown a picture of a person with whom they can identify themselves. They then have to answer questions about him in writing.

Rather similar to the group form of the above test is the Thematic Apperception Test.[22] Essentially it consists of a series of pictures which are shown to the subject, the pictures being of persons of the same sex and about the same age as the subject (so that he can identify himself) in a variety of differing situations. The subject is asked to write about events leading up to the situation, the outcome, and the thoughts and feelings of the character. In order that there may be plenty of fantasy on the part of the subject, the pictures are somewhat ambiguous. The subjects tend to identify themselves with the characters and reveal conscious and unconscious interests, needs and so on.

The most popular of all visual tests is the Rorschach Inkblot Test.[33] In this a series of cards, on which are a number of meaningless blots, some black on white, others coloured, are presented to the subject and he has to say what he thinks of each and what makes him say so. Guilford[34] is of the opinion that the validity of the test is near zero whether used to diagnose different types of mental patients, or to make predictions about nonclinical subjects.

A test often used with children is the Lowenfeld Mosaic Test.[35] The child is given a box containing some 400 small pieces (squares, triangles, diamond shapes, of differing colours) and a tray lined with white paper. He is told to make whatever he likes and to continue until he is satisfied with what he has made.

Summing up the results obtained from the use of projection tests we may suggest that some users can give penetrating, but subjective, accounts of personality, although it seems impossible for them to lay down instructions regarding interpretation so that others can follow. At the same time it is very difficult to make any estimate of the reliability and validity of these tests. Nunnally (op. cit.) suggests a typical finding for reliability is around ·60 with a few reliabilities as high as ·80. He is also of the view that, at most, projective techniques have only a low level of validity in predicting particular criteria.

Projection tests are not suitable for use by teachers, but by clinical psychologists and psychiatrists. Indeed, teachers can apply only a few of the methods that we have described. They rely mainly on ratings of past behaviour in assessing the personality as described under (c), but they

[32] The present form of the test was first described by Morgan, C. D., and Murray, H. A., in *Arch. Neurol. & Psychiat.*, 1935, **34**, 289–306.

[33] See Mons, W., *Principles and Practice of the Rorschach Personality Test*. London: Faber, 1948.

[34] Guilford, J. P., *Personality*. London: McGraw-Hill, 1959.

[35] Lowenfeld, M., 'The Mosaic Test,' *Amer. J. Orthopsychiat.*, 1949, **19**, 537–550.

can also use, provided care is taken, tests of attitudes and interests, some of which they can devise for themselves.

(g) *The interview and its variations.* The personal interview probably remains the most frequently used method of assessing personality either for educational or vocational guidance. Generally there is just one interview conducted either by a single person (for example a Headmaster, College Principal, or prospective employer) or by a small group. On other occasions there are a series of interviews, between which the interviewees are kept under observation either at school, at work, or in some social situation. During the interview those conducting it observe the manners and appearance of the candidate, listen to his speech, note his ability to answer questions, assess his social attitudes and range of interests, and check his past record.

Yet in spite of its long history and popularity, the interview is much less reliable and valid than most people believe.[36] Vernon[37] after reviewing the considerable amount of evidence that has accumulated from personnel selection in the British and American Armed Forces, the British Civil Service, and through the selection of students in this country and America, concludes that some interviewers are moderately good at assessing personality, but that most people, however confident they may be of their own power to sum up interviewees, are not. There is little doubt that many members of school staffs, psychologists and prospective employers are bad interviewers and judges of personality. Unfortunately it is not possible at present to forecast who will make a good interviewer and who will not, it is largely a matter of finding out by trial and error. However, Allport[38] has listed some characteristics of the good judge of character. In his view this ability to judge others is linked with experience and maturity which gives a rich store of contacts with human nature; intelligence; similarity with the person judged so that members of the same sex, race, colour and so on are the best judges of one another; and the cognitive complexity of the judge since people cannot judge others more complex and subtle than they. The good judge is also reasonably warm and friendly in his social relationships, but also to a considerable extent detached. Often he is an introverted person, and although he can adjust successfully to others, he himself is often enigmatic and hard to judge. Usually the reliability of the interview (i.e. the correlation between two independent interviews) is around 0·5 to 0·6 but if special care is taken it can rise to 0·7 to 0·8.

Its validity is still less favourable, although some people make better assessments than others and some interviewing boards take more trouble

[36] Ulrich, L. and Trumbo, D., 'The Selection Interview since 1949,' *Psychol. Bull.*, 1965, **63**, 100–116.

[37] Vernon, P. E., and Parry, J. B., *Personnel Selection in the British Forces.* London: University of London Press Ltd., 1949. Vernon, P. E., *Personality Assessment.* London: Methuen, 1964.

[38] Allport, G. W., *Pattern and Growth in Personality.* New York: Holt, Rinehart and Winston, 1961.

than others to ensure that the interviews are made as valid as possible.[39] Numerous instances are reported where the interview added nothing to the forecast of future performance made from objective tests. On the other hand, as Vernon points out, the interview can do some things efficiently. It can gather and check the details of the candidate's educational and occupational career, and it can assess the quality of a person's speech, while manners, social assurance and general bearing are revealed. These latter qualities are often of great importance as, for example, speech when students are being selected for training as teachers. But the interview is a poor instrument for disclosing more fundamental traits like industriousness and emotional stability. Yet in spite of its limitations, it will continue to be used, for it is a very flexible technique; it is difficult to replace, and it appears to be fair to the interviewers and the candidates.

During and since the 1939–45 war, use has been made of group observational techniques. The general idea is that a group of examinees are watched over a number of days by a group of Interviewers in a number of different situations. The best known example is the War Office Selection Board technique for the selection of officers. Groups of about eight candidates for commission were studied for two or three days by a psychologist, a psychiatrist, and various military officers. Besides being given objective tests of abilities, also questionnaires and projective tests of personality, and having their past records assessed, the candidates were watched in certain group exercises. Some task such as getting a heavy log over a wall would be set, and the group left to work out its own method of attack. In these exercises the candidates were not marked for ingenuity or initiative but rather for the manner in which they worked together as members of a group. Some would try to 'boss' the group, others would get the group to work as a unit, some merely acting as passengers. The exercises were chosen to be like those which arise in social situations of army life. A similar approach has been employed in the selection of certain grades of Civil Servants. Here the candidates had to carry out activities like those of actual civil servants, such as for example, studying documents and making a report on them.

In general, these group observational techniques give rather better estimates of personality than does the ordinary interview. But their success depends upon the skill of the observers and on the behaviour which the interviewee thinks he should display in the situation. However, like the interview, the method appears fair to all concerned. Occasionally, a similar approach was used in the selection of border-line cases at the 11 plus examination. The candidates were called together for a day. They took part in group games, dramatic activities and so forth, but we have no evidence that these situations brought out qualities relevant to grammar school success.

[39] Some useful suggestions for making the interview as valid as possible are given by Vernon and Parry, *op. cit.*

A technique that has been used successfully with children is that known as Time-Sampling.[40] In this, certain limited categories of behaviour are first laid down such as solitary play, marked aggressiveness and so forth. Each member of a group is then assessed for these traits for one minute, say, in each half-hour during which the members are playing together or engaging in some other activity. It is better for the children to be observed through a one-way screen so that they are unaffected by the presence of people watching. Eventually some definite statements can be made about the observed behaviour of a particular child; for example, Susan engages in solitary play for thirty per cent of the time. The method is rather easier to use with younger than older children because the behaviour of the former is simpler and easier to classify. The technique is reliable, too, in the sense that it is generally possible to get observers to agree over the kind of behaviour shown at a given moment, provided they are well trained and impartial, and that the categories of behaviour to be assessed are rigidly defined. On the other hand its reliability is poor when we measure the *consistency* of a child's behaviour. Susan may not engage in solitary play as much with fresh companions, with different toys, or in another setting. Often the behaviour of young children is largely determined by the situation. With care the method can be used with adults and adolescents; indeed, a similar approach is used in time and motion studies —not of personality but of behaviour at work. For other forms of direct-observation such as *incident sampling* and *conrolled diary*, see Guilford, *op. cit.*, Chapter 7.

Assessment of Self-concepts. The individual's Self-picture is a learned structure. It grows mainly through training, identification with individuals and peer groups, the comments of other children and people, the acquisition of social roles, and the inferences drawn from his experiences. Although it may appear from these comments that the Self is unitary, in fact we have a number of 'social selves'. Strang[41] distinguishes the Basic Self concept or the concept of a person he thinks he is; the Transitory Perception of the Self the individual holds of himself at a particular instant, influenced perhaps by passing mood; the Social Self or the Self as the person thinks others see it; and the Ideal Self or the Self the person would like to be. Phillips,[42] also Vernon,[43] have reviewed the studies dealing with Self-concepts in children, adolescents and adults, and there is no doubt that such concepts are now thought to be of great importance

[40] See Olson, W. C., and Cunningham, E. M., 'Time-Sampling Techniques,' *Child Developm.*, 1934, 5, 41–58. For examples of its uses with junior school children see Gardner, D. E. M., *Testing Results in the Infant School*. London: Methuen, 1942. Also Gardner, D. E. M., *Long Term Results of Infant School Methods*. London: Methuen, 1950.

[41] Strang, R., *The Adolescent Views Himself*. New York: McGraw-Hill, 1957.

[42] Phillips, A. S., 'Self-concepts in Children,' *Educational Research*, 1964, 6, 104–119.

[43] Vernon, P. E., *op. cit.*

in motivating behaviour, in maintaining mental health, and in influencing the learning situation. A discrepancy between a child's picture of his Ideal Self and Actual Self may have an unfavourable effect on his school work and personality development.

Vernon (*op. cit.*) has proposed some interesting possibilities, whereby it might be possible to get a person (e.g. Jack) to reveal his picture of himself; the sort of person he (Jack) expects to be in ten years' time; the picture he (Jack) thinks a typical person (Bill) of his own age, sex and social class would have of himself (Bill); and how his (Jack) acquaintances would describe him (Jack). The analysis of the findings may reveal a person's main trends and would be perfectly feasible with older children. Unfortunately, all approaches to the study of Self-concepts encourage a somewhat artificial, introspective attitude.

Chapter Five

OBSERVING AND ATTENDING

IN everyday life one occasionally meets a person who is described as being very observant. It is implied that as he goes about he uses his ears, eyes, nose, and other sense-organs in order to get to know his world. In fact we may define observation as being the process of knowing the environment by means of the senses. Teachers frequently speak of training their children to be observant and later in this chapter we shall see how far this can be effected. Actually, observing is dependent upon two steps. First, the subject has to *attend* to some limited aspect of his environment at a given moment, and then he has to *perceive* some object, episode or fact. Consequently, it is desirable that attention and perception should be discussed in some detail.

Attention. Teachers frequently tell their pupils to pay attention. By this they mean that they want their scholars to ignore most of the signals[1] reaching their sense-organs at that instant and to concentrate on the lesson or on what the teacher is saying. The words of the teacher may, of course, appeal far less than, say, a comic or some happening outside the classroom. Attention may therefore be defined as the selection of a particular stimulus or group of stimuli, and the ignoring of the rest. Note that human beings are never completely inattentive during consciousness. They are always paying attention to something, if only to their own thoughts.

The range of attention. Most of us often wish that we could attend to many different things at the same time, but our capacity is limited and we are only able to attend to one main object or activity at once. We breathe and read our newspapers at the same time, it is true, for the former activity is one to which we do not have to attend. But a girl who usually knits and reads together (the knitting has become an automatic action) has to abandon her book temporarily and pay attention to her knitting when she drops a stitch.

Sometimes there is a rapid switch of attention from one activity to another, so that we appear to be attending to two things at once although we are not doing so in reality. Thus if we try to read and listen to a conversation at the same time we probably listen to a few sentences of the conversation, turn our attention to the book for a few lines then switch our

---

[1] It must be remembered that there are signals from the organs of the body, or internal stimuli, reaching the central nervous system as well as external stimuli.

attention back to the conversation again before we have lost the gist of what is being said. When two tasks are attempted, such as adding numbers and listening to a story with a view to remembering its details, which demand this switch of attention, there is nearly always some loss of efficiency in the sense that neither task is completed as well as it would have been if performed independently.

We can, of course, pay attention to a number of objects if they together make up a more complex organisation which is our main object of attention. Thus a number of sheep in a field are seen as a small flock.

The span of apprehension. The span of apprehension is the number of objects that can be estimated at a glance without counting. Experiments with the Tachistoscope—an instrument which enables groups of dots, letters, numbers, or whole words to be exposed for brief periods of up to 1/50 second—show that the number of different items which we can discriminate in a brief period depends on how well we can group them. Hoffman's[2] work with schoolchildren showed that even the older ones could only read 4 or 5 jumbled consonants when the consonants were exposed for a brief period. But up to 20 letters could be detected when they formed familiar words, for here the subjects recognised each word as a whole, and did not have to attend to single letters. The span of apprehension also increased with age and ability. Again, if black spots are scattered over a white card and exposed for 1/10 second the average span for keen adults is about 8 with a range from 6 to 11[3] But 4 similar patterns each made of 5 dots are immediately reported as 20 dots. Burt's[4] experiments with children also confirmed individual differences in the range of attention. He found that some children could give the correct number only if 4 or 5 dots were displayed, others could manage 9 or 10. For a given individual, too, the span of apprehension is likely to vary somewhat from moment to moment about the average value.

The focus and near margin of attention. While we can only attend to one main thing at a time, that is, we are more conscious of it than of anything else at the given moment, we are often dimly aware of other objects, scenes, sensations and thoughts to which we are not actually attending. Thus a person may be attending to a television programme and be vaguely aware that he feels cold or hears the ticking of the clock. In addition, various physiological processes such as heart beat and breathing are taking place of which he might not be aware at all. At any given time, then, there is usually a definite focus of attention, a near margin of attention, and subconscious activity.

[2] Quoted by Woodworth, R. S., and Schlosberg, H., in *Experimental Psychology*. London: Methuen, 1954.
[3] Woodworth, R. S., and Schlosberg, H., *op. cit.*
[4] Burt, C., *The Backward Child*. London: University of London Press Ltd. 1937.

The near margin of attention is of considerable practical importance. When a child or adult is reading, for example, he is actually attending to a group of words and their meaning but in the near margin of attention must be the words, together with their meaning, which he has just been considering. Indeed, it is the passage now in the near margin of attention which helps him to interpret the current sentence. The ability to hold several ideas in this margin and to be able to marshal the relevant associations quickly seems to be dependent upon mental age. Again, as operations become automatic, they are carried on at the margin of attention so that attention may be paid to the tackling of more complex problems.

Factors involved in attention. At the end of the last century, it was still thought that there was a separate faculty of attention, but by the early years of this century, by which time a beginning had been made on the analysis of human abilities, some[5] seemed to be of the opinion that general intelligence and attention were identical. Though the latter viewpoint could not now be accepted as it stands, we shall suggest in a moment that attention is certainly linked with intelligence.

Sometimes a child finds a story or object so interesting that he attends to it spontaneously, while he attends to other things because he realises it will benefit him if he does so, or because he will be punished if he does not. In the latter case the child has, as it were, to 'make himself attend', and it is volitional rather than spontaneous attention.

When teachers speak of developing their pupils' powers of attentiveness, they are speaking of an attention which can be probably resolved into:[6]

(a) The mental age of the children or general intelligence plus verbal ability. Lack of attention and inability to concentrate for long periods is most noticeable among younger and duller children.

(b) The pupil's interest in the topic or object under attention, his general motivation and seriousness of purpose, and the manner in which the teacher presents the material. While volitional attention is bound up with motivation, persistence, and capacity to attend in the present for the reward that it will bring at a later date, teachers must remember that some inattention is due to their failure to make their subject matter interesting.

The factors which cause a person to tend to pay attention to one thing more than another may be divided up into two main groups. First, there are those that depend upon the object, or objective factors; and secondly, those that depend upon the interests, habits, temperament, and mood of the individual. The latter we call subjective or internal factors. In connection with objective factors the following points should be noted:

(a) Other things being equal, the greater the intensity and size of the stimulus the more likely it is to command attention. Thus a bright light,

[5] See Burt, C., 'Experimental Tests of General Intelligence,' *Brit. J. Psychol.*, 1909, **3**, 94–177.
[6] Vernon, P. E., *Structure of Human Abilities*. London: Methuen, 1961, 2nd Ed.

loud noise, large sign or notice are more likely to attract our attention than smaller and less intense stimuli.

(b) Repetition of a stimulus tends to create attention. We are more likely to take notice of someone shouting 'Fire! Fire! Fire!' than to a single shout of 'Fire!'. But beyond a certan point repetition becomes monotonous and loses its effect.

(c) A stimulus that changes or has movement usually gets attention. Examples range from the change in pitch of an interesting voice to flashing electric signs.

(d) A novel stimulus or a familiar object in an unusual setting will create attention. Thus most people will read 'sky writing' and look intently at a man dressed in strange garb.

(e) A stimulus which is very different from its surroundings is likely to get attention; for example, a moment of quiet coming in a period of general noise, or a white patch on a black background.

(f) Completed and symmetrical patterns more often command attention than those unfinished and without shape.

Subjective factors include:

(a) *Interests.* We generally attend to those things that interest us. Thus, the musician listens to the orchestra and the botanist attends to the wild flowers in the hedge.[7]

(b) *Habits.* The engineer listens to the sound of his engines because he has been taught to do so.

(c) *Natural tendencies and biological needs.* Anything which appeals to our natural tendencies will probably get our attention. The picture of the glamour girl appeals to the male, and the bonny baby to the maternal tendency in the woman. Advertisers make great use of this.

(d) *Temperament and mood.* The extravert will more often have his attention aroused by other people and by happenings outside himself than will the introvert. Again, when we are angry or depressed we are more likely to attend to such things as dirt on the floor or a black look on another's face than we should if we were in a happier frame of mind.

Very often objective factors will create the attention in the first instance, but the object or spectacle usually has to appeal to our habits, interests or natural tendencies if it is to hold our attention over a period. Teachers especially should bear in mind that whatever appeals to the interests and natural tendencies of children, whatever children feel is worthwhile, is more likely to obtain and hold their attention. But note that in sustained attention, eyes and ears are not rigid and motionless, rather there is movement within a definite and limited field. Prolonged and sustained attention cannot, however, often be expected from the young and the dull, and while genuine interest in the subject is the ideal sustainer of attention, there are times when children have to be compelled to attend to the matter in hand—material, perhaps, which cannot easily be made interesting.

[7] Indirect interests, sentiments or character may also force one to attend.

Perception. Having attended to some selected aspect of his surroundings the subject must get to know, or perceive, the objects or objective facts by means of his senses. But we must be careful here to distinguish between sensation and perception. Stimuli coming from various external objects and happenings affect one or other of the sensory areas of the brain (see Chapter 19) and we experience a sensation. But our interpretation of the environment or perception is much more than the sensations received; it is sensation reinforced by ideas, images, and past experience. Of course, we do not recognise the receipt of sensations and perceptions as separate processes. Perception is, therefore, likely to be affected by mental set, attitude, expectation or desire at a given moment, so much so that we sometimes perceive, quite falsely, that which we have been expecting to perceive. Thus if we believe in ghosts and we walk down a lonely country lane on a dark night, the right ideas and images are available to link up with some small sensory cue, such as a tree with a lightish bark, to give the very percept that we have been expecting. Again, if the words like Shakesbeth and Macphere are shown for a very short period they will be reported as the familiar Shakespeare and Macbeth.

Up to about the beginning of this century, psychologists tended to look upon objects as if they were isolated from their background. We now know that the look, sound, and feel of something cannot be divorced from its surroundings. In other words, the effect produced by a given stimulus varies with the nature of the accompanying stimuli. Early in this century attacks were being made on the theory that the same stimulus always gave rise to the same sensation. The most important group of critics of this hypothesis was the Gestalt[8] School of Psychologists, led by Kohler (1887–1967), Koffka (1886–1941) and Wertheimer (1880–1943),[9] and they have amply shown the effect of background on a figure and the effect of one figure on another. Thus a Gestalt, or whole, is more than the mere sum of its parts, whether the perception arises in the field of sight, sound, or through any of the other senses.

The building of a whole by combining parts. When sensations are fed into the brain we tend to group them according to certain principles of organisation. We shall illustrate this by taking our examples from the field of visual perception.

(a) *Proximity.* If we have lines 1–6 as in Figure 7 those that are close together seem to form figures, and the intervals between 2 and 3 and 4 and 5 seem to serve as background. It is difficult to see 2 and 3, also 4 and 5 as figures although we can do so if we try.

[8] See Katz, D., *Gestalt Psychology*. London: Methuen, 1951.
[9] The German word 'Gestalt' is often translated rather loosely as 'form' or 'configuration'.

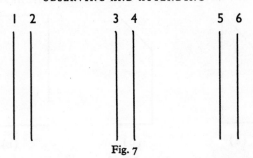

Fig. 7

(b) *Similarity*. In Figure 8 (a) we tend to see columns and in Figure 8 (b) rows. That is, we tend to group similar sensations together.

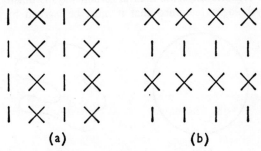

(a)   (b)

Fig. 8

(c) *Continuity*. Objects that lie on a straight line or on a continuous curve are easily grouped, Figure 9.

Fig. 9

(d) *Completeness*. A closed figure stands out more clearly from its background and is more easily seen as a unit than an uncompleted one. Compare Figure 10 (a) and (b). Further, if a figure has a small number of gaps in it, these tend to be overlooked. See Figure 10 (c). This tendency to close a gap is regarded by some as an important principle of brain dynamics.

(e) *Symmetry*. A regular figure is more easily seen against the background than an irregular one. Compare Figure 11 (a) and (b).

These principles also operate in the auditory field. If we hear a number of taps close together in time, they are heard as a group, but if they occur with long intervals between them we hear them as separate taps.

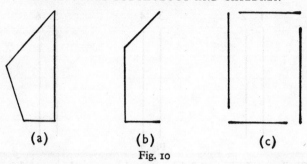

(a)   (b)   (c)

Fig. 10

Gestalt Theory. There has been much argument over whether or not this tendency to organise the sense field in certain ways is innate. In the last century psychologists assumed that it must be learned by experience.

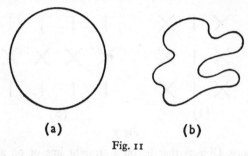

(a)   (b)

Fig. 11

Gestalt psychologists, however, believe that there is a natural tendency for incoming sensory stimuli to organise themselves into patterns of *Gestalten* at the physiological level, before they reach consciousness. Thus for a visual Gestalt we have:

Stimulus pattern ⟶ physiological Gestalt ⟶ Percept (object seen)

Gestalt or configuration theory maintains that this tendency to organise is unlearnt and that the organisation always takes place in such a way that the Principle or Law of Good Pattern holds. By this we mean that the individual always forms as good a pattern as possible. Thus, when a person sees a pattern, he will see it in such a way that the resulting figure is as stable, simple, regular, unified and so forth, as possible. Gestalt psychologists do not completely ignore previous learning, desire, attitude, expectancy and mental set, but they tend to minimise them.

In recent years there have been criticisms of Gestalt theory. For instance, Hebb,[10] while maintaining that the Gestalt psychologists have certainly

---

[10] Hebb, D. O., *The Organisation of Behaviour.* London: Chapman & Hall, 1949. See also Piaget, J., *The Child's Construction of Reality.* London: Routledge and Kegan Paul, 1955; and Watson, A. J., 'Perception.' In *Experimental Psychology* (Ed. Farrell, B.A.). Oxford: Basil Blackwell, 1955.

shown that there are innate factors involved in perception, thinks that they have gone too far in ignoring the part played by learning and experience in the perception of simple figures such as, say, triangles. For normal human beings this learning takes place in infancy and makes unified perception possible.

When children first learn to read some tend to see whole words or Gestalts at first; these must later be broken down as in the phonetic approach to reading (*see* Chapter 16). Again, the Gestalt principles of organisation are applied by geography teachers (perhaps unwittingly) when teaching their pupils to draw and reproduce maps. Indeed, they are used to some extent by all teachers when presenting material visually.

We should do well not to belittle the effect of previous learning and experience when children are organising their sense fields. The more familiar a child is with given material the more easily will he be able to group it and incorporate new and relevant material. The more knowledge he has of a given subject and the greater his facility in, and experience of, handling words, the longer and more complex are the sentences that can be used in talking to him about it.

Conclusion. In concluding this chapter we shall attempt to answer two very practical questions. First, how can we improve children's powers of observation in any particular field? The following suggestions are made:

(*a*) Since observation depends upon attention, and the latter on interest, we must do all that is possible to widen and strengthen the interests of children. Whatever children feel to be worth while will tend to get their spontaneous attention; the wider their interests and greater their knowledge, the more subjects and facts there are to which they will attend.

(*b*) While observation must not be thought of as a trainable faculty, poor observation may be due to:

    (i) Getting a general impression instead of studying some specific object or aspect of the problem. Children must always know what to look for and be trained to attend precisely to the point in question.

    (ii) Mood, preoccupation or prejudice. Thus, a child who is fully occupied with his own thoughts and feelings has less chance of attending to his environment and because of this, his observation is likely to be poor. Note, though, that expectancy or set is necessary, or the observer will attend to nothing in particular.

    (iii) By being put off by false cues. Children must be taught to attend to the data carefully and not in a hurried manner.

(*c*) Train children to check up on the results of their own observations, and to correct mistakes.

Secondly, how can we get and hold the attention of children? Our suggestions are summarised as follows:

(*a*) In so far as is practicable and sensible, make use of the information given in our discussion of objective and subjective factors involved in attention.

(*b*) Give children some training in the habit of attending.

(*c*) With young and dull children do not expect attention for long periods. Lessons of all kinds with such children should be for short periods, but during these periods attention should be demanded.

(*d*) Since the range of attention is limited, see that when some point is being taught the children are not distracted by unnecessary difficulties concerning it. For example, when reading for comprehension, the attention must not be put off by difficult words in the text or by too complex sentences. Likewise, when teaching a new technique in mathematics, practice with small numbers at first so that attention will not have to be paid to the new technique and to large numbers at the same time.

Chapter Six

IMAGERY AND THINKING

Images and Percepts. We saw in the last chapter that when our sense organs are acted upon by the appropriate stimuli, this leads to perception. But, after the stimuli have ceased, if we recall the perception and thus 'see in our mind's eye', or 'hear in our mind's ear', we are said to *image*. Thus if we recall the sight of a favourite mountain scene, or the sound of church bells, or feel that we are going through the motions involved in boxing, we are said to experience visual, auditory and kinaesthetic imagery respectively. There is also imagery associated with taste and smell but this is not usually well developed.

Images, although seemingly similar to percepts in some ways, are in reality very different, and we may classify these differences as follows. First, perception ends when the appropriate stimulation ends, whereas imagery goes on independently of sense organs and stimulation so that even a person who has become blind some time after birth may be able to form well-pronounced visual images. Second, images are usually less persistent than percepts; they can generally be brought into the mind or dismissed and are on the whole less vivid than percepts. Third, images are usually isolated. For example, we may suddenly 'hear' a tune as we go about our daily tasks. But had the tune arisen as a percept, it would have occurred in some wider context such as listening to an orchestra, radio or record player. Indeed, the distinction between an image and a percept is often made on the basis of behaviour and context.

Images and After-Images. We must also distinguish between images and *after-images.* Suppose we look at a coloured patch and then close our eyes, or else look at a larger uniform grey or white surface, the form of the coloured patch appears and persists for a few moments as an after-image. By varying the conditions of the experiment we can get an after-image of the same colour, or of the complementary hue. The former is called a positive after-image and the latter a negative one. An example of a positive after-image can easily be obtained by looking at a lit electric light bulb for a short while and then switching off the light, when an after-image of the illuminated bulb will be seen for a few moments.

Memory and constructed images. If we visualise the beach of a town where we spent an enjoyable holiday, or have an auditory image of running water, we are experiencing memory images. But if we make our images out of elements which have their counterparts in our past life and visualise a mermaid, or a city with streets paved with gold, we are experiencing constructed images. In some forms of mental disorder, memory images are particularly vivid and are taken for perceptions. For example, a patient may claim that he hears voices or sees visions. These false perceptions are called hallucinations.

Individual differences in imagery. There are as many different kinds of imagery as there are sensations, and people differ greatly in their ability to form these images. For most people, visual imagery seems to be clearer and to arise more frequently than other types, so that if they form images at all, they most frequently think of, say, a friend by calling up the image of his face. Others, however, would remember him by recalling the sound of his voice, while some might find kinaesthetic imagery of most help when thinking, say, of their movements in swimming or dancing. Nevertheless, most use mixed imagery to some extent, visual on some occasions, auditory or kinaesthetic on others. Again, although many people get poor images of touch (tactile imagery), taste (gustatory imagery), and smell (olfactory imagery), they may occasionally experience very powerful images of, for example, the taste of a lemon or the smell of garlic. Some investigations have suggested that those who are good in one type of imagery tend to be good in other types too; that is, that there is a general factor of imagery. Other experiments have not always supported this viewpoint, and in the writer's opinion the evidence for any general factor of imagery is very slender as yet. But imagery is a difficult subject to study and the methods of investigation used still need to be improved.[1] Stewart and Macfarlane Smith have produced evidence that the vividness of spatial imagery is associated with the amount of alpha rhythm suppression as revealed by the electroencephalograph. This study also supports the view that 'k' ability is linked with the capacity to obtain and utilise visual spatial imagery.[2]

When some people examine a picture or other object for 30–45 seconds and then turn away and look, say, at a grey screen, they can project on to that screen a realistic and vivid image of the object, and they can describe it in great detail and answer questions about it. At times the image might change position, shape, size, and colour, but generally it conforms very closely to the original. This phenomenon is known as eidetic imagery[3, 4] and is sometimes regarded as a special type of imagery, although we do

---

[1] For some of the common methods that have been used in the study of imagery see Woodworth, R. S. and Schlosberg, H., *op. cit.* Richardson, A., *Mental Imagery.* London: Routledge and Kegan Paul, 1969. Kessel, F. S., 'Imagery: a Dimension of Mind Rediscovered,' *Brit. J. Psychol.*, 1972, **63**, 149–62.

[2] Stewart, C. A. and Macfarlane Smith, I., 'The Alpha Rhythm, Imagery, and Spatial and Verbal Abilities,' *Durham Research Review*, 272–286.

[3] See Allport, G. W., 'Eidetic Imagery,' *Brit. J. Psychol.*, 1924, **15**, 99–120.

[4] Teasdale, H., 'A Quantitative study of Eidetic Imagery,' *Brit. J. Psychol.*, 1934, **4**, 56–74.

not really know whether or not it is qualitatively different from the more ordinary strong visual imagery. Eidetic imagery was believed to be strong in childhood, but that the frequency of occurrence fell during adolescence and in adults it was rare. Now (1972) it is realised that it is not as common in childhood as was thought (cf. Kessel, *op. cit.*).

Difficulties due to differences in imagery. It is likely that imagery may sometimes lead us to assume that others see theoretical and practical issues in the same way as ourselves, and that this may lead to difficulties in understanding their thoughts. Differences in imagery may be one cause of political, religious, and aesthetic intolerance. Similar difficulties may happen in teaching. A teacher who experiences visual imagery might at times have trouble in getting over his ideas to pupils who experience in the main auditory and kinaesthetic imagery. The difference in the way of 'seeing' things must also affect normal social intercourse between friends and acquaintances. Indeed, it has been suggested that it might be a source of trouble between husbands and wives! But just how serious is the problem caused by imagery differences is not known.

The value of imagery in education. The experimental work on images suggest that it is of great help to some in their thinking but not to all. Indeed the recent experimental work in imagery in the late nineteen sixties and early seventies (e.g. the work of Paivio or Bower) all argues that imagery has significance for learning and language. It is suggested that:

(a) There is no clear evidence that by exercise the capacity to form images can be increased. Naturally, if a child finds that he has a capacity for vivid imagery in any form he should be encouraged to use it whenever possible.

(b) Visual imagery is clearly connected with spatial ability in some way but the form of the relationship is unknown. Such imagery is likely to be of help in all cases where objects have to be manipulated imaginatively. It seems possible, then, that it will be of help to the engineer, architect, chess-player and artist, yet it is by no means certain that they necessarily have to employ it in their thinking.

(c) Images may be necessary for most people when thinking about past, future or possible objects or events. At least, such ideas need to be supported by images. Many people, too, employ images of words, numbers or other symbols in mathematical or other abstract thinking. For example, the notion of a country's 'balance of payments' may be illustrated by a simple visual aid: and for some people an image of this aid will be retained and be of great help when the concept is employed again. Note that the images used in abstract thinking are not always visual ones; there may be auditory images, or else actual words or numbers may be reproduced. Others may solve their problems without much use of imagery at all.

(d) Very often images seem to aid memory. One may, for example, through imagery be better able to recall a poem, a chemical formula or the movements involved in handling a plane. But the value of imagery in this connection must not be overstressed. If there is insufficient intelligence for learning to take place, the power of vivid imagery will be of no avail in remembering. But as we said in (c), graphs and other visual presentations of material are of great help, for they make the learning easier and provide a picture which can be imaged later.

(e) Imagery plays a considerable part in the appreciation of the arts—music, sculpture, painting or literature. The greater the variety and vividness of images that can be experienced, the more likely is the work of art to evoke an emotional response and to be appreciated.

(f) The writer and his students have produced evidence that visual reproductive (memory) imagery of static events is in evidence before the development of mental operations (see later in this chapter) which develop around 7–8 years of age in most children. But visual imagery that is anticipatory in nature, and involves movement of transformation from one state to another, is only in evidence after this age. Examples of such imagery would be the forecasting of the movements of two trains in a tunnel from their relative speeds on entering the tunnel, or the forecasting of the stages an arc of wire would pass through when bent into a straight piece of wire. The findings suggest that while flexible anticipatory imagery may be an aid to true thought, it cannot be a cause of operational thought or be responsible for the continued functioning of such thought. Indeed, it appears that thought itself, in the form of mental operations, makes it possible for the individual to experience such imagery. The evidence supports the views of Piaget and Inhelder[5] in this matter and perhaps explains some of the findings of earlier research on imagery.

Thinking. In everyday speech the terms 'to think' and 'thinking' imply the use of the mind, or the having of ideas, and they are used in a number of contexts. For example, I can say that I am thinking about a certain mountain pass, and little may come to my mind except some faint visual images. Or, I might tell some pupils to think about what they were taught yesterday. This means that they must try and recall yesterday's lesson. Again, a man, on being questioned, might say that he thinks it will rain. After examining the sky and his barometer, he draws a conclusion and announces the result. In this instance the activity of his mind was directed to some end, i.e. the giving of an opinion regarding the likelihood of rain falling, and his visual perceptions plus his thinking, yielded the answer. In psychology we keep the term 'thinking' to denote a connected flow of ideas directed towards some definite purpose or end, so that our third example contained the greatest amount of true thinking. The difference between dreams and daydreams on one hand, and thinking on the other, emphasises that the latter is directed to a definite or real purpose. In the

[5] Piaget, J. and Inhelder, B., *Mental Imagery in the Child*. London: Routledge and Kegan Paul, 1971.

former our thoughts and images wander, are sometimes unconnected or even fantastic, and are not consciously checked. For example, a person might experience fantasy about what he would do if he won a large sum of money in the football pools. Unrealism is the mark of such mental activity although dreams and daydreams may well be controlled by unconscious desires and serve some useful purpose. At the same time it must be made clear that all our thinking is affected by past experiences, present emotional mood and physiological state, and by unconscious influences.

Perceptual and pure ideational thinking. Thinking has sometimes been divided into *perceptual* and *pure ideational* thinking, although the difference between them is one of degree rather than of kind. In the former, the subject actually sees some objects, say some books, and his mind deals with them in a way which depends on the meaning such books have acquired for him in his past experience, If he sees a new book on a topic about which he is keen he will probably read it because, on the basis of past experience, he expects to find it interesting and enjoyable. Animals seem to be capable of perceptual thinking. In one famous experiment a chimpanzee was observed fitting two sticks together to make a longer one in order to gather food otherwise outside its reach. Here the animal was using his previous experience with sticks and distances. In perceptual thinking, then, the organism is always in actual contact with the relevant part of the environment. This kind of thinking is what Piaget terms *sensori-motor thought* (see later in this chapter), and is the only kind of thought available to children under about 2 years of age. Contrasted with this is *pure ideational* or *imaginative* thinking, in which mental activity does not depend upon sensations from the present environment. This kind of thinking seems to be confined to human beings. Note, however, that both kinds of thinking depend upon meanings derived from past experiences. This will be stressed again in the section which deals with the development of thinking, but in the meantime we must go on to consider the parts played by concepts and language in relation to thinking.

Concepts. When we hear the word 'bird' we do not conjure up ideas relating to all the different kinds of birds there are. To the normal adult, the term implies a class of animals which have feathers, two legs, and can usually, but not always fly. That is to say, we have developed the concept of 'bird'. By concept, then, we mean any term that can be recognised as a recurrent feature in an individual's thinking to represent a class of experiences, providing the individual can go back over the mental action through which the term was derived and anchor it in his first-hand experience. Note carefully that a child could use the term 'bird' as a piece of learned verbal behaviour; he could also use it to indicate one animal without having any concept of 'bird' in the sense in which the term concept has just been defined. Indeed, two-year-olds do use the word 'bird' in just this way. They indicate any one bird by the name without having any notion of the class of birds. Thus concepts enable words to stand for whole classes or categories of objects, events or qualities, and are of enormous help to human beings in their thinking.

Concept formation is probably best thought of as a blend of abstraction and generalisation. In the former process, the features common to a class of objects make their impressions upon the observer, who thus gradually acquires a picture in which the common features stand out strongly and the variable characteristics are no longer noticed. Thus if we have a number of circles of different diameters, made of different materials and painted different colours, the common feature is a circle and the recognition of this feature in all the objects constitutes the essence of concept formation. On the other hand, in generalisation, the concept stands as a hypothesis (e.g. circle or insect) which the observer proceeds to test by trying it out on fresh specimens of the class. It is better to draw these two ideas together since abstraction and generalisation are often difficult to distinguish in the actual behaviour of the individual. Concept formation is dealt with again later in this chapter from a Piagetian viewpoint.[6]

Language. Language is the means by which we express our thoughts to others either in vocal or written forms, but perhaps even more important, it immensely extends the range of thought. If we were confined to perceptual thinking or even to ideational thinking that merely involved images, our thinking would remain at a relatively low level. But through the use of language and other symbols (e.g. numbers) we can develop complex and abstract concepts like honesty and justice. This usually occurs through discussion of the essential characteristics of the concepts, and learning why these terms can be applied in some cases but not in others. True, imagery may help with such concepts (e.g. scales for justice), but many able people seem to think of concepts without any images. Generally, the concepts which we can form without language or other symbols are only the most rudimentary ones, and they are insufficient for any complex thinking. As our life tends to become more complex so we develop new concepts from time to time. Thus the concept of 'automation' has become more widely known among the general public since the early 1950's.[7] At the same time, however, it must be pointed out that for Piaget language is the symbolic vehicle by which thought is carried; and while language aids and abets the growth of concepts and of a system of communication which is constituted by concepts, it is in itself insufficient to bring about the mental operations which makes the formation of concepts possible. The general

---

[6] For a useful study of many aspects of the growth of concepts, see Wallace, J. G., *Concept Growth and the Education of the Child*. London: N.F.E.R., 1965.

[7] It must be realised that concepts such as 'democracy,' 'justice,' 'equality of man,' 'sanctification' are outside the understanding of many children and adults. At least up to adolescence, pupils' grasp of these concepts will be limited. Teachers must be very careful about the concepts they use.

question of the relationship between language and thought will also be raised again later in this chapter.

Young children often show the part played by language symbols in thinking as they talk aloud when working on some problem. Adults occasionally do this too. Usually, though, as children grow up they learn to talk subvocally, that is, they use silent speech, and finally they learn to think with very little movement of lips or tongue at all. It used to be considered that thought and silent speech were identical activities. That this is unlikely is shown by the fact that one can read a page of print in far less time than one can pronounce the words, however rapidly. Thought certainly comes before speech and is not identical with it. Nevertheless, some silent speech does enter our thinking at times, and slight speaking movements will occasionally take place in very serious thinking (cf. page 113).

Mention should also be made of another type of symbol, namely maps and diagrams, which often play an important part in the representation of complex situations and variables.

Problem solving and reasoning. If we keep to our definition of thinking, we may fairly say that thinking takes place whenever we attempt to solve a problem, and that problem-solving usually, but not always, demands some reasoning.

A problem can be said to exist when the way to attain some desired end or object is not immediately clear. For most simple problems that arise in everyday life the application of concepts, principles and techniques learnt from past experience will give the answer, but in more difficult instances this is not so. On these occasions a 'trial and error' or 'hit and miss' approach at the ideational level is sometimes successful, but on other occasions more serious thinking is required. If sufficient data for a solution seems to be available, the subject should first try to work out the types of approach that are likely to be successful, bearing in mind both the data and the required end. If one approach proves useless, then attempts should be made with a different one. Sometimes it is of help to invent some theory and work out its consequences in order to see if it yields the required result. If it does, then the theory offers a solution to the problem, though not necessarily the only one. Again, if the problem has been *thoroughly* studied and all possible relevant information collected yet without result, it is often helpful to put the problem aside for a while and come back to it again later (to 'sleep on it' as we say). In these circumstances a solution to the problem will sometimes come quite suddenly. Why this occurs we are not sure. It may be that the unconscious mind is at work on the problem the whole time, or it may be that the subject comes back to the problem physically and mentally fresher without some of the bias, mental rigidity, and set, which affected his earlier efforts.

When we reason correctly we find relationships between items confronting us and work out new correlates. So we find, as we should expect, that reasoning power is closely dependent upon general intelligence. The number of problems which demand reasoning for a solution are legion; but one simple example is:

Tom is older than Susan. Susan is older than John.
Who is the youngest?

The youngest here depends upon the fact that we are told the relationship between Tom's age and Susan's age, also between Susan's age and John's age. Susan is here what might be called the 'connecting' or 'middle term'. Reasoning often, but not always, depends upon such a term. If the connecting term is ambiguously related to the other items in the problem then our reasoning may be at fault. Teachers often speak about improving a child's reasoning ability. All-round reasoning ability cannot be altered unless the child's academic aptitude or general intelligence can be raised, although he can be trained to tackle certain kinds of logical problems.

The development of thought.[8] We now discuss the development of thought and the process of concept formation in children. Use will be made of Piaget's views,[9] as these appear to be of great importance. Some of his works are listed in the bibliography. In his earlier works, written between 1925 and 1932, he studied the development of thought, language, and moral judgment of the child largely by verbal methods. But in his later studies from about 1939 onwards, he has investigated the development of the concepts of space, weight, volume, number, time, movement, speed, etc. experimentally. His experimental work was carried out upon his own children, and those attending Geneva schools.

Piaget has been concerned with the growth of the general ways of knowing or of the intellect. Such cannot be taken directly from the blackboard, textbook or film by merely perception or acquired by drill; rather these general ways of knowing have to be constructed by the child through interaction with the environment. When forged, these general ways of knowing are never forgotten in mental health. For example, a child never forgets that a subset is subsumed within a set (he will not use these words), or that if $A > B$ and $B > C$ then $A > C$. These are, so to speak, the logical tools. Against these there is particular knowledge, such as knowledge about, say, the Norman Conquest. Particular knowledge necessitates interaction between the individual and specific aspects of the environment; indeed, all kinds of teaching procedures may be employed. But the development of the general ways of knowing or of logical thought determines the manner in which particular knowledge is assimilated. Moreover, such knowledge may be forgotten.

[8] In connection with the ground covered in the remainder of this chapter readers may also like to study: Lunzer, E. A., 'Children's Thinking.' In *Educational Research in Britain*. (Ed. Butcher, H. J.). London: University of London Press Ltd., 1968.
[9] Compare with Bruner, J. S., Olver, R. R., and Greenfield, P. M., *Studies in Cognitive Growth*. London: Wiley, 1966.

As the baby interacts with his environment he builds up organisations or structures of actions (as in touching, grasping, moving) which are transferred or generalised by repetition in similar or analogous circumstances. These are called *schemes*. In the post-infancy period as we shall see in a moment, it is mental acts—actions in the mind—which form structures. It must also be noted that for Piaget the terms *assimilation* and *accommodation* indicate fundamental processes. The former implies the absorption and integration of new experiences into previously organised structures, while the latter term indicates the modification of structures or the build-up of new ones.

Several well-defined stages in the intellectual development of children are recognised by Piaget and these are now briefly outlined[10]:

Sensori-Motor Intelligence (Birth–2 years). During this period the child puts a structure on his actions, and on his sensations received from the sensory organs, and then incorporates the outside world into this structure. Acts of sensori-motor intelligence consists solely at first in co-ordinating successive perceptions and overt movements. For example, a child will pull an object to himself without any real knowledge of the act. There is, as it were, a succession of states, which may be linked with brief anticipations and reconstructions but which can never permit the young child to arrive at any real understanding of the overall situation. But slowly throughout this period the child builds up a picture of the world as a collection of objects which continue to exist even when they are out of sight. Furthermore, he learns that they maintain the same size and shape even when there are changes in their appearance due to a new orientation in space. Indeed, during the first two years of life, the child slowly builds up a repertoire of actions, and accumulates much experience of their effects, so that by the end of the period he can work out how he is going to do something before he does it. In other words the child can now represent to himself the results of his own actions before they occur. This is the beginning of true thought—a connected flow of ideas directed towards some definite end or purpose—since actions have become internalised. Thus by 18 to 24 months of age children can carry out many perceptuo-motor tasks. They can solve many problems that are open to direct perception and physical manipulation. Moreover, because of the emergence during the second year of life of the ability to represent to himself the outside world through imitation,[11] language and symbolic play, we adults can actually observe the child represent to himself the results of his own actions before

---

[10] Peel, E. A., *The Pupil's Thinking*. London: Oldbourne, 1960. Flavell, J. H., *The Development Psychology of Jean Piaget*. London: Van Nostrand, 1963. Piaget, J. and Inhelder, B., *The Psychology of the Child*. London: Routledge and Kegan Paul, 1969. Beard, R. M., *An Outline of Piaget's Developmental Psychology*. London: Routledge and Kegan Paul, 1969.

[11] When a child can execute a movement he tends, if he sees an analogous movement in another person or object, to assimilate it to his own. For Piaget imagery arises out of imitation and is in fact 'internalized imitation'.

they occur, in simple and familiar situations. But with the advent of language there now has to be a tortuous redevelopment of all that has been done before, so that actions can now be carried out in the mind, and not only by the aid of imagery, but with the use of language. Thought then becomes much more flexible; it is no longer tied to specific situations actually present, because the child can increasingly use 'signs' (language) which in themselves do not in the least resemble objects or situations.

Pre-conceptual Thought (2–4 years). The child now uses notions which lie between the concept of an object and the concept of a class of objects. For example, he is as likely to say dog as dogs without deciding whether the dogs met during the course of an afternoon walk with his mother are one individual or a distinct class of individuals. Furthermore, the reasoning displayed at this stage is neither inductive nor deductive, but 'transductive', that is, by direct analogy. If X is like Y in some respects then the child is likely to claim that X and Y are alike in all respects. For example, if mother is cleaning her shoes she must be going out, since that sequence of events was experienced previously.

Intuitive Thought (4–7 years). Between the fourth and eighth birthdays there are marked changes in the nature of children's thinking. At the former age thinking may be characterised as semi-logical rather than as logical or systematised. The following experiment neatly illustrates this. A number of dolls are arranged on a table in a fixed pattern which is neither a circle nor a straight line. Each doll wears a different coloured dress, and in front of each doll is a counter of the same colour. A toy lorry moves among the dolls. The driver picks up the counters and places them carefully in the lorry in the same order as they are picked up. If four- and five-year-olds are asked, 'Why is the blue counter first?', 'Why is the green counter next to the yellow one?', they can answer correctly. But when they are asked to retrace the journey made by the lorry, that is, deduce the route the driver took from the layout of the counters in the lorry, they fail. They grasp that the order of the counters is determined by the route the lorry took, but they are unable to understand that the order of the counters determines the route taken.

Again the four- and five-year-old knows that if a piece of wire is taken and twisted into a different shape, 'it's the same thing, the same piece of wire'. But it will be seven years of age before he will agree that the piece of wire remains the same length if twisted into a shape that is, perceptually, very different. In other words, the child has acquired qualitative identity but not conservation of length.

At five years of age the child is unable to hold in mind two relationships at a time pertaining to a given situation and thus has great difficulty in making a judgment. Accordingly his thinking is greatly dominated by what he sees. This is illustrated by the following experiment. Suppose we have two similar bottles of lemonade which the child agrees contain the same amount of liquid. The content of each bottle is poured into a separate glass, the glasses being of very different shape. Obviously the amount of lemonade in each glass will *appear* to be different on account of the height it reaches or because of its surface area. Because of this the child is likely to say that the glass in which the height of the liquid is greater contains more lemonade than the other. By six years of age we find that children are not so easily deceived by appearances in this way. They may give the correct answer in some instances but not in others, depending on the extent of the difference. However, by seven years of age or so a real change has taken place. The child now says that the amount of liquid is the same whatever the shape and size of the recipient vessels. He'll say, 'You've only poured it', 'You haven't added any or taken any away'. He can appreciate that, say, tall-narrow can be transformed to short-wide and vice versa. At this age the generalisable action patterns taking place in the mind—the schemes—are very different from those of a five-year-old. A different kind of thinking is now taking place. Thought now conforms to a system, it obeys certain rules, it is consistent or, as adults say, it's logical.

Concrete Operations (7–11 *years*). This is the stage when the child develops what adults call logical thought. Piaget uses the term *operational* thought, the term *operations* means actions which can be carried out in thought, which are reversible and which form part of an integrated system of actions. The child develops new and more complicated intellectual structures, and he can look in on and monitor his thinking. He becomes *aware* of the sequences of actions in his mind, and he becomes aware of the part played by himself in ordering his experience. For any action carried out in the mind he can see that there are other actions that will give the same result; that is, he sees equivalences. Thus he understands that $5+2 = 7 = 6+1 = 9-2$; or he can measure the same distance in feet, also in inches, and see that the different set of figures mean the same thing. The child's thinking now begins to conform to a system and his thought becomes internally consistent. But note that his logical thought applies only to the perceivable or imageable world of things and events. Hence he can understand that if stick A is longer than stick B, and stick B is longer than stick C, then stick A is longer than stick C. Moreover, because the child can see the part he plays in ordering his experience, he can now begin to build the concept of class, relation, weight, time and the like. But it is only concepts that can be derived from first hand reality that can be elaborated by him.[12]

Formal Operations (12–15 *years*).[13] From about 12 years of age in able

---

[12] For a more detailed treatment of the topic of concrete operational thought see, Lovell, K., 'Systematisation of Thought'. In *Development in Learning—2* (Eds. Lunzer, E. A. and Morris, J. F.). London: Staples, 1968, 225–265.
[13] See Lovell, K., 'Growth of Formal Operational Thinking'. In *Advances in Educational Psychology* I. London: University of London Press, 1972.

pupils, and from 13 to 14 years of age in ordinary ones, even more complex structures become available to many adolescents. Such pupils can co-ordinate actions (in the mind) upon relations, which themselves result from the co-ordination of actions on reality. So, for any action in the mind, a far greater range of equivalent actions become apparent to them. The individual now no longer needs concrete material or imagery for he has acquired a capacity for abstract thought and he can reason by hypothesis. New intellectual abilities emerge which enable adolescents (the more able of them) to manipulate, mentally, a number of variables in turn, and to consider all possible combinations of variables. This enables them to use the inductive method and derive generalisations from a number of instances; intellectual skills not normally available to the junior school child.[14] The broad stages in the development of logical thinking proposed by Inhelder and Piaget have been confirmed although the evidence is clear that the least able secondary school children do not reach the stage of formal operations or reach it in isolated instances.[15]

With the advent of these new thinking skills a more complex kind of concept becomes available. At the junior school stage, the child built concepts that derived from first hand contact with reality. If these concepts can be completely divorced from their concrete contexts, and manipulated as 'pure' terms in the mind, then at the stage of formal thought a more abstract kind of concept can be elaborated from the less abstract concepts of earlier years. Thus the concepts of *proportion* and *heat* (it is the concept of *temperature* that is derived at junior school level) become available to the adolescent; concepts not derivable from immediate contact from the physical world.

The present writer used physical apparatus of the type devised by Inhelder and Piaget in studying the growth of formal operations. But Case and Collinson[16] have also shown, among secondary modern school pupils and students in a college of further education, that the stage of formal operations is clearly reflected by the changes in the type of inference drawn when the subjects were asked questions about passages in history, geography and literature. Hallam,[17] too, in a very careful study of the responses of comprehensive school pupils to varied passages in history, has demonstrated the change in type of inference which can be drawn by pupils at different stages of intellectual growth. Likewise Goldman[18] showed that the responses of children and adolescents displayed the in-

[14] Inhelder, B. and Piaget, J., *The Growth of Logical Thinking*. London: Routledge and Kegan Paul, 1958.
[15] Lovell, K., 'A Follow-Up Study of Inhelder and Piaget's *The Growth of Logical Thinking*,' *Brit. J. Psychol.*, 1961, **52**, 143–154.
[16] Case, D. and Collinson, J. M., 'The Development of Formal Thinking in Verbal Comprehension,' *Brit. J. Educ. Psychol.*, 1962, **32**, 103–111.
[17] Hallam, R. N., 'Logical Thinking in History,' *Educ. Rev.*, 1967, **19**, 183–202.
[18] Goldman, R. J., 'Researches in Religious Thinking,' *Educational Research*, 1964, **6**, 139–155. Also *Religious Thinking from Childhood to Adolescence*. London: Routledge and Kegan Paul, 1964.

tuitive, concrete operational, and formal operational stages of thinking, when they were questioned about Bible stories. The subjects also showed great change with age, in respect of the quality of the concepts they held of the Bible, God's nature, God's concern for man, Jesus and prayer.

When the adolescent has reached the stage of formal operations,[19] verbally presented abstract arguments and concepts become the important kind of learning experience for him, for he now has the language and capacity to appreciate the form of an argument. At the stage of concrete operations, his observations directed his thoughts; now thought directs his observations and actions.[20]

There is thus a development of thought from sensori-motor acts of intelligence though various stages of thinking. One could not, however, expect the development to be rapid or discontinuous, and Piaget has indicated that concepts which develop in, say, the 7–11-year-old period, depend in part upon the schemes built up as a result of motor activities taking place before the age of eighteen months. He is thus in disagreement with the Gestalt psychologists who believe that the grasp of a structure (e.g. a triangle), is an almost immediate act which cannot be analysed and in which learning plays only a minor role. On the contrary, the mental skills, that is, the schemes or structures of mental actions which make up our thinking are end-products depending upon our experience.

In some of his earlier works he studied the growth of *precausal* thinking in the child, i.e. forms of explanation that come earlier than those depending on physical and objective causes of phenomena. Piaget's views on this matter have often been criticised, but in a more recent and very thorough study by Laurendeau and Pinard,[21] many, but not all, of Piaget's findings in this field have been substantiated. Laurendeau and Pinard studied 500 children aged between 4 and 12 years of age, investigating the concepts of dream, and life; also the understanding of the origin of night, the movement of clouds, and the floating and sinking of objects. They found that *realism* (regarding one's own perspective as immediately objective and absolute) was not outgrown until about $6\frac{1}{2}$ years of age; *artificialism* (the child posits the explicit action of a maker at the origin of things) was frequently found in the younger children and did not disappear until 9 years; while *animism* (the child gives life and consciousness to surrounding objects) was also found frequently in the younger subjects and still persisted at times at 11 and 12 years of age. The lack of synchronism as between the disappearance of the different forms of precausal or illogical thinking suggests a lack of systematisation in the child's thinking. He has,

[19] For a detailed treatment of the topic of formal operational thought see also Lunzer, E. A. 'Formal Reasoning'. In *Development in Learning*—2 (Eds. Lunzer, E. A. and Morris, J. F.). London: Staples, 1968, 266–303.

[20] See also Peel, E. A., *The Nature of Adolescent Judgement*. London: Staples, 1971.

[21] Laurendeau, M. and Pinard, A., *Causal Thinking in the Child*. New York: International Universities Press, 1962.

even during the junior school years, no theory of the external world and the concepts he develops are not well organised.

In his later works[22] on the growth of such concepts as quantity, number, weight, volume, time and space, Piaget used an experimental population of between 4 and 12 years of age. Experiments were performed in front of the children using familiar material like counters and modelling clay, and they had to forecast their outcome. Thus, in a study of the development of the concept of quantity, two balls of equal size made of modelling clay might be shown to the child, both of which he recognises as containing the same amount of material. One of the balls is then altered in shape to become that of, say, a sausage. At first the child will not admit that the two objects contain the same amount of clay, that is, he denies conservation of quantity in the example. When he is rather older, he will admit it in some cases but not in others; later still, he will agree to the conservation of quantity in all instances. In the first two stages, his thinking seems to be influenced by cross-section, shape, or thickness, and the concept of conservation of quantity is only formed when he realises that the clay sausage can be returned to its original shape and what has been lost in one dimension has been gained in another. For Piaget this 'reversibility' of thought is, as we have already seen, a fundamental of thought and is essential for any form of mental experimentation and logical inference. He claims that the concept of quantity appears on the average between 7 and 8, that of weight between 9 and 10, and that of volume between 11 and 12 years of age.

Studies by Lovell and Ogilvie[23] of the conservation of substance and weight in which almost every child in a junior school was examined, individually, have confirmed the broad stages proposed by Piaget. But, the growth of these concepts is much more complex than Piaget allows, and depends much more on the experience of the physical world, and of working with many different media in varied situations, than he suggests. Likewise experiments carried out under the writer's direction have shown that the development of the concept of time follows much the same sequence as Piaget suggests; yet it is more complicated than he reckons in that an understanding of simultaneity, equality of synchronous intervals, and order of events, does not come in all situations and in all media at the same age.[24, 25]

[22] Piaget, J., *The Child's Conception of Number*. London: Routledge and Kegan Paul, 1952. *The Child's Conception of Movement and Speed*. London: Routledge and Kegan Paul, 1969. *The Child's Conception of Time*. London: Routledge and Kegan Paul, 1969.

[23] Lovell, K., and Ogilvie, E., 'A Study of the Conservation of Substance in the Junior School Child,' *Brit. J. Educ. Psychol.*, 1960, 30, 109–118. Lovell, K., and Ogilvie, E., 'A study of the Conservation of Weight in the Junior School Child,' *Brit. J. Educ. Psychol.*, 1961, 31, 138–144.

[24] Lovell, K., and Slater, A., 'The Growth of the Concept of Time: a Comparative Study,' *Journal of Child Psychology and Psychiatry*, 1960, 1, 179–190.

[25] For a relevant study in respect of the concept of *speed*, see Lovell, K., Kellett, V. L. and Moorhouse, E., 'The Growth of the Concept of Speed: A Comparative Study,' *Journal of Child Psychology and Psychiatry*, 1962, 3, 101–110.

In other experiments Piaget and his students claim to show that by about 7 years of age, the concept of number is formed. Children aged 5, 6, or 7 years of age would be required to place a blue counter against each of a number of red counters. A child of 5 may be able to count and find the number of blue counters to be the same as the number of red counters when they are matched in a one-to-one correspondence. But if, say, the red counters are spread out somewhat, he will deny that the number of blue counters is now equal to the number of red counters. At first it appears that number and space form a perceptual whole for the child. It is not until the pupil can separate number from spatial orientation, and recognises that total quantity is independent of the way in which the elements of the quantity are arranged, that he is ready for the concept of number. At 6 years of age the child sometimes separates number and space, and at other times fails; at 7 the concept of number is stable.

Again, the work of Piaget and Inhelder suggests that a child's concept of space develops in the following sequence. In the early years (3–4) his ideas are topological[26] so that he can distinguish open from closed figures, and inside from outside. Later there is an increasing co-ordination of perspective so that there is a better understanding of projective or non-metrical space. Thus the child comes to comprehend the terms *direction, before, behind, right, left,* and so forth, and he begins to make relational judgments and say that one thing is in front of another. And in the last stage the child develops his ideas of measurement and the metric representation of space (Euclidean space) so that he can draw a rectangle and measure the length of its sides. However, the later studies of Lovell,[27] Lunzer[28] and Fisher[29] have thrown doubt on some aspects of their thesis in respect of the growth of the child's conception of space although the recent thorough study of Laurendeau and Pinard,[30] also of Olson, should also be studied.

In other work Piaget and Inhelder[31] show the growth, from 4 to 10 years of age, of the child's ability to classify objects. Many of their findings have been broadly confirmed by the writer.[32] The ability to classify objects seems to depend upon the capacity to compare two judgments simultaneously; and this skill may well develop from the child's increasing

---

[26] Topology is the science of that group of spatial properties that remain invariant in any spatial transformation, e.g. open and closed.

[27] Lovell, K., 'A Follow Up of Some Aspects of the Work of Piaget and Inhelder into the Child's Conception of Space,' *Brit. J. Educ. Psychol.,* 1959, **29**, 104–117.

[28] Lunzer, E. R., 'Some Points of Piagetian Theory in the Light of Experimental Criticism,' *Journal of Child Psychology and Psychiatry,* 1960, **1**, 191–202.

[29] Fischer, G. H., 'Developmental Features of Behaviour and Perception,' *Brit. J. Educ. Psychol.,* 1965, 69–78.

[30] Laurendeau, M. and Pinard, A., *The Development of the Concept of Space in the Child.* New York: International Universities Press, 1970. Also Olson, D. R., *Cognitive Development.* London: Academic Press, 1970.

[31] Piaget, J., and Inhelder, B., *The Early Growth of Logic in the Child.* London: Routledge and Kegan Paul, 1964.

[32] Lovell, K., Mitchell, B., and Everett, I. R., 'An Experimental Study of the Growth of Some Logical Structures,' *Brit. J. Psychol.,* 1962, **53**, 175–188.

ability, from the age of a few weeks onwards, to co-ordinate his retro-actions (the process whereby an individual revises an earlier action in the light of later actions) and his anticipations. It is the conviction of the Geneva school that the motor actions carried out by children on objects lead to mental operations (actions carried out in the mind). Moreover, the grouping and co-ordination of these operations manifests itself in what we call intelligence. The more complex the operations that can be grouped and co-ordinated, the more intelligent the person.

Readers are strongly urged to repeat some of the Piaget-type experiments. Many thousands of experiments have now been carried out under the writer's direction,[33] and his students have all testified to the insight which these experiments have given them into problems associated with child thinking.

Although Piaget's work has been discussed at some length it must be remembered that many other people have investigated the development of concepts among children. Usually the tests applied have estimated the child's ability to deal with objects at the 'conceptual' or at the 'concrete' level. At the former level, he perceives an object as one instance of a class or category but as the latter, he does not. Thus Thompson[34] found that children between 9 and 11 years of age were usually able to form groupings of objects demanding abstraction or generalisation, whereas children between 6 and 8 years of age were more likely to bring things together in a concrete situation; for example, 'I use a knife and fork to eat with'.[35] Goldman and Levine[36] have shown that, among American children, there is a great increase in the ability of first grade children, compared with kindergarten pupils, to sort objects into categories. The first categories made are in the context of personal experience, i.e. the objects are placed together because they are normally found that way (situational), or because they have similar uses (functional), or on the basis of perceptual reality (shape and colour). Later, concepts are developed that are relatively free of immediate personal contexts and are based on abstract ideas. The authors also warn us to be very careful over the use of language with young children. For example, we do not know if the words 'similar', 'belong to', etc., are understood differently at varying age levels.

Suchman[37] has tried to establish if learning can be facilitated during the latter part of the stage of concrete operations. Using motion pictures he

[33] See Lovell, K., *The Growth of Basic Mathematical and Scientific Concepts in Children*. London: University of London Press Ltd., Fifth Edition, 1966.

[34] Thompson, J. T., 'The Ability of Children at Different Grade Levels to Generalize on Sorting Tests,' *Brit. J. Psychol.*, 1941, **11**, 119–126.

[35] For a study of the growth of children's concepts of country and nationality, see Jahoda, G., 'The Development of Children's Ideas about Country and Nationality,' *Brit. J. Educ. Psychol.*, 1963, **33**, 47–60, 143–153.

[36] Goldman, A. E. and Levine, M., 'A Developmental Study of Object Sorting,' *Child Developm.*, 1963, **34**, 649–66.

[37] Suchman, J. R., 'Inquiry Training in the Elementary School,' *Sci. Teacher*, 1960, **27**, 42–47.

demonstrated a number of physical experiments: e.g. a small amount of water was placed in a thin-walled can and boiled, then corked and cooled, with the result that the sides of the can collapsed. After a specific type of training programme devised by Suchman, he found that the pupils asked more questions; were more accurate in describing what they saw; were more skilled in indicating the changes in the situation that might be crucial; and were more able to formulate relationships between objects and events before them. It might be possible with such a training programme to speed up the transition from concrete to formal operations, but as yet there is no certainty that this can be done.

Many studies have also been carried out to see if it is possible to speed up the growth of concrete operational thinking in 5–7-year-old children. Usually the subject have been given some definite training programme and their performance after the training compared with that before. It appears from these experiments that specific training is not very effective unless the child's thinking is nearly ready for it; i.e. unless this psychic organisation can be restructured by that experience. Unless this is so, any improvement that takes place seems to have limited transfer to other analogous situations.[38] Using Piagetian terms, *accommodative* modifications in central processes of the brain take place only when the child encounters circumstances which so match his *assimilated structures* that he is motivated by them, and can cope with them. In the educational setting, our teaching should be a little ahead of the child's development although not so far ahead that he cannot understand at all.[39] Vygotsky[40] distinguished the child's *spontaneous* concepts, developed mainly through his own mental efforts, and *non-spontaneous* ones that are decisively influenced by adults.

It may also be asked how speech affects learning, and that, in turn, the growth of concrete operational thinking. In the Russian[41] view an essential step in the formation of mental actions is the mastering of the actions on the plane of speaking aloud. The action having been verbalised, or the action taking place by means of the manipulation of verbal concepts, is an important step in the transference of the action to the verbal plane. There it undergoes further changes until it acquires the characteristics of an internal thinking operation. Perhaps in the West we pay too little attention to the role of speech, i.e. the verbalisation of the action, in the development of concrete operational thinking. In our fear that children, through mere verbosity, might delude us as to the level of their thinking, we may

[38] See Inhelder, B. and Sinclair, H. 'Learning Cognitive Structures'. In *Trends and Issues in Developmental Psychology* (Eds. Mussen, P. H., Langer, J. and Covington, M.). New York: Holt, Rinehart & Winston, 1969.

[39] Some educational implications of Piaget's system are brought out by Almy, M., *Young Children's Thinking*. New York: Teachers College Press, 1966, Ch. 7.

[40] Vygotsky, L. S., *Thought and Language* (English Translation). New York: M.I.T. and Wiley, 1962.

[41] Galperin, P. Ia., 'Experimental Study in the Formation of Mental Operations.' In *Psychology in the Soviet Union*. London: Routledge and Kegan Paul, 1957.

have overlooked the part that verbalisation might play in the development of mental operations. Wohlwill[42] is explicit that, in his view, mastery of the verbal labels 'one', 'two', etc., to indicate the numbers one, two and so on, plays an important part in passing from the stage where number is responded to wholly on a perceptual basis (two blue circles can be matched with two blue circles), to the stage where number is responded to conceptually in the sense that four green squares can be matched against four red triangles.

But alongside the Russian view must be placed the position of the Geneva school. First, language training, like other forms of training, certainly directs the child's interactions with the environment and thus helps to focus the child's attention to relevant aspects of the problem (compare Wohlwill's view indicated above). Second, there is little evidence to support the view that language training, in itself, contributes to the growth of mental structures so that, say, conservation concepts are possible. On the other hand, there seems likely to be a feedback of language on mental structures at the level of formal operational thought when reasoning seems so much more closely tied to language. Furth and Youniss[43] have recently shown the facilitating effect of linguistic use on certain formal operations that are expressed in symbols, but not in other formal operations, e.g. probability. But more information is needed in this field. Thus for Piaget and his colleagues[44] the view would be that up to the end of the period of concrete operational thought, logical structures determine the nature of the linguistic structures rather than the other way round. Language may, so to speak, prepare an operation, and help in the selection, storage and retrieval of information; but it does not play a central role in the growth of operational thought.

Thinking and feeling. In concluding this chapter, we must note the interaction of thinking and feeling. Thinking can never be detached from the total personality, and we cannot think independently of our emotions, needs, and values, any more than without being affected by past experience. Goldschmid studies the relationship between level of development in respect of conservation of substance, weight, number, area, distance, etc., and certain personality variables. It was found, as would be expected, that conservation was positively related to IQ, MA and verbal ability.[45] But more interesting was the fact that children with well developed conserva-

[42] Wohlwill, J. F., 'A Study of the Development of the Number Concept by Scaleogram Analysis,' *J. Genet. Psychol.*, 1960, 97, 345–377.

[43] Furth, H. G. and Youniss, J., 'Formal Operations and Language,' *Int. J. Psychol.*, 1971, 6, 48–64.

[44] Sinclair, H., 'Developmental Psycholinguistics.' In *Studies of Cognitive Development* (Eds. Elkind, D. and Flavell, J. H.). New York: Oxford University Press, 1969.

[45] Goldschmid, M. L. 'Different Types of Conservation and Non-conservation and their Relation to Age, Sex, IQ, MA and Vocabulary,' *Child Developm.*, 1967, 38, 1229–1246.

tion tended to be more objective in their self-evaluations (i.e. responses to requests such as 'Tell me what you are like', 'Tell me the way you would like to be'), less dominated by their mothers, more favourably described by their teachers, preferred by their peers, and regarded as being more attractive and passive than children with a poorly developed sense of conservation.[46] Such evidence suggests the importance of affective as well as of environmental factors in the child's intellectual growth. Another relevant study is that of McKillop,[47] which involved over 500 adolescents in New York, well mixed in respect of social-economic status and race. The findings suggest that attitude affects perception, that material is more easily learnt and remembered if it conforms to one's point of view, that attitude affects judgment and the ability to reason logically, and that the more ambiguous and less rigidly defined the data is, the more important attitude becomes. Further study, by different authors, has shown that it is much harder to draw conclusions from syllogisms involving people about whom we have strong feelings than from syllogisms involving, say, Socrates. But there is a two-way traffic, for while a child's feelings influence his perceiving and thinking, his capacity to perceive and think affects his feelings.

The importance of thinking as calmly and objectively as possible about any subject, and of being able to write or speak without the frequent use of emotional charged words, is well brought out by R. H. Thouless in his book *Straight and Crooked Thinking*.[48]

[46] Goldschmid, M. L. 'The Relation of Conservation to Emotional and Environmental Aspects of Development,' *Child Developm.*, 1968, **39**, 579–589.

[47] McKillop, A. S., *The Relationship between the Reader's Attitude and Certain Types of Reading Response*. New York: Teachers College Bureau of Publications, 1952. See also Thouless, R. H., 'Effect of Prejudice on Reasoning,' *Brit. J. Psychol.*, 1959, **50**, 289–293.

[48] Thouless, R. H., *Straight and Crooked Thinking*. London: English Universities Press Ltd., 1930.

Chapter Seven

MATURATION

MOST teachers will at some time or other meet a child who is unable to tackle, say, simple fractions at 9 plus years, but who can do so when one year older. It is reasonable to suppose that at the earlier age failure was not altogether due to inexperience in arithmetic but rather due to lack of maturity, while at the latter age success came as the result of the increased maturity plus any additional experience. A similar situation arises in reading. A given child may not have sufficient maturity to be ready to read at 5 years of age and yet might be able to learn at $5\frac{1}{2}$ years. We may thus agree with McGeoch[1] that in psychology,[2] increase of maturity, or maturation, means the changes in behaviour with age which depend primarily upon organic growth factors rather than upon prior practice and experience. Such a definition does not rule out the effects of experience. Indeed, if maturation is defined as development which takes place in the absence of specific experience, then as Ausubel[3] reminds us, it can be thought of as consisting of development which is attributable to genetics and/or incidental experience.

In many day-to-day situations, it is impossible to make a clear-cut distinction between maturation and learning, since both influence behaviour. Nevertheless it is possible that certain kinds of behaviour are relatively more influenced by maturation, others by learning. Gesell[4] seems very definitely to be of the opinion that maturation is of greater importance in determining child-behaviour than is the culture pattern, or to use his term, *acculturation*. But he seems to ignore the fact that relevant environmental conditions always influence maturity in action. However, despite the difficulty of separating maturation and learning, the study of maturation is important for two reasons. First, maturation includes organic factors over which we have little or no control but which, nevertheless, markedly affect human development. Second, maturation seems to limit, to a great extent, an individual's rate of learning and to determine his ultimate levels of achievement.

[1] McGeoch, J. A., *The Psychology of Human Learning*. New York: Longmans, 1942.
[2] The term maturation has a different meaning in genetics.
[3] Ausubel, D. P., 'Maturation and Learning in Adolescent Development,' *Int. J. Educ. Sci.*, 1966, **1**, 47-60.
[4] Gesell, A., *The Child from Five to Ten*. London: Hamish Hamilton. Gesell, A., In *Manual of Child Psychology*. Editor Carmichael, L. London: Chapman & Hall, 1954.

The influence of maturation in animals. It is much easier to deny animals normal training or practice than children. Indeed, it would be completely unethical to deprive children of normal experience, and this is one reason why the effects of the environment on some important human traits cannot easily be determined. Resort has been made, therefore, to experimentation with animals, although we shall see a little later that some experiments have been carried out with children also. Obviously, conclusions drawn from experiments involving animals cannot be applied directly to children. But they are often provocative, and stimulate research with human beings.

Several experiments have indicated that it is maturation rather than practice which enables a tadpole to perfect its swimming technique. Practice given to younger tadpoles is much less effective than similar opportunities provided for older ones, for the latter are at a stage at which they are more ready for swimming. Cruze[5] showed that practice is more effective in helping a chick to peck at pellets of food at the age of four days than is a comparable amount of practice immediately after hatching. Further, there was a progressive increase in the ability of the chicks with age (the groups ranged in age from 1 to 21 days) to find their way through a maze or to solve problem boxes. Nevertheless Cruze also concluded that normal experience and training did play a part in bringing about an increase in proficiency with age.

Generalising from the experiments with animals we may say that within certain age limits the older the organism, and therefore the greater its maturation, the more rapidly and effectively does it learn. But in certain instances (for example, the flying ability of buzzards) it seems that if practice and experience are denied beyond a certain critical degree of maturation then the performance of the animal in that field suffers permanent retardation. To what extent this finding holds true in the case of children is not known with certainty. If it is true over a large field of human behaviour then it has the most important educational implications.

The influence of maturation in children. In studying the effects of maturation on learning in children, use has been made either of identical twins (where one gets training and the other does not), or of trained and untrained groups which have been matched for age, sex, intelligence, initial performance and so forth. The upshot of these experiments is that many motor activities are greatly affected by maturation. Such activities include locomotion, bodily coordination, sitting and standing, and specific motor skills like climbing a tree and bouncing a ball. Thus the study of Gesell and Thompson[6] on cube-manipulation and stair-climbing, Hilgard's[7] work on

[5] Cruze, W. W., 'Maturation and Learning in Chicks,' *J. comp. Psychol.*, 1935, **19**, 371–409. Also Cruze, W. W., 'Maturity and Learning Ability,' *Psychol. Monogr.*, 1938, **50**, No. 5.

[6] Gesell, A., and Thompson, H., 'Learning and Growth in Identical Infant Twins,' *Genet. Psychol. Monogr.*, 1929, **6**, 1–124.

[7] Hilgard, J. R., 'Learning and Maturation in Pre-school Children,' *J. Genet. Psychol.*, 1932, **41**, 36–56.

climbing, cutting with scissors, and buttoning clothes, and McGraw's[8] investigations of a variety of motor activities, all show the great influence of maturation at an early age. But in the case of more complex skills, the picture seems rather different. Thus in Mattson's[9] experiment, in which children aged between 4 years 10 months and 6 years 0 months had to roll balls through mazes of increasing complexity, the trained group performed better than the untrained group, and the differences between the perform- ances of the two groups increased as the tasks became more complex. In such tasks practice and training assume a more important role, and children left to depend upon maturation alone for increased skill are likely to be at a disadvantage.

Dennis,[10] has provided evidence concerning a situation where children are unnaturally restricted. At the time of his studies most (but not all) infants in the Hopi Indian Village in Arizona were bound to a cradling board on the first day of life. The restriction imposed was such that a child could move only his head, and he was kept in that position almost continuously for the first three months of life, the mother carrying the board on her back and often hanging it to a tree while she was at work. Though all Hopi infants walked one or two months later than white children, those who had been cradled walked no later than those who had not under- gone the restriction. This, too, suggests that maturation is of greater importance than experience as far as walking is concerned.

From a consideration of the simpler types of behaviour that we have mentioned, it seems that within the period of childhood deferred training is more economical than early training. Thus one week of practice later may get the same results as six weeks at an earlier date. But it is not likely to be true of the more complex activities. McGraw, who has done a great deal of work in this field, concludes that maturation is of the greatest importance in patterns of behaviour that emerge during infancy, such as sitting, standing and walking. Within fairly broad limits, these appear to be unaffected by special exercise. On the other hand skills which emerge later like swimming, balancing, riding a tricycle and so on, which an individual often acquires but does not of necessity have to acquire, seem to be considerably influenced by the practice given at certain maturational levels. But even here practice seems to be more effective if not given too early.

In concluding this section, however, it must be stressed that experience and learning are of *some* consequence even in so fundamental an activity as walking. Indeed, external stimulation, opportunities for learning and for

[8] McGraw, M. B., *Growth: A Study of Johnny and Jimmy*. New York: Appleton-Century-Crofts, 1935.

[9] Mattson, M. L., 'The Relation between the Complexity of the Habit to be acquired, and the Form of the Learning Curve in Young Children,' *Genet. Psychol. Monogr.*, 1933, 13, 299–398.

[10] Dennis, W., and Dennis, M. G., 'The Effect of Cradling Practice upon the Onset of Walking in Hopi Children,' *J. genet. Psychol.*, 1940, 56, 77–86.

gaining experience are essential for the development of all activities, motor or intellectual, but in some activities maturation is relatively more important than in others. Thus Dennis has more recently shown (1960), through studying children in an orphanage where they had little chance to receive stimulation or undergo experience, that motor development does not just consist in the automatic unfolding of a behaviour sequence based on the maturation of structures. Experience affected not only the age at which motor skills appeared but also their very form.

The influence of maturation on educational achievement. The discussion in the previous section dealt mainly with motor abilities. Unfortunately we know very little about the best ages to introduce the various school subjects. Such experimental evidence as is available from America at the moment does not, in the writer's view, accord with practice in this country, although it does accord with the evidence from recent studies of concept formation. For example, Washburne[11] reports the study made of some thousands of children in the U.S.A. which claims to determine the mental age levels at which various topics in arithmetic might be taught to children. It is concluded, for example, that the working of simple addition exercises with totals greater than ten should not be attempted until the child has a minimum mental age of 7 years 4 months. Other American studies[12] suggest that a child needs a minimum mental age of $6\frac{1}{2}$ years before he is ready for reading.[13] Most teachers in this country would probably agree with the writer that the latter mental age is unneccessarily high. Though mental age is a factor in determining the child's readiness for reading, it is not the only one. Previous relevant experience, motivation, the quality of teaching, and the pupil-teacher relationships are also important. Sanderson[14] has more recently maintained that the whole notion of reading readiness should be critically examined; while Lynn[15] has surveyed evidence suggesting that accurate perception and learning of whole words are readily accomplished by a mental age of $2\frac{1}{2}$ to $3\frac{1}{2}$ years. He further argues that the concept of reading readiness as such is not worth maintaining and thinks that the reading difficulties of children may be due to

[11] Washburne, C., *The Work of the Committee of Seven on Grade Placement in Arithmetic.* National Society for the Study of Education, 38th Year Book, 1939.

[12] For example, Gates, A. I., 'The Necessary Mental Age for Beginning Reading,' *Elem. Sch. J.*, 1937, 37, 497–503; or Morphett, M. V., and Washburne, C., 'When should Children Begin to Read?' *Elem. Sch. J.*, 1931, 31, 496–503. A critical analysis of the American work is given in *Studies in Reading*, Vol. I. Scottish Council for Educational Research. London: University of London Press Ltd., 1948.

[13] A number of tests said to assess a child's readiness for reading have been devised, mainly in America. Such tests seem to be useful in picking out children who are likely to have difficulties in learning to read. A typical test is that by Monroe, M., *Reading Aptitude Test.* Boston: Houghton Mifflin Co., 1935.

[14] Sanderson, A. E., 'The Idea of Reading Readiness,' *Educational Research*, 1963, 6, 3–9.

[15] Lynn, R., 'Reading Readiness and the Perceptual Readiness of Young Children,' *Educational Research*, 1963, 6, 10–15.

fundamental characteristics of the visual system and not due to maturation as such.

At the moment, then, we know very little about the influence of maturation on the complex mental abilities involved in the study of school subjects. We need to know, for example, far more about the best age or ages to introduce various mathematical steps,[16] or when to start the study of a foreign language. Research into the causes of backwardness has shown that the introduction of some new learning experiences (for example, reading) to a child before he is ready and capable of making progress, may frustrate him so much as to cause a permanent dislike of the study. Most children in our society seem to be ready to read by about $5\frac{1}{2}$ to 6 years of age but we have little exact knowledge about the best ages for introducing other subjects and topics.[17] However, we must not necessarily defer the teaching of reading to children until they are, say, 8 years of age. It is certain that they will learn quicker at 8 than at $5\frac{1}{2}$ years, but during those $2\frac{1}{2}$ years the children will have obtained much joy out of their reading; for, once they can read, a whole new world is opened up to them. The extra time required to teach a $5\frac{1}{2}$-year-old instead of an 8-year-old is of no real economic worth, and if he is held back in reading it is certain that he will be held back in other fields as well. Further, there is a danger that if he finds that he can do without reading until 8 years of age, he will be tempted to go on without being able to read.

While Piagetian studies have thrown much light on the growth of mathematical, scientific, and other concepts in children, far more knowledge is needed. The evidence is clear that there are great individual differences in the chronological ages of children when they attain a given concept, and that concept formation depends on factors other than mental age.

The best clues for parents and teacher are the signs that a child is attempting to engage in some particular activity, mental or physical, on his own. When such are observed, it usually means that he is mature enough to commence it. On the other hand, some children are mature enough but show no interest, and these do need encouragement to attempt the activity.

Summary. The problem of maturation is a complex one, but it is of the greatest importance in human affairs because intrinsic factors are involved, largely outside our control, which considerably affect our behaviour. Motor activities that emerge during infancy seem less affected by specific experience, while those that emerge later are more easily modified by

[16] Rosskopf, M. F., Steffe, L. P. and Taback, S. (Eds.), *Piagetian Cognitue—Developmental Research and Mathematical Education.* Washington: National Council of Teachers of Mathematics, 1971.
[17] The effectiveness of the teaching of formal subjects in Scottish schools throws doubt on the minimum ages for introducing various topics suggested by some American psychologists. See Vernon, P. E., O'Gorman, M. B., and McLellan, A., *Brit. J. Educ. Psychol.*, 1955, **25**, 195–203.

training and practice. Much more information is needed about the effect
of maturation on mental activities, and practically nothing is known about
the influence of maturation on the social-emotional adjustment and character training of children. It is by no means certain that we should be wise
in delaying the teaching of tool subjects until the period when the teaching
could be done most economically in terms of time. However, it must be
remembered that the greatest part of children's behaviour probably comes
through interaction of maturation and learning. Looking at the issue from
a Piagetian viewpoint, most school learning must follow on intellectual
development. The latter, in turn, results from the interaction of the child
with the environment involving a very large range of incidental experiences
—at least up to the onset of concrete operational thought.

Chapter Eight

LEARNING

WE may define learning as a change in behaviour which is more or less permanent in nature, and which results from activity, training or observation. To say that learning must have taken place when there is a change in behaviour is not enough; such a change must persist for a while. Momentary changes in behaviour due to sensory adaptation may take place but learning it not necessarily involved. We must also specify that the changes are due to activity, training or observation to distinguish them from the changes brought about by maturation discussed in the previous chapter. Learning occurs in many different situations; for example, in connection with memorisation, the acquisition of physical or intellectual skills, solving problems, learning by trial and error, rather sudden or 'insightful' learning, the establishment of attitudes, interests and character traits, and the acquisition of mannerisms and gestures.

The two main approaches to learning theory. Although we are going to discuss some theories on how learning is brought about, it must be made clear at the outset that most of our knowledge about learning has been determined empirically and has not been derived from any psychological theory. The experiments of psychologists have certainly taught us a great deal about how animals and children learn, but none of their theories are yet comprehensive enough to tie together all the known facts, or to answer all the questions that we would like to ask. Such information as we have about learning can, however, be put to good use even if we have no complete theory to explain the process, in the same way we can put electricity to excellent use although we do not have, as yet, any comprehensive theory to explain its nature.[1]

At present, then, there are two main approaches to learning theory. One of these is the Stimulus-Response Associationist type of theory and the other is the Field-Cognition type of theory. These terms may seem somewhat technical but in the following two sections we hope to make them clear.

[1] For an account of the theoretical approaches to the psychology of learning see: Hilgard, E. R., *Theories of Learning.* London: Methuen, 1966, Third Edition. Hall, F. W., *Learning: A Survey of Psychological Interpretations.* London: University Paperbacks, 1963. For an advanced and critical account of theories of learning see Lunzer, E. A., In *Development in Learning—2. The Regulation of Behaviour.* London: Staples, 1968.

Stimulus-Response Association[2] *theories.* On many occasions in everyday life one event follows closely upon another, for example, lightning and thunder. In such situations, we are said to associate one event with another, and the basic principle of associationism is that if A and B are presented together in space or in time the subsequent presentation of A tends to evoke B. Moreover, the strength of the association between A and B will depend upon the frequency, recency and vividness of previous associations. Our symbols A and B include amongst other things, ideas, perceptions, moods, and emotions. Associationism has been a topic of great interest to philosophers and thinkers from the time of Plato, but we can consider here only the more recent and relevant aspects of the problem.

In 1896 E. L. Thorndike began his studies of animals. In his well-known experiments with cats, he would place a young, lively, and hungry animal into a cage and put a piece of fish outside. Plenty of action on the part of the cat would be observed; it would push its claws through the bars, bite the bars and try to squeeze through them. Sooner or later it would touch the button which held the cage door, the door would swing open and the cat get out. When the animal, still hungry, was replaced in the cage, it would still attempt a 'trial and error', or 'trial and success', approach to the problem, but there were fewer actions and the door was opened sooner. With further trials the successful movements were 'stamped in' and useless ones eliminated, so that on being placed in the cage once more the animal got out in a couple of seconds.

As a result of his many experiments, Thorndike was led to formulate, in the early years of this century, his three famous laws. These are:

(*a*) *Law of Exercise.* The response to a situation becomes associated with that situation, and the more it is used in a given situation, the more strongly it becomes associated with it. On the other hand, disuse of the response weakens the association.

(*b*) *Law of Effect.* Responses that are accompanied or closely followed by satisfaction are more likely to happen again when the situation recurs, while responses accompanied or closely followed by discomfort will be less likely to recur.

(*c*) *Law of Intensity.* The greater the satisfaction or discomfort, the greater will be the strengthening or weakening of the bond between the situation and the response.

It will be seen that the Law of Exercise really embodies the principle of association applied to the situation and response. The Law of Effect is also one of association, for it really states that the satisfactory or unsatisfactory outcome of an act respectively strengthens or weakens the association already existing. Note carefully that the cat was motivated; it was learning more quickly since it was acting under the influence of the hunger

---

[2] It seems that associations are due to linkages formed in the cerebral cortex, between nerve cells and their ramifications.

drive. Later, in 1932 and 1933, Thorndike[3] made a fresh study of the Law of Effect, using human beings instead of animals. His new evidence led him to give much greater weight to reward than to punishment. The latter did not so much break the bond between the situation and the response; rather it caused the learner to try other moves which would bring him reward. Some psychologists think that the Law of Effect is the most important single principle in learning theory today.

Also working with animals at the beginning of this century was I. P. Pavlov (1849–1936), the Russian physiologist. He found that saliva flowed from a dog's mouth not only when food was placed in it, but also when the dog heard the approaching footsteps of the person bringing food, or if he heard a bell[4] rung just before food was brought. Now the normal flow of saliva when food is in the mouth is a reflex action and we may write:

Unconditioned stimulus →   Unconditioned response
     (food in mouth)   (reflex action of saliva)

But when the animal learns to associate the sound of a bell with food soon to be eaten, and commences to salivate before food is actually in the mouth, we may say that the complete sequence is:

Conditioned stimulus →   Conditioned response →
(Sound of bell or footsteps)   (Advanced flow of saliva)
→ Unconditioned stimulus →   Conditioned Response
     (Food in mouth)   (Reflex action of saliva)

This learning took place because of *reinforcement*, that is, because food was always given after the bell had sounded. By conditioning, then, we mean that the organism learns to respond to a secondary or neutral stimulus which has become associated in time with a primary stimulus. We may, therefore, regard conditioning as a special case of association by contiguity.

Among other important findings, Pavlov showed that if the conditioned stimulus is an electric bell, and is replaced by, say, a buzzer, conditioned responses are still evoked but they are weaker. The fact that other stimuli, more or less similar to the original conditioned stimulus, can bring about the same conditioned response is known as *stimulus generalisation*.

Pavlov was of the opinion that in the animal, knowledge of the external world is obtained almost exclusively by stimuli which come into the special cells of the sense organs which receive incoming signals, and the changes which these signals cause in the cerebral cortex. This type of signal activity must also play a great part in the life of man. But in human beings there is an important addition, for arising out of his social life and work, there

[3] Thorndike, E. L., *The Fundamentals of Learning*. New York: Teachers College, Columbia University, 1932. Thorndike, E. L., *An Experimental Study of Rewards*. New York: Teachers College, Columbia University, 1933.
[4] The stimulus must be of a nature to attract the animal's attention.

has developed what Pavlov called *second order* signals, in the form of oral and written language. Thus speech or written words represent an abstraction from reality and allow of generalisations and the build-up of concepts (cf. Chapter 6). In Pavlov's view laws established in the work of the first signal system should also govern the second signal system.

We may now explain in terms of Pavlovian theory how a child comes to use, say, the word 'horse' correctly:

Father says 'horse' → Child says 'horse'—an imitative response.
Sight of *horse* plus the word 'horse', frequently said by father, →
Child says 'horse'. (This sequence repeated many times.)
Sight of *horse* → Child says 'horse'—a conditioned response.

For a long time it was thought that Thorndike's trial-and-error learning was quite different from the conditioned response of Pavlov. Later, however, Clark Hull[5] worked out a very elaborate theory of learning which, while taking into account stimulus-response theory, also makes use of Thorndike's Law of Effect. He maintains that learning will not take place without reinforcement[6] or reward, and that it depends on a reduction in the individual's needs, primary or secondary, in accordance with the Law of Effect. Thus if a response reduces a need, say, hunger, which is strong at the time, then the same stimulus will bring about the same response in the future. This can be illustrated simply by considering a rat placed in a maze which has a number of blind alleys but also a correct path which leads to food. At first the rat will be seen to explore by trial and error, but eventually it reaches food and is rewarded. Next day if, when hungry, it is put in the maze again, it finds the food rather more quickly. Its correct choices are rewarded by food and its 'errors' (going up blind alleys) are penalised by its being temporarily denied food. After being put into the maze a few more times, it will go along the correct path without error. Thus Hull's theory of reinforcement provides a neat hypothesis of why learning takes place. Hull made a contribution to learning theory, and he modified his views from time to time as experimental evidence demanded.

Summing up this section, we may say that in the Stimulus-Response Associationist type of learning theory, learning takes place through the establishment or strengthening of bonds between the stimulating conditions and the responses. But for this to happen the stimulus, the response and the reinforcement must take place together in time. Responses which are followed by reductions of needs tend to be repeated, and those not followed by reward or need-reduction tend to disappear.

The Field-Cognition type of theory. Consider once more the rat placed in the maze. On the first few occasions, when it goes up blind alleys, its

---

[5] Hull, C. L., *Principles of Behaviour: An Introduction to Behaviour Theory.* New York: Appleton Century, 1943.
[6] 'Reinforcement' is here used in the more restricted sense of reward or drive-reduction.

behaviour would be regarded by Tolman as a kind of exploration rather than as 'errors'. Even on the first run through the maze the rat appears to learn something, for on the second run less exploration is necessary. In a way, then, the rat becomes *aware* of his surroundings, and on later runs he behaves as though he was aware that certain responses would bring him to food, that is, as if he was guided by a kind of 'knowing' or *cognitive theory*.

For Tolman,[7] learning depends upon what he calls 'cognitive maps', which are built out of experience. The previous association of environmental events appearing in time suggest to the individual that by responding in a certain way to a particular situation, other specific events will follow. As a result of experience, the learner builds up new expectancies, realisations or cognitions; that is, he learns 'what will lead to what'. These 'cognitive maps' may be simple or comprehensive, depending upon the structure of the brain, motivation, relevant experience and practice, and the nature of the external stimuli. The more comprehensive the map, the more likely it is that transfer of training will take place. Tolman questions the whole notion of trial and error learning which appears to operate without meaning and purpose. When animals are put into a situation in which they can respond in different ways, he claims that they show systematic if not appropriate behaviour. If one type of systematic attack does not bring the animal to its goal, say a food box, then another kind of systematic attack is used. Indeed, the animal seems to act in accordance with a series of 'hypotheses' (so called by Krechevsky) or 'provisional maps'. Each of these hypotheses is linked with the one that went before it, so that as each is tried out the number of potential approaches is cut down until the problem is finally solved.

Field theorists like Lewin and Tolman believe that all behaviour is 'purposive' or 'goal directed'. Their theories are connected historically with Gestalt theory, which in turn suggests that the psychological field is always organised as well as possible. This is sometimes difficult as there may be conflicting factors in the field, but even so we do as well as we can. Thus in learning, field theory opposes the idea of blindness or randomness in the organism's movement. Even when the individual's responses are badly adapted to the environment (as in the neurotic), field theory maintains that there is an attempt to deal with the environmental situation, and that the attempt is purposeful to the individual concerned.

Insight. Learning to solve problems is a matter of great interest to everyone connected with education. In this kind of learning some goal has to be reached but the way is not immediately clear. The individual often makes use of some of the following: the observation of relations, reasoning,

[7] Tolman, E. C., *Collected Papers in Psychology*. Berkeley, Calif.: University of California Press, 1951. Also Tolman, E. C. 'Cognitive Maps in Rats and Men,' *Psychol. Rev.*, 1948, 55, 189–208.

generalisation, and what the Gestalt psychologists call 'insight'. This term requires some explanation and to understand it we must go back to Thorndike's experiments mentioned before. It will be remembered that Thorndike believed that the cat used a purely 'trial and error' approach when attempting to get out of the box to eat the fish. Kohler,[8] however, in 1927, pointed out that Thorndike's problems were so arranged that it was hardly possible for the animal to solve them without such activity. A comparable situation for a human being would be to put him in a room, the door of which could be opened only by his treading on a small electric switch in the floor, the whole of the floor being covered by a carpet. The man would not be able to see at first even how to set about the problem, and a certain amount of examining the door, lock, walls, floor and so forth would be necessary however intelligent the man might be. Kohler maintained that, had the animal been able to survey the whole problem right from the start, in order to obtain a grasp of the situation as a whole from the beginning, then it would have been in a position to solve the problem.

In his own experiments, Kohler found that a chimpanzee, after looking at a problem for a while, would suddenly solve it at a first attempt without making any false moves. This Kohler called *insight*. Thus a chimpanzee quickly learnt after studying the situation, how to use a box as a stool from which to reach up to a suspended banana; but the stacking of several boxes to reach a higher object proved much more difficult for many of the animals. Even if they reached the objects, the boxes were often stacked in such a manner that they were unstable. In other words some had sufficient insight to solve the problem geographically but even so they could not always solve it mechanically.

One characteristic of good insight is *reproducibility*, that is, the animal when confronted with the situation once more, will quickly resort to the same solution. Another characteristic is the capacity to transfer the method of attack to other similar problems. Gestalt psychologists have generally spoken disparagingly of 'trial and error' behaviour, although they admit that such activity may change the situation in some ways so that a clearer view of the whole problem is obtained. Actually it seems that 'trial and error' behaviour is a necessary component of most problem-solving, though it may take place as a mental event rather than as overt behaviour. Gestalt theory holds that the organism *does* always organise its psychological field, and that the exploration and manipulation observed in 'trial and error' learning helped in such organisation. After each move, the psychological field is again reorganised until insight suddenly occurs. Looking at the matter another way, we may say that the animal sets up a series of 'provisional maps' or 'hypotheses' to solve the problem. Many of these may be tried out by behaviour internal to the animal which cannot be detected by the observer; others have to be tried out by external 'trial and error' behaviour. Note that previous relevant experience is of help; it

[8] Kohler's criticism had been anticipated by Hobhouse in 1901.

permits of more comprehensive 'hypotheses' on which the animal can work.

Learning in children. We have seen, then, that there are two main schools of learning theory. Field cognition theorists suggest that the active learner attempts to give meaning to his experiences, and the insight that he is able to display is as 'good' as it can be in the circumstances. The function of the teacher is to present situations to his pupils in which the relationships involved are not beyond their power of mental organisation. The children will then learn by direct insight. But the associationist would suggest that the job of the teacher is the forming of bonds of association and the 'stamping in' of those associations by repetition. Hence there is an emphasis on drill work and the need for motivating the learner. Each school has something to contribute to learning and teaching in the classroom where the children are mainly engaged in cognitive activities.

There is no doubt that the establishment of many simple habits like feeding, elimination, and sleeping, can be explained in terms of conditioning. Attempts have also been made to solve certain behaviour problems in children by means of conditioned response procedures. For example, a few experimenters have used a technique involving conditioning in curing enuresis (bed wetting).[9] In a typical study wire mesh sheets, separated by gauze, were placed in an electric circuit which included a bell. When the child commenced to urinate the gauze became wet and acted as a conductor of electricity; at the same time the bell rang (unconditioned stimulus). The child was awakened and went to the toilet to complete the passing of urine. After a number of trials bladder tension (now the conditioned stimulus) was enough to wake the child before the urination began. One worker reports that thirty cases between 3 and 13 years of age were cured by this means within two to three months. This technique would be most likely to be successful when enuresis is due to faulty training and not to emotional maladjustment. But in the usual classroom situation, the learning process is much more complex and cannot be explained on conditioning alone. Indeed, there is usually an interplay of associationist and field cognition theories.

It is possible for almost all children to have some degree of insight. If apes can show insight so can the dull child. Since Pavlov's dog organised its field of experience and noted relevant experiences in a situation that first appeared vague and meaningless, so insightful behaviour is possible at all levels of intelligence in children, provided the learning task is at the correct level of difficulty. On this view, the task of the teacher is to start from whatever insight his pupils possess and to direct them to new situations of the appropriate complexity which they can solve by insight. Essentially the new situation must be so arranged that the children are

[9] Compare Mowrer, O. H., and Mowrer, W. M. 'Enuresis, a Method for its Study and Treatment,' *Amer. J. Orthopsychiat.*, 1938, **8**, 436–459.

stimulated to ask themselves the right questions and to find for themselves the correct answers. They thereby tend to look upon themselves as organisers of their own environment and gain self-confidence. This helps children to think well of themselves and acts as a source of motivation. It is quite true that drill work will often be necessary, for successive repetition may bring 'partial insights', and each of these may in turn provide opportunities for further acts of insight. In other words drill often helps to reduce the complexity of the overall situation and through a succession of partial insights we get complete insight—in short we piece together a number of small cues. This is very different from regarding the function of repetition as the mere 'stamping in' of correct associations. Again, once there has been some understanding of the situation, or some achievement in solving the problem, repetition does away with conscious attention to the repeated act and leaves the child free to turn his attention to more complex issues.

Duncker,[10] Wertheimer[11] and many other psychologists have stressed that the most effective thinking occurs when use is made of insightful learning and their suggestions should be carefully noted by teachers. On the other hand, there will be occasions when the teacher will have to give the greater part of the material to his pupils in direct fashion, and learning will be likely to take place in the manner suggested by Hull. Learning then depends upon adequate motivation. Indeed, when entirely new material has to be learnt in which the child has no sophistication at all, then learning seems to take place along the lines suggested by Hull, and reinforcement has to be immediate and informative. But if the child finds himself in a situation, fairly simple for him, and he has a rich background relative to the situation, then learning will take place using a field cognitive approach.

Skemp[12] has drawn attention to the fact that *schemata*—organisations of past impressions, and themselves the result of experience and learning—give meaning in all future learning. He points out that when a child first enters a new field, the elementary schemata first built up are of great consequence to all future learning in that field. Schematic learning is more efficient than rote learning, for at each stage the child builds a platform from which further advance may be made. The problem, practically, is how best to help a child to build adequate schemata at the beginning of a new learning situation. If such schemata could be built then we should certainly have more efficient learning, more efficient recall, and a preparation for future learning. Moreover, while stimulus-response association theories may well account for some learning of content *within* any of the stages of thought outlined in Chapter 6, they seem unable to explain the

[10] Duncker, K., 'On Problem Solving,' *Psychol. Monogr.*, 1945, 58, No. 270.
[11] Wertheimer, M., *Productive Training*. Revised Edition. London: Tavistock, 1961.
[12] Skemp, R. R., 'The Need for a Schematic Theory of Learning', *Brit. J. Educ. Psychol.*, 1962, 32, 133–142.

move from one stage of thinking to the next. Likewise it seems that such theories are unable to explain how the child acquires adult language structures.

The way in which children actually solve problems is of great interest to teachers. Very often the solution depends upon their discovering some underlying principle or recognising some relationship. Many different types of experiments have been devised in this field, ranging from puzzle problems involving the use of apparatus, to problems demanding abstract reasoning; and ranging from simple to insoluble problems. The upshot of such investigations is that some sort of exploratory or manipulative behaviour is frequently used, helped by verbalisation. But in other instances the various hypotheses are tested covertly; there is much transfer from other situations, and the child works out the correct moves.[13]

The following are among the most important factors influencing the learning process in children. These have been found by experiment and are not deduced from learning theory:

(a) *Intelligence*. The more intelligent the child, the more easily will he spot relevant relationships between objects or ideas, and apply them to new but similar situations. Thus we find, as we should expect, that bright children are superior to dull children in trial and error learning, and their superiority is even greater in insightful learning.

(b) *Age*. Mental Age increases with chronological age up to about 15–16 years. Thus learning takes place with increasing facility up to the school leaving age providing motivation is maintained. In some instances, mental age increases after 16 years (*see* Chapter 3).

(c) *Relevant experience*. The greater the relevant experience in some field, the easier in general will be the learning of fresh material in that particular field or in one closely allied to it.

(d) *Motivation*. The extent to which a child is motivated determines the energy he will put into the learning process. Either primary or secondary needs may be involved. Further, unless he is motivated (even if only to avoid punishment) he cannot be rewarded, hence there can be no reinforcement. Indeed, it is no exaggeration to say that one of our chief problems is to discover the best ways of motivating children so that they will learn.

(e) *Observation*. Noting the characteristic features of the learning situation, or spotting the exact nature of the stimuli, is essential. Furthermore, observation of results is important, since these results act as a reinforcement and serve as a guide towards better performance. Any of the factors listed in Chapter 5 which aid attention and observation also aid learning.

(f) *Reinforcement*. Reward plays a great part in determining which activities will be learnt. If a learnt activity is not rewarded, that activity tends not to reappear in future behaviour. The form that the reward can take depends upon the motivation, at that instant, of the particular child.

[13] See Duncker, K., *op. cit.*

The term *reinforcement* also refers to knowledge of results. This is very important in making learning efficient. There is much evidence to suggest without such knowledge little learning takes place. The knowledge is not always given externally (e.g. by the teacher) but sometimes by the pupil himself, as when he knows if he can recite a verse of poetry.

(*g*) *Repetition*. The learning of very simple activities may be accomplished on the first occasion when they are attempted. But with more complex activities, repetition, suitably spaced, help the learning process considerably. This point is further developed in Chapter 9.

(*h*) *Concern*. There is evidence that a pupil's concern for the outcome of his study brings about conditions that help learning. We do not, of course, want anxiety in our pupils, let alone neurotic anxiety, but when they do not feel uncomfortable in 'not knowing' they are unlikely to learn. Indeed, there can be little reinforcement. The concern or tension must, of course, be relieved after making the correct response.

(*i*) Further practical suggestions for making the learning process as efficient as possible are given in the following chapter.

Programmed Instruction. In recent years there has been a great increase of interest in the use of programmed instruction. Some of the approaches originate from the work of B. F. Skinner in the training of animals. In a way he stands in the tradition of Thorndike, and his rules for training may be stated briefly as follows:

(*a*) Reinforce the desire behaviour as quickly and as frequently as possible.

(*b*) Shape the behaviour in the desired way through a series of small steps.

(*c*) Reinforce as far as possible by reward rather than by punishing. Some forms of automated teaching put these principles into effect.

In a typical teaching machine, there passes in front of the pupil a number of items illustrating, say, printed materials, diagrammatic materials demonstrating principles, statements of fact etc., and a question is asked about each. In the Skinner or 'linear' type of programme the student has to make up his response (a creative response) to each question, which he can then evaluate against the correct response given by the machine. Moreover, the step between each item is so small and well graded that the pupil can scarcely go wrong. In the 'branching' type of programme devised by Crowder, however, there is a multiple-choice type of response. If the subject is correct he moves on to the next item; if he is wrong he has to work through a further item (selected by the machine) that will eradicate his error.

Wittrock and Twelker[14] studied the effects of prompting, i.e. the giving of extra information or prompting before the subject makes his response;

[14] Wittrock, M. C. and Twelker, P. A., 'Prompting and Feedback in the Learning, Retention, and Transfer of Concepts.' *Brit. J. Educ. Psychol.*, 1964, **34**, 10–18.

also the effect of the giving of information after the response has been made, i.e. knowledge of correct response or reinforcement. It was found that prompted rules produced an effect on learning, retention, transfer, and time taken to learn. When little prompting had been given, knowledge of correct response also enhanced learning, whereas knowledge of correct response added to prompting did little to learning, retention and transfer, although it did not appear to reduce these. Such findings suggest that it is the initial presentation of the material that is important. They also run counter to the view that material should be so presented that learners make few mistakes *and* that it should receive immediate reinforcement.

The programmed textbook is another form of automated teaching. The correct response to each question appears on a later page (or in the margin) together with the next item in the sequence. The instructions to the student might well read, 'Read each item, write your response on a separate sheet of paper, and turn to the page to see if the answer is correct'. Programmed textbooks are devised along the lines of either Skinner or Crowder. In the latter type of text an incorrect answer leads to a new piece of information related to, or a further discussion of, the question just asked, while a correct answer leads to new information and another question.

Programmed instruction in school is probably better for structured subjects like mathematics; it has also a considerable future in further education, such as instruction in industry or the services. At the moment programmed textbooks are much cheaper than teaching machines. Simple but comprehensive surveys of the principles underlying automated teaching including forms of such teaching which are developments beyond those of the 'linear' approach of Skinner and the 'branching' approach of Crowder, are listed below.[15] Moreover, these references review much relevant research.

There have been, of course, many critics of programmed instruction. Cronbach[16] has pointed out that automated teaching is the antithesis of the discovery method, while Wohlwill[17] has criticised the movement on

[15] Green, E. J., *The Learning Process and Programmed Instruction*. New York: Holt, Rinehart and Winston, 1962. Another useful series of articles by Williams, J. D., Curr, W., Peel, E. A., Leith, G. O. M., under the general title 'Aspects of Programmed Instruction,' can be found in *Educ. Res.*, 1963, 5, 163–99. A guide to the writing of programmes, including matrix construction and flow diagrams, is given in Thomas, C. A. *et al.*, *Programmed Learning in Perspective*. London: City Publicity Services, 1963. Also *Educational Review*, Vol. 16, 1964 and its Supplement. Austwick, K. (Editor), *Teaching Machines and Programming*. Oxford: Pergamon Press, 1964. DeCecco, J. P., *Educational Technology*. New York, Holt, Rinehart and Winston, 1964. Leedham, J. and Unwin D., *Programmed Learning in the Schools*. London: Longmans, 1965. Kay, H., 'Programmed Instruction.' In *Educational Research in Britain* (Ed. Butcher, H. J.). London: University of London Press Ltd., 1968. Kay, H., Dodd, B., and Seine, M., *Teaching Machines and Programmed Instruction*. Harmondsworth: Penguin, 1968.
[16] Cronbach, L. J. *Child and Education*. Copenhagen: Munksgaard, 1962, 145–146.
[17] Wohlwill, J. F. 'The Teaching Machine: Psychology's new Hobbyhorse.' *Teachers College Record*, November 1962, 139–146.

the grounds that the programmers do not come to grips with what it is the child learns. Progressive steps in a programme are not related to each other by virtue of similarity of appearance or location (as in training animals). Rather, the steps are arranged in supposedly meaningful sequence, governed by the internal structure of the material to be learned and the semantic and syntactical characteristics of the verbal stimulation of which they are composed. It is an assumption that the principles that govern learning in the former situation, govern it in the latter. It is unlikely, however, that Cronbach's criticism is now valid. It seems possible to develop programmes that contain sufficient intuitive content of data and enough variety of actions to be performed by the child to facilitate the acquisition of new coordinating schemes using this term in the Piagetian sense.[18]

Programmed instruction of some kind has come to stay; it is both likely to prove a valuable aid in schools and to be of particular help in areas where teachers are in short supply. It seems likely that it must be considered in perspective along with other educational techniques and aids, each having its own advantages (or disadvantages) for specific tasks. Perhaps research should be directed towards the discovery of ways in which automated teaching can be combined with other educational methods so as to provide the best possible instruction for different tasks and different student characteristics.[19]

Computer Based Learning (CBL). At a number of centres in the U.S.A. computer aided instruction is in use, at least on an experimental basis, even if the experience gained so far under practical classroom conditions is limited. A beginning in this field has also been made at the University of Leeds.

In essence CBL consists of information or a problem being displayed to the child, his response being evaluated by the computer, and a feedback message sent automatically to the child and a new item displayed. This new data may contain remedial material if his response was incorrect, or help if the child requested this, or it may be new information or a fresh problem. The information given to the subject can be by teletype or a cathode ray tube, while the computer can control a slide projector and a tape recorder. Thus while the slide is projecting fresh information or a new problem on the screen, the appropriate information can be given orally as well. The child for his part, can make his response by typing, pointing with a 'light pen' on a cathode ray tube, or use other rather sophisticated devices. Moreover, the large computers now available allow a number of pupils to work at the same time, each having his own teletype,

[18] Compare Leith, G. 'Developments in Programmed Learning.' *Trends in Education*, 1966, April, 20–26.
[19] See Coulson, J. E., 'Programmed Instruction: a Perspective.' *The Journal of Teacher Education*, 1963, **14**, 372–378.

cathode ray tube, etc. Moreover, different pupils can be working at different school subjects.

CBL can use different logics depending upon the teaching strategy it is wished to employ. For example, material can be presented which merely requires the child to respond. Another logic presents problems which the child has to solve; but he may require additional information and so has to question the computer, which in turn responds by giving the help requested. The success of CBL is largely dependent upon the skill of the person who writes the lessons. He has to specify the teaching strategies that will cause the computer to select appropriate sequences of instruction to match each child's pattern of responses.

When the teaching material is structured as in elementary arithmetic, it is often possible for the computer to generate material from certain specifications which are stored in the computer. In the area of arithmetic these will include, say, the number of digits and the operations involved. Depending upon the pupil's performance, the computer can then adjust the task difficulty so that as the pupil becomes more competent the complexity of the task is increased. Such developments may show great profit in the future as the computer takes more part in the teaching.

The computer can also make an analysis of the path each child took through the programme, the frames he used, the questions asked, the help requested, and the time taken. Indeed, the computer can present a wealth of detail about each pupil's path, performance and progress that no other means could provide so quickly and accurately. Such information is likely to throw light on children's learning and on their problem-solving strategies; also to pin-point specific difficulties for each child and thus enable a remedial programme to be written where this is necessary.

It must not be thought that CBL will be a panacea. There are many psychological problems involved in CBL, computers are expensive to purchase and service, and programmes take much skill and time to write. But it appears that it might play a major role in educational technology in the future.[20]

Neuroticism, Introversion and Learning. Many studies have been carried out among children to see if there is a relationship between scholastic performance and the personality dimensions of stability-neuroticism and introversion-extraversion. The earlier studies involved few pupils and the results were not clear cut.

A later study by Entwistle and Cunningham[21] involved 2,707 children

[20] Coulson, J. E. 'Computer-based Instruction.' *Int. Rev. of Education*, 1968, **14**, 140–152. See also *Programmed Learning and Educational Technology*, 1968, **5**, whole number. Also Apter, M. J. *The New Technology in Education.* London: Macmillan, 1968. Atkinson, R. C. and Wilson, H. A. (Eds.) *Computer Assisted Instruction.* New York: Academic Press, 1969.

[21] Entwistle, N. J. and Cunningham, S. 'Neuroticism and School Attainment— a Linear Relationship,' *Brit. J. Educ. Psychol.*, 1968, **38**, 123–133.

aged around 13 years in Aberdeen schools. Their evidence showed a linear relationship (i.e. a straight line relationship) between school attainment and neuroticism scores, the correlation coefficient being $-\cdot16$. Thus children with high neuroticism scores tend to be less successful in scholastic attainments than children with low scores, although the size of the correlation is small. The finding was, however, true for both boys and girls. Further, Entwistle and Cunningham found that girls who are 'stable extraverts' and boys who are 'stable introverts' show the highest mean attainment scores. This data can, perhaps, be treated with more confidence than the earlier findings, which were often obtained from small and unrepresentative samples. Again Eysenck and Cookson[22] studied 4,000 11-year-old boys and girls. They found that both extraverted boys and girls did scholastically better than introverted ones, the product moment correlation coefficient being around $\cdot2$. In the case of the neuroticism dimension they found that the more emotional boys and girls did only slightly less well than the more stable ones although the significance of this dimension was marginal. These findings generally agree with those of Entwistle and Cunningham except that the latter found that boys who were stable introverts did better at school work.

[22] Eysenck, H. J. and Cookson, D., 'Personality in Primary School Children'. *Brit. J. Educ. Psychol.*, 1969, **39**, 109–130. See also a more general review; Eysenck, H. J., 'Personality and Learning.' In *Advances in Educational Psychology* 1 (Eds, Wall, W. D. and Varma, V. P.). London: University of London Press, 1972.

Chapter Nine

REMEMBERING AND FORGETTING

The Process of Memory. Let us suppose that a teacher has set aside half an hour during which his pupils have to learn a poem with a view to writing it out on the following day. First the children have to *learn* the poem, then they have to *retain* it overnight, and finally they have to *remember* it when they come to write it out. These three stages are always involved, though the first may often consist of experiencing some incident or situation (which we later recall) rather than deliberately learning it.

Logical memory dependent upon general intelligence. It used to be thought that memory was an independent faculty of the mind; indeed some still write and speak as if this were so. But experimental evidence now strongly suggests that logical memory, that is, the kind of memory we have for meaningful material such as the gist of a story, depends mainly upon general intelligence.[1] Nor is this surprising when it is remembered that the initial stage of the memory process is learning, and that if there is insufficient intellectual growth for learning, there can be no retention or remembering.[2] In contrast, however, there is clear evidence of rote memory abilities that are involved in remembering groups of numbers or sentences of varying length, but they do not have much bearing on learning, retention, or recall, in everyday life.[3]

Memorising or learning. Many experiments have been carried out where subjects have had to learn nonsense syllables or odd lists of numbers or words, and later recall them. While such material does not normally have to be learnt in school, a study of the evidence which has accrued from these investigations does throw light on the memorisation of more meaningful material.

If we read over a number of items, such as a group of digits, to a child, or let him read them once for himself, and then ask him to recall the items immediately, we measure what is known as his immediate memory

[1] Vernon, P. E., *The Structure of Human Abilities.* London: Methuen, 1961.
[2] It is noticeable that very old people who have usually suffered some decline in intelligence since adolescence often have the greatest difficulty in remembering the details of a story or of a passage of a newspaper which they have just read.
[3] The more recent work of Piaget and his colleagues involving recall memory supports the general argument outlined above. See Inhelder, B., 'Memory and Intelligence in the Child.' In Elkind, D. and Flavell, J. H. (Eds.) *op. cit.* See also Lovell, K., 'Some Studies involving Spatial Ideas.' In Rosskopf, M. R., Steffe, P. and Tayback, S., *op. cit.*

span.[4] An average child of five years has a span of about 4 digits whereas an intelligent adolescent might have a span of 8. In general, immediate memory span increases with age up to adolescence; it also increases with practice. Sometimes the subject is asked to recall the items in reverse order but this is a more difficult task. If we are given a list of items to learn which exceeds the memory span, it can be learnt by constant repetition until all the items are repeated correctly. But this is not the most intelligent or economical way to set about the task. It is far better to try to break down the list into smaller groups which are in some way familiar, similar, meaningful or characteristic. Thus, given a long list of digits to learn, one would try to spot a group of numbers which had meaning, e.g. 1066 or 1914. Again, in a list of nonsense syllables, it might be possible to attach meanings to some of them, or note two that rhymed or were in marked contrast to one another, or pick out some that were particularly odd. If this can be done and the respective locations of these syllables learnt, the learning of the whole list is enormously simplified.

The above discussion leads directly to the wider and more general question of how memorisation can be made as efficient as possible. This is of great concern to pupils and teachers alike, and our suggestions for answering the question are outlined below:

(a) The learner must find out exactly what he has to learn, that is, he must clearly identify his task. The value of this can be illustrated by an example drawn from a French lesson. Suppose that the children are given the following list of French words and their English equivalents,

1	*la classe*	the class	5	*le cahier*	the exercise book
2	*le livre*	the book	6	*le garçon*	the boy
3	*le crayon*	the pencil	7	*le maître*	the master
4	*le pupitre*	the desk	8	*la plume*	the pen

and told that in a later test they must be prepared to repeat the French words when the English equivalents are given and vice versa. The children accordingly learn the list without reference to the order of the words, and in such a test most children might do well. But if they were asked to write out the French words and their English equivalents in order, beginning at *la classe* and ending at *la plume*, many would do less well because they had paid attention to meaning and not to order.

(b) It is essential to spot the sense or meaning of the material as early as possible. Once the gist of the subject-matter has been grasped, details will quickly fall into place.

(c) Instead of constantly re-reading the material to be learnt, it is far better to recite the material either to oneself or to a friend, or write it out, making use of prompts whenever necessary. Relevant experimental evidence also suggests that with children and adults the more time devoted

[4] It will be recalled that Binet included tests to measure immediate memory span for digits in his Scales.

to recitation, the quicker, in general, will be the learning. But the actual proportion of the total time to be spent reciting depends upon the individual and the material to be learnt. Time can be wasted either in attempting to recite before one is ready or in continued reading after one is ready to recite.[5] Recitation is probably of value because it enables the learner to check on his efforts so that he soon knows what has been thoroughly learnt, what has been partially learnt, and what has not been learnt at all. Moreover, it is likely that the learner, realising that he is going to recite, is more stimulated to search for meaning and organisation among the material. Note carefully that the material should be recited or reproduced in the same way as it will be in the test. Thus one should write out specimen essays when revising for the usual essay-type examination.

(d) It is better to have intervals between the re-readings (spaced repetitions) than to read the material again and again without pause. We do not know why this is so; but presumably the pause gives time for consolidation of the associations already established in the brain. Nor do we know the optimum length of interval between repetitions; good results have been obtained with intervals varying in length from one minute to one day. Probably the longer the material, the greater should be the interval. Note that it is not short periods of study interspaced with short periods of rest that give the best results. Too short periods of study give no opportunity for 'warming up'. It is the repetition of the same material without interval that should be avoided.

(e) There has been much discussion about the relative values of *whole* and *part* learning. Is it, for example, more economical to read a whole poem through again and again until it is known, or is it better to learn a few lines at a time and then join the parts together? The former is likely to bring out the overall meaning more thoroughly, but part learning gives more immediate satisfaction and encouragement. Some people, although they like the 'part' method, find it hard to joint the parts together. The available experimental evidence does not show any clear-cut superiority for either approach. Thus McGeoch's work[6] with 9–10 year old children which involved the learning of poems showed that the scores obtained on writing out the poem were almost the same regardless of the method used. Another experiment, conducted by a different investigator, in which college students had to learn speeches on political and economic problems, also showed no consistent advantage for either method. No definite guidance, therefore, can be given on this point. One should note how big the 'whole' is, and take into account one's own preference for whole or part learning. If the latter method is used the 'parts' selected should be longer than the memory span, and the learner should from time to time

[5] See Gates, A. I. Quoted by Woodworth, R. S., and Schlosberg, H., *op. cit.*
[6] McGeoch, G. O., 'The Intelligence Quotient as a Factor in the Whole-part Problem,' *J. Exp. Psychol.*, 1931, **14**, 333–358. See also Northway, M. L., 'The Nature of "Difficulty"; with a Reference to a Study of "Whole-part" Learning.' *Brit. J. Psychol.*, 1937, **27**, 339–402.

read through the 'whole' in order to keep its meaning in front of him, and to ensure that the parts are seen in their proper perspective, both in relation to one another and to the whole.

(*f*) The learning of any material is aided by practice in handling that particular type of item. Practice usually brings success and the latter gives confidence; practice also gives experience in organising, and searching for meaning in, that kind of material. But practice effects in learning one type of material do not necessarily transfer to other material, as we shall see in the next chapter.[7]

Retention. The second stage in the memory process is retention. This is an unconscious activity, and we shall see in Chapter 19 that it is probable that as a result of experience and learning, our brains actually undergo changes, so that certain of the nerve cells are more likely to be excited again given the right stimulus. Retention, then, seems to be dependent upon chemical or physiological changes, and so long as these remain unimpaired we retain the power to remember each specific thing we have learnt.

Most material that we learn is slowly forgotten, presumably because these changes in the brain do not persist indefinitely. However, some things seem never to be forgotten. Others become ineffective, in the sense that we cannot recall them under normal circumstances. But apparently such changes as take place have not been obliterated completely, for when we have a high temperature or are under the influence of drugs we can remember incidents from the past that cannot normally be brought into consciousness. Note carefully, though, that there may be considerable discrepancies between what was originally learnt and what is later recalled, as will be shown later in this chapter.

Retention can be measured by finding out how much the subject can remember of what he has learnt. There are three ways of doing this. First, he may reproduce the material he has memorised as he does in the usual type of school examination. Second, he may recognise a statement as true or false, or say if some item belongs to a given context when the statement or item is brought to his notice. Third, there is the re-learning method. To illustrate this, let us suppose that a poem was learnt until it could be reproduced perfectly. After a period it is re-learnt until it can be reproduced without error once more. The difference in the time required to learn the poem originally, and the time required to re-learn it, gives a measure of the amount of retention. We find that when material cannot be recalled it can often be recognised, and when neither of these processes can be accomplished, re-learning shows that some retention has taken place.

Experimental studies[8] into the decline of retention of rote material

---

[7] Compare Magne, O. and Parknäs, L., 'The Learning Effect of Pictures,' *Brit. J. Educ. Psychol.*, 1963, **33**, 265–275.

[8] The work of Ebbinghaus (1885), and Boreas (1930) are among the best known in this field.

with time show that there is a rapid loss in the first few hours after learning and a much slower decline thereafter. The general form of the graph showing how *Percentage Retained* varies with *Time Since Learning* is shown in Figure 12. Although this curve was obtained by the re-learning method,

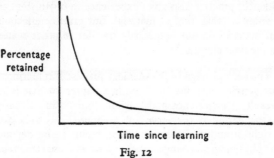

Fig. 12

other methods confirm the general trend. But there are great individual differences in the rate of forgetting, which are obscured in any general curve. Furthermore, material that has been over-learnt, that is studied attentively beyond the point where it can be repeated correctly, is retained better than material barely learnt,[9] while meaningful material is retained better than nonsense. Very important, too, is the fact that when material has been learnt, partly forgotten and learnt again, the rate of forgetting is lower after the re-learning; and it becomes lower still after further periods of reviewing. These findings lead us to suggest that, as far as school work is concerned, material should, ideally, be over-learnt in the first instance; it should be revised on the day after it is first learnt, revised after an interval of two days then after a week and so on. This ideal cannot be realised in practice, but teachers should attempt to have some revision soon after new material has been introduced, and should have further periods of revision at increasing intervals of time.

Other factors also influence the rate of forgetting. Retention is better during sleep than during consciousness, and this suggests that forgetting is partly dependent upon what takes place between learning and recall. It was shown by Müller and Pilzecker in 1900 that if this interval is filled by learning other material, less of the former material is recalled than if the interval had been spent in resting. This negative 'back action' effect of the second task upon the first is known as *retroactive inhibition*. It was thought at first that after each period of learning there was a period of consolidation; hence if a second lot of material was learnt before the first had 'soaked in' there would be interference with the consolidation of the first material.

[9] Krueger, W. C. F., 'The Effect of Overlearning in Retention,' *J. Exp. Psychol.*, 1929, **12**, 71–78.

Whether this theory is correct is uncertain,[10] but we do know that the greater the similarity of the second material to the first the greater is the interference effect. A point of practical importance not yet resolved is whether retroactive inhibition can be minimised by a short period of rest between the first and second learning task. In school it would seem wise that two lessons should not follow one another immediately if they consist of the same type of material, e.g. French verbs followed by Latin verbs. These findings indicate also that it would be advantageous, if one is not too tired, to learn difficult material just before going to bed, and read it over again in the morning. On other occasions it might be possible to follow a period of learning with another of an entirely different nature, such as a meal, a game, painting, music and so forth.

In 1913 Ballard,[11] working with children aged about 12 years, found that a partially learnt poem was recalled better after two or three days than immediately after learning. He called this phenomenon *reminiscence*. Some thought that this rise in score was due to rehearsal between learning and recall; but McGeoch's[12] experiments in 1935, also with children, suggested that this was not the whole explanation. Furthermore, it was difficult to understand how rehearsal could bring back a line of a poem not previously in the memory. Others pointed out that some items might be remembered at the second recall that could not be remembered at the first, although why this should be we do not know.

More recent work[13] showed that reminiscence might be due to faulty experimental design. Ballard's procedures measured recall immediately following the learning process and was itself a learning experience giving increased scores on later tests of recall. If groups are given poetry to learn, and some are tested as in Ballard's method, and others tested only after an interval of time, it is claimed that only the former show reminiscence.

Remembering. We have already noted that remembering must involve either recall or recognition. The former necessitates the reproduction of material that is not actually present before the senses at the moment, as when we write out the verses of a poem that we have learnt. But in recognition the material is presented, and the subject has to identify it as something that has been perceived before. This process is involved in answering the question:

In which year did William the Conqueror arrive in England,

597, 1588, 1066, 1492?

where the candidate has to recognise and underline the correct date.

[10] There was also the 'transfer' or 'interference' theory. This stated that the memory 'traces' of the original material and the interpolated material get confused.
[11] Ballard, P. B., 'Oblivescence and Reminiscence,' *Brit. J. Psychol. Monogr.* 1913.
[12] McGeoch, G. O., 'The Conditions of Reminiscence,' *Amer. J. Psychol.* 1935, 47, 65–89.
[13] Ammons, H. and Irion, A. L., 'A Note on the Ballard Reminiscence Phenomenon,' *J. exp. Psychol.*, 1954, 48, 184–186.

Recall is more difficult than recognition and is a more complex process, greatly affected by emotions and motivation, both at the time of learning and subsequently. Thus there may be considerable discrepancies between what was originally perceived and what is later reproduced.[14] The fallibility of witnesses and their differing accounts of the same evidence provide examples of this. Psychology has shown that evidence given in good faith is not necessarily accurate.

Fortunately, experimental investigations have established some of the principles that govern the restructuring of original perceptions. Bartlett[15] allowed his subjects to read a passage or study some diagrams for a fixed period of time. They then reproduced the material immediately and thereafter repeatedly at increasing intervals of time, for example, every day for a week and then weekly for a month. This was known as the method of *repeated production*. Among the changes found in the reproduction were the following:

(*a*) A tendency to 'round off' and simplify so that the elements of the story or diagram fall into general accord with the whole. Thus one of the factors in distortion seems to be the tendency to form a strong gestalt.

(*b*) Effects due to the subject's personality. Sex, interests, attitude and prejudice frequently play a part. For example, racial prejudice may affect the recall of a picture containing a Negro.

(*c*) A tendency to fill in any apparent gaps in the story or diagram, that is, a tendency towards progressive rationalisation.

(*d*) A tendency for repeated reproductions to be more consistent with the first reproduction than with the original.

Nevertheless in spite of inventions and distortions, the generalised structure and the salient details of the original remained, while a more recent experiment carried out by different investigators[16] showed that when repeated reproduction is carried out in front of an audience, the recalls tend to contain fewer inventions.

Bartlett also investigated *serial reproduction*. A story is read to a subject, who tells it to a second person, who in turn passes it on to a third and so on. He found that, in these circumstances the original style disappeared; there was much abbreviation, the filling in of apparent gaps in the story, and a continual search for meaning in the material. There was also a tendency for distortion towards the thoughts, beliefs, and standards of conduct prevailing in the subjects' social group.[17]

[14] The active organisation of past experiences operate and exert their influence upon the retention and reproduction of our perceptions.

[15] Bartlett, F. C., *Remembering*. Cambridge: Cambridge University Press, 1932.

[16] Hanawalt, N. G., and Ruttiger, K. F., 'The Effect on an Audience of Remembering,' *J. soc. Psychol.*, 1944, **19**, 259–272. Subjects seem to receive greater motivation from the audience and there is a greater striving for clarity. There is more care shown in identifying places, people, and times.

[17] Such influences are clearly marked in a cross examination using suggestive or 'leading questions'.

Other interesting suggestions have been made regarding recall. Stern[18] maintains that when memory images are put into words over-simplification and inaccuracy in recall are very marked. Freud and his followers believe that it is often impossible to recall events associated with a sense of guilt or shame. It is not the retention that is at fault here, but rather the repression of actual recall. The results of experiments designed to test this theory have not been conclusive. It is certain that feelings influence recall since they affect perception, and a person may not be able to recall an unpleasant scene because perception was affected in the first instance. Finally we may note that in some circumstances uncompleted tasks are much more readily recalled than completed ones, although no really satisfactory explanation of this can be given.

A beginning has thus been made in the study of recall and the many factors that affect it but much more needs to be done in this field.

Recognition is more simple and reliable than recall, but it is by no means infallible. Error is most likely to occur when the subject fails to distinguish between two similar expriences, as when half a dozen different figures are studied by a subject and these are shown again later interspersed with some similar and some dissimilar figures. Generally in recognition, the more quickly the response is made, the more likely it is to be correct.

A number of relevant experiments have been carried out in the Psychological Laboratory at Cambridge. The original experience consisted of an interesting story, and the interpolated material was a picture which illustrated part of the story although it was not in agreement with the story in every detail. The results indicated that the interpolated experience brought about changes in both recall and recognition of the original experience. Indeed, accurate recall and recognition is impossible with interpolated material of a similar nature. The memories of the related experiences merge to some extent as indicated in Bartlett's 'organised mass' of past experience (cf. footnote 14, page 142). This merging may be an irreversible process and any apparent separation of the two experiences is likely to be due to reconstruction by inference.[19]

The problem of training the memory. A question of importance is whether or not memory can be trained to operate more effectively. In answering this, one should again consider the three stages usually involved in the memory process. The learning stage can be helped by better management, that is, by observing the general principles and procedures which we have outlined. But in so far as learning depends on intelligence this cannot easily be raised. Retention can be aided by thorough learning, by

[18] Stern, W., *General Psychology from the Personalistic Standpoint.* London: Macmillan, 1938.
[19] Davis, D. R., and Sinha, D., 'The Effect of One Experience upon the Recall of Another,' *Quart. J. exp. Psychol.*, 1950, 2, 43–52. Davis, D. R. and Sinha, D., 'The Influence of an Interpolated Experience upon Recognition,' *Quart. J. exp. Psychol.*, 1950, 2, 132–137.

studying at a suitable period of the day, by constantly reviewing, and by avoiding circumstances likely to cause interference. Further, Winder[20] has produced some evidence suggesting that emotionally disturbed secondary school children lose ordinary learned material over a given period of time more rapidly than do more normal children. This suggests that whatever we do to aid a child's emotional adjustment is likely to aid his power of retention. Good mental and physical health are also likely to maintain the level of learning ability. But it does not seem possible to give any further advice about improving recall. The general question of training mental faculties is also discussed in Chapter 10.

Long and short term memory. There has been no discussion here of recent work on long and short term memory, as the problem is complex and its exact significance unclear for teachers at present.[21]

[20] Winder, W. E. P., 'Forgetting in Emotionally Disturbed Secondary School Children,' *Brit. J. Educ. Psychol.*, 1962, **32**, 82–83.
[21] For a current survey of the situation see the papers on 'Primary Memory' and 'The Relation between Long and Short Term Memory,' in *British Medical Bulletin*, **27**, No. 3, 1971, published by the British Council, London.

Chapter Ten

TRANSFER OF TRAINING

WHEN we speak of transfer of training we mean the effect which some particular course of training has on learning or execution of a second performance. Such an effect may be of a helpful nature, or it may hinder. In other words, it may be positive or negative in its action. This is a topic of importance to educationists and one which has been hotly debated in the past. At the end of the last century, when the theory of mental faculties was widely held, it was claimed that if the faculties of memory, reasoning, accuracy, quickness, observation, attention, judgment and so forth were trained, say, at the university, there would be little need for specific training in a given vocation, for the effects of training would be transferred from one mental function to another of the same type but in a different field. This doctrine was known as that of 'formal training' or 'mental discipline'. Latin and Greek were highly prized as they were said to develop the memory and improve verbal accuracy, or even to 'train the mind' all round. Other useful subjects were said to be mathematics which helped reasoning ability, and science which developed the powers of observation. However, not all educationists at that time accepted the doctrine of formal training, although a few still appear to believe in it even today. In 1890 the distinguished American psychologist, William James (1842–1910), challenged the efficiency of memory training, and in 1903 Thorndike claimed, as a result of experiments performed by himself and Woodworth, that a change in one mental function alters any other only in so far as the two functions have common elements. On this hypothesis one presumably might expect that multiplication of numbers would be aided by facility in addition, but great ability in adding numbers would not help arithmetic problems unless addition of numbers was involved.

Early experiments. In the first quarter of this century there were many investigations made to test the theory of formal training. These usually followed the design indicated below:

	Fore tests	Training	After tests
Group A	1	Y	2
Group B	1	—	2

The candidates would first take a test (1) involving memory tasks, and on the basis of the scores obtained two groups A and B would be formed so that they would be equally matched for ability to memorise. Group A would be designated the Experimental and Group B the Control group. The first group would then practise memorising suitable material, for example, poetry, prose passages, tables of weights and measures, and so on, while the other group worked at some other task not involving memorisation. After a given period both groups would take a second test (2) parallel to the initial one. If transfer effects had taken place, then Group A would have been expected to have a higher score on test 2 than Group B. But in many experiments this did not occur. In Sleight's experiment[1] (1911), which was typical of this general experimental design, schoolgirls of average age 12¾ years were studied; the experimental group practised memorising poetry and weights and measures, while the control group worked at arithmetic and other tasks not demanding memorisation. In the after-tests there did not appear to be any general improvement in memory as a result of practice, but those who had memorised poetry seemed better able to memorise nonsense syllables. Possibly this was due to their practice in using rhythm.

Evidence for Transfer of Training. Other investigations seemed to show that there was some transfer effect between one subject and another, depending upon the way in which the first subject was taught. Thus Judd (1908) maintained that there was a transfer effect if certain principles of generalisation were consciously formulated by the student; Winch (1923) found an improvement in logical reasoning following practice in problem arithmetic; and Johnston (1924) claimed that there was some transfer effect when pupils were taught, in geometry, consciously to use a technique of logical thinking. All these studies spoke of the need for organising the material used and for the conscious formulation and application of general principles. Another well-known investigation was that of Woodrow.[2] He used three groups of students and the design of his experiment was as follows:

	Fore tests	Training	After tests
Group A	1	Nil	2
Group B	1	Uninstructed practice	2
Group C	1	'Proper methods of memorising'	2

The fore and after tests included memory span for consonants, Turkish-English vocabulary, dates of events, poems and other items. Between the time of these tests, Group A did no work involving memorising; Group B spent 3 hours spread over 4 weeks on uninstructed memorising of poems and nonsense syllables, while Group C divided the same total time between

[1] Sleight, W. G., 'Memory and Formal Training,' *Brit. J. Psychol.*, 1911, 4, 386-457.
[2] Woodrow, H., 'The Effect of Type of Training upon Transference,' *J. Educ. Psychol.*, 1927, 18, 159-172.

instruction in proper methods of memorising and exercises in memorising poems and nonsense syllables. In the after-tests, Groups A and B scored about equally, but Group C scored higher marks than either of the other two on each test. Woodrow claimed that it was the special training that Group C received that accounted for these results and listed the features of that training as learning by wholes, the use of grouping and rhythm, the use of active self-testing, attention to meaning (including the use of images and symbols to help give meaning), and the development of the ability to memorise, and of confidence in that ability.

Other writers have stressed that *ideals* are important in transfer effects. For example, neatness made conscious as an ideal or aim in one subject, seems to carry over into other subjects. But without this ideal one might get neatness in, say, arithmetic but not in geography. Nearly all students in this field, however, stress the necessity of *conscious generalisation* before transfer effects can take place. Methods, principles and ideals are more likely to be transferred when the learner becomes clearly conscious of their nature and general applicability.

Transfer effects could also be of importance in industry. Is it, for example, possible to give an apprentice some generalised training, or is it necessary to give him training in each job or operation[3]? To answer this question. Cox[4] had, in effect, three groups practising operations connected with assembling and stripping lampholders. One part of the lampholder known as the 'container' was used for practice and training, and the remainder was used in the fore- and after-tests. All the groups were considered to be equal in ability in terms of their performance on the fore-tests. Group 1 was then set to do ordinary work, while Group 2 had uninstructed practice in alternately assembling and stripping certain material under standard conditions so many times per day, for 11 days. These operations were performed as quickly as possible. Group 3 had 11 daily periods of training of the same length as those of Group 2, but the aim of their training was to provide specific exercises in applying general principles to one assembly operation, that is, to the container operation. For example, the group was given general instruction in methods of laying out the material, in what to observe when engaged in certain operations; its members were taught to pay attention to the shape of various items and to the spatial relationships into which they had to be brought, and they were also shown how attention and effort could be most economically employed throughout the operation. In the after-test the trained group showed a marked improvement over both Groups 1 and 2, but Group 2 showed no superiority over Group 1. Moreover, Group 3 continued to make further relative gain later on. Cox concluded that systematic training

[3] Transfer effects can be negative as well as positive, but little has been said here about negative ones, as they do not often occur in education. But they do sometimes; e.g. finger-typing will hinder the learning of touch-typing.

[4] Cox, J. W., 'Some Experiments on Formal Training in the Acquisition of Skill,' *Brit. J. Psychol.*, 1933, **24**, 67–87.

in general principles had a positive transfer effect. The results of this experiment are particularly important to those engaged in teaching craft or coaching games. Instruction with a view to transfer is of more value than mere practice.

Recent studies, in which very simple learning situations of the stimulus-response type were involved, have shown that both monkeys and young children learn not only how to perform a task but also how to attack similar tasks efficiently. It appears that they acquire a technique of spotting relevant cues, and that this technique is transferred to other similar situations. Thus, in one of Harlow's[5] experiments, a monkey had to choose between two receptacles, of which only one contained food. On the cover of each receptacle was a different object. These objects acted as 'cues'. The positions of the objects were frequently changed and the monkey had to make many attempts before he became aware that the same object was always on the receptacle containing food. The next task involved the use of the receptacles with different objects on the covers. On this occasion the monkey required fewer trials before he associated a given cue with the food. Further tasks were given. It was found that the monkey required fewer trials with each task before he linked the correct object with food, so that after about 300 tasks, he nearly always picked the receptacle with food on the second trial. Experiments with children have shown that they too appear to learn a technique in such simple discrimination tasks which is transferred to other similar problems.

In another interesting investigation adults had to throw at a target under conditions of varying difficulty. The results indicated that transfer tended to be positive when moving from a relatively difficult initial task to a subsequent task which was easier, while transfer tended to be negative when the second task was harder than the first. While this is not the kind of task that we are normally concerned with in school or in other real life situations, the authors of the study do stress a point we have already indicated; viz., transfer does not inevitably and automatically follow upon the performance of a related task.[6]

Williams,[7] in a paper on the teaching of problem-solving, points out that it is usually assumed by teachers that variety in the kinds of problems used for training pupils facilitates the abstraction of essential principles of solution, thus making easier transfer to other problems. But after reviewing relevant literature he points out that when only a little training is given individuals transfer better after training on a single type of problem. When a great deal of training is given, however, individuals transfer better after training on a variety of problems. Thus when time is short, pupils are dull,

[5] Harlow, H. F., 'The Formation of Learning Sets,' *Psychol. Rev.*, 1949, 56, 51–65.
[6] Szafran, J. and Welford, A. T., 'On the Relation between Transfer and Difficulty of Initial Task,' *Quart. J. exp. Psychol.*, 1950, 2, 88–99.
[7] Williams, J. D., 'Teaching Problem-Solving,' *Educational Research*, 196, 1, 12–36.

or the technique is difficult, it seems that more training on fewer types of problem is indicated. When training to a high degree of proficiency is possible, the greater the variety of problems the better. Williams also points out that there is much experimental evidence showing that when a child discovers the solution to a problem himself, his chances of transferring the technique to the solution of other problems is increased (cf. Harlow's work).

It is also necessary to look at the problem of transfer of training in the light of findings given in Chapter 6. There it was seen that the complexity of the intellectual structures available to the child—or the complexity of the sequences of action that he can carry out in his mind—increases with age. Transfer of training is thus possible at all ages, but the quality of the transfer depends upon the complexity of the structures available to the child. The eighteen-month-old child will, like Harlow's monkeys, be able to show transfer in relation to certain perceptual differences. But the Junior School child can recognise the similarity between one number base and another and so show transfer from one to the other; while the adolescent can transfer a methodology that he has used to solve a problem in physics, to solve a problem in history.

Conclusion. We cannot say, then, in advance whether any subject will have an effect on performance in another subject, since it depends on the way in which the first subject has been taught. It seems that transfer effects are limited and that what is transferred are either specific elements or broader principles, methods, ideals and attitudes. But such broader transfer does not usually take place unless the learner has his attention drawn to these points and he becomes aware of their value and their applicability. Intelligence seems to be one of the main factors in transfer, for the more intelligent the child, the more likely he is to see the possibilities of transfer. Again, the extent of transfer effects is dependent upon the extent and thoroughness of the original training; indeed, a relatively low degree of original training may bring about a slight negative transfer effect.

When using tools and materials, suitable instruction in management of such work, with a certain amount of practice in the application of principles, builds up a technique that has positive transfer effects to other operations of a similar type. In all learning, too, increasing mastery of one subject or technique tends to build up a person's morale and lead him to a more confident attack upon other subjects or operations. It has also been shown that in very simple learning-situations, it is possible to acquire a technique of spotting the correct cue and that this technique is transferred to similar problems.

Stimulus generalisation, described in Chapter 8, can be made to give a plausible account of transfer of training.

Chapter Eleven

EDUCATIONAL ASSESSMENT AND GUIDANCE

Planning the course. It is obvious that any course of work must be carefully planned before it can be examined or assessed. Such planning usually involves at least the following three issues:

1. Clear objectives for the course must be written. While such words as 'to understand', 'to appreciate' are useful for an initial general statement of objectives, in more detailed objectives they must be replaced by words such as 'to name', 'to compute', 'to distinguish', 'to state'. Without clear objectives it is impossible to know what we are assessing.[1]

2. Thought must be given to the analysis of the tasks set. The knowledge and skills required by the pupil at any one point or stage must be considered, in order that the material can be appropriately arranged.

3. Decisions must be made regarding the facilities to be provided in respect of, say, help and revision.

Uses of traditional examinations. Education frequently involves the assessment of attainment. This is sometimes done by traditional written examinations or objective examinations (to be described later). Intelligence tests are not used since educational standards reached by children depend upon special abilities, temperament, industriousness, parental encouragement and support, quality of teaching and so forth, as well as on general intelligence.

Examinations were originally introduced to yield a more objective assessment of attainment than judgments based on personal opinion; also to do away with favouritism and patronage. But today they are commonly said to perform other functions,[2] and some of these are now listed:

(*a*) They indicate the extent of the factual knowledge acquired by pupils.

(*b*) They predict future educational achievement, and provide a means of selecting suitable candidates for certain educational courses or occupations.

(*c*) They test the efficiency of the teachers or of the methods used.

(*d*) Since a satisfactory level of performance in recognised examinations is thought to show intelligence, industriousness, perseverance and stability

---

[1] In respect of the writing of objectives see Bloom, B. S., Hastings, J. T. and Madaus, G. F. (Eds), *Handbook on Formative and Summative Evaluation of Student Learning*. London: McGraw Hill, 1971.

[2] Compare Vernon, P. E., *The Measurement of Abilities*. London: University of London Press Ltd., Second Edition, 1956.

of temperament, good results in such examinations are demanded by many employers.

(e) They provide an incentive whereby pupils and teachers are stimulated into working.

In the next section we shall see that the traditional written examinations often fail to fulfil these expectations.

Criticisms of traditional examinations. The value of examinations has frequently been challenged. Three common criticisms are;

(a) They tend to determine the curriculum and syllabuses.

(b) An unhealthy spirit of competition is engendered in pupils.

(c) Candidates do not always do themselves justice.

More important, however, is the fact that examinations do not always measure present achievement or predict future performance very accurately. There are several reasons why the later performance of pupils or students differs from that predicted by their examination marks. First, interests and attitudes change with time, and new abilities emerge. Second, performance in an examination depends to some extent upon the skill with which the teacher can spot likely questions and prepare for them. Third, some examinations are not reliable enough. It is the last point that is most serious. Vernon[3] claims that it is now well established that if one examiner sets and marks two examinations in the same school subject, the pupils taking the examinations are likely to get very different marks on the two occasions; also that the marks obtained by individual children are likely to show wide discrepancies when a single set of examination scripts are marked by two examiners. The main causes of poor reliability are:

(a) Changes in the mental and physical states of the pupils which affect their performance. This is usually small unless the time interval between the two examinations is large.

(b) Incomplete sampling of the candidate's knowledge. The greater the length of time for which the pupils are examined and the greater the number of questions asked, the more reliable the examination will be. This surely provides an argument for taking into account children's normal school work when making important decisions about their future.

(c) Inconsistencies in the standards of marking adopted by different examiners, or by the same examiner on different occasions.

(d) The most important cause is the differences in opinion among examiners about the relative value of the pupils' answers.[4, 5] There is

[3] Vernon, P. E., *op. cit.*

[4] In connection with points (c) and (d) we may note that examiners often look for different things in the essay-type answer. One may look for knowledge of facts, another for originality, while some may find it difficult to give credit for views expressed which are contrary to their own.

[5] Compare Hartog, P., and Rhodes, E. C., *An Examination of Examinations.* London: Macmillan, 1935, but remember that the value of some of their experiments was diminished because they took sets of scripts which were too homogeneous.

no doubt that in important public examinations the papers are marked more consistently than they are in minor examinations, but even so the results for a number of candidates who just fail or pass any type of examination would be different had their papers been marked and re-marked by different groups of examiners, or had they taken another set of examination papers.

However, more recent investigations have shown that reliability can be improved if sufficient care is taken. For example, if several examiners independently mark a set of essays, their various biases tend to cancel each other out, and the sum or average of their marks reaches the fairly high reliability coefficient of between ·8 and ·9.[6]

We next consider the validity of traditional examinations. This is a difficult problem since the objectives for examinations are rarely laid down. However, there is some evidence in respect of predictive validity. A number of investigations[7] has shown that the correlation between marks in school examinations and some later criterion, such as marks in a University Examination, vary considerably and seldom exceed ·5 to ·6. It must be remembered, though, that these studies often dealt with highly selected groups; if a more heterogeneous sample of candidates had been considered the best coefficient might rise to ·7 to ·8.

Again, it has been stated that if a candidate can pass examinations, he must possess traits of temperament and character that will be useful in other real-life situations. This is true to some extent, but intellectual brilliance, a stable temperament, and indifferent moral-social values can go together. Again, examinations can be passed by pupils of less stable temperament because of efficient coaching by teachers. Examination results do not, therefore, necessarily provide trustworthy evidence of temperament and character.

Finally, it may be asked if examinations stimulate pupils and teachers into working hard. In the writer's view this is so in many instances. On the other hand, examinations do not always stimulate desirable types of work. Some children merely cram in the last few weeks, and others are forced to overwork by parents and teachers. Moreover, subjects which may be of great educational value but which do not fall within the examination syllabus, tend to be neglected. A book dealing with many interesting

[6] See Wiseman, S., 'The marking of English Compositions in Grammar School Selection,' *Brit. J. Educ. Psychol.*, 1949, **19**, 200–209. Also Finlayson, D. S., 'The Reliability of the Marking of Essays,' *Brit. J. Educ. Psychol.*, 1951, **21**, 126–134. See also Britton, J. N., Martin, N. C., and Rosen, H. *Multiple Marking of English Compositions.* Schools Council Examination Bulletin No. 12, H.M.S.O., 1966.

[7] Valentine, C. W., and Emmett, W. G., *The Reliability of Examinations.* London: University of London Press Ltd., 1932. Scottish Council for Research in Education, *The Prognostic Value of University Entrance Examinations in Scotland.* London: University of London Press Ltd., 1936. Valentine, C. W., *Examinations and the Examinee.* Birmingham: The Birmingham Printers, 1938. Sanders, C., *Student Selection and Academic Success.* Sydney Commonwealth Office of Education: Education Series No. 1, 1948. Dale, R. R., 'The Prognostic Value of the University Examination,' *Brit. J. Educ. Psychol.*, 1952, **22**, 124–139.

aspects of examinations and their effect on the English educational scene has been edited by Wiseman.[8]

Objective examinations. Sometimes the ordinary descriptive examination answer is marked on a factual basis, a few marks being reserved for clear and logical expression, spelling or handwriting. In the type of examination now to be considered, this principle is extended by using a large number of short questions where the writing of pupils is reduced to a word or two, or where the answer consists merely of a figure, a tick or an underlining. Although some of these questions are likely to involve nothing more than knowledge of basic facts, a good paper will also contain questions that demand reasoning. Such tests are referred to as 'objective', examinations in contrast with the old or essay-type paper. A very few sample questions are given to illustrate their style:

(*a*) Multiple-choice.

Select the correct answer from the following:

Isotopes may be defined as

   (i) atoms of different elements which have the same atomic weight;

  (ii) atoms of different elements which contain the same number of neutrons;

 (iii) atoms of the same atomic number which contain different numbers of neutrons;

 (iv) atoms of the same atomic weight which contain different numbers of neutrons;

  (v) atoms of elements which contain equal numbers of protons and neutrons.

(*b*) Completion.

Fill in the words required to complete the following statements or answer the questions asked:

  (i) The quantity of electricity in coulombs =
current (in ......) × time (in ......)

 (ii) In Fleming's left-hand rule, if the forefinger represents the direction of the ...., and the middle finger represents the direction of the ...., then the thumb will indicate the direction of ....

Another well-known type of test of the Multiple-Choice kind is the Matching Test. A number of questions and a number of responses are listed in different order, and the questions and responses have to be fitted together. For example:

On the left is a list of the six longest rivers, and on the right a list of countries. After each country write the name of the river found in that country.

[8] Wiseman, S. (editor), *Examinations and English Education*. Manchester University Press, 1961.

(a) Missouri-Mississippi	China	....
(b) Amazon	United States	....
(c) Nile	India	....
(d) Yenisei	Central Africa	....
(e) Yangtse	Egypt and Sudan	....
(f) Congo	Brazil	....
	Western Siberia	....

In making up the test the following points should be observed:

(a) The instructions should be as brief and as simple as is consistent with clarity.

(b) The questions must be free from all ambiguity.

(c) It is desirable to start with a few easy questions to get the pupil into the way of answering, and to give him confidence.

(d) Different types of question such as multiple-choice and completion should be kept separate in order to avoid confusing the pupil.

In the objective examination which employs questions of the recognition type, some examinees can score marks by pure guesswork. If there were in each question, say, three alternatives, then 33 per cent of the marks could be obtained by random guessing. One way, then, to make allowance for guessing, is to give credit for scores above that figure only. But a fairer method which does not penalise the subject who omits a question in preference to guessing at it is to calculate the examinee's score corrected for guessing by the formula $R - \dfrac{W}{n-1}$, where R is the number of answers correct, W the number wrong, and n the number of alternative responses for each question.[9] When there are five or more alternatives, the correction is usually omitted since it is small. Gupta and Penfold[10] have suggested that when the number of alternative responses is two (as in a true/false test), and the subjects have been told 'do not guess', the formula $R - \cdot 5W$ is best for removing the effect of such correct guesses from the total score without penalising for erroneous information.

Taylor[11] has shown that in the case of a multiple-choice mathematics test there is no effect on the mean and spread of the marks obtained when secondary school pupils were encouraged to guess, encouraged not to guess, and merely given instructions that were neutral with respect to guessing. He concludes that a correction for guessing should only be applied when there is wide variability among examinees in their propensity to guess, fewer than five choices per item, or when the test is too difficult for the group tested.

[9] Compare Hammerton, M. 'The Guessing Correction in Vocabulary Tests,' *Brit. J. Educ. Psychol.*, 1965, **35**, 249–251.

[10] Gupta, R. K., and Penfold, D. E. M., 'Correction for Guessing in True-False Tests: An Experimental Approach,' *Brit. J. Educ. Psychol.*, 1961, **31**, 249–58.

[11] Taylor, P. H., 'A Study of the Effects of Instructions in a Multiple-Choice Mathematics Test,' *Brit. J. Educ. Psychol.*, 1966, **36**, 1–6.

Advantages and disadvantages of objective examinations.

Advantages.

(*a*) Marking is objective and takes little time.

(*b*) The whole syllabus can be covered by a paper containing, say, 150 questions in one hour. A large number of questions makes for higher reliability.

(*c*) The pupil spends his time thinking and not writing.

(*d*) So long as the questions cover all levels of difficulty evenly, the mark distribution will approximate to a normal one and can easily be converted to any other scale.

Disadvantages.

(*a*) Setting the paper is a skilled job. If the test is badly constructed it will not bring out originality, organising ability, capacity to interpret information or apply principles, but measure only rote knowledge and details. A well constructed test can bring out these more desirable characteristics.

(*b*) The examiner's personal opinions as to what is to be examined enters into the setting of the paper instead of into deciding at the end the good and bad points of the answer. In a sense, then, these questions are subjective.

(*c*) A great deal more reading is required from the candidate.

(*d*) These tests are somewhat artificial in their phrasing.

(*e*) Sometimes there is an undesirable effect upon study. Candidates tend to learn details as they will have to reproduce details. But well constructed tests cannot be charged with this to the same extent.

(*f*) Certain formal factors (compare Chapter 3) such as the examinee's previous acquaintance with this type of test, or other unknown group factors, affect performance in these examinations.

(*g*) No account is taken of lucidity of expression. However, if literary style, clarity of expression or handwriting are to be examined, separate papers should be set for this purpose.

Objective examinations are often criticised because they are thought to measure mere factual knowledge. But such criticisms are based on a wrong view of the organisation of human abilities. For in general those who have the capacity to learn facts are also those who show originality and grasp of general principles in the usual essay-type answer. To the writer, it appears that the traditional type of examination and the objective type should be used to supplement one another. Readers interested in the construction of objective tests and in the improvement of examining generally should consult Vernon.[12] In a further document, Vernon[13]

[12] Vernon, P. E., *op. cit.* For an introduction to some techniques of examining, see also Examinations Bulletin No. 3, *The Certificate of Secondary Education: An Introduction to some Techniques of Examining.* London: H.M.S.O., 1964.

[13] Examinations Bulletin No. 4 (by Vernon, P. E.). *The Certificate of Secondary Education: An Introduction to objective-type examinations.* London: H.M.S.O., 1964.

discusses the whole problem of the objective test against the background of the C.S.E. examination and succinctly summarises the strengths and weaknesses of such tests. He points out that the objective test may prove particularly helpful for pupils sitting this examination, for the candidates will be good readers but perhaps less good writers. Properly constructed objective tests could examine the pupils' ability to comprehend, apply, analyse and evaluate. If, however, the essay-type examination was relied upon exclusively, these candidates may be prevented from showing themselves in the best light, since European examiners generally look for the ability to formulate one's knowledge in the written medium.

It is important for the examiner to formulate what it is he is trying to measure. This necessitates a clear view of the objectives to which the education of the pupils should be directed. One interesting taxonomy of educational objectives has been put forward by Bloom.[14] This comprises:

   (i) *Knowledge* of specific facts, of terminologies, of conventions, of trends, of classifications and categories, of principles and generalisations, of theories and structures.

  (ii) *Comprehension*, interpretation and extrapolation.

 (iii) *Application* of scientific and social science principles to concrete problems.

 (iv) *Analysis* or breaking down the elements of the presented material, recognising their relations and significance.

  (v) *Synthesis* of elements and parts to form a whole so as to produce a new communication; e.g. an essay.

 (vi) *Evaluation* in terms of either internal or external criteria.

To examine (v) an essay-type question is set, otherwise objective-type questions may be used. The skills involved in attaining these objectives obviously overlap. One can, of course, draw up one's own list of educational objectives independent of Bloom's list. But it is helpful to think about these objectives in concrete behaviouristic terms rather than in vague mentalistic qualities; e.g. What should the pupil be able to do in each field of study? Having decided on the skills to be measured, the examiners must select the form of examination appropriate for each: essay-type, objective-type, a mixture, practical, etc.[15]

Standardised Tests of attainment. It is important to realise that standardised tests of attainment reflect the average performance of pupils and in no sense reflect agreed standards of work. Such tests are available for mathematics, reading (recognition and comprehension), spelling, and other aspects of English. The problem of constructing and standardising a psychological test was discussed in Chapter 3, and it is only necessary to

[14] Bloom, B. S., *Taxonomy of Educational Objectives*. New York: Longmans Green, 1956.
[15] A most helpful book for examiners in which there are stated objectives, and ways of assessing if these objectives have been attained is provided by Bloom, B. S., Hastings, J. T. and Madaus, G. F. (Eds.) *op. cit.*

remind readers that by means of such a test, an Achievement Quotient can be obtained in the basic skills.[16]

Other modes of assessment. The assessment of pupils need not be by timed examinations, traditional or objective, or under conditions in which they have no access to information. For example, one can have:

(*a*) Open-book examinations in which pupils take texts into the examination with them.

(*b*) Questions set which have to be answered in pupils' own time within, say, a fortnight.

(*c*) Assessment of course work. This involves a form of continuous assessment.

(*d*) Oral examinations.

(*e*) Small projects.

However, all that has been said about reliability applies to these modes of assessment as well. The assessors also have to formulate what it is they are trying to measure in terms of the objectives of the course, or there are no grounds on which to judge the validity of the assessment.

Criterion-Referenced Tests. Most tests with which teachers are familiar are termed norm-referenced tests. The pupils are, so to speak, spread out along a dimension of performance, some doing much better than others. But in the case of criterion-referenced tests we are interested in whether or not a pupil has reached a certain standard or criterion, whether he has attained some level of understanding, and whether or not his performance is better or worse than another pupil is immaterial. Criterion-referenced tests could gain wide acceptance in curriculum evaluation, and in establishing developmental levels in cognitive and attainment growth.[17]

Level of achievement. There are few long term studies of achievement. But Bloom's[18] analysis of those that there are suggests the great importance of the pre-school period and the first few years of school life on the development of learning patterns and general achievement. Further, Bloom suggests that two long term influences contributing to differences in scholastic achievement between children are: the meaning which education comes to have for the child in respect of his own personal advancement and role in society; also the level of education of, and value placed on education by, parents and other significant adults in the child's life, and the extent to which scholastic achievement is motivated and reinforced by these adults.

[16] For a list of standardised attainment tests see: Vernon, P. E., *The Measurement of Abilities*. London: University of London Press Ltd., Second Edition, 1956, pp. 173–178. Jackson, S., *A Teacher's Guide to Tests*. London: Longmans Green, 1967. N.F.E.R. *Catalogues*. Publishers *Catalogues*.

[17] See Ward, J., 'On the Concept of Criterion Referenced Measurement,' *Brit. J. Educ. Psychol.*, 1970, **40**, 314–23.

[18] Bloom, B. S., *Stability and Change in Human Characteristics*. London: Wiley, 1964. See also Peaker, G. F., *The Plowden Children Four Years Later*. Slough: N.F.E.R., 1971.

Bloom's views are reinforced in part by Wiseman[19] who studied 10-year-olds who had taken a number of standardised tests both at that age and at 7, 8, and 9 years of age. He found that the home circumstances of the child affected school attainment more than school conditions did. The quality of maternal care seemed particularly important, as Wiseman[20] had found earlier in his study of the attainment of secondary school children. The presence of dirt and crime in the home are more important than poverty *per se* from the point of the child's scholastic progress. Wiseman also found among the primary school pupils that economic level and social class are less important to children's school progress than are aspects of parental attitudes; e.g. their attitudes to education, books and reading. Moreover, since these adverse influences operate from the earliest years, it seems that nursery schools could be a means of countering such influences providing such schooling begins early enough, and providing research throws up more precisely the ways in which such early influence can be overcome.[21, 22]

Ross and Simpson[23] report details of a follow-up study of 3,465 pupils from birth to 18 years of age. They show that although the major part of the differences in ability and attainment associated with parents' education and family size may be traced to the years before 8, these two factors continue to influence rate of progress over both the 8–15 and 15–18 periods. Finally, we may note that Pidgeon[24] has reviewed much evidence that teacher expectations might affect pupil performance. In other words, teachers need to think well of their pupils and set standards of work which are high for them, since teacher expectations seem to be to some extent self-fulfilling. However, not all studies have confirmed this viewpoint.

The Cumulative Record Card and its uses. Teachers have kept some sort of notes about their pupils (either mental or written ones) ever since schools started. But in more recent years there has developed a more efficient technique for recording their assessments of pupils in a more systematic

[19] Wiseman, S. In *Children and Their Primary Schools*. London: H.M.S.O., 1967, Vol. 2, Appendix 9.
[20] Wiseman, S., *Education and Environment*. Manchester: University of Manchester Press, 1964. Wiseman, S. 'Environmental Handicap and the Teacher.' In *Advances in Educational Psychology* 1. London: University of London Press, 1972.
[21] For a survey of what is known of the psychology of the culturally disadvantaged, and for comments on what seems possible approaches to ameliorative action see, Jenson, A. R., 'The Culturally Disadvantaged: Psychological and Educational Aspects,' *Educ. Res.*, 1967, 10, 4–20.
[22] The interesting work of Skeels suggests that action taken during the first two years of life might be able to overcome the handicaps of severe cultural deprivation in some instances. See, Skeels, H. M., 'Adult Status of Children with Contrasting Early Life Experiences: A Follow-Up Study,' *Monogr. Soc. Res. Child Developm.*, 1966, 31, No. 105.
[23] Ross, J. M. and Simpson, H. R., 'The National Survey of Health and Development: 2,' *Brit. J. Educ. Psychol.*, 1971, 41, 125–135.
[24] Pidgeon, D. A., *Expectation and Pupil Performance*. Slough: N.F.E.R., 1970.

fashion, and of preserving them in a usable and readily accessible form. This is now done by means of the Cumulative Record Card.

In a comprehensive survey of the nature and uses of the cards, Walker[25] reports that in 1950 about two-thirds of the L.E.A.'s in England and Wales were using some kind of cumulative record in at least one stage of the infant, junior or secondary school life, although the form which the record took varied from one authority to another. The cumulative record, which shows how children have developed over a number of years, is more informative than the results of a single examination, providing the assessments are reliable and are in a form which can readily be interpreted. Thus it can be of the greatest help when guiding children educationally within a given school, when transferring them to another school, and when advising school-leavers about the kind of employment that they should enter.

The following information, in some form or other, is usually recorded on the cards:

(a) Personal details. Name, address, date of birth, sex, and as far as possible, conditions within the home and attitudes of parents.

(b) Attendance and Medical Record. Names of schools attended with dates. Details of the medical record should be filled in by the School Medical Officer, but it seems that this is seldom done since the School Medical Service has its own record card. Sometimes teachers are asked to record special disabilities and defects.

(c) General intellectual capacity. Most cards require the results of standardised tests of intelligence for junior and secondary school children. With infants the teacher has to make notes on, or grade on a five-point scale, certain aspects of intelligence listed on the card.

(d) Attainments. The result of standardised tests of attainment should be given wherever possible. Often, however, this is quite impossible and a five-point grading system has to be used, or the rank order of the child's performance stated, or examination marks expressed as a percentage. Strictly, when non-standardised tests are used, the marks should be brought to standard scores (see Chapter 20) with a mean of, say, 50 and a standard deviation of 10.

(e) Special abilities. These are often not clearly discernible until towards the end of the junior school stage. They include special skill or deficiency in handling words or using numbers, skill in manipulating shapes imaginatively, mechanical skill, manual dexterity, musical ability, physical athletic ability and skill at games.

(f) Interests. Children's interests are wide and rather unstable. Not until adolescence do they become more specialised and fixed. Bearing this

[25] Walker, A. S., *Pupils' School Records*. London: Newnes, 1955. Other publications dealing with record cards are: Fleming, C. M., *Cumulative Records*. London: University of London Press Ltd., 1945. Ministry of Education, *School Records of Individual Development*, Circular 151. London: H.M.S.O., 1947. Glassey, W., and Weeks, E. J., *The Educational Development of Children*. London: University of London Press Ltd., 1950.

in mind, also the fact that aptitudes and interests frequently do not go together, a record should be made of the following interests: intellectual (academic school subjects), practical (various crafts, domestic activities, gardening), aesthetic (music and dancing, poetry, painting), physical (games, athletics, swimming), social (conversation, club activities).

(g) Temperamental qualities and character. Almost all record cards ask for an assessment of traits like sociability, emotional stability, and self-confidence. Or they may ask for details of personal habits or a grading of conduct or behaviour. These qualities are usually assessed on a five-point scale with the teacher giving additional comments.

(h) Other relevant information.[26]

The frequency with which assessments are made varies, but as a rule they are entered annually and assessments must be made as objectively as possible. Standardised test results should be entered whenever this is feasible, for assessing general mental capacity and attainment. Moreover, the names of the tests used and the dates of testing must be clearly stated. If examination marks are recorded, then the number of children in the class should be given, the 'stream' or 'set', if any, indicated, and the range of marks shown. Better still, the marks should be brought to standard scores. When gradings are used, details of the number of children in the class, the 'stream', and the percentage in each grade should be stated. Remember that the data recorded has to be interpreted some years later by a different person.

The assessment of temperament and qualities of disposition is particularly difficult. Personality traits, as we have seen, change somewhat with the social setting. Thus assessments are needed from a number of teachers who see the child in different situations. An individual may be conscientious in one activity but not in another. It may, therefore, be safer at times to make an assessment of personality traits in relation to a specific situation or activity, for example, 'extremely persevering in metal-work'.

Again, there is the greatest danger that 'halo effect' will operate. Walker[27] studied the junior school record cards of an entire age-group of over 800 children. Assessments were made on observation, reasoning, perseverance, self criticism, English, arithmetic, conscientiousness, IQ, co-operation, artistic ability, sociability and other traits. Intercorrelations were calculated separately for boys and girls and then factor-analysed. Both sets of correlations yielded a large general factor which accounted for some 70 per cent of the variability in the assessments. Walker suggests that this factor reflects 'the ability to satisfy a teacher by alertness, careful thought, hard work and the willingness to accept and comply with adult standards. . . . Of only slightly less importance are attainments, and friendly, sociable

[26] See Eyre, J. H., 'The Prediction of Vocational Suitability from Secondary Modern School Record Cards,' Brit. Educ. Psychol., 1966, 36, 48–62. Also see Copeland, R. E., 'School Reports,' Educ. Res., 1966, 8, 196–208.
[27] Walker, A. S., op. cit.

characteristics'. The high correlations between the traits and the general factor (ranging from over ·9 to ·74 in both boys and girls) show the 'strong and all-pervading nature of the "halo effect"'. Walker also brings evidence to show that teachers make too many favourable and average assessments and fail to differentiate over the whole scale.

Effects of Streaming on Attainment in Junior Schools. There has been much controversy about the effects of streaming on the attainment of junior school children. Pupils can, of course, be put into homogeneous groups in more than one way, and in any discussion of the effects of streaming the overall school organisation should be considered.[28] In a report prepared by the N.F.E.R.[29] and presented as evidence to the Plowden Committee[30] —nearly 30,000 pupils were studied—children in streamed junior schools were found to do slightly better on attainment tests than pupils in unstreamed schools. Although the differences were statistically significant, they were not large. The Plowden Report (Vol. 2, page 575) suggests that, on the average, the streamed group got two or three more correct answers in tests of 30 or 40 items. It will be realised that there may be many other educational and personal advantages gained by non-streaming and these may outweigh any slight gains in attainment.

A further study[31] by the N.F.E.R. involved the follow-up of approximately 5,500 children who were initially tested at 7 and then annually until the end of the junior school course. It was found that about half the staff in the non-streamed schools held attitudes like those in the streamed schools, and this was important since they appeared to create a 'streamed atmosphere' in their non-streamed classes. However, the upshot of the investigation was that no significant difference in academic learning could be found between children of any ability level in either type of school, or under the two types of teacher. At the same time, non-streamed schools were superior in respect of: outweighing the disadvantage of a poor home background; relationships between pupils and teachers; motivation to do well; and participating in non-academic activities such as sports and orchestras, providing the teacher was sympathetic to non-streaming. Moreover, the benefits were found most among pupils of average and below average ability.

Ferri[31] followed through some 1,700 of these pupils to the end of the second year in the secondary school. They were then scattered over 83 schools; only a relatively small number of these were non-streamed and

[28] Yates, A. (Ed.), *Grouping in Education.* London: Wiley, 1965.
[29] Lunn, J. B., 'The Effects of Streaming and other Forms of Grouping in Junior Schools. First and Second Interim Reports,' *New Research in Education,* 1967, 1, 4–45; 46–75. This work also deals with the types of organisation found in junior schools at the time of the study.
[30] *Children and Their Primary Schools.* London: H.M.S.O., 1967, Vol. 2, Appendix II.
[31] Lunn, J. B., *Streaming in the Primary School.* Slough: N.F.E.R., 1970. Ferri, E., *Streaming Two Years Later.* Slough: N.F.E.R., 1971.

even these frequently employed 'setting'. Both boys and girls from both types of junior school had poorer attitudes to school and were less motivated to do well. The marked differences found among pupils in streamed and non-streamed junior schools in respect of extra-curricular activities had largely been obliterated. However, in the non-streamed schools pupils were playing a greater part in school activities, so school organisation was operating in much the same way in secondary school. Finally, the type of secondary school organisation had little effect on pupils' aspirations, but pupils from lower social classes and in non-selective secondary schools (secondary modern) had the lowest aspirations.

Selection for Secondary Education in Retrospect.[32] Selection for secondary education and its associated problems was one of the most controversial issues in education. Now the tripartite system of secondary education, as we have known it, is disappearing. Of course, psychologists, *qua* psychologists, were unable to pronounce on many aspects of the issue at all, since sociological and other questions involving value judgments were concerned. But psychologists tendered advice to educationists which largely determined the nature of the selection procedures, and they were greatly concerned with the nature and validity of current selection techniques. Given the job of selecting a proportion of 10–11-year-olds for grammar schools, psychologists were, in the main, successful in their efforts, although their advice overlooked two points. First, general intelligence or academic aptitude can be affected by schooling and environment generally (compare Chapter 3). Second, selection had unfortunate effects upon the primary school. The curriculum could be dominated by examination requirements, parents and teachers could exert undue pressure on children to obtain a grammar school place, and there could be an unnecessary amount of practice and/or coaching for intelligence and attainment tests. Another effect was that of 'streaming' children on entering the junior school and of keeping the 'A' classes with the best teachers throughout.

It should be noted at the outset that the provision for grammar school education[33] varied from about ten per cent of the age group in some areas to about 40 per cent in others, with an average of about 20 per cent for the whole country. This was a serious defect in the system. Psychology was in no position to say exactly what proportion of children could benefit from an academic education, and widely differing estimates were put forward.[34] It depends not only upon the level of intelligence, but upon

[32] For a very thorough study of the whole problem as seen in 1957, see Vernon, P. E. (Editor), *Secondary School Selection*. London: Methuen, 1957.

[33] In Scotland the Senior Secondary School was roughly equivalent to the English Grammar School, but it usually accepted a considerably larger proportion of the school population.

[34] Compare McIntosh, D. M., *Educational Guidance and the Pool of Ability*. London: University of London Press Ltd., 1959. Macpherson, J. S., *Eleven-Year-Olds Grow Up*. London: University of London Press Ltd., 1958.

the cultural and vocational attitudes of the home and the community, temperament, quality of teaching and school morale.

Moreover, the extensive Swedish evidence suggests that the development of ability depends to some extent on the structure of the educational system. It was found in Stockholm that if selection for an academic type of schooling is made at 11 years, a large amount of talent is 'lost'. If selection is made at 13, or by means of flexible arrangements in a comprehensive school, more pupils commit themselves to a longer school career.[35]

Methods of selection that were used. In many L.E.A.'s in England and Wales, the general scheme of selection was as follows.[36] The head-teachers of the junior schools reported to the Education Office on all the $10\frac{1}{2}$–$11\frac{1}{2}$-year-old children, and provided estimates of their intelligence, attainment, special abilities, personal qualities and interests. But the most important parts of the selection procedure were the tests of verbal intelligence, English and Arithmetic. These were marked by selected teachers and raw scores converted to standard scores (*see* Chapter 20). The standard scores also made an allowance for age. Thus the three standard scores added together gave an order of merit for filling the number of grammar school places available. At the 'border-line' zone the school reports were taken into account, or the children (perhaps with their parents) were interviewed,[37] and eventually the complete list of those selected for grammar schools was obtained.

Naturally the procedures varied between L.E.A.'s in some of the details. A few authorities did not employ an intelligence test, and several preferred traditional examinations to objective attainment tests; some conducted their examination in two parts, with only those children who did reasonably well in the first part being allowed to continue to the second; some set essays for all candidates, or had all possible candidates for grammar schools interviewed and not only the borderline cases (others set a further examination for those[38]).

In Scotland, selection took place on much the same lines as it did in England although there were two differences. First, selection was a year later; and second, teachers' estimates of their pupils' attainment were scaled[39] in order to equalise the standards of judgment of teachers in

[35] Husen, T., 'Educational Structure and the Development of Ability.' In *Ability and Educational Opportunity*. O.E.C.D., 1961.

[36] National Unions of Teachers, *Transfer from Primary to Secondary Schools*. London: Evans Bros., 1949.

[37] Bearing in mind our comments in Chapter 4 on the reliability and validity of the personal interview, the interviewing of children and/or parents is strongly deprecated.

[38] For interesting and detailed accounts of the methods of selection employed by certain L.E.A.'s see a series of articles on Selection at 11 in *The Times Educational Supplement*, September 9th, 16th, and 23rd, 1955.

[39] See McClelland, W., *Selection for Secondary Education*. London: University of London Press Ltd., 1942. Also McIntosh, D. M., *Promotion from Primary to Secondary School*. London: University of London Press Ltd., 1948.

different schools. These scaled estimates were then added to the test results.

A few L.E.A.'s selected for secondary technical schools at 11 but the majority selected at 13 years of age. When selection was at the earlier age, the evidence showed that it was very difficult to differentiate between pupils who should go to grammar and those who should go to technical schools. Although some boys showed a clear bias, such cases were rare, and most who were selected for either type of school were good 'all-rounders'. In a few cases only did spatial tests distinguish between boys suited to technical rather than grammar schools.[40]

When selection for technical schools took place at 13, the examination often consisted of tests of intelligence, English, and Arithmetic, followed by spatial or performance tests. At this age the position is not complicated by the need to select for grammar schools at the same time, and spatial tests did help to distinguish between those likely to succeed at practical work in technical education. On the other hand, some of the practical tests set were of unknown reliability and validity.

Tests of interests have also been devised in an attempt to differentiate further between practical and academic interests. For school children the best known British ones were the Devon Interest Test devised by Fitzpatrick and Wiseman,[41] which distinguished between academic 'likes' and 'dislikes', and the Lambert and Peel[42] General Information Test which measured interest in technical and academic pursuits by the amount of knowledge the candidate displays. Thus in the latter test several sets of questions are given to the candidate and he is told to answer half the questions in each set. He can choose to answer the questions dealing with literary or with technical subjects and his interest is assessed by the proportion of choices and the correctness of his answers. (See also a later section of this chapter headed *Educational Guidance*.)

Validity of selection. In the investigations of the validity of selection procedures, marks obtained in secondary school subjects were usually studied. Obviously there are many objections to taking school marks as the sole criterion of ability to profit from a particular type of education. A child may have profited considerably from his stay in a secondary school, yet his subject marks may not be high. However, the criterion is as good a one as we can get and to some extent a valid one.

[40] Compare Dempster, J. J. B., *Selection for Secondary Education*. London: Methuen, 1954. Also Macfarlane Smith I., 'The Validity of Tests of Spatial Ability as Predictors of Success on Technical Courses,' *Brit. J. Educ. Psychol.*, 1960, **30**, 138–145; this paper suggests the value of spatial tests at 11.

[41] Fitzpatrick, T. F., and Wiseman, S., 'An Interest Test for Use in Selection for Secondary Education,' *Brit. J. Educ. Psychol.*, 1954, **24**, 99–105. Also Wiseman, S., 'The Use of an Interest Test in 11 plus Selection,' *Brit. J. Educ. Psychol.*, 1955, **25**, 92–8.

[42] Peel, E. A., 'Assessment of Interest in Practical Topics,' *British J. Educ. Psychol.*, 1948, **18**, 41–47.

No selection procedure for children at eleven or at any other age can be made foolproof. During the secondary school stage the health, interests, attitudes, and motivation of children change; moreover, there is good evidence that certain aspects of home background greatly affect school achievement.[43]

The upshot of many studies suggests that, in general, the selection procedures were good. There was usually a correlation of between ·8 and ·9[44] between marks obtained in entrance tests and marks obtained in school subjects one to five years later. A typical investigation is that reported by Emmett.[45] Children who sat a County Transfer Examination in February 1948 were assessed in July 1951 according to a common criterion for each type of school. There were then 985 pupils assessed in grammar schools and 939 in modern schools. The correlations (corrected to values which would obtain had *all* the children of the year-group been assessed on the same standards) between performances in the County Examination in 1948 and in the secondary schools in 1951, were ·83 and ·85 for the grammar and modern school groups respectively. If, however, attention is confined to pupils within each of the two types of school, that is, to the more restricted range of ability within each, the correlations were ·52 and ·73 respectively. This allows for a considerable change in the performance of some pupils within either type of school, especially the grammar school. For example, a child originally placed in the 'C' form of a grammar school might rise to the 'A' stream and vice versa.

Later tendencies in selection procedures. Many people wanted all examining to be abolished and children transferred to different types of secondary schools as a result of teacher-estimates.[46] Such a procedure allows the school great freedom in choosing its own curriculum and teaching methods; it also permits the child's potential to be judged after considering his work over a number of years rather than by examination. But great care must be taken; for while teachers can reliably place their own pupils in rank order they are unable to make absolute judgments and compare their pupils with children in other schools. This difficulty can be overcome by giving each primary school a quota based on its past average of places

[43] See Morrison, A. and McIntyre, D., *Schools and Socialization.* Harmondsworth: Penguin, 1971, Ch. 1. Also Bynner, J. M., *Parents' Attitudes to Education.* London: H.M.S.O., 1972. Also Frazer, E., *Home Environment and School.* London: University of London Press Ltd., 1959. See also Wiseman, S., *Education and Environment.* Manchester: Manchester University Press, 1964.

[44] These correlations are statistically corrected to show validity over the whole range of ability. Within the selected grammar school groups only, they are much lower, namely around ·4 to ·5, as in Emmett's study described in the text.

[45] Emmett, W. G., 'Secondary Modern and Grammar School Performance Predicted by Tests given in Primary Schools,' *Brit. J. Educ. Psychol.*, 1954, **24**, 91–98. See also Richardson, S. C., 'Some Evidence Relating to the Validity of Selection for Grammar Schools,' *Brit. J. Educ. Psychol.*, 1956, **26**, 13–24.

[46] Compare Bosomworth, G., 'The Use of Teachers' Assessments in Allocating Children to Secondary Schools,' *Durham Res. Rev.*, 1953, **4**, 50–53.

obtained in grammar schools under the examination system. Otherwise, teachers' estimates have to be scaled against an external examination, usually an intelligence test. Unfortunately, this method also raised difficulties. First, the scaling of teacher estimates is very unreliable in a small school where there are few candidates. Secondly, teachers seem unable to make proper allowances for age differences[47] (the pupils' ages may range from 10 years 6 months to 11 years 5 months) when the estimates are made. However, some L.E.A.'s did drop examinations in English and Arithmetic and selected children on the basis of an intelligence test score and scaled teacher estimates.[48]

Some educationists wished the essay to be part of all selection examination procedures. The essay can be marked fairly reliably if enough care is taken, as we have already indicated, although there is little clear evidence as yet that the inclusion of an essay improves the overall validity of the selection technique. At the same time, however, the essay may improve the forecast of performance in certain subjects.[49]

In 1959 Vernon[50] summarised the tendencies in the provision of secondary education at that time:

1. Measures believed (by some) to reduce emotional strain by making the examination form part of the school routine and not holding it on certain days.

2. By giving more weight to junior school assessments and less to tests.

3. The introduction of more bilateral, intermediate comprehensive (as in Leicestershire), and fully comprehensive schools, in order to reduce, delay, or avoid segregation.

4. Improving facilities in the Modern school to make it more attractive.

While any form of selection for secondary education continued there would always be those who develop late (*see* Chapter 17), border-line cases,[51] and misfits. Thus there arose increasing opportunities for transfer between different types of secondary school, and for the more able children in modern schools to pursue an academic course and prepare for external examinations.

After 1959 an increasing number of L.E.A.'s prepared plans for abolishing the system whereby children were selected for different types of

[47] See Clark, H., 'The Effect of a Candidate's Age upon Teachers' Estimates and upon his Chances of Gaining a Grammar School Place,' *Brit. J. Educ. Psychol.*, 1956, 26, 207–217.

[48] In keeping with the N.F.E.R. technique. See Yates, A and Pidgeon, D. R., *Admission to Grammar Schools*. London: Newnes, 1957.

[49] Nisbet, J. D., 'English Composition in Secondary School Selection,' *Brit. J. Educ. Psychol.*, 1955, 25, 51–54. See also a series of papers under the general title, 'Symposium: The Use of Essays in the Selection at 11,' *Brit. J. Educ. Psychol.*, 1956, 26, 128–136, 163–171, 172–179.

[50] Vernon, P. E., 'Trends in Selection,' *The Times Educational Supplement*, March 13th and 20th, 1959.

[51] For a discussion on the position and size of the borderline group see Pilliner, A. E. G., 'The Position and Size of the Borderline Group in an Examination,' *Brit. J. Educ. Psychol.*, 1950, 20, 133–136.

education. Moreover, in July 1965 the Department of Education and Science issued the now famous Circular 10/65 (the relevant circular for Scotland was published a little later). This document requested L.E.A.'s to submit plans for the reorganisation of secondary education on comprehensive lines, and it suggested six main forms of comprehensive education which had emerged from experiment and discussion. It thus appears that selection for secondary education may disappear, although it will be appreciated that further political decisions may affect the outcome. Indeed, according to a recent N.F.E.R. survey, published in 1972, some 50 L.E.A.s do not operate any selection procedures, 56 operate one in part of its area, and 55 operate selection procedures throughout its area. At the time of the survey, verbal reasoning tests and teacher estimates and assessments remain the almost universal means of selection. But it must not be forgotten that some form of grouping pupils in respect of attainment may still be necessary in some subject areas within the comprehensive secondary school unless mixed-ability groups are used throughout. This is also true in the case of 'middle schools' which, at the time of writing, are increasing in number.

A criticism of the selection of children at 11 years of age. A major criticism levelled against selection at 10–11 years of age was that whatever methods are used children will most likely suffer some psychological stress. To what extent this was true is not known. Birch[52] did not find any increase in the incidence of nail-biting at 10–11 years of age, and there was no evidence that there is an increase in the number of children referred to Child Guidance Clinics at this period. But Bowyer[53] claimed that roughly seven per cent of her sample suffered stress over the 11+ examination and nearly three-quarters were anxious in varying degrees. She also makes the point that there are two kinds of children in particular who are likely to undergo stress as a result of the examination, viz.: able children who have a tendency to anxiety as part of their all-round sensitivity, and the border-line candidates who are in a situation of unavoidable anxiety. On the other hand, some children may suffer from anxiety about their future, and when they did not get to the type of secondary school that they wished to attend they may have suffered disappointment and bitterness which affected their future motivation and attitude to school. Yet symptoms of maladjustment may not have been in evidence.

Educational guidance. In Great Britain, then, children about 11 years of age or later were, and sometimes still are, selected for different types of education. With the disappearance of these selection procedures, it will

[52] Birch, L. B., 'The Incidence of Nail Biting Among School Children,' *Brit. J. Educ. Psychol.*, 1955, 25, 123–128.
[53] Bowyer, R., 'Individual Differences in Stress at the Eleven-plus Examination,' *Brit. J. Educ. Psychol.*, 1961, 31, 268–280.

be appreciated that some kind of grouping of pupils has still to take place within the secondary stage of education unless all subjects are to be studied in mixed ability groups. Sometimes pupils are 'set' for subjects; in other instances pupils may be unstreamed *within*, say, the top third of the school as judged for attainment, also *within* the middle third, and *within* the bottom third. Indeed, many different patterns of organisation are emerging within the secondary comprehensive school. However, once within secondary schools pupils are often left without much guidance. Skilled advice is needed when children are transferred from one group to another, and when deciding if they should specialise in particular subjects. The present position in respect of these matters is not altogether satisfactory. Wise educational guidance should be cumulative and continuous and should take into account special abilities, temperament, declared interests, family background and outlook, and other environmental influences. From 11 to 16 years of age there is rapid development in many directions, coupled with changes in the pattern of emotional drives which underlie many adolescent interests. Under present conditions in school there is often no organisation whereby all-round assessment of children can be made, in the light of which their future guidance could be arranged. Yet such guidance is vitally important in the education of adolescents. It seems likely that in schools there is a need for a counsellor whose function it would be to advise head-teacher, children and parents, on all aspects of educational guidance, and to see that a given child transfers from his 'course' or 'group' when such a change should prove necessary. Under present arrangements teachers have neither the time, nor are they trained, to devote much time to the educational guidance of their pupils. It is hoped that more persons trained to give guidance will be available in the future.[54]

It is difficult to be precise about the help that tests of interests can give in allocating children to courses or subjects, and those concerned should consult Wiegersma and Barr,[55] also Yates and Barr.[56] In the U.S.A. neither the Strong Interest Vocational Blank nor the Kuder Preference Record—two of the most popular interest scales in that country—have been very helpful in predicting school and college attainment. Correlation coefficients between interests scores and grades range from 0 to ·3 even in subjects like engineering, mathematics and science. It seems that interest is only one of many factors determining attainment. However, we can say for certain that measurement of interest can only supplement,

[54] For a discussion of the function of school counsellors see: 'The Counselling Function: a Symposium,' *Educ. Res.*, 1967, 9, 83–104. For a manual on educational guidance see: Jackson, R. and Juniper, D. F., *A Manual of Educational Guidance*. London: Holt, Rinehart and Winston, 1971. See also the Section in Ch. 18 on counselling.

[55] Wiegersma, S. and Barr, F., 'Educational Guidance—II: Interest Testing in Educational and Vocational Guidance,' *Educational Research*, 1959, 2, 39–64.

[56] Yates, A. and Barr, F., 'Selection for Secondary Technical Courses—A Report of a Pilot Investigation,' *Educational Research*, 1960, 2, 143–148.

and not replace, tests of general and special abilities; while interests reveal only a general disposition to choose to study or enter a group of educational courses.

Vocational guidance. When young people leave school they obtain their employment in the following ways:

(a) Largely by chance. Another reason which sometimes dictates the decision is the size of the pay packet. In both these instances no real thought is given to the problem, nor is any worthwhile advice sought. However, as we shall show in Chapter 17, many school-leavers do think about their future and get useful advice.

(b) Acting on the advice received from relatives and friends who know something of the conditions and requirements of various forms of employment. The value of such advice varies greatly.

(c) Acting on information received from the 'Careers Master' at school. Such teachers should know the kinds of work available locally (some L.E.A.'s publish notes on these matters) and the qualifications required. Such masters or mistresses must also know about the entrance requirements of the universities and other professional bodies. All teachers, in whatever type of school, who advise pupils about their future should be interested in aptitude tests and know something about the subject of vocational guidance.

(d) Via the Youth Employment Service. This is operated in most places by the L.E.A. but its policy is controlled by the Youth Employment Council (made up of officers of the Department of Education and Science, the Department of Employment and Productivity, and the Scottish Education Office). Youth Employment Officers attend schools and interview leavers. Their knowledge of local opportunities varies greatly, as does their skill in advising pupils. It is to be hoped that they will get more day-to-day technical advice from psychologists in the future.

(e) Acting on advice received from the National Institute of Industrial Psychology. The applicant has to submit himself to a very thorough psychological examination.

(f) By applying to a firm and being selected. Sometimes the applicant undergoes a testing programme. This procedure should be referred to as vocational selection, not as vocational guidance.

Whoever advises young people about their future employment should be able to assess the following:

(a) The psychological and physical characteristics of those seeking guidance.

(b) The psychological and physical characteristics required for success in the employments available.

Apart from professional psychologists few are well qualified to fulfil requirement (a), and there is a need for one member on the staff of each secondary school to be competent in administering relevant tests, collecting data, and in interpreting school records. As for (b), much is now known about the levels of intelligence and attainment, special abilities, physical and temperamental qualities needed in a number of occupations. But a great deal more knowledge is required on certain points; for example, studies of criteria of occupational success are needed. Indeed, we should admit that many current guidance procedures are poorly validated at present, and that careers masters and Youth Employment Officers are often working blindly. Nevertheless, in spite of the difficulties, all follow-up studies of carefully worked-out schemes of vocational guidance have demonstrated their great value to young people and adults.[57]

In a study of 330 boys and girls in the 15–18-year age group, and working in 75 firms, Maizels[58] found in 1965 (although the results were not published until 1970) that many young people had made up their own minds what to do, and did not refer to the help of anyone. However, it appeared that the influences of the home and school were at work. At the same time many pupils had no idea of what conditions would be like, or what the prospects would be, and many had expected a better service from the youth employment officer. Such findings argue a case for better advice to be given in school.

[57] Hopson, B. and Hayes, J. (Eds.), *The Theory and Practice of Vocational Guidance. A Selection of Readings.* Oxford: Pergamon, 1968. Vaughan, T. D., *Educational and Vocational Guidance Today.* London: Routledge and Kegan Paul, 1970. Also Edmonds, P. J. (Editor). *Careers Encyclopedia.* London: Macmillan and Cleaver. Fifth Edition, 1967. Hayes, J. and Hopson, B., *Careers Guidance.* London: Heinemann, 1971.

[58] Maizels, J., *Adolescent Needs and the Transition from School to Work.* London: Athlone Press, 1970.

Chapter Twelve

DULLNESS AND BACKWARDNESS[1]

Some Definitions. The Minister of Education, in the Handicapped Pupils and School Health Service Regulations, 1945, has laid down that the following classes of children require special educational treatment: the blind, the partially sighted, the deaf, the partially deaf, the delicate, the diabetic, the educationally sub-normal, the epileptic, the maladjusted, the physically handicapped and those with speech defects (the diabetic are now excluded). Although we are here concerned only with the educationally sub-normal child, it is well to remember that there are many other types of handicap from which children suffer. The regulations define educationally sub-normal, or E.S.N., pupils as those who, by reason of limited ability or other conditions resulting in educational retardation, require some specialised form of education wholly or partly in place of the education normally given in ordinary schools. This definition is not an exact one but it is suggested[2] that special educational treatment should be given if the child is so retarded that his standard of work is below that achieved by average children 20 per cent younger than he is, that is, with an Educational Quotient of 80 and under.

It was pointed out in Chapter 3 that an intelligence test should, for a representative group of children, give a mean IQ of 100 and have a standard deviation (or spread) of 15 points of IQ. Using such a test, we find that the IQ's of most children fall between 70 and 130. Children with IQ's above 130 are regarded as being of superior intelligence, those whose IQ's fall between 85 and 70 are considered dull, while those whose IQ's are within the range from about 80–55 will usually be classified as educationally sub-normal. Finally, children whose IQ's lie between about 55 and 25 are termed moderately sub-normal, and those with an IQ of less than about 25, severely sub-normal; the last two groups being generally regarded as not being suitable for school education, although the moderately sub-normal attend training centres. But it must be stated emphatically

---

[1] For a review of research into backwardness in Britain during the period 1962–66 see Lovell, K., 'Backwardness and Retardation.' In *Educational Research in Britain* (Ed. Butcher, H. J.). London: University of London Press Ltd., 1968, 119–132.
[2] *Special Educational Treatment.* Ministry of Education Pamphlet No. 5. London: H.M.S.O., 1946. The Ministry of Education suggests that some 10% of registered pupils could be classified as educationally sub-normal (E.S.N.).

that the demarcation lines between the various groups cannot be rigidly fixed at certain IQ levels. For example, mild mental sub-normality depends upon the extent to which the individual can make adequate social adjustment as well as upon IQ level.[3]

Causes and incidence of the more severe forms of mental sub-normality, mild sub-normality, dullness, and backwardness among children.

The more severe forms of mental sub-normality. Children suffering from the more severe forms of mental sub-normality have IQ's below about 55. Such conditions should be regarded as outside the normal range. Although teachers will not meet such children in ordinary or special schools, they should know a little about the causes of such disorders. Moreover, the education of all mentally handicapped pupils is now the responsibility of the Department of Education and Science so that there is likely to be closer liaison between special schools and training centres. Altogether there are roughly one per cent of children in this category. These conditions tend to occur in normal families and their causes can be divided into five main groups:

(a) Parental developmental disorders. The available evidence suggests that malformations in the foetus (i.e. during growth within the mother's uterus) can be brought about by injury, chemical conditions, temperature conditions, interference with oxygen supply and nutrition. It is the time at which the noxious agent is applied that seems to determine what kind of malformation will occur. Under-development in the size of brain, as in the microcephalic, is an example of parental developmental disorder, although such disorders are sometimes due to genetic causes. In recent years, evidence has accumulated showing that the Rhesus factor is a cause of some cases of mental deficiency. Toxic substances are produced in a mother if her blood is Rhesus negative and she is carrying a foetus whose blood is Rhesus positive. These poisons, when they reach the foetus,[4] may cause damage to the blood, liver and brain. At birth such children may have anaemia, jaundice, or a form of paralysis. Effective treatment can be given in many cases but sometimes mental defectiveness and spasticity may result.

(b) Birth injuries. The majority of spastic and other cerebral palsy defects in children are due to birth injuries. Cerebral palsy is a disorganisation of the motor control system as a result of damage to the central nervous system. In some cases, damage interferes only with motor development, and not with intellectual growth. Birth injuries are, as a rule, brought about by a variety of complications either just before or during the birth process.

[3] See Fitzpatrick, F. K., 'An Investigation Bearing on the Laws Relating to Feeble-mindedness, and their Application,' *Brit. J. Educ. Psychol.*, 1955, 25, 117–122.
[4] Often it is the next child that is affected.

(c) Infectious diseases. Most children suffer one or more of the infant infections, such as measles, scarlet fever, mumps, whooping cough and others, without much lasting effect. But a few children are affected permanently, and if the damage to the nervous system occurs in the first two years of life, they may be greatly retarded in learning to speak and walk, and in all-round intellectual development.

(d) Metabolic and other disorders. A number of metabolic[5] disorders have been discovered which are a cause of mental deficiency, e.g. amaurotic idiocy, gargoylism, and phenylketonuria.

(e) Chromosome unbalance. Mongolism is a common and well defined example of mental deficiency. Short growth, slanting eyes, depressed nose bridge, dry lips, open mouth, enlarged and fissured tongue, flat facial features and short neck are characteristic of this condition. Mongol children occur in about 1 in 900 pregnancies and their IQ's are usually in the range 40–60. A number of mongol children studied in Great Britain, France and Sweden, have been found to have 47 chromosomes in the body cell instead of 46.[6] Fundamentally the trouble seems to originate when the ovum is formed, so that after fertilisation the body cells of the embryo contain an unusual number of chromosomes leading to abnormal development. The incidence of mongolism increases with the age of the mother at the time of conception.

The whole treatment of the causes of the more severe forms of mental sub-normality has been dealt with in simple and generalised terms, although it is based on current knowledge. It must be remembered that there are many other varieties of mental defect, the causes of which could be classified under our five headings, but they have not been mentioned in the text. Readers who want more information on this subject should consult textbooks which deal specifically with the problem.

Mild sub-normality. Children are usually classified as mildly sub-normal when their IQ falls within the range 75/80 down to about 55, though adequacy of social adaptation is also taken into account and the category may thus include brighter and even duller children. These children may also be termed educationally sub-normal although we have seen that the E.S.N. category is defined in terms of attainment rather than in terms of IQ. These pupils should not be looked upon as patients or ill people, but rather as having weak intellectual capacity. Some Education Authorities have special schools for them, but elsewhere they are accommodated in ordinary schools.

Mildly sub-normal children frequently suffer discouragement, contempt and neglect from an early age. This is very likely, in turn, to affect their

[5] Metabolism may be defined as the process by which nutritive material is built up into living cells, and protoplasm broken down into simpler substances which perform definite functions.
[6] Some mongol children do have 46 chromosomes. See Lovell, K., *An Introduction to Human Development*. London: Macmillan, 1968, Ch. 1.

emotional and social growth. Again, since they cannot respond as adequately to the environment as can normal children, they are likely to feel isolated and to be excluded from some social activities from early childhood. The mildly sub-normal mother sometimes has a large family, neglects the children, gives them inadequate food and overlooks early infections. She may be promiscuous and the father may be a drunkard; either parent may leave the home. Such parents are often responsible for what is known as the 'problem family' which is frequently found associated with juvenile delinquency.[7] At the same time it must be stressed that the majority of mildly sub-normal children have parents who are dull or of average intelligence, and not mentally sub-normal parents.

It is important that mild sub-normality should be detected at an early age in order that special attention may be given to speech, reading, writing and simple number work. Given an intellectually stimulating atmosphere and an opportunity to develop good social and emotional adjustment, many mildly sub-normal children can be made to grow up into self-respecting and self-supporting adults. But denied the opportunities to develop, they sometimes get into trouble with the law, have poor work records as adults, and live lives below their capacities. The infant or junior school-teacher who suspects that a child is mildly sub-normal should refer him to the Child Guidance Clinic at the earliest possible moment. If the teacher's opinion is sustained by examination at the Clinic, then such facilities as are available for helping these children ought to be made available as soon as possible.

Chazan[8] has shown that the mildly sub-normal pupils in E.S.N. Special Schools are drawn mainly from the lower socio-economic groups. Rather over a third in his sample were maladjusted, or about three times as many as in a control group of pupils in ordinary schools matched for age, sex and socio-economic background. In the E.S.N. Special School children there was a higher incidence of depression, emotional tension, hostility to adults, speech defects, behaviour problems and delinquency compared with the controls, while low sociometric status (see Chapter 13) often went with maladjustment. Chazan points out that this evidence confirms the great need to deal with the personal and social needs of these children.

There are two main causes of mild sub-normality:

(a) Many of the children in this class are normal from the biological standpoint and are merely the antithesis of those of high intelligence.

(b) Injuries, early infections, metabolic disorders, severe emotional disturbances and poor upbringing.

---

[7] Some mildly sub-normal women make good housewives and mothers. See Brandon, M. W. G., 'The Intellectual and Social Status of Children of Mental Defectives,' *J. Ment. Sci.*, 1957, **103**, 710–738.

[8] Chazan, M., 'The Incidence and Nature of Maladjustment among Children in Schools for the Educationally Sub-Normal,' *Brit. J. Educ. Psychol.*, 1964, **34**, 292–304. Chazan, M., 'Factors Associated with Maladjustments in Educationally Sub-normal Children,' *Brit. J. Educ. Psychol.*, 1965, 277–285.

Dullness. Dull children, that is, those whose IQ's range from 85 down to about 75/70, constitute a serious problem for the teacher, since they are usually kept in ordinary schools and yet do not respond to ordinary teaching methods. Dull pupils only rarely reach standards of work equal to that of their age group, while in later life as adults they are liable to find life rather difficult and bewildering. Genetic endowment, coupled with poor upbringing in the early years, probably accounts for the majority of cases of dullness, but adverse conditions in the uterus during pregnancy, infection in early life and other causes, may play a part in some instances.

Backwardness and Retardation. Burt[9] defined backward children as those who, in the middle of their school career, are unable to do the work of the class next below that which is normal for their age. This was an arbitrary but very useful suggestion. Burt also introduced the term *educational age* which may be defined as the 'age' the child has reached in school subjects as measured by standardised tests of attainment. Thus children aged 10·0 should have an educational age averaging the same figure, and ranging from 9·5 to 10·5 years. Those in the next lowest class will have, on the average, an educational age of 9·0 varying from 8·5 to 9·5 years. A 10-year-old who cannot do the work of the class next below him must have an educational ratio below 8·5/10·0 (educational age/chronological age), that is, below 85 per cent. This figure can be applied regardless of age and so it is more precise to define a backward child as one whose educational age drops below 85 per cent of his own age.

Consider next, a bright child of 9·0, who has a mental age of 13·0 and a reading age of 10·0. Such a child is not backward but has been described by some as retarded (e.g. Schonell). Today, we know that we should not use the term in this way. Vernon[10] proposes that since measured intelligence and attainments differ in the degree to which they depend upon upbringing and opportunities, we must expect attainment to be sometimes greater, and sometimes less, than would be expected from measured intelligence, just as attainment in English may be higher or lower than in Mathematics.

Much research has been carried out into the causes of backwardness. The principle cause of dullness is the poor quality of the neural mechanisms with which the child is born, although this condition is partly brought about by lack of environmental stimulation as well. Thus children who are dull are likely to be backward in the more academic school subjects. Other possible causes of backwardness are now listed, although it must be stressed

[9] Burt, C., *The Backward Child*. London: University of London Press Ltd., 1937, pp. 77–78.
[10] Vernon, P. E., 'The Relation of Intelligence to Educational Backwardness,' *Educational Review*, 1958, **11**, 7–15. See also Crane, A. R., 'An Historical and Critical Account of the Accomplishment Quotient Idea,' *Brit. J. Educ. Psychol.*, 1959, **29**, 252–259.

that the problem is very complex and some of the conditions listed are likely to be 'conditions associated with' rather than 'causes of'.

(a) Irregular attendance at school; this may be due to illness or truancy.

(b) Frequent changes of school due to change of address.

(c) Poor quality of teaching or unsuitable teaching methods, including lack of continuity of method from one class to the next, and too quick or too slow promotion. Lack of continuity is, of course, reduced when mixed-ability groups are used.

(d) The introduction of basic skills, such as formal reading and early processes in arithmetic, before some pupils have a sufficiently high mental age, and before they have had enough experience to make the work meaningful to them.

(e) Lack of harmony between home and school.

(f) The socio-economic background of the home. Such conditions as great poverty, poor feeding, insufficient sleep, and general neglect are known to be causes of backwardness. Though we have less certain information on some of these matters, it is likely that stability of the family, parental attitudes to the child, home discipline, parental interests and parental attitudes to school and work are equally important. Thus, psychologically unfavourable home conditions frequently seem to be the cause of academic failure in secondary schools (cf. page 158).

(g) Defective physical conditions such as poor hearing, bad vision, impediments of speech, adenoids and recurrent catarrh.

(h) Certain conditions associated with temperament, e.g. a tendency to emotional instability.

(i) The emotional attitude of the child to school and school subjects. A poor adverse attitude may arise from dislike of a teacher, or teachers, from dislike of a subject due to unsuitable teaching methods, or from a sense of failure. The latter is only too likely to make worse a disability already present.

Most of the earlier investigators into the causes of backwardness in school work, whether general or in specific subjects, suggest that failure rarely arises from a single cause but from a number of interacting conditions. It is true that a single cause may stand out as being of primary importance, cf. dullness; but usually there are, according to Burt, at least three adverse factors operating. In his London group of backward children, Burt found that three-quarters suffered from low intellectual capacity, three-quarters from unfavourable physical conditions, two-thirds from unfavourable social conditions, about one-third from adverse temperamental states, and only one-sixth from unfavourable school conditions. Schonell's[11] investigation into specific backwardness in reading, spelling and composition in a group of 15,000 school-children also suggested that many causes were at work, causes linked with mental, physical and

[11] Schonell, F. J., *Backwardness in the Basic Subjects*. Edinburgh: Oliver and Boyd, 1942.

environmental conditions. However, our views on the causes of backwardness in some children may have to change.

There is now increasing evidence that backward readers may, in some instances, be suffering from inadequate development or functioning of certain areas within the brain.[12] Such children do not necessarily have low IQ's; indeed some are quite bright. For example, Birch and Belmont[13] have shown that backward readers are less able to make auditory-visual equivalences (match a pattern of taps with the corresponding pattern of dots) than normal readers. Their findings suggest that the development of auditory-visual integration has specific relevance to reading, although it is not the sole factor underlying poor reading. This view is also supported by the evidence of Lovell and Gorton.[14] They gave a number of tests to a random sample of all the backward readers aged 9–10 years found in the primary schools of a L.E.A., and to a matched group of average and good readers. The data strongly suggest that some backward readers have a specific neurological impairment which detracts, among other things, from the ability of the child to make auditory-visual equivalences. This impairment is clearly linked with reading failure. This failure in development or functioning could be brought about by genetic or adverse prenatal or paranatal conditions. Thus Kawi and Pasamanick[15] found a greater incidence of adverse prenatal and paranatal conditions among children with reading disabilities than among those without, over the IQ range 84 to 120. Moreover, there is evidence that there are more boys than girls with reading difficulties. This has been shown by Lovell[16] et al., while in a longitudinal study of nearly 5,000 children, Douglas[17] has shown that although boys have a larger vocabulary than girls at both 8 and 11 years of age, nearly three times as many boys as girls have to be given remedial reading.

The incidence of dullness and backwardness. Child[18] has made a number of interesting observations on the incidence of post-war backwardness, but

[12] Critchley, M., *Developmental Dyslexia*. London: Heinemann, 1964. Money, J. (Editor), *Reading Disability*. Baltimore: Johns Hopkins Press, 1962. Vernon, M. D., *Reading and its Difficulties*. London: Cambridge University Press, 1971, Ch. 7.

[13] Birch, H. G. and Belmont, L., 'Auditory-Visual Integration in Normal and Retarded Readers,' *Amer. J. Orthopsych.*, 1964, **34**, 852–861.

[14] Lovell, K. and Gorton, A., 'A Study of Some Differences between Backward and Normal Readers of Average Intelligence,' *Brit. J. Educ. Psychol.*, 1968, **38**, 240–248.

[15] Kawi, A. A. and Pasamanick, B., *Prenatal and Paranatal Factors in the Development of Childhood Reading Disorders*, Monographs of the Society for Research in Child Development, 1959, No. 73. See also Davie, R., Butler, N. and Goldstein, H., *From Birth to Seven*. London: Longman, 1972.

[16] Lovell, K., Gray, E. A. and Oliver, D. E., 'A Further Study of Some Cognitive and other Disabilities in Backward Readers of Average Non-Verbal Reasoning Scores,' *Brit. J. Educ. Psychol.*, 1964, **34**, 275–279.

[17] Douglas, J. W. B., *The Home and the School*. London: MacGibbon and Kee, 1964.

[18] Child, H. A. T., *Studies in Education* No. 7. London: Evans, 1955.

it is to the work of Schonell[19] that we turn for more detailed information in this field. He has summarised the results of many surveys into the number of children with IQ's below 70, the number of dull children with IQ's 70–85, and the incidence of backwardness, i.e. the number of children with an educational ratio less than 85. Schonell draws the following conclusions:

(a) The incidence of children with IQ's less than 70 consistently gives an average figure of 2/3 per cent for the whole country (this excludes the majority of those with an IQ below 55).

(b) Estimates of the incidence of dullness vary according to the IQ limits taken and the standard deviation of the test employed. If we take the IQ range as 70–85, then some 12–14 per cent of the children in our schools are likely to be classified as dull.

(c) General backwardness, or deficiency in most school subjects is, according to Burt, likely to be about 15 per cent. But Schonell thinks that if figures were available for a representative sample of the population for all age groups and all basic subjects, the figure might be nearer 20 per cent.

(d) Some 5 per cent of children of average, or above average intelligence are backward in one, or in a number of allied subjects.

(e) For every ten backward children in a class, three or four have an IQ greater than 85. These with help can sometimes be brought up to normal attainment levels in various subjects, but the remainder will less often reach average standards of work. On the other hand, Child[20] suggested that in a sample of London primary schools in 1953, the number of children who were backward but not dull had risen to nearly one-half. Child's view has been confirmed by the writer,[21] who in studying large groups of 9–10-year-olds, also 14–15-year-olds,[22] has found that about half of the backward readers have average or higher non-verbal reasoning scores.

(f) These findings suggest that some 20–25 per cent of pupils need special help in one or more school subjects for a limited or extended period. These figures broadly agree with those found by Wiseman[23] among 14-year-olds (1951). He gave the number of pupils backward in both reading and arithmetic in secondary modern and all-age schools as 19 and 22 per cent respectively.

The problem of backwardness in reading is one of great importance, particularly since at the end of World War II it was generally contended in Great Britain that the proportion of illiterates and backward readers had

[19] Schonell, F. J., 'The Development of Educational Research in Great Britain,' Brit. J. Educ. Psychol., 1949, 19, 82–99.

[20] Child, op. cit.

[21] Lovell, K., Shapton, D. L. and Warren, N. S., 'A Study of Some Cognitive and Other Disabilities in Backward Readers of Average Intelligence as assessed by a Non-Verbal Test,' Brit. J. Educ. Psychol., 1964, 34, 58–64.

[22] Lovell, Gray and Oliver, op. cit.

[23] Wiseman, S., Education and Environment. Manchester: Manchester University Press, 1964.

risen gradually. Obviously any figures that we obtain will depend upon the type of test used in examining children, and on the standards adopted to define these conditions. An important survey of reading ability was undertaken by the Ministry of Education, the results of which were published in 1950.[24] In this, a silent reading test was applied to some 3,500 children close to 15 years of age, and 2,500 close to 11 years of age in over 200 schools, thus ensuring a representative cross-section of children at each age-level. A backward reader was defined as one whose reading age was more than 20 per cent below his chronological age, while an illiterate was defined as a person with a reading age less than 7·0 years. The proportion of backward readers (including illiterates) at 11 and 15 years was 23 and 30 per cent respectively, while the proportion of illiterates at 15 years of age was 1·4 per cent. Since then, however, a number of other surveys have suggested that the proportion of backward readers and illiterates has fallen somewhat. This can, no doubt, be explained by the fact that the early education of the children who were examined in 1948 had been upset by the war. In 1957 the Ministry of Education gave the results of a survey made in 1956 with the same test as was used in the survey described above.[25] Altogether, 1,741 pupils aged 15, and 1,374 aged 11 years were tested. It was found that at 11 years of age there had been a gain in reading age of 9 months, and at 15 years a gain in reading age of 5 months, compared with 1948. Moreover, the proportion in the semi-literate and illiterate categories at 11 years of age had decreased from 5 per cent in 1948 to 1 per cent in 1956, while the corresponding figures at 15 years of age showed a drop from 6 per cent to 4 per cent. In 1964 the same test was again given to a representative sample of 11-year-olds. The data showed that in that year, boys and girls of 11 reached, on the average, the standard of pupils 17 months older in 1948.[26] It is fair to say, then, that standards of reading rose, although a core of backwardness still remains. However, according to the results of a study carried out by the N.F.E.R. for the Department of Education and Science, there was no improvement in reading standards between 1964 and 1970/71.[27]

Ascertainment of educationally sub-normal and backward pupils.[28] It is usual for educationally sub-normal pupils either to be sent to a Special School or to receive special educational treatment in an ordinary school. However, when such a child comes from a satisfactory home, is likely to attend school regularly, and has an IQ above about 75/80 he is unlikely to be sent to a special School. If a teacher suspects that a child qualifies for a Special School place, he should send him to the Child Guidance Clinic

[24] *Reading Ability*. London: H.M.S.O., 1950.
[25] *Standards of Reading*, 1948–1956. London: H.M.S.O., 1957.
[26] *Progress in Reading*, 1948–1964. London: H.M.S.O., 1966.
[27] Start, K. B., *The Trend of Reading Standards*. Windsor: N.F.E.R., 1972.
[28] See Williams, P., 'The Ascertainment of Educationally Subnormal Children,' *Educ. Res.*, 1965, 7, 136–146.

where his intellectual level will be ascertained by an educational psychologist who will use an individual test. The final decision as to whether a particular child should go to a Special School rests with the L.E.A. after he has been examined by an approved School Medical Officer who, in turn, has received recommendations from teacher, psychologist and other specialists.[29] If it is decided that the child is capable of being educated in an ordinary school then he will naturally become the responsibility of the teachers in that school.

In the case of children who are dull but not educationally sub-normal, and brighter backward children, the teacher has an important part to play in diagnosing pupil-difficulties. First, he should gather as much data as possible bearing on the child's scholastic record, his home life and his overall personality. Amongst other things he will find out as much as he can from the child concerning his interests, leisure pursuits, out-of-school activities, attitude to school and to his own disabilities; he will also make estimates of the child's temperamental traits and his degree of emotional stability. Second, he should proceed along the following lines:

(a) Obtain at least two estimates of the child's IQ from the use of group verbal intelligence tests providing his reading age is sufficiently high. Most well-known group verbal intelligence tests which are often used in junior schools need a reading age of $9\frac{1}{2}$ years before the intelligence test score can be regarded as valid. With poor readers, group non-verbal or group oral intelligence tests should be used.

(b) Assess the child's attainment ages by using standardised tests of arithmetic, spelling, reading and other English tests.

(c) Use diagnostic tests to discover the main types of errors and difficulties. Such tests[30] are available for studying weaknesses in arithmetic, reading, spelling and other aspects of English.

In addition, the following information might be obtained if the child is sent to the Child Guidance Clinic:

(a) A report on the socio-economic conditions of the home and on the general quality of home life obtained as a result of visits to the home by a psychiatric social worker.

(b) A more complete picture of the child's emotional attitudes and temperamental traits obtained through the use of projection tests, and from observations of reactions in play situations; also by interpretation of the child's drawings and paintings. Unfortunately, all personality assessments made by these means are to some extent subjective.

When as much information as possible has been gathered about the child, remedial teaching should be arranged to suit his particular needs as far as the facilities of the school permit.

[29] The interests of the parents are safeguarded and an appeal can be made to the Minister.
[30] The development of such tests in this country was due in great measure to F. J. and F. E. Schonell.

Organisation involved in the remedial teaching of junior and secondary school children.[31] Many experiments have been carried out in connection with the teaching of E.S.N. and backward children. The evidence suggests that when such children meet with continued failure in an ordinary class, loss of self-respect usually results and the condition becomes self-perpetuating. Hence, it is necessary to take them away from the competition of more successful pupils and to put them in a small group where they can get more individual help, have more intimate pupil-teacher relationships, have some opportunities for exercising responsibility, and experience success through the use of appropriate teaching methods. A number of methods for organising such work has evolved in Britain:

(*a*) Special Schools. These may be day or residential schools. Excellent work is being done in these schools, for the whole work and atmosphere is suited to the needs of the child in question. Yet some people take the view that special classes in ordinary schools are preferable to special schools.[32] It is said that here he can join in out-of-school activities with normal children, can join in school gatherings and participate in non-academic pursuits, thereby acquiring a sense of normality which will help him to increase his self-respect and happiness. Indeed, some now suggest that all handicapped children should, whenever possible, attend the same schools as normal children, and the word 'special' should be dropped from the official names of separate schools for the handicapped.

(*b*) Special classes in ordinary schools. These are small classes of approximately 15-20 pupils. Many head-teachers now arrange for these classes to be kept as small as possible. In small schools, however, the problem is more difficult, since the number of teachers or rooms may not permit the formation of such classes.

(*c*) Setting for subjects. Pupils are put into different groups of similar attainment levels for specific subjects. This method is often used in the case of pupils backward in reading or mathematics.

(*d*) Children may be withdrawn from their classes and given coaching by members of the regular teaching staff or by peripatetic teachers.

(*e*) A variety of methods involving teaching outside the school. For example, there may be individual coaching at the Child Guidance Clinic, or there may be a class under a qualified teacher attached to the clinic. Central remedial teaching classes have also been used. Children from different schools attend these classes during a certain number of sessions per week. Finally, there is the remedial teaching centre. Here, teaching in school subjects can be combined with some therapeutic work through dramatics, painting or puppetry.

At the present time the bright but slow learning child and his duller

[31] For a thorough discussion of this subject see Cleugh, M. F., *The Slow Learner.* London: Methuen, 1957. Also see Segal, S. S., 'Dull and Backward Children: Post-War Theory and Practice,' *Educ. Research*, 1961, 3, 177-194.

[32] See Schonell, F. J., McLeod, J., and Cochrane, R. G. (Editors), *The Slow Learner. Segregation or Integration.* St. Lucia: University of Queensland Press, 1962.

companions still tend to receive the same treatment although some L.E.A.'s may make special provision for the former.[33]

General methods used in remedial teaching. Here we can only discuss general methods used in remedial teaching and readers must refer to other sources[34] which deal with remedial teaching in specific subjects. The results of experimental work carried out in this field, together with the findings of child psychology generally, suggest the following points as the most important:[35]

(*a*) The teaching material must be very carefully graded, even more so than in the case of ordinary children.

(*b*) There should be short frequent lessons, especially in the basic skills. Thus two periods per day of 20 minutes each is better than one period of 40 minutes.

(*c*) There should be ample use of visual aids, models and concrete material generally.

(*d*) The work being done, and the teaching method employed, should always appear meaningful and purposeful to the children. Thus both material and method should be related to real situations that the pupils can understand and appreciate. Such an approach often helps to create a desire to learn and helps to do away with the apathy so often noted in dull and backward children. Thus reading material must be related to the interests and outlook of such pupils. This means that reading material suitable for dull 15-year-olds is very different from that suitable for dull 9-year-olds.

(*e*) In some cases good results have been obtained through art, music, puppetry and drama, in the development of the social qualities of such children, in helping to restore their confidence, and in stimulating their interest. And because of these changes they go to their more formal work with greater zest.

(*f*) Backwardness is often associated with adverse emotional attitudes towards subjects, teachers, or the school. Obversely, in the case of emotional maladjustment, the level of school work is usually below that suggested by the level of intellectual capacity. Thus it is essential that there should be an individual friendly approach in remedial teaching. Further, the work should be so well graded that every pupil can tackle it with good chance of success; indeed with such children 'nothing succeeds like success'.

Experience shows that small classes can make some progress in basic subjects with the use of appropriate materials and methods. In addition where such methods are adopted there is often less absence from school and better emotional adjustment in the pupils themselves. Nothing is more

[33] See Collins, J. E., 'Remedial Educational Provision for Children of Average or Above Average Intelligence,' *Educational Review*, 1954, 6, 133–146.
[34] E. G. Tansley, A. E., and Gulliford, R., *The Education of Slow Learning Children*. London: Routledge and Kegan Paul, 1960.
[35] See Schonell, F. J., 'The Development of Educational Research in Great Britain. Part V. Handicapped Children,' *Brit. J. Educ. Psychol.*, 1949, 19, 82–99.

helpful to the child in emotional difficulties than a building up of his self-respect and an attempt to make his interests more objective.[36]

On the other hand it should be clearly understood that in remedial classes and in the ordinary classroom situation, although some backward children make rapid progress, most make limited gains, and some make no progress at all. Naturally, special treatment may well give security and support to the child, to his class teacher and his parents. It may be excellent, too, for his emotional and motivational life. Teachers of backward children in ordinary schools would, however, do well to emulate the work of the enlightened E.S.N. Special Schools and seize upon any relative strength of the child and try to build him up as a person. In essence, then, we must do what we can, with the facilities we have, to aid his personal and social growth.

It is necessary from the point of view of the mental health of young teachers to stress that for most of our backward children progress will be limited. At a Unesco Seminar at Hamburg in 1956 Hans Thomai of Erlangen reported the results of a longitudinal study covering the first five years of school life of more than 3,000 children. It was shown that during this age range attainment tends to be constant and varies only within a limited range. Rapid changes were rarely observable. The Swedish study given by Malmquist (1958) is also in keeping with this point of view. It was found that in following 399 pupils, an entire age group of junior school children in two Swedish towns, that all those who were backward in reading at 7 were, with one exception, backward at 11.

It is an assumption that children, apart from the mentally sub-normal, can reach the varying levels of reading skill that *we* think they ought, or that they can attain certain degrees of facility—that *we* think they should—in handling mathematical concepts and skills. The human race has had far too little experience of mass education to know whether our assumptions are reasonable. It is likewise presumption to say that because a child is 9, 10, or 11 years of age and a non-reader, he will never read. He may well have attained a reading age of 11 years by sixteen. We just do not know enough to judge any case in advance. But once a child is backward with respect to his age group, and rank bad teaching and/or prolonged illness can be ruled out, we need to be cautious regarding the progress, and the speed of progress that he will make in the basic subjects.[37, 38, 39]

[36] For a study of the psychology of handicapped children generally see Cruickshank, W. (Editor), *Psychology of Exceptional Children and Youth.* London: Staples, 1956. Dunn, L. M. (Editor), *Exceptional Children in the Schools.* London: Holt, Reinhart & Winston, 1963.

[37] Compare Lovell, K., Johnson, E., and Platt, D., 'A Summary of a Study of the Reading Ages of Children Who Had Been Given Remedial Teaching,' *Brit. J. Educ. Psychol.*, 1962, **32**, 66–71.

[38] Lovell, K., Byrne, C. and Richardson, B., 'A Further Study of the Long Term Effects of Remedial Teaching,' *Brit. J. Educ. Psychol.*, 1963, **33**, 3–9.

[39] Cashdan, A., Pumfrey, P. D., and Lunzer, E. A., 'Children Receiving Remedial Teaching in Reading,' *Educational Research*, 1971, 3, 98–105.

Methods of Selecting Children for Remedial Education. Children selected by teachers or educational psychologists for remedial education have frequently been selected on the grounds that their 'age' in, say, reading, was $1\frac{1}{2}$ or 2 years below their mental age. We should, however, never select children merely by subtracting such ages. If we do we shall often pick out more bright children for remedial education than dull ones. A clear and simple discussion of this problem has been provided by Phillips.[40] If it is not possible to make the necessary calculations to overcome the above snag, it is better to select children on the basis of a discrepancy between reading age and chronological age, at the same time taking into consideration all other relevant evidence about the child's attainments, attitudes, background, etc.

[40] Phillips, C. J., 'Retardation and the Use of Tests,' *Educational Review*, 1958, 2, 16–29.

Chapter Thirteen

SOME ASPECTS OF THE SOCIAL BEHAVIOUR
OF CHILDREN

WE are said to behave *socially* when our behaviour is influenced by others and we, in turn, influence their actions. Social behaviour may thus be defined as the physical and psychological interaction of two or more persons in a common environment.[1] Although we are here only interested in human beings, social behaviour can also be observed in many animals ranging from monkeys to ants.

Some difficulties in the field of social behaviour. Our moral and social values determine what aspects of social behaviour we deem to be important, and thus our views about the relative importance of certain aspects of the social behaviour of children will depend upon the value judgments of our culture or sub-culture pattern. Just as in personality study we have no satisfactory theory of personality development but a good deal of useful knowledge, so we know a good deal about the social growth and behaviour of children which is of great help in day-to-day situations, although we have no comprehensive theory as to how children develop their stable patterns of social behaviour. One theory is that of Miller and Dollard,[2] which stresses the development of such patterns through imitation of other children. Thus when a child is forced into some action by a need, he often sees another child experiencing a similar type of need and getting apparent satisfaction from a certain kind of response. This behaviour pattern of the second child acts as a cue, and the first child tends to repeat the response whenever the cue is presented. If the response also reduces his need, then he will tend to repeat the response whenever the need is felt again. This theory of imitation is an interesting one and can explain certain aspects of the growth of social behaviour in children, but in other ways it is quite inadequate. Furthermore, instinct and psychoanalytic theories of behaviour do not carry one very far either.[3]

Some general trends in the social behaviour of young children. In later

[1] The study of social interactions which take place within some clearly defined group, such as a classroom, has been termed 'group dynamics'.

[2] Miller, N. E., and Dollard, J. E., *Social Learning and Imitation.* New Haven: Yale University Press, 1941.

[3] For a more detailed treatment of social learning see Morris, J. F., 'Social Learning and Perspectives in Adolescence.' In *Development in Learning*—2 (Eds. Lunzer, E. A. and Morris, J. F.). London: Staples, 1968, 330–385.

chapters reference will be made to the social life of young children up to and including adolescence. In this section we give a brief account of some general trends in the social development of pre-school children, and mention one means of assessing the degree of social maturity which an individual has reached.

Not until children are four or five months old do they begin to take notice of each other. Moreover, when under one year of age an infant seems to be unable to make social contact with more than one other infant simultaneously. But soon after the ninth month, social interactions between young children increase and become more personal, so that the infant will then offer his companion a toy, while by the end of the second year of life he can usually keep up social contact with two infants at the same time.[4]

Parten[5] used Time-Sampling technique (*see* Chapter 4) to study the kinds of social behaviour which pre-school children engage in. Their behaviour was classified either as unoccupied, onlooker (watching other children but not making any contact with them), parallel activity (playing alongside other children with the same kinds of material), associative activity (sharing materials with other or 'taking turns'), and co-operative play (children all working towards some common end). Parten found that, in general, as the pre-school child grows older, he engages less and less in the former types of activity and more and more in the associative and co-operative activities. Intelligent children tended to develop faster than the less bright ones, but at all stages and ages there were large individual differences. Again, Hattwick and Saunders[6] analysed the ratings of the behaviour habits and personality traits of 555 children between the ages of 2 and 4½ years. Above this age-range the children showed decreasing desire to be fed by others and to avoid playing with others, and at the same time an increasing tendency to gain the attention of others, to obtain praise, and to 'boss' others.[7]

Doll[8] has devised a useful scale which estimates a person's degree of social maturity. This scale was originally devised to help pick out mental defectives who were socially incompetent, but it can be used with ordinary children. The items of the scale have been proved to be typical of the average (American) person of the age indicated. Thus:

---

[4] Compare Bühler, C., *From Birth to Maturity*. London: Kegan Paul, Trench, Trubner, 1947.

[5] Parten, M. B., 'Social Participation among Pre-school Children,' *J. abnorm. soc. Psychol.*, 1932, **27**, 243–269.

[6] Hattwick, L. A. and Saunders, M. K., 'Age Differences in Behaviour at the Nursery School Level,' *Child Developm.*, 1938, **9**, 27–47.

[7] For a study that shows how the dominant behaviour of young children changes with the composition of the group, see Gellert, E., 'The Effect of Changes in Group Composition on the Dominant Behaviour of Young Children,' *Brit. J. Soc. Clin. Psychol.*, 1962, **1**, 168–181.

[8] Doll, E. A., *Vineland Social Maturity Scale*. Vineland, N. J.: Training School, Educational Test Bureau, 1936.

Dries own hands 2½ years
Makes telephone calls 10½ years

In the case of children, the examiner (who is trained in the use of the scale) gets the required information from a parent or other responsible person who knows the child well. A Social Age and Social Quotient are worked out. The latter correlates rather highly with IQ but it has been shown that the scale is a useful reliable and valid instrument that assesses aspects of behaviour which are not measured by intelligence tests.[9]

In 1966 Lunzer[10] made available the Manchester Scales of Social Adaptation. While he acknowledges his debt to the Vineland Scale, he has provided a revised scale based on samples of British children.

Play. All children play at some time or other. Indeed, play is the principal means by which children experiment with social situations. Various theories as to why children play have been put forward but, once again, no really satisfactory explanation has yet been suggested. Some of these theories are now briefly noted[11]:

(a) One of the oldest and most widely held views is that which defines play as an excess of energy which the young person has in abundance. Because children are free from economic pressure and free from the need to devote their energies to self-preservation because of parental protection, they are said to have energy to spare which they express in play, that is, in activities which do not subserve the serious needs of life.

(b) Karl Groos, following earlier writers, stressed the part played by instinct as a motivating factor in play. He held that play was an important part of the training of the higher animals so that when the child plays at 'homes' he is preparing himself for a grown-up activity. Karl Groos thus maintained that play arose in children as a result of the urge of certain instinctive tendencies which would only later express themselves in mature form.

(c) The Recapitulation Theory found its most brilliant expositor in Stanley Hall, who maintained that the child relived the life of his ancestors in his play. Thus he plays at hunting, fishing, and home-making, these activities representing the ways in which primitive people lived.

(d) The Recreation Theory suggests that play refreshes and restores the mental and physically tired. While sleep and rest are necessary, a change to a more interesting and active pastime is more restful than mere idleness. This view was upheld and extended by the Relaxation Theory which maintained that many of the activities that children (and adults)

[9] Doll, E. A., *The Measurement of Social Competence*. U.S.A.: Educational Test Bureau, 1953. Kellmer Pringle, M. L., 'Social Maturity and Social Competence,' *Educational Review*, 1951, 3, 183–195; also 'Social Learning and its Measurement,' *Educational Research*, 1960, 2, 194–206.
[10] Lunzer, E. A., *The Manchester Scales of Social Adaptation*. Slough: N.F.E.R., 1966.
[11] Compare Lowenfeld, M., *Play in Childhood*. London: Gollancz, 1935.

now engage in, such as abstract reasoning, writing, number work, and so forth, are comparatively new in the long history of the human race. Children must revert from time to time to more primitive forms of behaviour (that is, racially older), in which physical activities assume a major role. Thus physical forms of behaviour form the basis of much of children's play.

(e) It has been suggested that play is a safety-valve for pent-up emotions. This is known as the Theory of Catharsis. Certain of our natural tendencies, such as pugnacity, are inhibited by the very nature of social life, but in fighting play, or in fantasy play, the child gets an opportunity to express this tendency and the emotion subsides with it.

On reviewing these theories, we realise that there is something to be said for each, but every one of them is also inadequate in some respect. For example, it is difficult in (a) to explain why children play games to the point of exhaustion, and very difficult to explain in terms of the Relaxation Theory the joy that some children get out of mental activity and intelligent play, such as is involved in chess.

One view of play advanced by Mitchell and Mason,[12] based upon current psychological findings, suggests that play is the means by which human beings seek self-expression. People are essentially active, physically and mentally, and their physiological condition and psychological inclinations predispose them to certain forms of play-activity. These inclinations are, in turn, dependent upon primary needs like hunger and sex, also upon acquired needs, habits, attitudes, sentiments, and desires. The most prominent social needs include the wish for new experience; for recognition in terms of social status; for security; for participation in activities with others; for receiving appreciation from, and giving appreciation to, other individuals; and for the beautiful. In short, human beings, so predisposed, seek life or self-expression in play and continue in their play-activities as long as these bring satisfaction to them.

Whatever may be the correct theoretical explanation of play, there is no doubt about its value to children. Among the physical benefits resulting from some kinds of play, we may list the activity of larger muscles, which, in turn, stimulates growth and increases the demand for oxygen, thereby creating greater respiratory activity; the improvement of digestion and assimilation, also the stimulation of excretion; the increase in circulation throughout the body; the strengthening of the heart muscles through the exercise of the skeletal muscles; and finally the improvement in neuro-muscular control which in turn affects strength, accuracy and skill. Psychologically, too, play is of the greatest importance. Many kinds of play act as a kind of relaxation in that they provide a change; through free play the child learns how to adapt himself to his playmates, to co-operate with them, to lead or to be led, to make compromises, to defend his rights or those of

[12] Mitchell, E. D., and Mason, B. S., *The Theory of Play*. New York: A. S. Barnes, 1948.

others, and to withstand antagonism. Again, play helps the child to build up his own picture of himself which is of vital importance in determining his behaviour. For example, a child of limited attainment in the classroom may feel in play that he has, after all, some ability, some prestige, and that he can do some things. On the other hand, if he is somewhat inept in his play and performs poorly in games, feelings of inadequacy already present may be further increased. Moreover, play often provides a means by which children can satisfy their needs either in a socially acceptable way or in fantasy, and this helps in maintaining good mental health. For example,[13] Moore studied a large group of 4–6-year-olds using doll play. He found that children of this age show considerable oscillation between untrammelled fantasy and realistic limitations, aggressive destruction and constructive reparation, emotional involvement and objective or humorous detachment. Further, Moore suggests that play could be a regulative factor in that it can admit affect-laden thought to the ego in such doses as the latter can assimilate through play without being overwhelmed. Play, too, provides a wide range of experiences which are very useful to the child and the teacher when the former comes to some of the more formal school topics (for example, counting in number work). Finally, during play, and especially through organised games, the child learns many useful lessons in the field of morals. For example, he must learn to be unselfish in passing the ball, to be a reliable member of a team, to be loyal and obedient to the captain, to control himself, and to be prompt and courageous. But we must be very careful not to infer that these traits will necessarily carry over or transfer into other real life situations. Because a child 'plays the game' on the playing-field, it does not always mean that he will do so in the classroom or as an adult. Whether he does so depends upon the extent of the transfer of the training, and upon his needs at a particular moment.

In the early years there certainly seems to be a close connection between the type of play which children engage in and the level of their intellectual growth. Piaget[14] argues that there are three successive classes of play: practice play, symbolic play, and games with rules. Practice play is characteristic of a poor stage of verbal development and it involves no mental representation (e.g. 'dressing up'). But in symbolic play the child understands the difference between the action he is pretending to perform and the action he is actually performing. Moreover, there is a clear interest in the thing symbolised (e.g. 'the cowboy', 'the nurse') and this helps the child to assimilate aspects of reality to his own needs and interests. The amount of time spent on these forms of play decreases with age and by about 7 to 8 years of age the child develops modes of play characterised by rules as a result of his co-operation and interaction with other children. For

[13] Moore, T., 'Realism and Fantasy in Children's Play,' *J. Child Psychology and Psychiatry*, 1964, 5, 15–36.
[14] Piaget, J., *Play, Dreams and Imitation in Children*. London: Heinemann, 1951.

Piaget, play emphasises assimilation over accommodation and so is fun, since play need not fit the demands of reality.

Throughout the ages there have been educationists who have used various 'playway' approaches in teaching their pupils. Such methods try to harness the natural and acquired tendencies of the child to provide the motivation, and in situations where these tendencies are satisfied, learning takes place more readily. During the present century there has been a remarkable growth in 'playway' and 'activity' methods. Those who advocate these methods point out that children learn most rapidly when their tendencies and interests are catered for, while at the same time their personality is more likely to develop healthily in an environment where they work as members of a group. Social psychologists have also stressed that in the ordinary classroom situation involving class teaching, the child's natural impulses and social tendencies, especially the need for security and acceptance, are likely to be frustrated, with the teacher tending to dominate the situation.[15] In these circumstances the motivation of children declines, and all manner of incentives have to be applied such as competition, threats and punishment. Instead, social psychology suggests that greater use should be made of group work, for within the small group the child feels more secure, maintains his self-esteem more successfully and gets the opportunity of talking to others and so relieving his own anxieties to some extent. Moreover the teacher takes on the part of a wise and experienced member of a group rather than that of the traditional teacher. Again the greater opportunities for discussion between pupils and teacher is likely to increase the latter's understanding, and language performance. Small group work is, of course, imperative in some areas of the curriculum (e.g. mathematics) when classes are composed of mixed-ability groups.

Social relationships within a group of children. In later chapters we shall discuss the social relationships of children in greater detail. It is sufficient here to say that young children are brought together and form loose groupings because they live near one another, go to the same school, attend the same church, or belong to some organised group such as Cub-Scouts. In adolescence it is common interests and skills rather than mere physical proximity which brings young people together, so that a number of older boys and girls who are keen on, say, swimming, may come from different parts of the town and meet at the swimming baths.

Since the early 1930's considerable study has been made of the social relationships between children within a group. Psychologists have developed *sociometric techniques*,[16] that is, methods of plotting the social

[15] See Oeser, O. A. (Editor), *Teacher, Pupil and Task. Elements of Social Psychology applied to Education*. London: Tavistock Publications, 1955. Fleming, C. M., *The Social Psychology of Education*. London: Routledge, 1944.

[16] Compare Moreno, J. L., *Who Shall Survive?* Wash., D.C.: Nerv. & Ment. Dist. Publ. Co., 1934. Also Jennings, H. H., *Sociometry in Group Relations: a Work Guide for Teachers*. Wash., D.C.: Amer. Counc. Educ., 1948. Hallworth, H. G.,

relationships within a group of children such as a school class. These techniques usually involve asking each child to name his or her friend or to say with whom he would like to sit. Sometimes the 'guess who' technique (*see* Chapter 4) is used, or the actual social relationships within a group are observed. The data is plotted on a *sociogram* as follows (Figure 13). A small triangle represents each boy and a circle each girl, while arrows run between these shapes showing how each child chooses his friends. If many arrows point to a child then he or she is popular with the others, that is, a child is a 'star'. If few or no lines point to a child it means that he or she is either socially unacceptable to the others, or is a social nonentity in that particular situation and may be regarded as an 'isolate'. This is illustrated

Sociogram

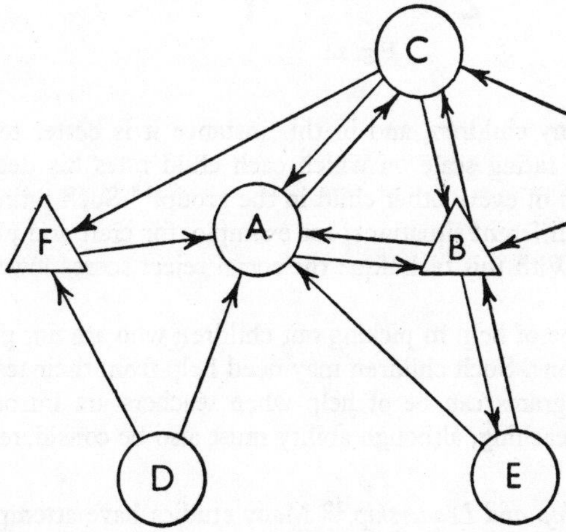

Fig. 13

in the accompanying diagram. If, say, three or four children have a number of arrows running to and from one another, it implies that strong bonds exist between the members of this sub-group within the class. Further, if this sub-group is popular with the remaining members of the class, it might exert a great deal of influence on the activities of the whole class. Thus, in our diagram, A, B, and C are popular children, whereas no one chooses G or D for a companion.

One must be very careful about generalisations drawn from the sociogram, for the social interrelations are relative to the group in which they were obtained. In a different group, or even with the same group in an entirely different situation, children D and G might well have been more

'Sociometric Relationships among Grammar School Boys and Girls,' *Sociometry*, 1953, 16, 39–70. Richardson, J. E., Shulka, K. J., Forrester, J. F., and Higginbotham, P. J., *Studies in the Social Psychology of Adolescence*. London: Routledge and Kegan Paul, 1951.

acceptable to their colleagues.[17] Nor must it be forgotten that a child may play with an 'isolate' merely because there is no one else to play with. If we wish to distinguish between a child who is socially unacceptable and one who is just a nonentity then we may indicate attraction by an unbroken line and rejection by a broken line. This is illustrated in Figure 14. It is difficult to show both attraction and rejection on the same diagram

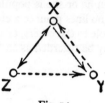

Fig. 14

when there are many children, and in this instance it is better to use a five or seven point rating scale on which each child rates his degree of acceptance-rejection of every other child in the group.[18] Such ratings can be made for many different situations; for example, for craft and physical education lessons. With this technique the social reject scores lower than the nonentity.

Sociograms can be of help in picking out children who are not popular with their companions. Such children may need help from their teachers. Furthermore, sociograms can be of help when teachers are introducing group methods of teaching, although ability must also be considered.[19]

Popularity, Friendship and Leadership.[20] Many studies have attempted to find out why some children are more popular than others. All the evidence indicates that popular children are those who can adapt their behaviour to the needs of the situation and to the needs of their companions. They are thus usually friendly, happy, talkative, energetic, enthusiastic and daring. It seems, then, that popular children are those who are able to make good personal adjustments to their fellows according to the standards and values

[17] But this issue is complex. See Northway, M. L., 'The Stability of Young Children's Social Relations,' *Educ. Res.*, 1968, **11**, 54–57.

[18] Thompson, G. G., and Powell, M., 'An Investigation of the Rating-Scale Approach to the Measurement of Social Status,' *Educ. Psychol. Measmt.*, 1951, **11**, 440–455.

[19] For a comprehensive treatment of the topic of sociometry in the classroom see Gronlund, N. E., *Sociometry in the Classroom*. New York: Harper, 1959.

[20] For an English study of sociometry, popularity and leadership see Evans, K. M., *Sociometry and Education*. London: Routledge and Kegan Paul, 1962. See also Evans, K. M., 'Sociometry in School,' *Educational Research*, 1964, **6**, 121–128. Hartup, W. W., 'Peer Interaction and Social Organisation.' In *Manual of Child Psychology* (Ed. Mussen, P.). London: Wiley, 1970, 3rd Edn. This paper covers friendship and leadership.

of our society, whereas unpopularity among other children may be a sign of emotional maladjustment in a child. The above is not necessarily true in adults. An adult may be unpopular because he takes some stand on a moral issue against the views of the majority, yet he may be very far from maladjusted or neurotic.

Children tend to select their friends from among those who live reasonably near them and, within broad limits, from the same socio-economic group as themselves. Friends are also found to be generally similar in age, intelligence and interests. But research strongly suggests that the essential feature underlying friendship between children (or adults) is their ability to satisfy each other's psychological needs. For each individual these needs are many and varied, so that each child in a group cannot be friends with every other child. Moreover, children's needs change with time so that children tend to 'drop' some friendships and take up new ones with the passage of time.

Finally we must consider the concept of leadership which is a difficult one to define. Leadership is not a clear-cut characteristic which a person possesses, like the colour of hair or eyes, but rather a trait resulting from the interaction of the personality and the environment. Thus a child may show leadership on the playing fields but not in a classroom where more academic studies are pursued. However, in a given situation a leader shows some competence and behaves in such a manner that he satisfies his own needs and those of his companions. Such behaviour is adaptable and flexible; the leader does not try to 'bully' but rather uses his energy and talents in the interests of the group. The leader is thus likely to be a person who shows an exceptional degree of emotional maturity for his age. It will be remembered that in Chapter 4 the War Office Selection Board technique for picking out potential officers was described. There, men were looked for who displayed the kind of behaviour that has just been outlined. The teacher who can both satisfy his own psychological needs and those of his pupils will be able to maintain true discipline as distinct from mere order, for he will have the capacity to create disciples.[21]

[21] For a comprehensive survey of research findings on the leadership, function, actions and patterns of small groups, see Cartwright, D., and Zander, A., *Group Dynamics*. Third Edition, Evanston: Row Patterson, 1968. In the future there is likely to be more teaching in small groups, more seminars, and more discussion generally, in secondary schools. Group dynamics is likely to become a topic of greater importance in teacher training. See also Ottoway, A. K. C., *Learning through Group Experience*. London: Routledge & Kegan Paul, 1966.

Chapter Fourteen

SOME ASPECTS OF THE PERSONAL DEVELOPMENT OF CHILDREN

THIS chapter may be regarded by some as the most important one in the book. It is certainly not an easy one to write for two reasons. First, one can only attempt to cover certain selected aspects of the problem and, secondly, the psychologist *qua* psychologist, cannot decide on the goals at which one should aim in personality-development. Nevertheless, the psychologist can give useful information concerning the influences which affect the personal and social growth of children, and is often in a position to suggest how a given goal might best be reached.

In the first part of this chapter we are to consider some aspects of the development of personal relationships and social attitudes, and the chief factors which influence this growth. Some take the view of the philosopher A. N. Whitehead that the basis of all experience is emotional,[1] and therefore believe that the basis of all education is emotional.

If this is so, then perhaps educationists and psychologists have concerned themselves too much with the cognitive side of the personality and too little with the emotions. Again, others point out that it is more important than ever today that good attitudes as well as knowledge and skills should be built up in children. It is argued that social changes are taking place very rapidly, life is nowadays far more complex than it was in simpler communities; there is less chance of children learning by experience without the help of others; while under present urban and city development the family is now often part of a community which means nothing to them, and to which they feel no sense of belonging. Under these conditions, children are likely to develop anxieties unless special care is taken over their emotional upbringing. As anxious adults they are liable to be aggressive, or to run away from difficulties, or surround themselves with a protection of material possessions.

The Influence of the Home. Psychoanalytic theory suggests that some of the first emotional attitudes are brought about by the relationships involved in feeding and tending, while some psychoanalysts have maintained that a

---

[1] The actual words of Whitehead are, 'The basis of experience is emotional. Stated more generally, the basic fact is the rise of an affective tone originating from things whose relevance is given.' Whitehead, A. N., *The Adventures of Ideas*. Cambridge: Cambridge University Press, 1933, p. 226.

predisposition to anxiety is present in the infant at birth. It is claimed that in the early tending process, security or insecurity (the latter leading to further anxiety) is engendered, and that the better the child-mother relationships are, the more likely it is that the child will achieve the capacity to give and receive affection. But however good the mother, the child will always suffer some frustration (caused by the mother herself, or other adults) associated with feeding, to which he will react with anxiety or aggression. Thus there develops in each individual an ambivalence, or double feeling, towards those he loves, born out of the original feeding situation where the infant learned both to love the individual who fed him, and hate the person who withheld things from him. In later life the harbouring of ill feelings towards those we love is unacceptable to us; they are repressed, and often issue in the form of unconscious guilt or reparation.

Again, theory suggests that the child, in fantasy, builds up images not of his ordinary parents, but of exaggerated personifications of the 'good' and 'bad' qualities, that is 'good' and 'bad' in the sense of the parents' attitudes being gratifying or frustrating to him. These parental figures are then internalised so that some of the parental qualities or their opposites are built into the child's personality. It is through the incorporation of these images, together with the internalisation of the demands of near relatives and other children, that the ego and super-ego develop. In a mature individual the ego is sufficiently developed to enable him to give a rational interpretation of the world, and for him to exercise what is termed *will*. On the other hand, if the images are very disapproving or punishing in their attitudes, then the super-ego or conscience might be over-severe. In these circumstances the ego may not be able to perform its proper functions; the individual may have difficulty in his relationships with others, and his mental health may suffer.

Finally, there is a considerable amount of literature which suggests that prolonged separation from, or change in, the mother-figure in approximately the first five years of life, is likely to affect the mental health of the child and lead to delinquency and emotional maladjustment. This viewpoint is discussed again in later chapters.

While we must bear in mind psychoanalytic theories regarding emotional and social development, it must be pointed out that the more ordinary stresses and strains, frustrations and so forth, which the child constantly meets, must also be considered as having valuable effects on the child's personal development. Furthermore, some scepticism regarding the above theories is justified in so far as they neglect the role of genetic factors in determining the quality of the central nervous system with which the individual comes into the world. Thus, certain individuals are more likely to succumb to stress and strain than others because of poor constitutional equipment. Although there is undoubtedly a relationship between early upbringing and later personality traits, we are in no position yet to say precisely what types of personality are due to particular kinds of upbringing.[2]

To support what has just been said, reference may be made to the well-designed experiment of Hewitt and Jenkins.[3] Their evidence is valuable even if we cannot accept their thesis in full. They applied factorial analysis to the traits of five hundred problem children, of average age between 11 and 12 years, with a mean IQ of 94. Clear relationships were found between:

(a) Unsocialised aggressive behaviour in children (assaulting tendencies, cruelty, defiance of authority, malicious mischief, inadequate guilt feelings), and parental rejection (illegitimate or unwanted pregnancy, mother hostile to child, mother sexually unconventional, lack of contact between parents).

(b) Socialised delinquent behaviour in children (bad companions, gang activities, stealing, truancy from school, staying out late), and parental negligence (untidy or dirty home, lack of supervision, lax or too harsh discipline, mother mentally dull, slum area).

(c) Over-inhibited behaviour in children (seclusiveness, shyness, worrying, sensitiveness, submissiveness), and 'family repression' on the part of the parents (father hypercritical, parents unsociable, mother demanding, sibling rivalry).

Hewitt and Jenkins maintain that children exposed to different environmental situations will exhibit different patterns of behaviour and adjustment. But the experiment was not designed to show this. What they have shown is that there is a connection between certain kinds of behaviour in children and certain kinds of upbringing and environment. Similar relationships might, however, have been obtained through the action of inheritance, and the authors seem to have fallen into the trap of assuming that the correlation between two variables shows the cause responsible for the correlation.

Given the society in which we live, with its attendant standards and values, it is suggested that the following will aid the personal and social growth of children:

(a) Give the child the maximum amount of love and security without being over-indulgent.

(b) Give the child his proper place in the family, neither petting nor ignoring him.

(c) Have a clear but permissive authority in the home. Every individual, whether child or adult, needs clearly defined barriers which protect him

[2] Compare Orlansky, H., 'Infant Care and Personality,' *Psychol. Bull.*, 1949, 46, 1–48. Also Stevenson, I., 'Is The Human Personality More Plastic in Infancy and Childhood?' *Amer. J. Psychiat.*, 114, 152–161. See also, *Deprivation of Maternal Care: a Re-assessment of its Effects*. World Health Organisation, Public Health Papers, No. 14, 1962.

[3] Hewitt, L. E., and Jenkins, R. L., *Fundamental Patterns of Maladjustment. The Dynamics of their Origin*. Illinois: Green, 1946.

from himself and from others. These rules aid mental health since they enable the individual to build up habitual responses for dealing with threatening or frustrating situations, and also limit the attacks which others can make upon him. An atmosphere in which the child is left to do as he likes may well contribute to maladjustment. At the same time the atmosphere should be co-operative and democratic, and the child should be given sound reasons for the rules as far as the level of his mental development permits. There must also be a consistent exercise of authority; this consistency being of importance in inculcating moral-social values in the child.

(d) Help the child at each stage in his development to exploit his potentialities fully, thus enabling him to pass more smoothly to the next stage. There is some evidence that over-protective mothers have a bad effect on the social-emotional growth of their sons, unless the fathers also play a considerable part in their sons' upbringing.

In short we may say that one should aim at a calm, harmonious, well-adjusted atmosphere in the home, where the child is accepted and played with; where consistent control is exercised, and where the child is aided to maturity. Against this, in homes where there has been overprotection of children, inharmonious relationships and defective authority, we tend to find adjustment difficulties, aggression, unco-operativeness, rebellion and delinquency in the children. But we must be very careful at present not to assume that the type of upbringing wholly determines personality.[4]

The Influence of the School. The twentieth century has seen many changes in our educational system, and one important change has been that in the personal relationships between pupils and teacher to the benefit of both. Schools are far happier places than they were at the beginning of the century, and psychology must take some credit for bringing about this change. Some of the main investigations underlying this trend will first be outlined.

Lewin, Lippitt, and White,[5] exposed four groups of 10-year-old boys to what they described as *authoritarian, democratic* and *laissez-faire* group atmospheres. In the authoritarian atmosphere the leader determined the policy and most of the boys' activities, and he remained aloof from the group except when actually participating in some activity. Within the democratic group there was discussion about policy; the leader suggested alternative procedures; the boys could form their own groups and the leader tended to be a group-member without depriving the children of initiative. The leader in the laissez-faire group provided material and gave information, but only when asked. The individual members arrived at

[4] See Lovell, K., *An Introduction to Human Development.* London: Macmillan, 1968, Ch. 6.

[5] Lewin, K., Lippitt, R., and White, R. K., 'Patterns of Aggressive Behaviour in Experimentally Created "Social Climates",' *J. soc. Psychol.,* 1939, **10,** 271–299.

their own decisions, and the leader made little effort to interfere with the group at work or to participate in their work.

Summing up their findings, we can say that in the authoritatian atmosphere a good deal more emotional tension was built up. It would appear that the authoritarian leader is able to prevent the outbreak of open aggression, but is unable to stop the building up of latent aggression. The democratic leaders were liked more than the authoritarian leaders, and good morale was established in their groups. For morale involves working together for the common good and for common goals, and relations of friendliness rather than of hostility to other members of the group. In the laissez-faire group there was considerable frustration and disruption. The absence of constructive group-activity led to idleness, and this in turn led to some good-natured horseplay. Such behaviour tended to frustrate those who were trying to start constructive work.

Anderson[6] has studied what he termed *Dominative* and *Integrative* Behaviour in the classroom and in group play. In the former the child tries to satisfy his own needs when seeking some goal, regardless of anyone else. Energy has to be expended against other children; the dominative child has to fight his way through either by physical or verbal attacks. But in integrative behaviour the child discovers ways of reaching the goal which are satisfying to himself and to other children. Anderson found, as others have also, that integrative behaviour on the part of one child elicits integrative behaviour in others. This kind of behaviour should surely be encouraged, since it satisfies the needs of the members of the group and minimises the amount of conflict between them. Indeed, it is the basis of co-operative enterprise.

Anderson[7] and his associates have also studied the effect of the teacher's classroom personality on his pupils. Thus J. E. Brewer has brought forward evidence which indicates that integrative behaviour on the part of the teacher tends to bring about integrative behaviour in the child. Obversely, dominative behaviour in the teacher tended to bring about resistance on the part of the children and more classroom mis-behaviour. Conflict between pupil and teacher was stimulated, and incentives and spontaneity on the part of the children stifled.

Such studies involving authoritarian and democratic classroom management have their weaknesses, since it is difficult to control the many variables involved.[8] Indeed, it has been suggested that the manner in which the teacher brings about classroom order and management is more

[6] Anderson, H. H., 'Domination and Integration in the Social Behaviour of Young Children in an Experimental Play Situation,' *Genet. Psychol. Monogr.*, 1937, **19**, 341–408.
[7] Anderson, H. H., and associates, *Appl. Psychol. Monogr.*, No. 6, 1945: No. 8, 1946: No. 11, 1946. Stanford, Cal.: Stanford University Press.
[8] The experiments mentioned were carried out in the U.S.A. and it cannot be assumed that the findings are necessarily applicable to other culture patterns. Dunham points out that the teachers' function as leader remains debatable. See Dunham, J., 'Appropriate Leadership Patterns,' *Educ. Res.*, 1965, **7**, 115–126.

important than the method itself. The idea of a task-orientated teacher, who, while maintaining self control, remains at the same time friendly and encouraging to pupils, seems to be forgotten in many studies when democratic teaching is contrasted with an authoritarian approach. Davey[9] points out that up to the year 1969 there was no evidence that either democratic or authoritarian leadership was consistently associated with higher achievement. But all agree that the group spirit of a class influences the conduct of its members. For example, Connor[10] has demonstrated among New Zealand children that pupils in classes with 'good' climates interact more with one another and with the teacher, have better emotional rapport with the teacher, are more socially cohesive as a group, and have a better attitude to school as a whole, compared with pupils in classes with 'poor' climates.

Thus from the work of Anderson and Lewin in the U.S.A. and others, we gain a somewhat clearer knowledge of the way in which pupils tend to react to different kinds of teachers; we also know that pupil attitudes are differently affected by different teachers. We should realise, then, that the child does not have a completely fixed personality, but varies considerably in his behaviour according to the treatment he receives from his teachers. At the same time the reaction of other boys and girls to him are of great importance. Indeed, studies show that the child's concept of himself is a learned structure, growing mainly from comments made by other people and from inferences drawn from his experiences. Furthermore, the teacher is influential in this respect, and it is possible to teach so that changes can be made in the Self-Picture.[11]

The implications of these findings are obvious from the point of view of the teacher. Pupils need to feel secure, to receive appreciation as individuals in their own right, to be able to contribute to the group life through co-operative enterprise, and they need an atmosphere in which authority is exercised in a clear and protective but democratic way.[12]

To satisfy these needs is not always an easy task for the teacher in our present educational organisation. He may succeed in setting work of the appropriate standard, so that all pupils in the class can get a measure of success, and this certainly helps to build up confidence and morale. But it is the matter of personal relationships with children and the exercise of authority that create the greatest difficulties for some teachers. Morris,[13] in a most stimulating discussion written mainly from the standpoint of

[9] Davey, A. G., 'Leadership in Relationship to Group Achievement,' *Educ. Research*, 1969, 11, 185–92.

[10] Connor, D. V., 'Behaviour in Class Groups of Contrasting Climate,' *Brit. J. Educ. Psychol.*, 1960, 30, 244–249.

[11] Staines, J. W., '"The Self-Picture" as a Factor in the Classroom,' *Brit. J. Educ. Psychol.*, 1958, 18, 97–111.

[12] This discussion on the influence of the school can be supplemented by studying Morris, J. F., 'The Social Psychology of Learning.' In *Development in Learning*—3 (Eds. Morris, J. F. and Lunzer, E. A.). London: Staples, 1969.

[13] Morris, B., in *Studies in Education*, No. 7. London: Evans, 1955.

psychoanalysis, suggests that teachers suffer from the fact that during their working hours they are in constant contact with immature minds. The well-adjusted teacher is able to react to immature behaviour with mature attitudes; the maladjusted teacher finds more difficulty in doing so. Again, when in authority, the teacher tends to behave as his parents and teachers behaved to him; and when under authority, as he behaved as a child. Here, too, resolution of the conflict between the parental and childish roles calls for personal maturity. There is, however, good evidence that teachers vary as widely in their personality traits as would any group of unselected people. Except that they tend to be of superior intelligence and verbal ability, they do not conform to any one personality type. Thus a proportion of teachers now selected for training, or likely to be so selected in the foreseeable future, are almost certain to be in some degree emotionally immature. Irrational reactions to teaching are likely to occur from time to time and to affect pupil-teacher relationships adversely. For example, through fear of aggression which a teacher may feel to be latent in his pupils, or through projection on to his pupils of his own unconscious aggression, he or she may continually display dominative behaviour and be afraid to relax and exercise more permissive control.[14]

On the other hand, not all maladjusted teachers seem to affect their pupils adversely. Indeed some may, because of their condition, go out of their way to help maladjusted pupils. According to Gladstone[15] whether or not the maladjusted teacher has an ill effect on his pupils depends upon the manner in which he tries to resolve his psychological tensions. The teacher who tries to make his adjustments through *intropunitive* patterns of behaviour (aggression or punishment directed towards the self with associated emotions of guilt and remorse), *or impunitive* behaviour (repression of the frustrating situation with no apparent aggression), there may be no bad effect on the pupils, although the teacher may not be happy himself. But when there are *extrapunitive* responses (aggression directed to an external object or person with the associated emotions of anger and resentment) it seems certain that there will be an adverse effect upon the pupil-teacher relationships and on the psychological adjustment of the pupils.

It is not possible in this book to discuss ways in which teachers may best be helped to come to terms with the child within themselves, to reduce their own anxiety and consequently their own aggression, and to handle their own ambivalence. But the very fact that people are made aware of the personal problems which they are likely to encounter may affect, for the good, their conscious behaviour, since some degree of insight is a

[14] Long ago A. Freud wrote, 'I hold, . . . that the teacher . . . should have learnt to know and control his own conflicts before he begins his educational work. If this is not so, the pupils merely serve as more or less suitable material on which to abreact his own unconscious and unsolved difficulties.'

[15] Gladstone, R., 'Do Maladjusted Teachers cause Maladjustment? A Re-review,' *J. except. Child.*, 1948, **15**, 65–70.

prerequisite of rational conduct. Wall[16] has suggested that the psychology course in the training of teachers should, amongst other things:

(a) Help students to understand the unconscious elements in their own mental life which determine their attitudes and behaviour.

(b) Show the importance of personal relationships between individuals and groups in school life.

(c) Help students to carry over to the classroom what they have learnt about themselves and the psychology of groups.

Continuity of Personality Dispositions. A number of long-term studies of the same children are now available which throw some light on the question of the continuity of personality development. Peck and Havighurst[17] showed that the degree of conscience development and emotional independence at 10 years of age were highly correlated with similar variables at age 16, suggesting the stability of these personality dispositions over the six-year period. Further, Kagan and Moss[18] have reported their findings in respect of 44 males and 45 females who were studied from the early months of life until adolescence; indeed, 71 were studied until they were at ages varying between 19 and 29. The most consistent of their findings was that many kinds of behaviour shown by the child between 6 and 10 years of age, and a few during the 3–6 period, were moderately good predictors of related behaviour exhibited during adulthood. For example, passive withdrawal from stressful situations, involvement in intellectual mastery, anxiety in social situations, dependence on family, ease with which anger is aroused, identification with one's sex-role, and pattern of adult sexual behaviour, were related to analogous behaviour dispositions during early school years. But the stability of these dispositions was greatly dependent on the extent to which the culture pattern encouraged them. For example, the stability of behaviour in respect of aggression and sexuality was greater in males than in females, for Western society frowns on these dispositions in the girl more than in the case of a boy. Cultural roles thus play a great part in determining both behaviour change and stability of behaviour.

The Cinema. Many studies have been made of the effects of the cinema on the behaviour of children, whether for good or for ill. In the United Kingdom the best known investigation is given in the Wheare report.[19] In this it is suggested that the cinema is not a primary cause of delinquency or moral laxity among children under 16, although it may be a contributory factor in a complex of moral and social factors which underlie delin-

[16] Wall, W. D., *Education and Mental Health*. London: Harrap, 1955.
[17] Peck, R. F. and Havighurst, R. J., *The Psychology of Character Development*. New York: Wiley, 1960.
[18] Kagan, J. and Moss, H. A., *Birth to Maturity*. London: Wiley, 1962.
[19] *Report of the Departmental Committee on Children and the Cinema*. London: H.M.S.O., 1950.

quency.[20] It is shown that nightmares, over-excitability and other forms of nervous strain do frequently follow on children's visits to the cinema.[21] Moreover, the report makes it clear that the amount of hooliganism, sexual stimulation, or mischievous behaviour directly attributable to films, and imitated closely from them, is not large. Nevertheless, manners, standards of behaviour and moral values are all affected. This investigation, together with the results from American studies, strongly suggests that the cinema, by presenting false standards of living, gives a significance to strength, luck, beauty and money, out of all proportion to their place in real life. Any ill effects of the cinema may be cumulative and difficult to measure; sometimes, too, it may bring about a small change in the environment which may precipitate anti-social behaviour among children who are already disposed to delinquency.

Moreover, more recent work suggests that a display of aggressive behaviour in films may have ill effects. Bandura and Walters[22] have surveyed a number of studies in which children or adolescents have viewed aggressive behaviour mediated via the film. These studies uniformly indicated that *vicarious* participation in aggressive activity increases, rather than decreases, the frequency and intensity of aggressive responses in the viewers. Experimental evidence thus gives little support for the hypothesis that aggressive behaviour in others may have a cathartic value for the viewer. Most studies have, however, been carried out before the spate of violence and sex currently seen in films, so the position may be worse than Bandura and Walters suggest.

But the cinema also has potential for good. Much useful information is presented, and the lives of great and good people are often portrayed. Investigations also suggest that attitudes to intolerance[23] and gambling[24] can be changed for the better by means of films. An important factor seems to be the attitude taken by the actor with whom the children identify themselves. If his attitude is one of condemnation towards undesirable conduct, children are more likely to be influenced in the same direction.

Radio and Television. Many large-scale studies have been carried out in the U.S.A. (but not the U.K.) into effects of radio on the personal develop-

[20] Healy and Bronner also concluded that only a very small percentage of delinquents are clearly motivated by what they have seen in the cinema. See Healy, W., and Bronner, A. F., *New Light on Delinquency and its Treatment*. New Haven: Yale University Press, 1936.

[21] Generally confirmed by the findings of Renshaw *et al*. See Renshaw, S., Miller, V. L., and Marquis, D., *Children's Sleep*. New York: Macmillan, 1933.

[22] Bandura, A. and Walters, R. H., 'Aggression' in *Child Psychology*: the Sixty-second Yearbook of the National Society for the Study of Education. University of Chicago Press, 1963.

[23] See Rosen, I. C., 'The Effect of the Motion Picture "Gentlemen's Agreement" on Attitude towards Jews,' *J. Psychol.*, 1948, **26**, 525–536.

[24] Thurstone, L. L., 'Influence of Motion Pictures on Children's Attitudes,' *J. soc. Psychol.*, 1931, **2**, 291–305.

ment of children. The upshot of these is that most programmes hardly affect their social and personal development. Some items, such as discussion of current affairs, programmes involving the lives of great people, or the appreciation of the arts, may be of positive help. Programmes involving violence, however, are sometimes thought to provide an outlet for 'pent up' feelings. Others maintain that if this kind of programme is repeatedly experienced the cathartic effect is lost. Indeed, unrealistic and unsocial situations on the radio, as in films, may have a cumulative effect working against sound personal development.

The investigation sponsored by the Nuffield Foundation[25] in the U.K. was a thorough study into the effects of television on children in the 1950's. In brief it suggested that T.V. is not as black as it is painted nor is it the instrument of great enlightenment that it is sometimes claimed to be. It is not generally true that T.V. makes children do badly at school or that it makes them listless, passive or more aggressive. It does not generally keep children from youth clubs, and while it does not stimulate much activity it can broaden interests. After T.V. has been in the home for some while viewers read as many books as children without sets, but they read fewer comics. The report urges parents to set a good example and help children to view selectively, and points out that since 75 per cent of 10–11 year olds view until 9 p.m., and one-third of 13–14 year olds watch until 10 p.m., more care should be exercised in planning adult programmes.

Increasing numbers of social scientists in the U.S.A. now seem to be of the opinion that continued exposure to violence in films or on T.V. is likely to increase the use of violence among children who watch. At the time of writing, however, no published results are available regarding the newer studies, nor are data available as yet from a current British enquiry into the relationship between long-term exposure to T.V. violence and the behaviour and attitudes of adolescent boys.

Reading Material. Surprisingly enough, little direct evidence has been reported of the desirable effects of good reading matter, although in the writer's opinion it is hardly possible to deny that good literature may be beneficial to children. There are, however, many who stress the evil effects of bad literature. In reading the child can turn back again to the most lurid parts and read them again, whereas the most sordid parts of a film or radio or television programme can only be seen or heard once. Thus Healy and Bronner[26] consider that cheap novels and magazines have a bad effect on character-development.

Comics and comic-strips have come in for much criticism on both sides of the Atlantic. Some of these are undoubtedly of help to children because they contain much information, or because they help children to solve

[25] Himmelweit, H. T., Oppenheim, A. N., and Vince, P., *Television and the Child.* London: Oxford University Press, 1958.
[26] Healy and Bronner, *op. cit.*

problems associated with the attitudes of others to them, or with their own feelings towards others. Most, probably, do not affect social and personal development for good or ill. But a few which repeatedly carry stories stressing crime, violence, sadism and sex, do harm. The cathartic value of such literature has occasionally been stressed, but against this many contend that the constant reading of unpleasant material must have an ill effect on some children. True it might be only one factor operating, but this is no reason why children should be exposed to harmful literature which might precipitate anti-social conduct.

Values.[27] Values may be defined as more or less stable patterns of attitudes built up around some object like a school, church or club; or around some type of behaviour such as being reliable, or being considerate to old people. They are attitudes which are dominated by the individual's interpretation of the worth of the person, object, or idea to him, in the light of his goals. Our values generally guide our behaviour although this is not always so. A child whose values lead him to tell the truth may lie when there is great pressure on him from the environment, or when he has some pressing personal need. Thus when personal needs are very strong, children who would not do so otherwise, may steal or cheat. Well-developed systems of values, however, are of the greatest importance to the child, for they help to make him feel secure, and, according as they are social or anti-social in nature, they largely determine his behaviour in situations where moral issues are involved.

Values seem to be built up slowly in much the same way as our secondary needs are acquired, according to Hull's theories. Everyone praises the child when he is honest; the child likes praise; so ultimately he considers it a good thing to be honest. For honesty reduced a need in the first place and later became a need itself. Furthermore, he slowly builds up a generalised concept of honesty arising out of his being honest in many different situations—in the home, at school and in the shop. However, other values seem to be built up through unconscious imitation of those whom the individual looks upon as his 'ideal'; and with the more able children through reflective thinking that results in generalised moral principles. Naturally, the values a child acquires will depend very much upon those which exist in the sub-culture pattern in which he is brought up. Each value will have an emotional attachment associated with it, and each will bring satisfaction, usually in the form of social approval. Broadly speaking, in our society moral-social values include honesty, loyalty, fair play, kindness, reliability and respect for human beings, among many others. Thus a thief has a bad character in our society as a whole, but he may be a good character (kind, loyal, etc.) to members of a sub-group of thieves.

[27] The remainder of this chapter should be read in conjunction with Lovell, K., *An Introduction to Human Development*. London: Macmillan, 1968, Ch. 7.

Character is thus personality evaluated against a system of moral-social values.[28]

Pringle and Edwards[29] report a study of 226 pupils aged 10–11 years and of wide ability range. They found that only 25 per cent chose the 'ideal person' from the family circle; more frequently the choice was a person from the films, television, radio, sport or books. This is the reverse of what was found 30 years earlier. The chief reasons for their choice of persons were that the 'ideal' was good (efficient); good (kind); and adventurous. Again, the chief types of actions regarded as morally wicked by the pupils were: murder, physical cruelty, stealing, cruelty to animals, lying and damage to property. However, the less able children more often choose their 'ideal person' from within the family circle, and their moral judgments were more blurred in complex situations; while bright pupils were found to pay more attention to motives than to results of actions.

Conscience. Psychologists are very careful today about the use of the term 'conscience' though they are fully aware of its importance. Conscience consists, fundamentally, in what the individual thinks ought to be done, and this may often conflict with what he actually does. It can control behaviour and also arouse guilt after a transgression has been committed.

It was seen earlier in this chapter that, according to psycho-analytic theory, the conscience or super-ego is built up by the child through his gradually interiorising certain pictures of his parents and others. Certain parts of the love-object are also copied or introjected by the child. This form of learning can be more permanent and generalisable to more situations than other forms of social learning; moreover it can exist in conflict with other aspects of the personality. Argyle[30] points out that the most plausible explanation of introjection is that parents teach and persuade children to react to their own behaviour in certain ways. For example, the parent might say, 'You are naughty and ought to be punished'. The child thereby acquires his own self-reactions, and he can enact, in fantasy, a parent's response even in the absence of the parent. Argyle thinks that introjection takes place for some children, but not for others, especially from the parent of the same sex and when there is a warm and dependent relationship. Permanent introjection does not take place until 5–6 years of age, and although there may be an upper age limit when parental exhortation is introjected, the reactions of a peer group to one's behaviour may, under similar conditions to those listed above, be introjected in adolescence. In more recent years, then, psychologists have come to doubt whether the

[28] Compare Hemming, J., *Brit. J. Educ. Psychol.*, 1957, **27**, 77–88, for an article under the general title 'Symposium: The Development of Children's Moral Values.' Articles by other authors appeared in later volumes.

[29] Pringle, M. L. K. and Edwards, J. B., 'Some Moral Concepts and Judgements of Junior School Children,' *Brit. J. Soc. clin. Psychol.*, 1964, 3, 196–215.

[30] Argyle, M., 'Introjection: A Form of Social Learning,' *Brit. J. Psychol.*, 1964, **55**, 385–390.

earlier years are all-important in forming conscience. Both Sherrif[31] and Kardiner[32] have said in so many words that conscience is at least partly developed by later conditioning and learning in the social environment, so that home, school, church and playmates all have a hand in its formation. In other words, the conscience of the older child or adult is largely determined by the moral-social values that have been established.[33]

Character-Development. When we attempt to build up values in children, one important guiding principle is that values are most likely to be developed and to guide behaviour when they are based upon individual or personal experience. Children seem to learn, as we have already said, what are the moral-social values which their society cherishes,[34] by experiencing satisfaction from those actions which are acceptable. Thus goals, rewards and punishments are essential in character-training as in other forms of learning.

Moral-social values, then, are best learnt when they are linked to specific actions, so that ultimately generalised moral-social values emerge out of the matrix of the child's own experience. These values cannot be presented to him like sets of facts learnt in school. Thus parents and teachers should use everyday experience to 'drive home' lessons relating to honesty, lying, cheating, cruelty, selfishness and so forth, and not merely preach to children.

Rewards seem to be somewhat more effective than punishment in developing good character, as in learning. It is, however, well established that certainty of reward or punishment following a given action is more important than the magnitude of the reward or the severity of the punishment. It is important that the attitude of home and school should be clear and consistent in its treatment of a given type of behaviour. No character worth having can develop where an action is rewarded one day (need reduced) and punished next day (need increased).[35]

Ideally, parents and teachers should do all they can to build up what we call conscience or internalised motivation so that a child's behaviour is no longer controlled merely by external rewards and punishments. One should attempt, as far as possible, to show the child how each new problem in conduct is related to the generalised values which he has built up, and which have sentiments and satisfactions associated with them. A given act

[31] Sherrif, M., *An Outline of Social Psychology.* New York: Harper, 1948.

[32] Kardiner, A., *The Individual and His Society.* New York: Columbia University Press, 1939.

[33] Compare Stephenson, G. M., *The Development of Conscience.* London: Routledge and Kegan Paul, 1966. See also Williams, N. and Williams, S., *The Moral Development of Children.* London: Macmillan, 1970, Ch. 4.

[34] Some sections of the community will have different moral-social values than others. Thus Christians and non-Christians of the same socio-economic class will agree about cruelty and unkindness, but differ, perhaps, about values associated with marriage and divorce.

[35] But see Wright, D., 'The Punishment of Children. A Review of Experimental Studies,' *J. Moral Education,* 1972, 1, 221–229.

of behaviour is then considered by the child as being in or out of keeping with his values.

Many studies have been made of the growth of moral judgments. For example, Piaget's[36] evidence suggested three main stages. There is first the period of heteronomy which lasts from about four to eight years of age. In this, rules and laws are regarded as having been given by adults and older children, and are sacred and fixed for all occasions. It is not the spirit but the letter of the law which must be observed. Piaget designated the second stage as one of equality. Rewards and punishments are now distributed equally in the sense that the latter must be related to the misdeed, and the pupil is no longer dominated by the letter of the law. The third stage is one of equity. Here the relationship is based not merely on equality, but extenuating circumstances are considered and allowances are made for individual motives and needs. Kohlberg's[37] work also follows in the tradition of Piaget, but he divides his moral judgments into six stages, for by using more difficult questions he was able to show that moral judgment increases to 17 or so.[38]

Whiteman and Kosier[39] have also studied the growth of moralistic judgments. They scored a response as mature or immature on the basis of whether a subject's decision concerning the naughtiness of another child was based on the latter's intentions in relation to the act, or on the material consequences of his behaviour (i.e. on the amount of, say, damage involved). It was found that the ability to formulate mature judgments increased with age over the 7–12 year period, and with increase in IQ at each age level. But the ability was not related to personality characteristics as rated by teachers, sex, or being a member of certain boys' and girls' organisations. But it did seem to be affected by their attendance in ungraded (American) classes since it brought children of different ages in close contact with one another. It seems clear from these studies that the growth of moral judgment is linked with cognitive growth. However moral judgment does not ensure moral behaviour.

It will be appreciated that moral judgment is but one aspect of moral development. Williams and Williams[40] suggest that other aspects include, say, concern for others, and conscience, all of which are likely to affect behaviour. Moral development and its antecedents form a very complex problem which is not well understood at present. Moreover, moral

---

[36] Piaget, J., *The Moral Judgment of the Child*. London: Kegan Paul, 1932.

[37] Kohlberg, L., 'The Development of Children's Orientation towards a Moral Order,' *Vita Humana*, 1963, 6, 11–33.

[38] Nothing written in this chapter is to be taken as necessarily contradicting the view held by some theologians that there is within all human beings a natural tendency to recognise some aspects of moral law. For example, all men and women seem to have some respect for human life.

[39] Whiteman, K. H. and Kosier, K. P., 'Development of Children's Moralistic Judgements: Age, Sex, IQ and certain Personal Experimental Variables,' *Child Developm.*, 1964, 15, 831–841.

[40] Williams, N. and Williams, S., *op. cit.*

judgment does not ensure moral behaviour as we shall see again later. The former is related to cognitive growth and social experience as we saw earlier. Readers interested in making a further study of the problem should also consult Hoffman,[41] Bull,[42] Graham and Kay[43].

An Experiment in the Measurement of Character. Reference must be made to the very thorough study of character of a large number of children by Hartshorne,[44] May and Shuttleworth. Although their results were reported in 1928, 1929 and 1930, their experiment has not been surpassed by later work either for experimental design or for thoroughness. But not all psychologists accept the interpretations which the authors give to their work.

The results are reported under three headings: studies in deceit, studies in service, and studies in the organisation of character. In the first investigation, they found that a child's deceitfulness or honesty seemed to depend upon the nature of the situation, its importance to the child, and his feelings at the time. He may, therefore, cheat in one situation but not in another. In the classroom the most common motive for cheating was the desire to do well. Here is a clear case of a personal need, the desire to be well thought of by others, causing a dishonest act. Furthermore, in classes where there was a friendly co-operative atmosphere there was less cheating than in classes where teachers used more restrictive methods.

From their evidence the authors suggest that much moral behaviour is specific to, and conditioned by, the situation. On the other hand moral knowledge did correlate to a moderate extent with moral conduct, and the authors found that many children showed a certain consistency or stability in moral conduct, which they termed *integration* (not to be confused with Anderson's Integrative Behaviour). It is not implied that integration necessarily denotes a good character, but rather that an integrated or consistent person gives responses that are organised in such a way that his conduct may be predicted. He may be a good or a bad character, although other things being equal, the integrated child tended to be honest. It seems, indeed, that integration is linked with the opposite of neuroticism.

In 1934 the data from the character tests was analysed by Maller.[45] He concluded that there was a general factor common to all the tests, which could be identified with the readiness to forego an immediate gain for the

[41] Hoffman, M. L., 'Moral Development.' In *Manual of Child Psychology* (Ed. Mussen, P.), 3rd Edition. Volume 2, 261–359. London: Wiley, 1970.

[42] Bull, N. J., *Moral Judgment from Childhood to Adolescence.* London: Routledge and Kegan Paul, 1969.

[43] Graham, D., *Moral Learning and Development.* London: Batsford, 1972. Kay, W., *Moral Development.* London: Allen and Unwin, 1970, Revised Edition.

[44] Hartshorne, H., and May, M. A., *Studies in Deceit.* New York: Macmillan, 1928. Hartshorne, H., and May, M. A., *Studies in Service and Self Control.* New York: Macmillan, 1929. Hartshorne, H., May, M. A., and Shuttleworth, F. K., *Studies in the Organisation of Character.* New York: Macmillan, 1930.

[45] Maller, J. B., 'General and Specific Factors in Character,' *J. soc. Psychol.,* 1934, 5, 97–102.

sake of a remote but greater gain. A similar definition of good character comes from Washbourne.[46] He concludes that those of good character possess 'impulse judgment', which he defines as the capacity to weigh an immediate satisfaction against a future satisfaction and arrive at a decision as to which of the two is more desirable.

Grinder's[47] more recent work in this field also suggests that although the growth of a mature moral judgment depends on the child's interaction with the social environment, such judgments do not guarantee correct behaviour. The evidence indicates that the behavioural and cognitive aspects of the mature judgment, especially in boys, seem to develop independently of one another. When faced with temptation, children's compliance with social standards seems to be more a function of social learning than of changes in cognitive structure.

Conclusion. Character then, as such, does not seem to be inherited. We inherit, it is true, a central nervous system, cerebral mechanisms, a glandular system, and organic drives of different strengths (e.g. sex drive), all of which will affect our capacity for responding to environmental stimuli and learning. Similarly, drugs and brain lesions can affect behaviour; while it is likely that something in the nature of social and altruistic tendencies is innate, so that there may be innate potentialities for acquiring moral values. Generally though, we build up character, within the limits set up by the above-mentioned factors, by reacting in different ways to our environment. Those concerned with promoting correct habits in children should give them ample opportunity to practise the kinds of behaviour society desires. Readers would do well to study *Citizens of Tomorrow*[48] for a summary of the influences affecting the moral and social developments of adolescents. The writers have provided a great deal of useful information, although here and there it is possible that the reports are coloured by surmise, prejudice and wishful thinking. One point stressed is that teachers might attempt to develop in the child the concept of work as an essential contribution to the health and wealth of the community.

One concept of personality structure provided by Eysenck[49] gives a plausible hypothesis regarding the link between the physiology of the central nervous system and our social attitudes and values. Following Pavlov he suggests that fundamental neurological structures determine, say, the degree to which the individual shows reminiscence, or the ease with which he can be conditioned. He gives evidence to show that extra-

[46] Washbourne, J. N., 'Definitions in Character Measurement,' *J. soc. Psychol.*, 1931, 1, 114–119.
[47] Grinder, R. E., 'Relations between Behavioural and Cognitive Dimensions of Conscience in Middle Childhood,' *Child Developm.*, 1964, 35, 881–891.
[48] *Citizens of Tomorrow.* London: King George's Jubilee Trust, 1955.
[49] Eysenck, H. J., *Sense and Nonsense in Psychology.* London: Pelican Books, 1957.

verts condition less easily than introverts. Thus under varying environmental influences, introverts are more likely to be easily socialised than extraverts, and thus are more likely to have greater persistence, a higher level of aspiration, and to control their sexual impulses better than extraverts, since these traits are valued in our cultural pattern. Finally, Eysenck suggests that there appears to be a definite tendency for introverted people to develop tender-minded attitudes (e.g. pacifism, go back to religion, etc.), and extraverted people to develop tough-minded attitudes (e.g. companionate marriage, Jews too powerful, harsh treatment for criminals, etc.).

Although he has developed his views still further, Eysenck[50] has clearly pointed out the need for experimental verification of his theory. But, if there is any degree of truth in his suggestions, then character education should not take the same form for all children. 'Spare the rod and spoil the child' may be quite appropriate to the extraverted, hard-to-condition type of child; whereas modern methods which are more free and easy might be more appropriate to the introverted, anxious, easy-to-please type child. Siegman[51] had reported a positive correlation between extraversion and anti-social behaviour in male students but not in a comparable female group. The author interprets these findings in terms of the male (or female) identifying himself (or herself) with the sex-role that the individual is expected to play. In the American culture aggression and acting out are more condoned in the male, and more frowned upon in the female.

[50] Eysenck, H. J., 'Symposium: The Development of Moral Values in Children VII—The Contribution of Learning Theory,' *Brit. J. Educ. Psychol.*, 1960, 30, 11–21.

[51] Siegman, A. W., 'A Cross Cultural Investigation of the Relationship between Introversion-Extraversion, Social-Attitudes and Anti-Social Behaviour,' *Brit. J. soc. clin. Psychol.* 1963, 2, 169–208.

Chapter Fifteen

THE PRE-SCHOOL CHILD

BIRTH usually occurs about 280 days from the end of the last menstrual period before conception. If birth takes place earlier the child is said to be prematurely born. But birth does not mark the beginning of the individual. Heartbeat commences four weeks after conception, the mother reports feeling definite foetal movements at about four and a half months, and respiratory movements can be evoked by the fifth to sixth month if appropriate stimulation is employed. A few studies have suggested that the foetus can be conditioned. Spelt[1] studied the responses of a number of foetuses aged between seven and nine months by applying small flat drums (tambours) to the mothers' abdomen. This study claimed not only that conditioned responses were obtained, but also their extinction and spontaneous recovery. A few investigators have pointed out the possibility that certain of the reflexes of the newborn are responses to conditioning before birth, although others reject this thesis and stress that the responses of very young babies are due to innate programming and maturation rather than conditioning.

The four weeks following a full-term delivery, are known as the neo-natal period.[2] During this time the child has certain physiological adjustments to make; for example, his breathing and bodily temperature are irregular at first, but we are here more interested in his psychology. There is evidence that the neonate is sensitive to some kinds of visual stimulation, and while there is also evidence that he can hear, there is no certainty that he can discriminate pitch although high-pitched notes bring out more responses than low-pitched ones. Certain conditioned reflexes can be brought about by environmental stimulation.[3] Moreover, by the end of the first four weeks of life the child begins to experiment by trial and error and to distinguish, for example, between things that are, say, suckable (e.g. cot blanket) from those that are not (e.g. rattle). It is in these early acts of discrimination that the origins of thinking are located. Some learning takes place in the neonate resulting from his sensori-motor experience although, as Hebb[4] has reminded us, the first learning of the newborn (like the early learning of the adult who suddenly receives his

[1] Spelt, D. K., 'The Conditioning of the Human Foetus in Utero,' *J. Exp. Psychol.*, 1948, **38**, 338–346.
[2] For fuller accounts of this period see Gesell, A., *The First Five Years of Life*. London: Methuen. Also Pratt, K. C. in *Manual of Child Psychology*. London: Chapman & Hall, 1954.
[3] See Lipsitt, L. P., 'Can Human New-Borns Learn?' *Bull. Brit. Psychol. Soc.*, 1966, **19**, 71–72.
[4] Hebb, D. O., *The Organisation of Behaviour*. London: Chapman & Hall, 1949.

sight after having been blind from birth) is very inefficient as far as detectable effects on behaviour are concerned. One of the most interesting findings is that the neonate does not appear to have differentiated expressions, e.g. rage or fear, but rather a general agitation or excitement whether stimulated by, say, hunger or pricking with a needle.[5] Or at the most, the emotional expression of the infant in the first four weeks is not differentiated beyond the pleasant and the unpleasant. It is later maturation and experience that will channel the emotional expressions into different patterns, so that responses emerge that correspond roughly to the emotional behaviour of adults and are given names like fear and joy. The fact that different patterns of emotional expression emerge after the age of one month does not in any way prove or disprove that such behaviour is due in part to innate tendencies. Before its first birthday the infant will show clear signs of anger, affection, fear, jealousy and other emotions, but it is very doubtful to what extent these are native or acquired.

Motor Development. There is evidence that the neonate's responses to stimulation tend to involve the greater part of the body. But during infancy and childhood there seems to be some development in the direction of increasing specificity of response, so that a given stimulus tends to bring about movement in limited parts of the body only. This trend in motor development has not yet been established as a general rule, but it seems to hold true in many instances. For example, when the five-year-old first attempts to write, he often contorts his tongue, lips, and legs, to get some degree of co-ordination with his arm, wrist, and fingers. Later, the arm, wrist and fingers can work independently of the remainder of the body. It is important to note that some workers (e.g. Gesell) consider that this trend from mass movement to a greater specificity of response is a result of maturation and little to do with learning. Others deny this and claim that the greater differentiation of response is acquired as a result of training and experience.

One very interesting response of the newborn is the palmar or 'grasp' reflex. Sherman, Sherman and Flory[6] report that rather more than 10 per cent of the infants in the sample they studied could support their own weight by grasping a thin rod. This response of some infants has long been known and has caused considerable curiosity because of its similarity to the behaviour of the apes. It does not, of course, prove that man or his ancestors lived in trees. The response seems to be an involuntary or reflex action, involving only the palm and fingers. As the infant gets older the involuntary type of grasp disappears and the voluntary type appears although later there is probably overlapping of these two.

It is in the over-all field of motor development that the child appears to

[5] See Sherman, M., 'The Differentiation of Emotional Response in Infants,' *J. comp. Psychol.*, 1927, 7, 265–284, 335–351; 1928, 8, 385–394.

[6] Sherman, M., Sherman, I. C., and Flory, D. C., 'Infant Behaviour,' *Comp. Psychol. Mongr.*, 1936, 12, No. 4.

make the most relative progress in the first year of life. At birth he is helpless, although it must be stressed that the baby comes into the world with sufficient equipment to survive in a normal environment. For example, its autonomic nervous system[7] is developed and soon after birth the following responses (among many others) may be observed: crying, swallowing, opening and closing mouth, sucking, opening and closing eyelids, widening or narrowing pupils in response to light, kicking.[8] But progress is rapid and by the time of his first birthday the child can usually stand upright. A great deal of our knowledge of the motor development in young children comes from the work of Gesell and his associates, also Piaget, although the stages listed below can be noted by any observant adult. Once again it is stressed that any ages which are given are averages and any single infant may depart significantly from them.

During the neo-natal period the infant seems to spend most of his time eating, sleeping and crying, and it is not until three to four months of age that he can hold his head steadily erect when his body is held in a sitting position. At the age of six or seven months he can sit upright for a short while, and as soon as this happens he can observe, from his cot or pram, a great deal more of his environment; after this time, moreover, adults increasingly play with a baby. These are important events from the point of view of a child's contact with the world and his general education. Soon after the ninth month many, but not all children, can be seen crawling on the floor. Sometimes this involves moving along the floor in a prone position; at other times the child moves along on hands and knees, or hands and feet. Again, some children move by rolling on their sides, while others seem to omit the crawling stage altogether. This is a particularly trying period for mothers, who are glad when the infant is up on his feet. By ten months or so the young child can usually pull himself erect by means of the bars of the cot or play-pen; at twelve months he can walk with help, and at thirteen months he can take a few steps on his own. Progress in walking thereafter continues steadily, but even at two years of age, although the child can walk a good deal and even run, he is still a toddler and unsteady at times. By the time of his third birthday, however, he is walking and running with ease.

The study of Gutteridge[9] into the acquisition of motor skills by nearly 2,000 children between 2 and 7 years of age is particularly illuminating. It was found amongst other things that rather less than half of the 3-year-

[7] The autonomic nervous system is self-governing and appears to act independently of the central nervous system although the two systems are intimately connected. It supplies innervation to the muscles of the heart, and to the involuntary muscles of the walls of the blood vessels, stomach and intestines. It also supplies the motor secretory nerves to different glands, and other organs not under voluntary nervous control. See Chapter 19.

[8] See Dennis, W., 'A Description and Classification of the Responses of the Newborn Infant,' *Psychol. Bull.*, 1934, **31**, 5–22.

[9] Gutteridge, M. V., 'A Study of Motor Achievements of Young Children,' *Arch. Psychol.*, N.Y., 1939, **34**, No. 244.

olds could jump, but nearly three-quarters of the 4½-year-olds, and four-fifths of the 5-year-olds had acquired this skill. Some 20 per cent of the 4-year-olds could throw a ball well, this percentage increasing to nearly seventy-five at 5½ years. At first when youngsters throw, there are mass movements of all the body; later they throw with two hands and finally with one. Gutteridge also found that almost all 4-year-olds could ride a tricycle with great skill. Other researches have shown that motor skills are dependent not only on height, weight, strength and neuromuscular maturity, but also on intelligence, motivation and social-emotional maturity. Furthermore, if children have plenty of toys and apparatus to play with and have the opportunity to watch other children using such equipment, then motor development is helped forward.[10]

Social-Emotional Development. It seems that the baby at first aims solely at the gratification of his biological needs. But during the first months and years of life, this tendency is slowly changed by the growth of the self or ego. The development of sense organs, the capacity to distinguish between sensations that arise within and without the body, the increasing ability to control what seems to be innate tendencies, the acquisition of language, and the greater control of motor activities, all help towards the formation of the self. So the developing ego, while still wishing to live by the pleasure principle, is more and more affected by reality—the relationships with adults and the demands of society. It seems likely, therefore, that the growth of the ego could be affected by the relationship between the infant and his parents; and workers such as Bowlby,[11] Goldfarb, Hadfield and Spitz, stress that the quality of the early relationship between mother and child is a determining factor in the development of personality (cf. Bowlby's views concerning causation of delinquency).

We accept the view that social and emotional development depend upon the environment as well as on maturation, while it is probable that the emotional relationships established between the child and his parents, especially with his mother, are important. Thus if he is sure of his parents' love he will, it is assumed, feel safe and secure and will be the more likely to stretch out and make advances to other people. On the other hand, if his parents are over-possessive and he becomes very dependent on them, or feels rejected by them, it seems possible that he will become retarded in establishing satisfactory social-emotional relationships with others. We have already seen in Chapter 14 that the evidence of Hewitt and Jenkins[12] is among the best we have supporting the view that parents' rejection, neglect or repression, is associated with later aggressive, delinquent or inhibited behaviour respectively in their children. But as we also pointed

[10] Jones, T. D., 'The Development of Certain Motor Skills and Play Activities in Young Children,' *Child Developm. Monogr.*, 1939, No. 26.

[11] See Bowlby, J., *Maternal Care and Mental Health*. Geneva: World Health Organisation, 1952.

[12] Hewitt, L. E, and Jenkins, R. L., *Fundamental Patterns of Maladjustment. The Dynamics of their Origin*. Illinois: Green, 1946.

out, the design of their experiment was such that it could not reveal whether the relationship found between parent attitude and child behaviour was due to inheritance or upbringing.

Again, it has been suggested that one effect of a child's being deprived of his mother during infancy is poor academic work at school. Such a child does not necessarily appear unintelligent, but seems to lack interest and does not care very much what others think of him. Such children are sometimes termed 'affectionless', and it has been pointed out that the capacity for feeling what others think of one may, in part, determine the effort that a child will put into his school work. It has also been suggested that the over-protected infant develops into the hard-working schoolchild, although such may show signs of instability. However, what workers in this field have not established is whether the traits which these children exhibit are in fact due to their having been deprived of maternal love or over-protected. Such children may have had parents who were, on the average, more emotionally unstable than usual and who handed on these characteristics by heredity.[13]

Finally, we may note that Lewis[14] after studying 500 deprived children, has suggested that even when the child is deprived of his mother in the first one or two years of life, any damage may be compensated to some extent by good substitute mothering. These points are stressed, for while the child-mother relationships seem to be of importance, marked individual differences do occur in very young babies, and it would be incorrect to suggest on the evidence available at present that these relationships are the only vital issues, that they can completely offset innate differences in temperament, or that in all cases they can determine behaviour patterns emerging at different ages.[15] Schaefer and Bayley,[16] in a study of 27 boys and 27 girls carried through from three days of age until adolescence, indicated that the personality of the boy develops well if the mother is loving at an early age, and if at adolescence he is also granted autonomy. But their data

[13] For a cautious and critical review of relevant literature on maternal deprivation see: Rutter, M., *Maternal Deprivation, Reassessed*. Harmondsworth: Penguin, 1972.

[14] Lewis, H., *Deprived Children*. London: Oxford University Press, 1954.

[15] Bowlby has clearly indicated that children separated from parents before 4 years of age due to illness, but presumably not rejected, do not commonly develop into affectionless and delinquent characters. *See* Bowlby, J. *et al.*, 'The Effects of Mother Child Separation: a Follow Up Study,' *Brit. J. Med. Psychol.*, 1956, **29**, 211–247. *See also* Kellmer Pringle, M. L. and Bossio, V., 'Early, Prolonged Separation and Emotional Maladjustment,' *J. Child Psychology and Psychiatry*, 1960, **1**, 37–48. They show that early physical separation does not always lead to emotional difficulties. See also Yarrow, L. J., 'Maternal Deprivation: Toward an Empirical and Conceptual Revaluation,' *Psychol. Bull.*, 1961, **58**, 459–490. See also *Deprivation of Maternal Care: a Re-assessment of its Effects*. World Health Organisation, Public Health Papers, No. 14, 1962. Casler, L., 'Maternal Deprivation: A Critical Review of the Literature,' *Monogr. of Soc. for Res. in Child Developm.*, No. 80, Vol. 26, 1961.

[16] Schaefer, E. S. and Bayley, N., 'Maternal Behaviour, Child Behaviour, and their interrelations from Infancy through Adolescence,' *Monogr. of Soc. for Res. in Child Developm.*, 1964, No. 87.

suggest that in the case of the girl there is less carry over from the effects of early maternal behaviour. However, the adolescent girl seems to reflect more the present attitudes of the mother and that of the girls' interpersonal relationships at that time.

During the first year of life the child is markedly dependent upon the mother biologically (e.g. for food) and psychologically, but by the time of his first birthday he likes to have others around him and he has a great tendency to repeat antics which bring laughter to his audience. It seems, then, as if his own perception of other people's emotions helps him to establish his own early social relationships. By the age of fifteen months there is evidence of considerable curiosity. The infant, although he has begun to 'toddle' is by then developing an interest in the outside world away from himself and his parents. He will look into cupboards, overturn baskets, and generally pull and push any object that he is capable of moving. This seems but another phase in the process of the child's accommodating himself to the world around him.

From about the age of eighteen months to two and a half years, the child passes through what has been thought of by some as a period of self-will or aggression. It is certainly a time of concern to some parents. Broadly we may say that the child hates restraint, has frequent temper tantrums, builds up rituals around himself, is defiant, is slow to respond when called, or when he is told to perform some act, and generally seems to be unreasonable. Of course, the child is now running about, and not only are his demands increasing with age, but he is in a better position to make his demands felt. Furthermore, at this age, other children may be born into the family and there may be some sibling rivalry. In his play he is also impetuous, for he will run about for no apparent reason, play with a toy for a moment and then abandon it. Naturally, some control is necessary and parents and other adults encourage children to control their tempers by kind but firm action. Some frustration will help the child to set up a controlling force within himself and to adjust himself to the reality of the environment.

By the time of the third birthday or thereabouts, there is a considerable change in the child's behaviour, to the great satisfaction of his parents. He is more friendly, more obedient, and generally more amenable in his personal relationships with others. He now studies the emotional expression of adults and will try to please them, instead of being wilful and contrary as earlier. Further, while the two-year-old tends to be solitary in play and to remain aloof from other children, the three-year-old shows an interest in playing with others of his own age. Indeed, there is both a growth of sociability and independence throughout the third year of life. Between four and five years of age, the child likes to play in groups of two to five children, but sometimes he can be seen talking to, and playing with, some imaginary companion. Another characteristic of this age is that the child occasionally confuses fantasy with reality in his play. At the same time he is very talkative, is inclined to be 'bossy', and displays little regard for other children. Sometimes he shows a certain callousness and indifference, and he has been described at this age as ego-centric. Temper tantrums and outbursts of crying still occur, but not as frequently as they did at two years of age.

We now turn to discuss briefly the fears of young children. Arising out of the child's increasingly differentiated responses to his environment, we may observe what adults call fear by about six months of age. Bronson[17] has reviewed the studies which have been made of the development of fear in man and in certain other animals and concluded that three states can be detected. The first—a precursor to fear—is noted in the signs of distress which the infant makes to many different types of irregular and un-patterned stimuli involving, say, noise, movement or sight. Any action by the mother which involves contact with the infant seems to reduce these 'distress reactions'. In the second stage there emerges a fear of novelty presented visually; for example, strange objects or something familiar but in a strange setting. Here the visual presence of the mother can reduce the tension. The third and final stage is marked by the increasing ability of the child to handle novelty even when the mother is not present. Fear of animals appears a little later, but whether this fear is innate or acquired is not known with certainty. Valentine[18] seems to be of the opinion that it is innate, but others think that this fear arises from the fact that the child's first experience of an animal might be an unpleasant one or that the child has come to associate an animal with a strange noise, e.g. the barking of a dog. Lorenz[19] suggests that fear of snakes is due to an 'innate release mechanism' (see page 24) and begins to operate at about 3 years of age; this I.R.M. operating in some 50 per cent of people. During the first year or two of life, fear of the dark seems to be rare, but as the child grows older this becomes of greater importance. Another fear which makes its appearance at about the age of twelve months is that of being left alone, or of being abandoned by one's parents. Much has been said and written about the ill-effects resulting when young children are in hospital and separated from their parents. While such separation causes anxiety in some children, others spend much time in hospital without apparent ill-effects. It is possible, although we cannot be certain on this point, that anxiety following on separation is merely part of the symptoms of a child who is actually, or potentially maladjusted in any case.[20]

[17] Bronson, G. W., 'The Development of Fear in Man and other Animals,' *Child Developm.*, 1968, **39**, 409–431.
[18] Valentine, C. W., *The Psychology of Early Childhood*. London: Methuen, Third Edition, 1946.
[19] Lorenz, K. Z., *Discussions on Child Development*. London: Tavistock Publications, 1953, Eighth Discussion.
[20] See Edelston, H., 'Separation Anxiety in Young Children: A Study of Hospital Cases,' *Genet. Psychol. Monogr.*, 1943, **28**, 3–95. Some psychoanalysts may not necessarily agree with Edelston that while neurotic disturbances may be caused by separation anxiety, many children spent time in hospital without apparent ill-effects.

In Chapter 18 we suggest ways by which adults can help children who are emotionally disturbed. Here we merely repeat three general principles to be observed in bringing up young children in order to ensure as far as possible sound social-emotional development. First, give the child love and security. Secondly, recognise the stage at which the child is, let him develop as fully as possible at that stage and do everything feasible to facilitate his passing to the next stage. Thirdly, realise that it is sometimes necessary to restrain and frustrate the child (as in punishment). Loving but firm treatment as required aids psychological maturity; over-pampering and over-indulgence retards it.

Finally, it must be remembered that although children appear to pass through the same or similar stages of development, great individual differences do occur in any age group.

Language Development.[21] The acquisition of speech sounds by babies seems to depend upon maturation, for Lenneberg[22] has indicated that neither deafness nor deaf parents greatly reduces the amount of sound activity in the first six months of life. Indeed, for the first three months of life the speech sounds of deaf children are, qualitatively, almost identical with those of hearing children, and even up to the twelfth month many of the sounds uttered by the deaf are much like those of hearing children. However, a baby tries out many sounds; those that he hears adults use become incorporated into his language; those not heard eventually become extinguished. Moreover, by three months of age the rate of vocalisation is increased by encouragement.[23] But it also seems that the child imitates and acquires only those sounds that appear in his spontaneous babbling. Vocalising (which is very different from crying) of some sort or other takes place very early, and as soon as the infant finds that he can make one sound he will attempt others. One or two months after birth, sounds such as 'ah' and 'eh' can be distinguished, while two-syllable sounds like 'da-da', where the second syllable is a repetition of the first, can be heard a few months later. Gesell reports that sounds denoting pleasure first occur between the third and sixth month. Somewhere between the second and fourth month the infant appears to take greater interest in the human voice speaking to him, but it is not until the ninth or tenth month that very elementary imitation of sounds commences.

Most students agree that infants can understand what is said to them

[21] In connection with language development see: Lenneberg, E. H., *Biological Foundations of Language*. London: Wiley, 1967. Also Lovell, K., *An Introduction to 'Human Development*. London: Macmillan, 1968, Ch. 4. McNeil, D., 'The Development of Language.' In Mussen, P. (Ed.), *Manual of Child Psychology*, Vol. 1. London: Wiley, 3rd Ed., 1970. McNeil, D., *The Acquisition of Language*. New York: Harper and Row, 1971.

[22] Lenneberg, E. H., 'The Acquisition of Language,' *Monogr. Soc. Res. Child Developm.*, 1964, **29**, No. 1.

[23] Todd, G. A. and Palmer, G., 'Social Reinforcement of Infant Babbling,' *Child Developm.*, 1968, **39**, 591–596.

before they can use words. Indeed, there appears to be an increasing understanding of words from about the ninth month although the average child cannot use one word significantly until the eleventh month. It must be stressed that there is a great difference between making a sound and understanding the use of a sound in an appropriate situation. One and two syllable sounds are made much earlier than eleven months, but it is not until then that the child can produce a sound that can stand for an idea. Nearly all writers agree that the first word that the child uses is one like 'mama' where a monosyllable is repeated. Presumably the parent noting the child's babbling uses such a word to denote a definite notion (in this case a person) and the child comes to recognise that 'mama' stands for mother. But at the same time it looks as if there is a more complex significance attached to the earliest words spoken. Valentine[24] shows very clearly that a word like 'mama' may also be used in a generalised sense to denote all the things that a mother usually does for her child. The child may, therefore, use the word 'mama' when he needs something. Hence many of the earliest words that a child uses also stand for an emotional command, and are ejaculations or sentence nouns. Thus the child may not only shout 'mama' when he sees her, but also when he wants something, just as the adult uses the words 'Fire!' and 'Thief!' to denote not only the nature of the object but also that something must be done about the situation. It should also be pointed out here that, in Lenneberg's view,[25] the age of onset of speech is under maturational control although its development is affected by environmental conditions.

From the age of one year the number of words that a child can use increases slowly for a while. Note carefully that a child (or adult) at all ages is able to understand far more words when they are spoken to him than he can use in his own speech. The former may be described as his passive, and the latter as his active or oral vocabulary. From about the age of eighteen months, however, the oral vocabulary of a child increases rapidly. One of the earliest tests devised to estimate the extent of the active vocabulary of young children was that of Smith[26] and some of her findings are set out below:

Age		Average number of words in Oral Vocabulary.	Age		Average number of words in Oral Vocabulary.
yr.	mth.		yr.	mth.	
1	0	3	4	0	1,540
1	6	22	4	6	1,870
2	0	272	5	0	2,072
3	0	896			

[24] Valentine, C. W., op. cit.
[25] Lenneberg, E. H., Biological Foundations of Language. London: Wiley, 1967.
[26] Smith, M. E., An Investigation of the Development of the Sentence and the Extent of the Vocabulary of Young Children. Univ. Iowa Stud. Child Welfare, 1926, 3, No. 5.

These figures show fairly close agreement with Watts'[27] later estimates:

Age	Vocabulary	
	Watts (1st Study)	Watts (2nd Study)
4·0–4·5 yr.	1,760	2,712
4·6–4·11 yr.	2,080	2,910

We can be sure, at least, that the average child enters the English infant school with a working vocabulary of at least 2,000 words (though much fewer in children of low intelligence and in those coming from linguistically deprived homes).

The length of the spoken sentence also increases with age. The findings of Smith and others suggest the following norms for different ages:

Age		Average number of words	Age		Average number of words
yr.	mth.		yr.	mth.	
1	6	1	3	6	4
2	0	1–2	5	0	4–5
2	6	2–3			

There is evidence, too, that girls tend to make longer sentences than boys and are more generally advanced in language development than boys, age for age, although this is not always so.

A number of influences affect language development[28] and these are now briefly listed.

(a) *The level of intelligence.* As a rule mildly sub-normal children learn to talk much later than children of normal or superior intelligence. However, some bright children learn to talk late, and it by no means follows that a child who is late in talking will be mentally retarded.

(b) *Good cultural background.* There is a tendency for children who come from homes where there are books and cultural interests, to be spoken to and read to more, and to be told more stories; these activities greatly help children. Many studies showed that children born in unstimulating institutions show retardation in language development compared with similar children placed in foster homes. In such institutions the cultural level was generally lower than in foster homes and the child was less likely to have warm personal relationships with adults who will take an interest in, or talk to, him, or tell him stories. But institutions are now different places.

[27] Watts, A. F., *The Language and Mental Development of Children.* London: Harrap, 1948.

[28] Compare Sampson, O. C., 'A Study of Speech Development in Children of 18–30 months,' *Brit. J. Educ. Psychol.*, 1956, **26**, 195–201. Also Sampson, O. C., 'The Speech and Language Development of Five Year Old Children,' *Brit. J. Educ. Psychol.*, 1959, **29**, 217–222.

(c) *A good pattern of adult speech.* Adults should give up using 'baby talk' when speaking to children of more than a year. In particular they should make explicit what it is they intend to say. Adults should be careful to use language correctly when dealing with spatial and temporal relationships, and in using language to describe objects, persons or events not actually present.

(d) *Encouragement.* Adults can help children by encouraging the latter to imitate them and to try out new words and sentences. They can help even more by encouraging children to use language precisely when dealing with spatial and temporal relationships and when describing situations not actually present (cf. *c* above).

(e) When a child develops a system of gesture-language and the parents understand him, he may not take the trouble to talk. Moreover, anxious parents sometimes anticipate a child's needs without making him say clearly what he wants.

(f) There is some evidence to suggest that rapid motor progress (e.g. progress in walking) may hinder language development for a short while.

In the past most studies of children's language have been concerned with the size of vocabulary, the length and complexity of sentence, and articulation. Now, increasing attention is being focused on how a child acquires his language. Unfortunately, we know very little yet about the way in which the child learns the rules of adult grammar. In the more recent literature dealing with this problem, the reader will meet terms that are currently used in linguistics such as *phoneme* (or basic sound); *morpheme* (the simplest sound that has meaning); *morphological* rules (those that govern building up of words); *syntactical* rules (those that govern the building up of words into sentences).

The child's first two or three utterances seem to be abbreviated versions of adult sentences. 'Where's the dolly?' becomes 'Where dolly?'. Miller and Ervin,[29] like countless thousands of mothers of English-speaking children, observed that children use sayings like 'all-gone sweetie' instead of 'the sweetie is all gone'. Indeed, these workers, also Brown and Fraser,[30] Brown and Bellugi,[31] have indicated something of the nature of the child's earliest grammatical systems. At first he reduces the adult models as in the example given above. Yet even here he seems to omit certain classes of words (e.g. I, to, the, has) but keeps in others (mainly nouns, verbs and adjectives). Further, the need to reduce the adult model seems to be determined by his limited ability to plan and not by immediate memory span, since the child can use no longer utterances when he produces them

[29] Miller, W. and Ervin, S., 'The Development of Grammar in Child Language.' In *The Acquisition of Language* (Eds. Bellugi, U. and Brown, R.). Monographs of the Society for Research in Child Development, 1964, No. 92.

[30] Brown, R. and Fraser, C., 'The Acquisition of Syntax.' In *The Acquisition of Language* (op. cit.).

[31] Brown, R. and Bellugi, U., 'Three Processes in the Child's Acquisition of Syntax,' *Harvard Education Review*, 1964, 34, 133-151.

spontaneously. Obviously memory is not involved in the latter case. As the child gets older, however, longer utterances can be planned. In other instances the child makes an utterance, say, 'Daddy tea' and an adult expands this into 'Daddy has his tea', and the child copies this expansion. While children appear to learn in these situations it is not known if such expansions are necessary; simply listening to adult speech may be sufficient.[32] However, what was said earlier about the need for the adult to be explicit, and the need for the child to be explicit, seems to be important. But perhaps the most exciting and least understood aspects of children's language structure is the understanding and construction of sentences they have never heard. Brown and Bellugi (*op. cit.*) have tentatively proposed how this may happen: it seems certain that imitation and expansion are insufficient. Readers interested in the early grammars of children, i.e. those used between two and three years of age, should consult McNeill[33] or a summary of the work of McNeill and others given by Lovell.[34]

From the practical point of view the wise parent or nursery-school teacher will, until we are more sure of the facts, continue to expand the child's utterance into the adult grammatical form. Thus 'Where doggie?' could be expanded by the parent into 'Where is your doggie?'. Below are two examples of the speech of children at the University of Leeds Children's Centre.[35] The first concerns a child who had just reached his second birthday and was unable to accommodate to the teacher's model.

Child: 'I big boy. I paint.'
Teacher: 'You're a big boy—you want to paint.'
Child: 'Paint, paint. I paint. Want paint. Want paint.'

The second example refers to a child aged 3 years 1 month.

Child: 'I be finished tomorrow.'
Teacher: 'You will finish it tomorrow.'
Child: 'I will finish it tomorrow.'

In the second example the child was able to modify his own grammatical structure in the light of the adult model and yet it was not identical with the adult version. He was, of course, a year older. Moreover, this learning through dialogue goes on much later, and the learning of certain kinds of words seem to help the child to manipulate ideas in his mind. Thus in the 5-year-old one might find: 'I want to play'. The adult might reply, 'You can play *after* you drink your milk,' and this is followed by the child's comment 'I finished my milk'. Although the small words like *if*, *to*, *from* are among the last to be acquired, they are important, for they help the

[32] Cazden, C. B., 'The Acquisition of Noun and Verb Inflections,' *Child Developm.*, 1968, **39**, 433–448.
[33] McNeill, D. In *The Genesis of Language*. Boston: M.I.T. Press, 1966. Or *op. cit.*
[34] Lovell, K., *op. cit.*
[35] Provided by Miss E. Bailey, Warden of the Children's Centre.

child to turn round in his mind, past, present and anticipated experiences. It should be noted that it is around 2 years 10 months to 3 years of age that the normal child passes from the phrase-structure grammars consisting of simple affirmative sentences (e.g. 'I paint'), to transformational grammars in which by means of deletions, substitutions, etc., the child produces negative, passive, complex, etc., sentences (e.g. 'The boy was not bit by the dog').

In the pre-school period there is a danger that the adult will over-estimate the level of the child's thought, for the latter has often acquired the basic elements of adult grammar without being able to think like an adult. Even in the junior school years, children have difficulty with some constructions in spite of the onset of concrete operational thought. C. Chomsky[36] tested children's grasp of four structures: 'John is easy to see'; 'John promised Bill to go'; 'John asked Bill what to do'; 'He knew that John was going to win the race'. She found that the last was fairly uniformly acquired by $5\frac{1}{2}$ to 6 years of age, but that the first three sentences were subject to great individual differences in the rate of development. The first two were acquired between the ages of $5\frac{1}{2}$ and 9, but the sentence 'John asked Bill what to do' was still imperfectly understood by some children even at age 10. Her findings were upheld by Cromer[37] so we must conclude that active syntactical acquisition is taking place to 9–10 years of age at least.

Syntax is one component of grammar; the other is morphology. English is not as heavily inflected language as, say, Russian. Berko[38] first studied the growth of English morphology (in American children) by asking subjects to make new formations using nonsense words. For example, a child was shown a picture of an object and told, 'This is a wug'. He was then shown another picture of two objects and the experimenter continued, 'Now there are two of them. These are two ——'. The correct response is, of course, 'wugs'. Berko found that 4–7-year-old children knew the rules for forming the plural and possessive for nouns, and the past tense and third person for verbs.[39] Miller and Ervin (*op. cit.*) used the same technique with even younger children and found that the plural was usually known by three but there were large individual differences. The learning of the

[36] Chomsky, C., *The Acquisition of Syntax in Children from 5 to 10*. Cambridge: M.I.T. Press, 1969.
[37] Cromer, R. C., 'Children are Nice to Understand,' *Brit. J. Psychol.*, 1970, **61**, 397–408.
[38] Berko, J., 'The Child's Learning of English Morphology,' *Word*, 1958, **14**, 150–177.
[39] Among E.S.N. Special School children the position is very different. Even at 15 years of age they have only a limited knowledge of these rules, and a limited ability to interpret compound words (e.g. breakfast). Their poor performance in respect of morphology parallels the slow growth of logical thinking in these pupils. The position is entirely consonant with Piaget's view that it is the level of cognition that determines the language that can be used. See Lovell, K. and Bradbury, B., 'The Learning of English Morphology in Educationally Subnormal Special School Children,' *Amer. J. Ment. Def.*, 1967, **71**, 609–615.

plural for meaningful words always came before that for nonsense words that had a similar shape, but the interval between the two was small.[40]

Thus it seems that most children have learnt much of the fundamental structure of their language by about 4 years of age, certainly long before the onset of concrete operational thought. There then appears to be a long period of overlearning so that grammatical habits become automatic, and the child's thinking, as it were, catches up. Yet some patterns are not thoroughly established even in the 6-year-old. He will sometimes use 'buyed' and 'bought', or 'brang' and 'brought', interchangeably. And as we indicated above, actual syntactical acquisition is also taking place to at least 10 years of age. So far, workers in this field have paid relatively little attention to intonation patterns. These are among the first items in a child's speech and may yield information of importance.

Readers who are particularly interested in language development will have to acquire some knowledge of linguistics. Unfortunately linguists are not agreed on basic issues. One British school of linguistics is represented by the work of Halliday[41]; while American linguistics is dominated by the 'transformational grammar' of Noam Chomsky.[42] A transformational model of syntactic structures, used to describe children's grammar from under 3 to over 7 years of age as a self-contained system, and to indicate trends in development, has been provided by Menyuk.[43]

As stated earlier, most workers agree that children can imitate a sentence before they can understand it, and understand it before they can produce it. Fraser[44] et al. produced good evidence among twelve 3-year-old children that this was indeed the case. More recently in a study carried out under the writer's direction,[45] it has been shown that this is true in children between the ages of 2 and 6, also in E.S.N. Special School children aged 6 and 7. Moreover, the relative difficulty of the grammatical constructions remains much the same from age to age. In the test in question the use of the affirmative/negative came first, while the use of the passive voice remained difficult throughout the age range tested.[46]

[40] For a recent study among English children see Selby, S., 'The Development of Morphological Rules in Children,' Brit. J. Educ. Psychol., 1972, 42, 293–299.

[41] Halliday, M. A. K., McIntosh, A. and Strevens, P., The Linguistic Sciences and Teaching Language. London: Longmans, 1964.

[42] Chomsky, N., Syntactic Structures. The Hague: Mouton, 1957. Also Chomsky, N., Aspects of the Theory of Syntax. Boston: M.I.T. Press, 1965.

[43] Menyuk, P., 'Syntactic Rules used by Children from Pre-school through First Grade,' Child Developm., 1964, 35, 533–546.

[44] Fraser, C., Bellugi, U. and Brown, R., 'Control of Grammar in Imitation, Comprehension, and Production,' J. Verbal Learning and Verbal Behaviour, 1963, 2, 121–135.

[45] Lovell, K. and Dixon, E., 'The Growth of the Control of Grammar in Imitation, Comprehension and Production,' J. of Child Psychol. and Psychiat., 1967, 8, 31–39.

[46] For further reading on the acquisition and development of language see McNeill, D., The Acquisition of Language. London: Harper and Row, 1971. Also, Menyuk, P., The Acquisition and Development of Language. London: Prentice Hall, 1971.

Stammering and Stuttering. Stammering means hesitation in uttering words while stuttering means hesitation in speech with repetition of the first sound of the word. These conditions cause concern to parents and teachers. Many theories have been advanced concerning their origin; these range from general motor retardation which seems likely to be due to heredity, to psychological disturbance due to tension (e.g. attempting to force a child's language development) or shock (e.g. the arrival of a younger sibling). Strangely enough some cures are brought about by treatment based on each of these theories, but no form of therapy is effective in all cases. This surely suggests that we have yet a lot to learn about these conditions.

One study in which stutterers and non-stutterers were matched age for age, claimed that all the stutterers were maladjusted in some respects. It also indicated significant differences between the two groups of mothers in the methods of bringing up their children. The mothers of stutterers were more inconsistent in the matter of discipline; they pampered their children more; they also had more illnesses and accidents in their households. While this investigation strongly suggests that stuttering may be one symptom of maladjustment, it does not in any way prove that differences in upbringing were the sole cause of the maladjustment. The groups of mothers may well have differed in their degree of emotional adjustment and differences could well have been handed on by heredity.

It is, however, very important to remember that nearly all children between 2 and 5 years of age repeat some words or syllables in their speech. This is perfectly normal. A broad distinction between the harmless repetition of young children and stuttering lies in the effortlessness of the former and the tension associated with the latter. Again, some stammering is often a temporary phase, caused by the inability of the child to express himself quickly enough.

Perceptual and Intellectual Development.[47] Studies by Fantz[48] suggest that babies have an unlearned preference for visual stimuli that are patterned and complex rather than simple and homogeneous, although it must be noted that there is disagreement over some points of this work. For

[47] See Kessen, W. and Kuhlman, C. (Editors), *Thought in the Young Child.* Society for Research in Child Development, 1962, No. 83. Fowler, W., 'Cognitive Learning in Early Childhood,' *Psychol. Bull.,* 1962, **59**, 116–152. Gibson, E. J., 'Perceptual Development,' in *Child Psychology*: the Sixty-second Yearbook of the National Society for the Study of Education. Chicago: The University of Chicago Press, 1963, 144–195. Lovell, K., *An Introduction to Human Development.* London: Macmillan, 1968, Ch. 2 and 3. Kidd, A. H. and Rivoire, J. L. (Eds.), *Perceptual Development in Children.* London: University of London Press Ltd., 1967, 81–174. Dodwell, P. C. (Ed.), *Perceptual Learning and Adaptation.* Harmondsworth: Penguin, 1970.
[48] Fantz, R. L. In *Perceptual Development in Children* (Eds. Kidd, A. H. and Rivoire, J. L.). London: University of London Press Ltd., 1967.

example, later studies by Fantz,[49] also by Koopman and Ames,[50] indicate that it may be five months of age before children look longer at a clear black and white schematic drawing of a face than at a scrambled drawing of it in the same colours.

Gibson's[51] study suggests that perception of depth (e.g. the ability to recognise depth when looking through a glass plate on to a floor, say, six feet below), has developed by six months of age. Although it cannot be assumed on present evidence that it is unlearned, there are data indicating that in some animals depth perception is available to them on the first day of life.

During the early months of life the baby appears to observe his environment, to compare sensations obtained through his senses, and to begin to recognise similarities when he sees them. Slowly he builds up both percepts, which may be defined as interpretations given to sensory data, and concepts or ideas. Note that concept formation is aided to some extent by language, although in the view of Piaget language is not central to conceptual growth (see Chapter 6). During this period it must also be remembered that the child is learning much by trial and error: i.e. he finds out how to get a toy through the bars of a cot.

There is further evidence that a change in the child's perception takes place in the fifth or sixth month, for by then he can discriminate between simple shapes, e.g. a circle and a cross. Thus after six months of life some perception of shape has developed (for the shape can be recognised whatever its size), and this seems to be the first of all percepts to be formed. Older children can also manipulate and discriminate between shapes without being able to name them; hence shape concepts certainly precede verbal ones. By about 2½ years of age colour recognition seems to develop in most children, and it has been suggested that between about 3 and 5 years of age children tend to match on the basis of colour rather than of shape; but on this point not all investigators are agreed. The knowledge of colours and colour names seems now to come earlier due, perhaps, to the development of the plastics industry making so many coloured toys available.

Rice[52] has indicated that by the age of 5 to 6 years children can recognise shapes (e.g. diamond shapes) as being the same when they are differently orientated, and this may be the first sign of the emergence of spatial ability. More recently Olson[53] has made a detailed study of the capacity of six-year-olds to (a) discriminate and (b) reproduce, various patterns. In respect

[49] Fantz, R. L. and Nevis, S., 'Pattern Preferences and Perceptual-Cognitive Development in Early Infancy,' Merrill-Palmer Quarterly, 1967, 13, 77–108.

[50] Koopman, P. R. and Ames, E. W., 'Infants' Preferences for Facial Arrangements: A Failure to Replicate,' Child Developm., 1968, 39, 481–487.

[51] Gibson, E. J., op. cit.

[52] Rice, C., 'The Orientation of Plane Figures as a Factor in their Perception by Children,' Child Developm., 1930, 1, 111–143.

[53] Olson, D. R., Cognitive Development. London: Academic Press, 1970.

of the child's ability to discriminate he found that one horizontal or one vertical line was the easiest, patterns in which both 'up' and 'down' lines joined by a horizontal at the top or bottom were of intermediate difficulty, and oblique lines tending to converge the hardest to discriminate. In respect of reproduction, a line parallel and close to the edge of the paper was easiest, parallel to but distant from the edges of the paper of intermediate difficulty, and the diagonals of a square and an oblique cross, as in the letter X, the hardest. It was only the six-year-olds who could tackle the hardest tasks with a good chance of success.

From the age of 2 years onwards, intellectual growth proceeds aided by an increasing mastery of language as indicated in Chapter 6. Gesell[54] by studying a child's ability to arrange cubes, has shown that at 1 year the child picks up one cube and drops it, at 15 months he can build a pile of two cubes, at 2 years he can put three cubes in a row, and at 3 years he can build a bridge of three cubes. By the age of 3 years, too he can make very simple generalisations: for example, he is likely to say 'cars' when he sees a number of toy cars, although he does this much more frequently at 4 years of age. But even at the latter age his intellectual ability is limited, and it is not until he is 5 that the average child can count up to ten objects and have some understanding of the terms 'yesterday' and 'tomorrow'. The length of sentence which a child can repeat after hearing it said once gives some indication of the intellectual growth of children between 2 and 4 years. According to Gesell, a 2-year-old can usually repeat a sentence of three or four syllables (e.g. I have a doll), while the 4-year-old repeats one out of three sentences of twelve to thirteen syllables (e.g. When the train passes you will hear the whistle blow).

It will be appreciated that physical, perceptual, and intellectual development are all interrelated especially in the early months of life. For example, in the first four months of life physical maturation brings growing 'grasp control' and growing coordination of hand and arm to mouth. This enables the baby to discover the suckable from the non-suckable and so brings about the first discriminations which are at the very origins of intellectual growth. Again, physical maturation allows 'head turning' and 'eye following', and the coordination of sight and sound as the child turns his head to a noise to maximise the input into both ears. A few months later there is coordination between hand and eye in relation to objects outside the body so that the baby can perform actions with such objects. This happens at first when the child touches, say, a swinging rattle. Actions of grasping and shaking are then repeated as a whole. In such behaviour the infant begins to show the onset of some small anticipation of his own actions and the onset of intention.

Sensory deprivation, if serious and prolonged during the first year of life, does have a serious adverse effect on intellectual growth. Schaffer and

[54] Gesell, A., *op. cit.*

Emerson[55] consider that deprivation can start two types of change. The first is concerned with a depressing effect on alertness. This is both easily brought about and easily reversed and it seems to be the only effect of the less serious forms of deprivation. But extreme and prolonged environmental restriction can result in real deterioration of the developmental quotient.

The literature concerning the effect of child rearing practices on cognitive development during childhood has been reviewed by Freeberg and Payne.[56] They conclude that there are many issues connected with this important topic that remain unclear, and that it is only in recent years that small amounts of evidence have become available as to how such practices might affect cognitive skills. In our present state of knowledge we can only stress that parents and nursery school teachers can best help young children by providing them as far as possible with varied and stimulating experiences, and by encouraging language development.[57]

Psychoanalytic Theory and Infancy. This section deals with matter which is very controversial (compare Chapter 4). Broadly speaking, we may say that psychoanalysis aims at revealing the subject's unconscious mind and repressed wishes to his consciousness. The analyst, after getting rapport with the subject, tries to bring back forgotten incidents and to find the origin of psychological conflicts. For many years now it has been used as a form of psychotherapy on adults. Often it is claimed that the individual can recall childhood experiences as far back as the first year of life. Psychoanalytic methods have also been used with children[58] and it is claimed that from their behaviour, and the symptoms which they display, usually in play, it is possible to infer a great deal about their early upbringing. We may say, then, that psychologists have built up theories concerning the way in which early feeding and upbringing, the love and security that parents give and withhold, also the disciplines that society imposes, all mould the personality of the growing child. One important postulate of the psychoanalytic school is that psychological shock results from the severing of the child's foetal relationship with his mother, and some analysts hold that the ultimate cause of all anxiety is the birth process. Again Freud writes of the *oral* and *anal* phases of *pre-genital* development (*see* Chapter 4). In the former phase parts of the mouth dominate what

[55] Schaffer, H. R. and Emerson, P. E., 'The Effects of Experimentally administered Stimulation on Developmental Quotients in Infants,' *Brit. J. soc. clin. Psychol.*, 1968, 7, 61–67. See also Schaffer, H. R., 'Recent Changes in Developmental Quotients under Two Conditions of Maternal Separation,' *Brit. J. soc. clin. Psychol.*, 1965, 4, 39–46.

[56] Freeberg, N. E. and Payne, D. T., 'Parental Influence on Cognitive Development in Early Childhood: a Review,' *Child Developm.*, 1967, 38, 65–87.

[57] See also Kohlberg, L., 'Early Education: A Cognitive Developmental View,' *Child Developm.*, 1968, 39, 1013–1062.

[58] See Freud, A., 'Introduction to the Technique of Child Analysis,' *Nerv. Ment. Dis. Monogr.*, 1928, No. 48. Also Klein, M., *The Psychoanalysis of Children*. London: Hogarth Press, 1932.

may be called the sexual activity of the period (i.e. of the infant), while in the latter phase 'anal and sadistic tendencies' come to the fore. Freud and his followers have suggested personality traits which are likely to result from the child's being unduly deprived or frustrated in connection with these oral and anal tendencies.

Now it has long been known that pressures produced in the birth process may damage a child's brain. These injuries may be of a temporary nature, or they may have serious and lasting consequences. Again, it is very likely that the infant suffers for a few days after birth similar mental and physical conditions to those experienced by adults after a major surgical operation, although this condition of 'shock' following birth has not been proved. We may certainly agree that early upbringing and experience generally do affect the content of the unconscious mind and also the personality, for the former plays a considerable part in determining the behaviour of child or adult in any situation. But we do not possess knowledge of any clear relationships between types of upbringing (e.g. in relation to feeding, weaning, or bowel control) and specific personality traits later. Orlansky,[59] also Stevenson, have surveyed much of the data on the relationship between infant care and personality growth and show that little definite relationship exists. Other workers conclude that most of the investigations involving normal children have thrown great doubt on the value of generalisations made by psychoanalysts about child life.[60] Very interesting is the work of Goldman-Eisler.[61] She claims a definite relationship between early weaning, and therefore early oral deprivation, and a rather pessimistic, aloof introverted personality later on. But the design of her experiment does not necessarily show effects of treatment. If the tendency to be introverted is inherited, such a tendency might be passed on to the child; it is also possible that introverted mothers tend to cease to feed their babies earlier than extraverted ones.

On the other hand, psychoanalysts have contributed ideas which are stimulating and which may prove very fruitful. For example, we have already seen that the young child is supposed to take into himself (i.e. internalises) in fantasy, exaggerated personifications of the 'good' and 'bad' qualities of his parents, and in this way he gets the raw materials out of which he forms his own character. The difficulty lies not in the theories which the psychoanalysts propose but in the methods that they use to obtain the raw data on which the theories are built—theories which are so largely intuitive as to preclude objective verification. There is no way of checking that the responses of children are not made to fit a particular theory, and it is difficult for a third party to judge exactly what passed between the analyst and child (unless a tape recording is made), or to

[59] Orlansky, H., *op. cit.*; Stevenson, I., *op. cit.*

[60] Compare Ellis, A., 'An Introduction to the Principles of Scientific Psychoanalysis,' *Genet. Psychol. Monogr.*, 1950, 41, 147–212.

[61] Goldman-Eisler, F., 'The Problem of Orality and of its Origin in Early Childhood,' *J. Ment. Sci.*, 1951, 97, 765–781.

know to what extent the interpretation of the responses is coloured by the analyst's own personality. As Burt[62] has so shrewdly remarked when dealing with psychoanalytic theory in relation to delinquency, 'Intuition and ingenious speculation do not make a science'.

There is, however, a possible connection between psychoanalytic theory and the work of Lorenz and Tinbergen. We say in Chapter 2 that in some animals, there appear to be inborn patterns of behaviour (which often operate reciprocally between members of the same species), but the environment may help to prevent their appearance and determine the objects to which they are directed. Lorenz has suggested that the very lasting 'object-fixations' of human beings—for example, those few individuals with whom any one of us could fall violently in love—seem to be partly dependent upon early childhood impressions and seem also to be largely irreversible. In our example the loved one provides the 'key stimuli' which release patterns of behaviour that, in turn, bring about satisfaction of needs. Bowlby,[63] in particular, has elaborated some interesting, if speculative, possibilities in this field.

[62] Burt, C., 'Recent Discussions of Juvenile Delinquency,' *Brit. J. Educ. Psychol.*, 1949, **19**, 32–43.
[63] Bowlby, J., 'The Nature of the Child's Tie to his Mother,' *Intern. J. Psychoanal.*, 1958, **39**, 350–373.

Chapter Sixteen

THE PRIMARY SCHOOL CHILD

Social and Emotional Development.[1] A great deal more has been written about the pre-school child and the adolescent than about the middle years of childhood. This is regrettable, since the characteristics of the primary school child are of as great interest to parents and teachers as are those of the other age-groups. Gesell and Ilg[2] have attempted to specify the characteristic traits and behaviour for each of the years from five to ten. This is extremely difficult since individual differences between children at 7 years of age are probably much greater than the differences between average children at 6 and 8 years. On the other hand we can certainly distinguish the behaviour of the average 5-year-old from the average 10-year-old. In their investigations Gesell and Ilg studied 50 or more children in each age-group. But it should be noted that the groups were all likely to be above average in intelligence and, therefore, not truly representative samples; also it does not appear to be a follow-up study of the same children through the years. Generalising from a number of their findings, together with those of many other workers, we may suggest that the following changes tend to take place between 5 and 10–11 years of age:

(*a*) At 5 the child is still somewhat a creature of uncontrolled tendencies and his emotional outbursts are often violent though short-lived. By 11 the child is in a state of greater emotional equilibrium.

(*b*) With increase in age there appear to be more stable personal relationships between the child and others. There is generally less physical aggression, although boys still fight, but there is more verbal aggression and argument.

(*c*) While parents and family remain important, primary school children increasingly wish to be with friends of their own sex as they get older. Furthermore, in the infant school the approval or disapproval of a grown-up is of more consequence to the child than are the smiles of friends. At this age he has implicit trust in adults, while pupil-teacher relationships are personal and direct with each child. But as he gets older he assesses and evaluates his teachers and other adults, and is more and more interested in winning approval from his classmates.

[1] See Chazan, M., 'Children's Emotional Development.' In *Educational Research in Britain* (Ed. Butcher, H. J.). London: University of London Press Ltd., 1968, 45–68.

[2] Gesell, A., and Ilg, F. L., *The Child from Five to Ten*. London: Hamish Hamilton Ltd., 1946.

(d) At 5 years of age children still play in small groups in which the personnel may change rapidly, but by 8 years of age the groupings are somewhat more formal and they may or may not have a specific purpose in view. Note, however, that compared with some later adolescent groups, the group is still rather loosely-knit and is almost invariably of one sex only.

(e) From rather individualistic play, or in small groups, in the infant school, children develop an interest in team games which involve competition and skill.

(f) Up to about 8 years of age children are nearly always subjective in their personal relationships, but thereafter they become more objective. For example, a child of 6 will praise himself and expect praise on all occasions and will deprecate the other child. He cannot take the point of view of the other fellow because his own feelings are strong and urgent, and he uses the other children in the group for his own purposes. But by the age of 8 there are signs of a change, a hint of the beginnings of a team spirit, and from $8\frac{1}{2}$–9 years onwards there is an increasing appreciation of the other child and what that child does.

(g) Between 5 and 7 years of age a child can frequently be seen confusing fantasy with reality in his play. Thereafter he becomes more of a realist, although fantasy will continue.[3]

(h) There is an increasing divergence of interests and outlook of boys and girls (see later in this chapter).

To many, the child between 7 and 11 years is the most interesting of all schoolchildren. He appears to be very friendly, is full of life and energy, plays hard and sleeps soundly, and up to about 9 years of age is willing to undergo repetitive jobs in which he has no particular interest, e.g. learning multiplication-tables. The more turbulent emotions of earlier years are less in evidence and the difficulties of adolescence are not yet upon him. Indeed, he appears to be very much like the proverbial 'cork', for if depressed as a result of unkindness, antagonism, or injustice, he very soon regains his poise and interest in his surroundings. Furthermore, it must be stressed here that after about 8 years of age he becomes very interested in playing with others, and persistent solitary play (not occasional solitary play which all children want at times) after this age is often indicative of emotional maladjustment.

[3] An interesting and relevant study has been provided by Moore in a group of 115 children aged 4–6 years of age. Using standard doll play he investigated their fantasies and feelings concerning everyday situations, and the ability to solve simple problems involving interpersonal relationships (e.g. readiness to share at mealtime). At 4, many boys showed aggression or inhibition or an alternation of these, which prevented constructive solutions. Such indications were less often found in the girls but punishment was more frequent in their play. By 6, however, inhibition and anxiety had decreased in the boys, and there was an increase in both punishment and in constructive solutions to the problems, together with a clearer demarcation between fantastic and realistic forms of play. See Moore, T. and Ucko, L. E., 'Four to Six: Constructiveness and Conflict in meeting Doll Play Situations,' *J. Child Psychology and Psychiatry*, 1961, 2, 21–47.

But the primary school child like the pre-school child has his fears and anxieties. Jersild[4] et al., in a study of 398 children between 5 and 12 years of age, found the greatest incidence of fears in response to mysterious phenomena such as ghosts and corpses, although obviously none had actually suffered attacks from these. The second largest cause of fears was animals, although few of the children had suffered harm from animals. This investigation suggests that some of the fears of children at this age may be implanted there by adults by such threats as, 'I will give you to the bogey-man'. In another study, Jersild[5] found that 53 per cent of some 1,100 American children worried in case they should not be promoted at school although in fact only some one per cent would suffer that fate. Other studies in the U.S.A. have confirmed that 11- and 12-year-old children are anxious about school progress. True, some of this anxiety may reflect the fears of the parents. But if these findings in respect of school progress and promotion are true of children in Great Britain, we should have to consider afresh whether too much emphasis is placed upon competitive scholarship in school. Some teachers will think that it is a good thing to induce a little anxiety in children in respect of their school progress; others will disagree. What is certain is that we had too little objective evidence as to whether the examination at 10–11 years of age for entry into the Grammar School did worry many children, and to what degree; also whether there was much deterioration in the morale of those who were not accepted for a Grammar School (compare Chapter 11).

The Development of Abilities.[6] We saw in Chapter 3 that general intelligence increases steadily throughout the primary school period. Thus, throughout the years under review, the child's ability to grasp relationships increases, so that by about 8 years of age the average child is equipped to begin to tackle most kinds of intellectual work in school provided that it demands only concrete operational thought and that he has the vocabulary that is needed and that the ideas are within his experience. Burt found that there was sufficient mental maturity for simple syllogistic reasoning by the time a mental age of about 8·0 years had been attained, although it must be remembered that pre-school and infant-school children will occasionally reason provided the premises are few, fairly concrete, and familiar. As for special abilities, we have already noted that Stephenson first showed the presence of a verbal factor in girls aged 10–12 years. It seems likely that this ability emerges by 6 years of age or earlier, but it is not easy to measure at that age, since group verbal tests cannot be applied and individual testing

[4] Jersild, A. T., Markey, F. V., and Jersild, C. L., 'Children's Fears, Dreams, Wishes, Daydreams, Likes, Dislikes, Pleasant and Unpleasant Memories,' *Child Developm. Monogr.*, 1933, No. 12.
[5] Jersild, A. T., Goldman, B., and Loftus, J. J., 'A Comparative Study of the Worries of Children in Two School Situations,' *J. Exp. Educ.*, 1941, 9, 323–326.
[6] See also Chapter 6; Fowler, W., *op. cit.*; Kessen, W. and Kuhlman, C., *op. cit.*, Lovell, K., *The Growth of Basic Mathematical and Scientific Concepts in Children.* London: University of London Press Ltd., Fifth Edition, 1966.

is slow. At that age verbal ability and general intelligence are difficult to separate. There has been considerable discussion as to the age at which the spatial factor emerges, and Vernon,[7] after reviewing the position, maintains that the evidence for this ability by 11–13 years or even earlier is overwhelming. Nevertheless, as Burt pointed out long ago, general intelligence is by far the most important of the abilities in determining progress in school subjects in the primary school. Performance is, of course, also dependent upon interests, and on attitudes to subjects; and now, as in adolescence, these interests and attitudes are likely to fluctuate with change of teacher, with teaching method, and with the content of the subject.

Musical ability is also in evidence before the child leaves the junior school. Many musicians and other investigators have been interested in devising tests which will pick out children with musical ability. Wing[8] employs seven tests which fall into two groups. The first three deal with ear acuity; in these the subject is asked to give the number of notes in a played chord, to state whether a note rises or falls when a chord is repeated with one note changed, and which note of a repeated melody is changed. The last four tests deal with taste or preference. The subject has to compare a good version with a mutilated or weaker version and state which he prefers. There are changes in rhythm, harmony, intensity, and phrasing. Scores on the ear acuity tests show a steady growth with age from 8 years upwards although the tests of preference show negligible scores up to 11. The correlation between musical ability and intelligence among children seems to be about 0·3. Bentley[9] has also devised a battery of tests to measure musical ability in children. He uses tests of pitch discrimination, chord analysis, tonal memory and rhythmic memory. He found that musical abilities increased with age although the average yearly increase was small. Although rhythmic memory is more highly developed than tonal memory in childhood, both are more advanced than pitch discrimination, while chord analysis is weak in most children under 11 years of age. Like Wing he found a low correlation between musical ability and measured intelligence[10].

It is often suggested that memory is at its best during the primary school period, and some even talk as if there was a special memory ability emerging at this time. Perhaps these viewpoints arise because up to about 9 years of age the child will certainly learn material (e.g. poetry) in which he is not greatly interested. This is not so in adolescence or adulthood, for

[7] Vernon, P. E., *The Structure of Human Abilities*. London: Methuen, 1961, Second Edition.

[8] Wing, H. D., 'A Factorial Study of Musical Tests,' *Brit. J. Psychol.*, 1941, 31, 341–355. Wing, H. D., 'Some Applications of Test Results to Education in Music,' *Brit. J. Educ. Psychol.*, 1954, 24, 161–170.

[9] Bentley, A., *Musical Ability in Children and its Measurement*. London: Harrap, 1966.

[10] For a review of the literature dealing with the psychology of musical ability see Shuter, R., *The Psychology of Musical Ability*. London: Methuen, 1968.

then we are far more likely to attend to, and learn, that which interests us. Actually there is little evidence of a special memory ability of much consequence in school work. Logical memory (i.e. the capacity to remember meaningful material such as the gist of a story) seems to be accounted for by the growth of intelligence as we saw when dealing with memory. Again, there are few grounds for saying that memory is at its best during this period since logical memory increases as general intelligence increases and is likely to reach a maximum at about 15/16 years for most children in this country at present.

There does not appear to be any reliable difference between the sexes in general intelligence; such differences as there are seem to depend upon the test used. Thus in the Scottish Survey[11] which involved almost all the 11-year-old children in Scotland in 1947, there was a small but significant difference in score in favour of the girls on the group verbal test, but a significant difference in favour of the boys when 1,215 were tested by means of the Terman-Merrill test. General experience shows that girls do slightly better on tests which involve language although the differences are not always consistent. This may well be an effect of the culture pattern. Investigations into sex differences in arithmetic performance between about 8 and 12 years of age do not always show consistent results, but there is a tendency for boys to show a slight superiority in problem arithmetic; in mechanical arithmetic there is either no difference or a slight superiority on the part of the girls.

Sensory Capacities and Motor Abilities. In this section we propose to deal briefly with the development of a few of the sensory capacities and motor abilities, since these are of relevance to parents and teachers.

As a child grows up, there is generally an improvement in the acuity of vision. But care should be taken to see that vision is not strained by the reading of too small print. Colour discrimination also increases with age. For example, Smith[12] found a steady growth in the discrimination of colour saturation, hue and lightness from about $7\frac{1}{2}$ to 25 years of age. At the beginning of the primary school period, however, colour discrimination may still be ahead of colour naming, but children of this age have a greater knowledge of colours and colour names, than they had in the 1930s (cf. Cook[13]). In connection with hearing, it is instructive to note that some children suffer from high frequency deafness and cannot distinguish high notes. These children have difficulty in distinguishing between sounds such as 'ee' and 'oo', and because they do not find it easy to follow speech, their school work may suffer.

[11] *The Trend of Scottish Intelligence.* London: University of London Press Ltd., 1949.
[12] Smith, H. C., 'Age Differences in Colour Discrimination,' *J. genet. Psychol.*, 1943, 29, 191–226.
[13] Cook, W. M., 'Ability of Children in Colour Discrimination,' *Child Developm.*, 1931, 2, 303–320.

Some research findings strongly suggest that the growing child first gets co-ordinated control over large muscles and then over smaller ones. This is one reason why we first use manuscript writing or printing and later cursive writing or connected script. The former is satisfactory when children are allowed to make large strokes and groups of large muscles come into play, but by $7\frac{1}{2}$–8 years there is better control of the smaller muscles which control fingers and wrist, and children are then switched to cursive writing which is faster and more legible. Accuracy of adjusted movement (as in writing) increases rapidly from 5–9 years, and speed of adjusted movement from 7–10 years. After these ages the rates of increase decline. There is also evidence that muscle-sense shows an improvement over the age-range. This means that there is more information coming from the proprioceptors, or sense organs which continuously register changes in length, tension, compression, etc., of the body. Through the proprioceptors we become aware of, and judge, the position of our arms, legs, and other parts of the body, both in relation to one another and to the outside world. In this matter boys are, on the average, superior to girls between 8 and 11. Sex differences in muscular endurance also become more obvious during the period and it is not possible to ignore them in games or physical education after 9 years of age.

The concept of Organismic Age. Olson[14] brought forward some evidence that the child, of both primary and secondary school age, develops as a whole. That is to say, if we take a number of physiological and psychological measures of the child, we find that they are to some extent inter-related. Hence a backward child is often below the average on certain physiological measures as well. Thus Olson takes a child's mental age, reading age, height, weight, state of dentition, strength of grip and carpal or bone age (see next chapter) and derives what he has termed an *organismic age*. How valuable this concept will be in forecasting the educational, or other progress of children, only future research will reveal. The data provided by the study of Besch[15] *et al.* among twins is consistent with the hypothesis that there is no intrinsic biological relation between physical and intellectual development, and that the observed tendency for more intelligent children to be better developed physically is a function of common environmental influences.

Handedness. A topic of general interest is that of handedness. Most people use their right hand in preference to their left when performing many of the daily tasks. A great deal has been written on the question of handedness, but to date there does not appear to be any really satisfactory explanation as to why most people are right-handed. Left-handedness may be

[14] Olson, W. C., *Child Development*. Boston: Heath, Second Edition, 1959.
[15] Besch, O-F., Lenz, W. and Maxwell, J., 'The Correlation between Mental and Physical Growth in Twins,' *Brit. J. Educ. Psychol.*, 1961, **31**, 265–267.

something of a handicap for people living in a world where most apparatus is designed for right-handed people, although left-handed individuals say that the handicap is very slight or non-existent. It used to be thought that training a left-handed child to use his right hand involved a danger of the child's beginning to stutter or stammer. Now we know that this need not necessarily be so. If the training is done in an interesting fashion with no coercion, it seems that handedness can be changed without any psychological danger resulting. But such a change should not be undertaken lightly, for it does involve readjustment for the child, and most people can get through life comfortably as left-handed individuals.[16]

It is important that the writing paper should be aligned differently for left-handed children. Whereas for right-handed individuals the paper should be tilted so that the top left-hand corner is nearer the body, for left-handed people the top left-hand corner of the paper should be away from the body as indicated in Figure 15.

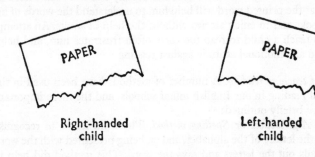

Right-handed child   Left-handed child

Fig. 15

The development of reading. After speech, reading is the most important of the basic skills and we must devote some space to certain aspects of the psychology of reading. Proper reading as distinct from 'barking at print' involves:

(a) The recognition of the visual pattern of the word and the ability to pronounce it.

(b) A knowledge of what words, and combinations of words, mean. This requires previous experience with situations in connection with which the words have been used. Thus the understanding of words is greatly conditioned by experience.

Reading readiness. It has already been pointed out that the concept of reading readiness as it has been understood, is now being challenged.

[16] Readers thinking of making a child, whose natural tendency is to use his left hand when writing, change to his right hand, should see: Trankell, A., 'The Influences of the Choice of Writing Hand on the Handwriting,' *Brit. J. Educ. Psychol.*, 1956, **26**, 94–103.

Since the Americans have shown that it is possible to teach some 2–3-year-olds to read, there is no doubt that the concept needs to be looked at again. No set age can be given for attempting to teach children to read for, as Watts[17] insists, the age at which a child wants to read depends upon his intelligence, the cultural background of the home, and the teacher. There are, therefore, large individual differences between children when it comes to the age at which they are ready to read. In a good environment where the child has had picture-books shown to him, had stories and rhymes read, and where the adult conversation around him has been stimulating, readiness for reading appears at about a mental age of 5½ to 6 years, that is, often by 4 years or earlier in a bright child. When ready to start reading, a child will show an increased interest in his picture-books, and in having stories read to him, and will perhaps hold up a book or paper in front of him and pretend to read. The teacher should watch carefully for these signs. A child does not usually learn to read before he realises that the printed word will help him to understand the words of his picture-book, and to enjoy stories without the help of adults. An attempt to start to teach a child to read too early often frustrates him, and helps to build up an emotional attitude against reading.

Methods of teaching reading. A number of methods have been used in the teaching of reading in our English infant schools, and the more important of these are briefly outlined:

(a) *The Alphabetical or Spelling method.* The child learns to recognise and name the letters of the alphabet, and on being presented with the word *dog*, he reads out the letters and says the word. This method did help in the learning of spe ling, but it is not used much today.

(b) *Look and Say*, or *Whole Word method.* In this method the child is presented with a card on which is a picture of, say, a dog, with the word *dog* printed underneath, and he has to establish the visual pattern of the word. Two or more cards are then put together to make a short, simple sentence. When one word only is used, the child is denied the use of any clues from the context, yet Schonell[18] thinks this the best method when reading is begun with the dullest 25 per cent of children.

(c) *Phonetic method.* This is an analytic method which aims at providing the different sounds of the letters of the alphabet. It was extremely popular for some years and then fell from favour somewhat, but there now seems to be a revival of interest in it again. Current readers based on a phonic approach are more interesting than were earlier ones. It has, however, one advantage in that it gives the pupil more ability in tackling many new words, although some irregular words must still be learnt by wholes.

[17] Watts, A. F., *The Language and Mental Development of Children.* London: Harrap, 1948.
[18] Schonell, F. J., *The Psychology and Teaching of Reading.* London: Oliver and Boyd, 1948.

(*d*) *Sentence method.* A short simple sentence based upon the experience of the child is used, e.g. This is Sam. Thus we start with a large unit and later make a study of the words making up the sentence. In this method, help is obtained from the context and it is thought by some to be the best method for bright children.

There has been a great deal of research both here and in the U.S.A. in an attempt to find out which methods should be used, but opinions are still divided. Some teachers in both countries favour the use of non-phonic methods to begin with, and their point of view can be summarised thus:

(*a*) It is best to start most children on the Whole Word or Whole Sentence method, the former with the duller and the latter with the brighter pupils.

(*b*) There is no point in beginning phonetic analysis before the child has a mental age of 7 years, as previous to that he seems to have great difficulty in analysing and synthesising words.

(*c*) Sooner or later most children must have some phonetic analysis. Able children might be able to analyse new words for themselves, but others will guess at sight when they meet new words unless they are taught to do otherwise.

(*d*) It is better to teach the analysis of new words as they are met in the context of a sentence, rather than to use the more formal method of introducing words singly and without context.

Others take the view that the phonic method, right from the start, provides the best approach for most children. Indeed, a recent study made by the N.F.E.R. suggests that in successful schools, the teaching of reading tended to be organised right from the start and early phonic training was common.[19] At the same time the work of Bruce[20] should be considered. He presented a series of words to infant school children with mental ages in the range 5 to 9. The words were of the form: S–T–AND, J–AM, FAIR–Y, in which the middle, first or last part of the word had to be omitted in pronunciation. That is to say, a particular letter sound had to be taken away. This detailed study suggests that a mental age of 7 is necessary before the child can attempt the task with a fair chance of success. Bruce also points out that teaching can have an effect on the word analysis up to a mental age of 9, after which the effect disappears. The study implies that bright children who have acquired sufficient vocabulary and reached sufficient general maturity, may well be ready to start phonetic analysis in the reception class of the infant school.

An important piece of research has taken place in which a phonemically regular and limited alphabet (the Initial Teaching Alphabet), with consis-

[19] Cane, B. and Smithers, J., *The Roots of Reading.* Slough: N.F.E.R., 1971.
[20] Bruce, D. J., 'The Analysis of Word Sounds by Young Children,' *Brit. J. Educ. Psychol.*, 1964, 34, 158–170.

tent spelling, was used with infants from the day of their entry into school, to see if the inconsistencies of English spelling are an important cause of reading failure. Wall[21] summarising the evaluations made of the research concludes that children were provided with a medium (not a method) and that they mastered certain aspects of reading faster than they would have done using traditional orthography. But abler children got more from the medium than did the less able, and he concluded, quoting Burt, that as far as the causes of poor spelling are concerned they reside more within the individual than within a method or a medium. In the evaluation of a second, and later experiment, Cartwright and Jones[22] conclude that on the whole, pupils taught via i.t.a. made better progress than those taught via traditional orthography. However, children taught by the former medium have eventually to transfer to traditional orthography and the results throw doubt on whether, in the long run, they have any advantage over children who begin with traditional orthography.

Conditions Influencing the Speed with which Children learn to Read.[23] The speed with which a child acquires facility in reading seems to depend upon one or more of the following influences which are not completely independent of one another:

(*a*) *General intelligence.*

(*b*) *Relevant background experience.* The child who has had stories read and told to him, has had a good supply of picture-books, has had a good deal of conversation with adults, who has been taken to places and shown things, will find reading easier because he will come across words which describe real-life experience.

(*c*) *Adequacy and continuity of teaching.*

(*d*) *Motivation,* i.e. the interest in wanting to learn to read. The motivation of children can be helped by paying attention to the points listed under (*b*) above.

(*e*) *Emotional stability and confidence.* The child must have enough staying power and confidence in himself to remain in a more or less frustrating position until learning occurs.

(*f*) According to Schonell,[24] auditory and visual discrimination are important. A characteristic of the lack of auditory discrimination is that a child may confuse sounds made by similar words, e.g. *set* and *sat*. In lack of visual discrimination, similar word forms are confused, e.g. *form* and *from*. Schonell talks as if auditory and visual discrimination were special abilities and suggests that they are partly inborn and partly acquired.

[21] Wall, W. D. In *The i.t.a. Symposium* (Ed. Downing, J.). Slough: N.F.E.R., 1967.
[22] Cartwright, D. and Jones, B., 'Further Evidence Relevant to the Assessment of i.t.a.,' *Educ. Res.*, 1967, **10**, 65–71.
[23] See Sampson, O. C., 'Reading Skill at Eight Years in Relation to Speech and Other Factors,' *Brit. J. Educ. Psychol.*, 1962, **32**, 12–17.
[24] Schonell, *ibid.*

But to what extent these abilities actually overlap with general intelligence at 5 to 6 years of age is not known. Davidson[25] has shown that the ability to discriminate adequately between up and down letters, p, q, as compared with b, d, and to distinguish between the letters b, d themselves, is partly dependent upon mental age. However, Thackray[26] found that among a group of 182 infant school children in their second term at school (average age 5 years 4 months), reading age correlated more highly with tests of auditory and visual discrimination (·53 and ·50 respectively) than it did with general ability (·47), home environment (·42), and emotional and personal attitudes (·10–·36). This evidence tends to confirm that an adequate level of auditory and visual discrimination must be available before reading is possible and that such discrimination is to some extent independent of general intelligence. Moreover, there is now good evidence (cf. Lovell and Gorton, *op. cit.*) that once the child is past the early stages of reading, then reading progress is dependent in part upon the capacity of the central nervous system to maintain an adequate level of auditory-visual integration; i.e. integration of the sound of the word with its written form.

The Motor Side of Reading. Reading is certainly a perceptual activity although it is more than that. Experiments have shown that when a child looks at a picture his eye movements are very irregular. These movements may be from left to right or vice versa followed by movements up and down. But in reading, a new pattern of eye movement develops. The eye moves along a line of print from left to right (except in languages where one reads from right to left) in a series of jumps broken by pauses. The jump from one part of the line to the next that is to be fixated is called a *saccadic* movement, and the pause, during which the eye is steady and sees a stationary pattern of print, is termed a *fixation*. But sometimes the eye jumps back along a line instead of going forward. Such a movement is called a *regression*. Buswell[27] produced evidence for children in the U.S.A. suggesting that the average number of fixations per line declines from about 15 at 6–8 years of age, to 7 at 9–13 years, while over the same period the average duration of the fixations decreases from about 0·5 seconds to 0·25 seconds, and the average number of regressions per line from 4 to 1·5. After 13 there appears to be a small decrease in the number of fixations and regressions per line, and in the duration of the fixations. But these are average figures and any one individual may show considerable departures from these norms. In general, the better the reader, the fewer

[25] Davidson, H. P., 'A Study of the Confusing Letters B, D, P and Q,' *J. genet. Psychol.*, 1935, 47, 458–468.
[26] Thackray, D. V., 'The Relationship between Reading Readiness and Reading Progress,' *Brit. J. Educ. Psychol.*, 1965, 35, 252–254.
[27] Buswell, G. T., 'Fundamental Reading Habits: A Study of Their Development,' *Suppl. Educ. Monogr.*, 1922. Quoted by Woodworth, R. S., and Schlosberg, H. in *Experimental Psychology*. London: Methuen, 1954.

the number of fixations and regressions per line. But when the child or adult is under emotional disturbance, perhaps in trouble over difficulties in the test or even very interested in, or excited by, the text, the eye movements will revert to a more irregular type of movement. Eye movements have, however, little to do with comprehension.

Note that a good deal of a line of print is not fixated directly and slight indirect vision is sufficient for most letters. Furthermore, when we are reading aloud, the eye keeps ahead of the voice. This can be demonstrated by taking synchronised records of eye movements and voice. Thus in the sentence:

Voice   Eye
↓   ↓
The tiger jumped over the stream

the eye may be taking in 'jumped' as the voice is saying 'tiger'. This eye-voice span varies from individual to individual. It increases with experience in reading, is larger in good than poor readers, and may reach eight words in an older mature reader. One would expect a small eye-voice span to give poorer reading for there is less guidance from the context. Hence the necessity for plenty of practice in silent reading for speed, rather than oral reading or reading for articulation, for in the latter the eye-voice span is necessarily small.

Growth of certain language skills. Watts[28] concludes that the size of usable vocabulary develops rapidly during the infant school stage, and the average child enters the junior school with some 4,000 words at his disposal. Thereafter vocabulary grows less rapidly, and Terman quotes an active vocabulary of 5,400, 7,200 and 9,000 words for average American children of 10, 12 and 14 years of age respectively.

When the child has acquired a small reading vocabulary and has mastered the phonetic approach to new words, his reading vocabulary tends to increase rapidly. Smith[29] has shown that in America (school age usually six), the average number of words recognised (according to Smith's definitions) increase from about 17,000 at 7 years of age, to over 30,000 at 11–12 years of age. Thus we get meaning both from hearing, and seeing in print, words that we cannot use orally.

Templin's study[30] of American children aged 3–8 years, published in 1957, shows the same pattern of growth in sentence length and complexity, and in the use of various parts of speech, as reported previously. But compared with 25 years earlier, children talked more, and used more

[28] Watts, A. F., *op. cit.*

[29] Smith, M. K., 'Measurement of the Size of General English Vocabulary, through the Elementary Grades and the High School,' *Genet. Psychol. Monogr.*, 1941, 24, 311–345.

[30] Templin, M. C., *Certain Language Skills in Children.* London: Oxford University Press, 1957.

complex sentences and adverb clauses. Possibly better education, mass media, or greater child-parent dialogue all contributed to this. Among her other interesting findings were:

(a) Significant differences in length of utterance as between boys and girls were rarely observed.

(b) The upper socio-economic groups used slightly longer utterances at most age levels tested, but at only two age levels were the differences statistically significant. Again, a slightly more advanced type of sentence structure was used by the higher socio-economic groups, but the differences were not great.

(c) There was a consistent decrease, with age, in the proportion of structurally incomplete but functionally complete remarks. Such remarks include: naming; answers in which words are implied because they are expressed in the question; expletives; and remarks which are not complete in themselves but which are clearly a continuation of the preceding remark.

(d) A steady increase with age in the use of more complex and elaborate forms of sentence.

(e) A great increase with age, over the five year span studied, of the use of subordinate clauses. This was true of both sexes and for upper and lower socio-economic groups. Adverbial clauses were most frequent, noun clauses next, and adjectival clauses least frequent.

Templin's work also confirmed McCarthy's conclusion that most of the usual indices of maturity such as vocabulary, articulation, sentence length, speech errors, are strongly related with the exception of vocabulary. Even so the correlations tend to decrease with age. The relation between language maturity and IQ or mental age depends on the intelligence test used. If it has a strong verbal content, the correlation will be higher than if a non-verbal test is used.

In 1964 Sampson[31] published the fourth of her papers dealing with the long term study of language development of 45 British children (22 boys and 23 girls). Speech was assessed at $2\frac{1}{2}$; spoken language at 5; vocabulary at 5, 8 and 10; written vocabulary at 10; reading at 8 and 10; non-verbal intelligence at 8; composition rating at 10 and subordination index (ratio of the number of subordinate clauses used to the total number of clauses used) at 10. As a general conclusion it seems that children's composition is fairly closely related to their other linguistic skills, past and present, but composition presents special difficulties and develops more laboriously than speech. At 10 years of age the mean inter-correlation between two measures of vocabulary, two written compositions (one factual, one imaginative) and the subordination index was ·53.

Readers are reminded that certain syntactical acquisitions continue to be made up to 10 years of age (see page 223).

[31] Sampson, O. C., 'Written Composition at 10 years as an aspect of Linguistic Development,' *Brit. J. Educ. Psychol.*, 1964, **34**, 143–150.

Interests and Activities. As children get older, boys and girls tend to develop different interests and join in different activities. Some of these sex differences must be due to physiological causes but it is probable that most others are due to the pattern of our culture. For example, boys are some ten per cent superior in vital capacity[32] to girls by the age of 10 years. This could partly account for sex differences in liking for activity and adventure. Again the greater interest of girls in dolls, and the greater aggressiveness in boys, could partly be due to physical influences (e.g. endocrine gland secretions). Indeed, it is hoped that future research will show us more clearly the part played by the culture pattern in these and other matters.

Throughout the primary-school period the child loves to be active and exercise his body in some way or other. The form of activity changes, however, with the years, and with the opportunities available to the child. Thus at 5–6 years the child runs, skips, dances, rides a tricycle or pushes a cart. There is also a good deal of imitation and play which involves 'pretending' (e.g. making a home or dressing up), and in connection with this we have already noted that the child will confuse fantasy with reality. By 5 years of age boys show an interest in games involving cowboys and Indians, guns, cops and robbers, and in the rudiments of ball play. Between 8 and 9 years they become somewhat less interested in unorganised running and chasing and more concerned with games that involve playing together, speed, and skill. Thus an interest in football, cricket, swimming, and boxing rapidly evolve after about 9 years of age. At the same time boys become increasingly keen on constructional activities such as making models, and playing with Meccano. Girls at 7 still continue to play at 'families' (with more elaborate dressing up now), but they also like playing at 'school', and at being 'teacher'. They show less interest in team games and in organised physical activities than boys do except for an interest in a few games such as netball. They do, however, frequently play at 'skipping'. By the age of 8 years, too, girls become active in sewing, knitting, and other domestic skills at an elementary level. Summing up, we may refer to the findings of Lehman and Witty[33] who surveyed the play activities of some 17,000 city and over 2,000 rural children. Their conclusions confirm that boys more often engage in active play and games involving skill and competition, while girls more frequently join in sedentary activities. They find, however, that the largest sex differences in interests occur between the ages of $8\frac{1}{2}$ and $10\frac{1}{2}$ years. After the latter age more activities become common to both sexes.

As soon as children can read, books open up a new world to them and it is hardly surprising that reading is a popular pastime with most children between 5 and 11 years of age. A survey made by the British Broadcasting

---

[32] The maximum quantity of air which can be expired after the deepest possible inspiration is called the vital capacity.

[33] Lehman, H. C., and Witty, P. A., *The Psychology of Play Activities*. New York: Barnes, 1927.

Corporation in November 1953 and reported by Kerslake,[34] gave information about the reading habits of some 3,700 children and young people. These were drawn from a hundred different localities spread over the British Isles and may be taken as a fairly representative sample. According to Kerslake, between 5 and 10 years of age, there is, among boys, an increase of interest in detective and mystery stories, in cowboys and 'western' stories, and in adventure, but a marked decline in interest in fairy tales. Girls showed an increase of interest in detective and mystery stories, school stories and adventure, but a much smaller decline of interest in fairy tales. Although not mentioned in the above survey, boys in the upper part of the primary school are interested in simple scientific and technical literature (e.g. the pictorial type of encyclopaedia). Both boys and girls are very interested in comics. But note that the reading material in which the various age groups are interested may change as fashions alter from one year to another, and as new materials become available.

But against this one must also note the findings (not complete at the time of writing) of the Sheffield University Institute of Education.[35] The reading habits of some nine thousand 10, 12 and 14-year-old children were studied. The most popular books were *Black Beauty, Little Women* and *Treasure Island*, followed by books like *Alice in Wonderland, Oliver Twist* and so on. But, while the favourites of today were the favourites of a century ago, the 9,000 children did mention 8,000 titles, so that new books are being read and new characters and heros enjoyed.

Teaching bright and gifted Primary School children. Teachers in primary schools meet, from time to time, very bright children who may be abler than they themselves. These children do present us with problems if we are going to do our duty to them and provide experiences and opportunities so as to develop their potentialities to the full. It must be remembered that from these children will come our future leaders in many fields, including those of science and technology. Perhaps we ought to provide such pupils with an 'enriched' school environment and curriculum. This problem has received a little study in this country although greater consideration has been given to it in the U.S.A.[36] Unfortunately most of the American texts are written from the point of view of a general school setting very different from that of ours.[37]

[34] Kerslake, E., 'Some Thoughts on Children's Reading,' *Look and Listen*, 1955, 9, 21–23. See also Carsley, J. D., 'The Interests of Children (aged 10–11) in Books,' *Brit. J. Educ. Psychol.*, 1957, 27, 13–23.
[35] Leader in *The Times Educational Supplement*, 6 August 1971.
[36] Cf. De Haan, F. R., and Havighurst, R. J., *Educating Gifted Children.* Chicago: Chicago University Press, 1961.
The Fifty-Seventh Yearbook of the National Society for the Study of Education, Part II, is devoted to the problem of *The Education of the Gifted.* See also *The Year Book of Education*, 1962. London: Evans.
[37] For an English author who has written on the topic see Wall, S. W., 'Highly Intelligent Children,' *Educational Research*, 1960, Vol. 1 and Vol. 2. Also Bridges, S. A. (Ed.), *Gifted Children and the Brentwood Experiment.* London: Pitman, 1969.

A study carried out under the writer's direction investigated some of the personality and cognitive characteristics of a group of 50 pupils aged 8 years 5 months to 11 years 7 months all of whom had WISC Verbal IQ's of 140 or more. The group was therefore comparable with Terman's group of gifted pupils (cf. page 52). The teachers rated their pupils on 25 personality characteristics using the same rating scale as Terman had used. British teachers gave their pupils almost the same mean ratings as had the teachers of Terman's group in California forty years ago. The subjects were rated very high for General Intelligence, Desire to Know, Originality, Desire to Excel, Truthfulness, etc., although on a few traits they came close to average, e.g. Freedom from Vanity and Egotism. In spite of their very high scores on conventional tests of intelligence and attainment, only ten per cent of the replies to questions involving logical thought were at the level of Piaget's stage of formal thought (see Chapter 6).[38]

[38] Lovell, K., and Shields, J. B., 'Some Aspects of a Study of the Gifted Child,' *Brit. J. Educ. Psychol.*, 1967, **37**, 201–208. Shields, J. B., *The Gifted Child*. Slough: N.F.E.R., 1968.

Chapter Seventeen

THE ADOLESCENT[1]

Physiological Changes and Physical Abilities. Soon after, or even before, the girl leaves the primary school (11-plus years) she begins to develop physically in some respects faster than before, acquires hair on the pubes and under the arms, and develops more mature breasts and a body more nearly like that of an adult. These changes mark the beginning of the adolescent period, which may be defined for both sexes, as that time in the teens when the individual approaches the peak of his physical and mental growth. Again, at this time the girls begin to menstruate, although the age at which this first happens cannot rigidly be laid down. Generally it begins between 12 and 14 years of age; but there are considerable differences, some beginning as early as 10 and some as late as 16–18 years of age, due in part to physiological conditions and in part to environment. There is evidence that inadequate diet, severe illness and other unfavourable environment factors tend to retard the onset of puberty (i.e. the age at which the individual becomes capable of reproduction). The onset of puberty in boys is less clearly marked by any one physical sign, but most investigators agree that it begins between 11 and 15 years of age. The voice breaks, hair makes its appearance on the pubes and face, and there is a rapid growth of the size of the genital organs. Adolescence is, however, a period of psychological as well as physiological change, and by the time the individual has reached the late teens or early twenties he has usually acquired a more stable outlook and assumed some responsibility for himself. With the coming of this psychological maturity and responsibility, as it were, we say that the individual has become an adult.

Growth was rapid in infancy and then slowed down in the middle years of school life. Thereafter comes a spurt in growth which starts in the sexes at different times. Girls grow at an increased rate from 9–12 and their rate of growth then decreases, whereas boys tend to grow most rapidly from 11–14 years. Girls tend to be taller than boys between about 11 and 12 years of age, while after about 15 the average male continues to develop into a taller and heavier individual than the average female. But it is important to remember that there is great individual variability in change of height, weight and other physiological functions during adolescence, and

[1] See also Wall, W. D., *Adolescents in School and Society.* London: N.F.E.R., 1968. In this, recent research on adolescence and on the influences affecting adolescent behaviour are considered and brought to bear on the problems of school organisation and curricula.

smooth curves tend to obscure individual variations. In view of these variations the method now used for determining the level of physiological maturity, that of skeletal analysis, is most useful. In this, the present status of bone formation (ossification) is studied by means of X-ray pictures of the wrist-bones, and/or other selected parts of the skeleton, and it is possible to arrive at what may be called a *bone age*. This technique shows that there is a close positive relationship between sexual and skeletal maturation. See also page 261.

Many investigations have been made into the physical abilities of children of secondary school age. Highmore and Jones[2] find evidence of a general athletic ability[3] among 11-year-old secondary modern schoolboys, and suggest that an estimate of a boy's athletic ability may be obtained from subjecting him to three tests—sprinting, long jump, and cricket ball throw—giving equal weight to each. Further evidence of a general factor of physical athletic ability has been found by Highmore[4] among male Training College students, and by Vernon[5] among Army recruits. Strength, which is usually measured by hand grip, increases rapidly during the first 20 years of life but at different rates from year to year. In boys there is evidence that manual strength roughly doubles during the primary-school period, and doubles again between 11 and 16. Girls are, of course, on the average, less strong than boys. This must be due in part to natural physiological differences, but it is also likely to be partly dependent on cultural conditions since in our society girls do not usually have the frequent and vigorous use of their muscles in bodily activity that boys have.

It is important to note that in our culture a typical adolescent boy is expected to have some interest, or to participate in, some form of physical activity. Such activity may range from rugby football to camping. True, some boys who have little interest in physical activities can compensate for this by performance in other directions, but unless this is done successfully the adolescent may find himself in difficulties over personal relationships with his contemporaries. Thus, encouraging interest, and imparting skill in games, athletics, and other physical activities, is one way of helping male adolescents to maintain mental health.

The Adolescent and Adults. The adolescent's relationships with adults, whether parents, teachers, or others, are a frequent source of difficulties. The boy or girl of 15–16 years is sexually mature, and is seeking independence and freedom from adult control. Like the child, he often has to

[2] Highmore, G. and Jones, B. W., 'The Athletic Ability of Boys in a Secondary Modern School,' *Brit. J. Stat. Psychol.*, 1959, **12**, 127–131.

[3] Athletic ability does not, of course, necessarily imply ability at games such as Rugby and Association Football. The former is involved in track and field events.

[4] Highmore, G., Unpublished Thesis, University of London Library, 1949.

[5] Vernon, P. E., *The Structure of Human Abilities*. London: Methuen, 1961. For a comprehensive survey of physical abilities see McCloy, C. H., and Young, N. D., *Tests and Measurements in Health and in Physical Education*. New York: Appleton-Century-Crofts, 3rd Edition, 1954.

accept the advice and decisions of adults even although he cannot understand them. Thus he is apt to scrutinise and criticise his parents and teachers, to flout their opinions, and disregard their authority. He alternates between resenting adult interference and wanting to confide in them; he is sometimes assertive and at other times shy and sensitive, still greatly needing help, but not wanting to ask for it. However, if his previous relationships with adults have been satisfactory, this phase will not last long.

It will be appreciated that the changes in thinking which take place in adolescence has repercussions in adolescents' relationships with adults. The former can now advance some hypothesis or build a theory without having seriously to consider whether it is practically or socially possible. Again, the adolescent can, for the first time, see the way in which adults run the world or do some specific thing as one of a number of ways. When he tries to communicate this to, say, parent or teacher the adult may not be able to consider the options. While we must certainly help adolescents to see possibilities not previously available to them, we must also remember that they do not have the experience to judge the value of the theories they propose.

The home is of the greatest importance to the adolescent. If it is a good home, it provides love and security; it transmits to him the *mores* and standards of society, and helps him in his adjustments to the outside world. The school and other environmental agencies are not as important as the home in these respects. While it is true that both parents and teachers can render great assistance to the adolescent by permitting him to work as an independent individual in as many ways and as frequently as possible, it is the attitude of parents, especially, which affects the growing up process.[6, 7] A certain amount of parental indulgence is helpful in that it provides an atmosphere of security while the individual is making increasing contact with the outside world. On the other hand, parental indifference or over-indulgence retards the process of adjustment to the world. It is vital that parents spend time with their adolescent children, discussing with them, giving their opinions on a number of issues and allowing their children to put their viewpoint too. Above all, adolescents must be made to feel that parents (and other adults) care about them and that they are not neglected. Note that the adolescent is particularly sensitive to injustice, sarcasm, or lack of understanding whether within or without the home. In many ways the conventions of the adolescent may conflict with those of the parents. Again, both sexes usually want to bring home their friends, although some do not because they feel ashamed of their parents, generally without good reason. Since these and other similar matters cause trouble

[6] Yet it is interesting to note that although parents exert such influence on the adolescent, he will, even when he has good parents, often prefer to confide in someone outside the family (e.g. a teacher).

[7] In boarding schools the pupils will naturally be more influenced by the attitudes of teachers than in day schools.

between adolescents and their parents, it is important that the latter should realise the need to handle adolescents with tact and understanding.

The majority of studies dealing with the attitudes of adolescents to their parents have been undertaken in the U.S.A. However, Musgrove[8] has shown among British children, that in early adolescence they increasingly prefer their coevals to their parents as leisure time companions. He also found that the peak of hostility towards the parent of the same sex occurred at 15 for boys, and at 14 for girls. These figures are in keeping with the American findings, but at no age did he find the high degree of hostility that some workers in the U.S.A. have found among adolescent girls. Up to 15 the British children made approving statements about their peers about as frequently as they did about adults in general, and less frequently than they did about their parents.

Another point which might be mentioned under this heading is the tendency of the adolescent to identify himself with an adult, e.g. teacher, or to ape a film star or well-known footballer. This phase of hero-worship is often valuable in that it leads to new deals and interests but it can lead to disillusionment. If, in the latter instance, his home life is also unhappy, he may, even more than usual, seek compensation perhaps in the form of excessive day-dreaming. Teachers can be of great help to adolescents by noticing, and guiding them through, such phases.

The Importance of Social Acceptance.[9] The adolescent has limited experience of life and often finds himself in social situations in which he does not know the way in which he is expected to behave. Further, as well as being sadly aware of his own limitations, he is often treated like a child. In these circumstances it is entirely reasonable that he should seek out companions of his own age who will give him the support and security that he needs. Among his equals he finds his greatest opportunity for social acceptance. Thus adolescents tend to be clannish and to develop their own styles of dress and ways of behaving. Moreover, if an individual wishes to be accepted by his equals he must abide by their standards. When a young person has been rejected by a group he will sometimes go to great lengths to become accepted again. Those who are faced with continued rejection, may display symptoms of aggression, social withdrawal or over-compensation in some other fields. Investigations have shown that with both sexes, sociable, friendly, enthusiastic children, are those most popular with their contemporaries. We have also seen that skill in physical activities is, among boys, a valuable attribute from the point of view of social acceptability. But it must be remembered that there are wide individual differences, both in the desire for social acceptance by their peers and in reactions to continued rejection.

[8] Musgrove, F., 'Intergeneration attitudes,' *Brit. J. soc. clin. Psychol.*, 1963, 2, 209–223.
[9] Compare Hemming, J., *Problems of Adolescent Girls*. London: Heinemann, 1960.

Role-Conflict in Adolescence. Musgrove[10] has made an interesting study of role-conflict in adolescence. A questionnaire had to be completed by fourth-year grammar and modern school children; also by a smaller number of junior school pupils and technical college students. They had to respond to four statements: Fit and good at games; Behave sensibly and generally 'act your age'; Be respectful, courteous and polite to your parents and elders; Be quite free to stay up late, or stay out late, if you wish.

The subjects were asked to rank each of the above four aspects of behaviour to show:

What they ideally wished to be (*role-conception*);
What they thought mothers, fathers, friends, bosses wished them to be like (*role-expectation*);
What in fact they thought they were like (*perceived role-performance*).

Thus under the column dealing with the ideal self, each subject placed in rank order the four statements given above. The same was done under the columns relating to mother, father, etc.; also under the column dealing with the actual self. Musgrove found that role-conflicts were consistently high in three widely separated grammar schools, and the role-conflicts in girls in three modern schools in the same area were consistently low. Grammar school girls and modern school boys were intermediate in degree of role-conflict. Overall the grammar school boys and girls were more at odds with themselves, with their friends, their parents and their teachers than were the modern school children. Musgrove argues that it seems to be the type of educational institution that increases or reduces role-conflict. The demands of the grammar school may make for a deeper sense of conflict than the modern school, for the former may promote more anxieties, tensions and uncertainties, and a greater separation from adult life. While the author may well be right, we have to be careful to eliminate social class as a variable since role-conflict may differ within such classes.

Adolescent Groups. We must now turn to considering the group life of adolescents in more detail. First, some groupings may be formed merely because children go to the same school or live in the same neighbourhood. These may be temporary affairs, or they may be long-lived; usually though not always, they contain members of one sex only. A second type of adolescent group is the clique. This is generally a small single-sexed or mixed group of young people, and there is usually an emotional element binding them together. These cliques may arise within a school, or in, say, the youth club, or among the young people of a church. Members usually have strong feelings of friendship for one another, and help one another in preference to outsiders. Thirdly, there are the larger adolescent groups formed by individuals who have common interests and ideals and not

[10] Musgrove, F., 'Role-Conflict in Adolescence,' *Brit. J. Educ. Psychol.*, 1964, 34, 34–42.

because they live near one another or go to the same school. These groups are likely to be older and to include both sexes.

A fourth and very important type of adolescent grouping is the gang.[11] Compared with other groups, this is usually more highly organised and sometimes has a headquarters at a definite place. Its members may have grouped themselves together for some good purpose, but because of conflicts and pressures from without, the group turns into a gang. The gang thus provides for the frustrated individual a pattern of behaviour, and offers rewards in the way of prestige and companionship. Thrasher[12] suggested as long ago as 1927 that the gang seems to be the child's answer to the failure of the family and neighbourhood to provide for basic needs and drives. Note that many gangs indulge in harmless activities and do not come into contact with the law, although they are more likely to do so than other adolescent groups because of the way in which they were brought into being. Members of a gang sometimes dress alike.

Attitudes of Adolescents in School. Allen[13] has summarised relevant literature bearing on the problem of how best we may maintain good adolescent attitudes in school. He concludes that ordinary adolescents must be made to feel that they are really being taught; that there are many worth while things to do; that their opinions and feelings count; that school recognises the status they wish to have, and often do have, outside school; and that school has a real bearing on what they will do when they leave. A more recent study by Edwards and Webb[14] among 232 grammar school pupils, 77 per cent of whom were over 18, suggests that these older adolescents have an ambivalent attitude towards guidance from their teachers. They demand both clear, direct instruction and informal discussion, and they want both advice and guidance, and independence. The majority rejected both permissiveness which seems synonomous with indifference by their teachers, and restrictive authoritarianism.

The Interests and Activities of the Adolescents. In interests and activities, as in other aspects of adolescent development, individuals differ greatly among themselves. Valentine[15] has pointed out that adolescent interests also tend to fluctuate. But the available evidence suggests that interests tend to become more stable at later ages. Conditions which affect such interests and activities include social and political happenings (e.g. nearness to the end of an economic depression or major war), the time of year (e.g. summer or

[11] Not to be confused with the primary-school gang which may be formed by the age of 7 years or earlier.

[12] Thrasher, F. M., *The Gang.* University of Chicago Press, 1927.

[13] Allen, E. A., 'Attitudes of Children and Adolescents in School,' *Educational Research*, 1960, 3, 65–80.

[14] Edwards, T. and Webb, D., 'Freedom and Responsibility in the Sixth Form,' *Educ. Research*, 1971, 14, 46–50.

[15] Valentine, C. W., 'Adolescence and Some Problems of Youth Training,' *Brit. J. Educ. Psychol.*, 1943, 13, 57–68.

winter sports), sex, physique and health, intelligence, educational opportunity, social background, past and present opportunities, and such
factors as urban and rural environment. Thus many of the reported findings in regard to interests apply to only a particular group of adolescents
at a specific period of time. Another difficulty is that an adolescent might
have an interest in an activity, but cannot engage in it for one reason or
another, e.g. poor performance in some skill.

It is often supposed that reading books is very popular at all ages during
adolescence, provided the young person is a competent reader and is not
actively discouraged by the home. But there is also evidence that some
adolescents, especially in the more congested areas of large cities, read very
few books out of school. In the survey reported by Kerslake *op. cit.*,
boys and girls between 12 and 15 years of age were interested in detective
and mystery stories, and adventure, and the girls were also interested in
school stories. But between 16 and 20 years of age, when the majority were
out at work, there was a sharp decline in interest in all types of books with
the exception of detective and mystery stories. A recent study by Yarlott
and Harpin[16] among 800 G.C.E. 'O' level and 200 'A' level candidates,
indicated that the six most popular categories of leisure-time reading
materials were humorous writing, mystery and suspense, novels with
serious themes, science fiction, love or romance, and historical novels.
Girls were more predominantly concerned with the last two categories
although the percentages of boys and girls were more nearly equal in the
others. Newspaper reading, however, seems to be firmly established by
13–14 years of age in both sexes,[17] and comics and magazines are the most
popular reading material of all during adolescence. But reading tastes and
popularity of certain newspaper items are likely to change from one period
of history to another; they also vary between ability levels and between
pupils of different cultural backgrounds.

It has often been suggested that there is a marked increase of interest
in religion and even of religious experience during adolescence, more
especially, perhaps, among the children of the upper working and middle
classes.[18] Whether actual 'conversion' is supposed to take place, or whether
the adolescent is particularly susceptible to the influences of the home,
church, or Bible class, is not known. It is certain that many adolescents
think about, and discuss, religion. Some investigators (e.g. Kuhlen and
Arnold[19]) suggest that changes in interest in religion during adolescence

[16] Yarlott, G. and Harpin, W. S., '1,000 Responses to English Literature (2),'
Educ. Research, 1971, **13**, 87–97.
[17] See Burns, D. G., 'Newspaper Reading in the Secondary Modern School,'
Brit. J. Educ. Psychol., 1955, **25**, 1–9. Williams, A. R., 'The Magazine Reading
of Secondary School Children,' *Brit. J. Educ. Psychol.*, 1951, **21**, 186–198; Alderson,
C., *Magazines Teenagers Read*. London: Pergamon, 1968.
[18] See Valentine, C. W., *Psychology and its Bearing on Education*. London:
Methuen, 1950, 567–569.
[19] Kuhlen, R. G., and Arnold, M., 'Age Differences in Religious Beliefs and
Problems during Adolescence,' *J. genet. Psychol.*, 1944, **65**, 291–300.

are due to the accumulated experience of life in combination with increasing intellectual maturity; hence the individual can better interpret the world of facts and ideas which he is meeting. Others suggest that the seemingly greater interest in religion is part of the search for controlling values around which the individual may integrate his life, and which is so typical of the adolescent. At the same time he becomes increasingly aware of his actual self and his limitations. Indeed, adolescence is frequently described as a time of conflict between youthful ideals and the real self.

It must be noted, too, that active interest in religion decreases during adolescence if we take church membership as a criterion. Thus Moreton[20] found that the commonest age for discontinuing church attendance was between 15 and 19 in both sexes, with more boys than girls ceasing to attend at an earlier age, and more females than males discontinuing between 19 and 24 years of age.

A more recent study among university students suggested that the religious beliefs of Arts and Pure Science students declined during the early years at the university; but the decline continued in the later years only for the science students. Medical students in their final years, and students training for the teaching profession—especially the Arts students —had the highest scores of all on an attitude test.[21] Another study[22] investigated changes in religious attitudes among a group of 106 students between their first and third years at the university (i.e. it was a longitudinal study). Movement away from religion appeared to be more common among women, and Nonconformist and Roman Catholic students than among Church of England students, although there was additional evidence to suggest that university education, in itself, is unlikely to be important in bringing about these changes. It is possible that some of these changes are due to the general decline in attitude to religion in recent years and not due to age as such. Wright and Cox[23] report on the changes in attitude to the Bible and religious education over the period 1963–1970. In the former year a survey was carried out among 2,276 boys and girls in the second year of the sixth form, while in 1970 the corresponding figure was 1,574. In the latter year there was much less support for the legal provision of RI in school and less favourable attitudes to it, together with less acceptance of the divine authority of the Bible. While the attitude of girls to RI and the Bible is still more favourable than that of boys, their attitudes have changed more than those of boys.

The majority of male adolescents are interested in physical activities

[20] Moreton, F. E., 'Attitudes to Religion among Adolescents and Adults,' *Brit. J. Educ. Psychol.*, 1944, 14, 69–79.

[21] Poppleton, P. K. and Pilkington, G. W., 'The Measurement of Religious Attitudes in a University Population,' *Brit. J. soc. Clin. Psychol.*, 1963, 2, 20–36.

[22] Pilkington, G. W., Poppleton, P. K. and Robertshaw, G., 'Changes in Religious Attitudes and Practices Among Students during University Degree Courses,' *Brit. J. Educ. Psychol.*, 1965, 35, 150–157.

[23] Wright, D. and Cox, E., 'Changes in Attitude towards RI and the Bible among Sixth Form Boys and Girls,' *Brit. J. Educ. Psychol*, 1971, 41, 328–331.

of some sort or other, and we have noted that such interest usually makes them more acceptable to members of their age-group. Girls are also interested in physical activities, but not to the same extent. Thus we find adolescent boys watching or participating in boxing, association and rugby football, and cricket; and both sexes interested, or taking part in, hockey, swimming, tennis, skating, cycling, walking, camping, or athletic events.

As boys and girls approach school-leaving age, they spend a good deal of time thinking and talking about what they will do when they leave school. Considerable fluctuation of vocational choice occurs among younger adolescents, but as they get older their choices become more realistic and they take more account of their own abilities and of the opportunities of the environment. Thus Wilson[24] in a study of over 1,600 secondary-modern school-leavers found that roughly three-quarters of the children made reasonable choice of vocation in view of their intelligence. According to their recollections of earlier wishes there had been frequent changes in vocational interests. Some of these were later realised as impractical, although they might continue to remain in the mind alongside more serious aims. Children with good social and emotional adjustment seemed to be more mature in their attitudes to vocations. Other important factors influencing vocational choice were found to be: parent's occupation, the experience and opinions of friends and relatives, interest and success in relevant school subjects, and the opportunity of seeing work done and trying it out. Other studies suggest that good immediate financial rewards, the opinions of older brothers and sisters, security and social prestige, are also important elements in influencing adolescents' vocational choice. Furthermore, the children of the higher income groups are more likely to follow in their father's footsteps (or in work of comparable social and economic status) than children of the lower income groups.

Tyler[25] has shown that among American children, interests that are characteristic of scientists become crystallised sometime between the tenth and fourteenth years. But the temperamental matrix out of which they emerge goes back to a much earlier developmental stage. Early acceptance of the masculine role seems to be a precursor of scientific interests. In the case of girls, career interests begin to take shape at or before the age of 14, although there may well be certain temperamental factors that precede them. Girls who develop such interests seem to be rather later than others in adopting the feminine role, for they make fewer feminine choices in the first grade but are indistinguishable from others on this basis at later stages.

The transition from school to work, however, is not always a smooth one. It many kinds of employment the physical conditions in which

[24] Wilson, M. D., 'The Vocational Preferences of Secondary Modern Schoolchildren,' Brit. J. Educ. Psychol., 1953, 23, 163–179.
[25] Tyler, L. E., 'The Antecedents of Two Varieties of Vocational Interests,' Genet. Psychol. Monogr., 1964, 70, 177–228.

adolescents work, and the hours they work, are very different from those obtaining in the schools; furthermore, foremen are people very different from teachers in outlook, and the moral temperature of the factory is often lower than that of the school. Tenen[26] found among adolescent factory workers, who had been unable to exercise much choice in deciding their work, considerable dissatisfaction and resentment arising in the work-situation itself, as a result of frustration of the adolescent's desire for satisfactory physical development, for security of social status in the factory, and for the acquisition of satisfactory skills in the work. Schools could help children by allowing them to get close acquaintance with actual work conditions, and by seeing that they get as much sound advice as possible (*see* Chapter 11). Note that the abler adolescents are, on the average, likely to be happier in their work because they are older and better educated, and are likely to go into jobs where more satisfactory working conditions and better prospects prevail.

Reference was made in Chapter 11 to the data of Maizels (*op. cit.*) gathered in 1965 but published in 1970. It also showed that apprentices—particularly those in large firms—most frequently described their jobs as interesting, varied, responsible. But boys and girls in unskilled manual jobs had work of lowest interest appeal. Unfortunately the study revealed that most pupils had no real ideal of what work conditions would be like or what the prospects were. Vocational aspirations were, on the average, higher than those subsequently achieved. The findings of the investigation again emphasise the need to help pupils appreciate the problems of real work conditions, and to give them as much sound advice as possible.

Veness[27] has provided evidence on the aspirations of school leavers. She used an interview, also an essay in which the adolescent had to consider himself at the end of his life and thus write his life story from the time he left school. The 'average' boy wanted a job with promotion prospects with the peak ambition lying in middle management or in a post of similar status. He wished to marry and have children who would then become the centre of his ambitions; his ultimate objective being an adequate pension and retirement to a cottage. For the average girl, marriage and maternity were central objectives. Her ambitions were almost wholly for her husband and children although she wanted a 'nice' home and 'nice' friends. If her husband survived with her she looked forward to ending her days in the country anticipating the occasions when her grandchildren visited her.

Adolescent Abilities. In Chapter 3 we saw that measured intelligence or academic aptitude grows rapidly during childhood, but that after about 12 years growth begins to decelerate. The age at which the level of intelligence reaches its maximum seems to be dependent upon the actual level of

[26] Tenen, C., 'The Adolescent in the Factory,' *Brit. J. Educ. Psychol.*, 1947, **17**, 72–82.
[27] Veness, T., *School Leavers*. London: Methuen, 1962.

intelligence, and the length and quality of the schooling which the child receives. In Great Britain, measured intelligence seems to reach its peak at about 15 or soon after for most people, but this might not be true when the compulsory school-leaving age is raised. Teachers might well ask themselves whether some secondary schools are stimulating their pupils as much as they might, for, as we suggested earlier, the degree of intellectual stimulation received at the secondary stage seems to vary more widely than at the primary stage. For example, Vernon[28] provided evidence showing a correlation of 0·79 between an assessment of goodness of schooling, or amount of intellectual stimulation received at each of a number of schools (made by the Chief Education Officer of the L.E.A.), and IQ gains or losses between 10–11 and 14 years of age. The results suggested that, on the whole, the secondary schools, together with the home environments from which their pupils came, provided a poorer stimulus to general intellectual development than did the grammar and technical schools and the environments from which their pupils were drawn. But as Vernon points out, these results may in part reflect the educational content of the intelligence tests used, for in another area where a less verbal type of test was used, there were very much smaller gains or losses.

Verbal educational abilities (the v:ed group), and spatial mechanical abilities (the k:m group), increase during adolescence, provided the individual is receiving adequate stimulation in these fields. As for later adolescence, we saw in Chapter 3 that the v:ed abilities (other than reading ability and vocabulary) remain stationary, or decline somewhat, in the years immediately following school-leaving, unless there is further training or relevant experience; while the k:m abilities increase until the late teens or early twenties with or without much training or experience. Teachers should note that the more homogeneous the children in a secondary-school class are in respect of general intelligence, the more important special abilities become in determining the relative progress that pupils can make in a school subject.

Wing[29] reported that scores on his musical test increase with age until 17 and then remain fairly constant. He also stressed the very important practical point that if musical ability does depend upon a specific ability or abilities, then the organisation of classes for school music should be by cross-classification rather than by normal streams for these are usually based on performance in the more academic subjects. Bentley (*op. cit.*) also supports the idea of regrouping pupils for music lessons.

Burns[30] made a useful study of the vocabulary of secondary modern school children. He has provided the percentage number of boys and girls, all in their third year at such schools, who were able to give, in writing, the

[28] Vernon, P. E., *The Times Educational Supplement*, May 6, 1955.
[29] Wing, H. D., 'Some Applications of Test Results to Education in Music,' *Brit. J. Educ. Psychol.*, 1954, **24**, 161–170.
[30] Burns, D. G., *Vocabulary of the Secondary Modern School Child*. London: National Foundation for Educational Research, Occasional Publication, 1960.

meaning of each of some 4,000 words. These words were such that they were unlikely to have known them when they entered the modern school, and yet needed to know almost all of them before they left. His results should be studied by all those interested in the vocabulary of such children. He also found that children of both sexes appear to know more words when judged by oral definition than they do when asked to write the oral definitions on paper.

As far as the growth of formal operational thought is concerned, all the available evidence suggests that schooling and culture are important influences.[31] Beyond some minimum chronological age set by neurophysiological conditions, the age of onset of formal thought seems to be linked to the concepts used in the community, the climate of expectancy and opinion in the society, the experiences received in the home or at school or work, and by social attitudes.

The Development of Heterosexual Relationships. In the previous chapter we noted that single-sex groups are formed before the child leaves the primary school although these groupings are usually loosely knit. Earlier in this chapter we saw that by early adolescence these groups become of more importance to the individual, but that they are usually still single-sexed. Indeed, at this stage, there is often some aloofness and even antagonism between the sexes, the girls thinking that the boys are rough and the boys thinking that the girls are 'soft'. There may also be rivalry between the sexes.

A little later many adolescents find themselves particularly attracted to a person of the same sex, of about the same age, and having the same interests. They exchange mutual confidences and generally become 'bosom pals'. This phase is particularly noticeable among girls, and is often referred to as a 'crush', or 'pash'. It must not be thought, however, that this happens only in boarding schools where boys and girls tend to be segregated from one another for long periods, nor must this homosexual stage be thought of as abnormal in any way. Indeed, it seems to be a perfectly natural stage in the development of heterosexual relations. At about the same time a girl may find herself particularly attracted to an older man or woman (e.g., a teacher), and more rarely, a boy may feel similarly about an adult. Such attractions are temporary affairs. There is also, as we have seen, a good deal of hero-worship on the part of the adolescent.

The next phase seems to be one where groups of boys appear to be interested in, and watch, groups of girls, and vice versa. For example, a group of girls may watch boys play football, or a group of boys may ride their bicycles up and down past a group of girls. There seems to be at this stage, sexual curiosity, but not sexual desire as such. Soon, however, the individual is attracted to a particular person of the opposite sex and the

[31] Peluffo, N., 'Culture and Cognitive Problems,' *Int. J. Psychol.*, 1967, **2**, 187–198.

pair begin to meet. In the early days the relationship is usually idealistic, and romantic, with the boy and girl often merely wanting to be together, to talk, hold hands, and to look into each other's eyes. Parents and teachers should look upon these friendships sympathetically; they should not be forbidden, and parents should encourage young people to take their friends home. Such affairs are often temporary and usually harmless, although the adolescent needs to be helped through this stage. Note carefully the effect of our culture pattern on the behaviour of the sexes at this stage, and compare such behaviour with the 'dating' of American adolescents. Finally, in later adolescence, there is a more mature 'falling in love', with the idea of a home and partner in the mind, and a greater urge for sexual intercourse. The writer has been careful to omit any ages in connection with these stages for there are great individual differences in psychological and sexual development.

It is necessary in this section to say something of the sexual behaviour of adolescents for there is no doubt that there is a widespread need for sex education. This book is not, however, the place to say by whom such education should be given, or the form that it should take, except to state that in the writer's view we tend to stress the teaching of facts rather than educating the feelings. Moreover, positive help and guidance would also be of help to many boys and girls in facilitating the rather difficult process of getting to know, and become adapted to, one another. Co-education helps enormously in this respect in educating the sexes together. Various studies (chiefly in the U.S.A.) have shown that adolescents are interested in the details of sexual intercourse, child bearing, and menstruation; also in the art of making friends, courtesy, manners, and social poise. Left to themselves, however, most boys and many girls in Britain get their ideas about conception from their friends.[32] Mothers are also an important source of information for girls, while teachers play some part in informing the members of both sexes.

Kinsey et al.,[33, 34] in their well known studies, report that a very high percentage of male adolescents (in the U.S.A.) are regularly sexually active[35] by 15 years of age. Between the onset of adolescence and 15 years of age, the frequency of sexual outlet is surprisingly close to that of the 21–30 year group of males, that is, the group (many of which are married) with the highest frequency of sexual activity of any. Indeed, if the popula-

[32] Schofield, M., The Sexual Behaviour of Young People. London: Longmans, 1965. Chesser, E., The Sexual, Marital and Family Relationships of the English Woman. London: Hutchinson, 1956.

[33] Kinsey, A. C., Pomeroy, W. B., and Martin, C. E., Sexual Behaviour in the Human Male. London: Saunders, 1948.

[34] Kinsey, A. C., Pomeroy, W. B., Martin, C. E. and Gebhard, P. H., Sexual Behaviour in the Human Female. London: Saunders, 1953.

[35] Sexually active means indulging in any activity leading to an orgasm and not just sexual intercourse.

For critical essays on the Kinsey reports see: An Analysis of the Kinsey Reports on Sexual Behaviour. Edited by Geddes, D. London: Muller, 1954. Also Kardiner, A., Sex and Morality. London: Routledge and Kegan Paul, 1955.

tion tended to marry earlier the authors think that it is likely that the maximum frequency of outlet in the male would, on the average, come in the early teens. In the female, however, they find in their total group a much smaller percentage had experienced sexual orgasm by 15 years of age, and this remains true even at 20. On the other hand a substantial proportion of American girls admit to having been erotically aroused in some form or other by 15. Thus Kinsey points out, after considering all his evidence, that the average adolescent girl gets along with about one-fifth of the sexual activity indulged in by the adolescent male. Indeed, the average frequency of sexual outlet in the women between 20 and 30 years of age, is still below the average for the adolescent boy and it must be difficult for many wives, mothers and female teachers to understand the sexual problems that boys have to face. The more recent study of British teenagers[36] (934 boys, 939 girls) aged 15–19 shows that in spite of all the strong social and physiological pressures towards sexual intercourse, most teenagers manage to resist these influences. Indeed, British secondary schools contain only a tiny minority that are sexually experienced. The incidence of such experience increases somewhat in the late teens, especially among couples who are 'going steady' or are engaged.[37, 38]

The effect of the culture pattern on the problems of adolescents. Earlier in this century it was maintained that adolescence must necessarily be a period of stress and strain, for the individual was undergoing great changes in many aspects of his life. Today, more people are of the opinion that if society permits the individual to play the part of an adult at an earlier age, then his maturity will come earlier. Partly responsible for this change in outlook is the work of Margaret Mead, Malinowski, and others, who have contrasted the development of adolescents in the more primitive cultures (e.g. among the South Sea Islanders) with that in Western Europe. In some cultures the period of adolescence appears to be made easier because young people are given status and responsibility at a comparatively early age. However, we must not forget that during adolescence there are major physiological changes occurring, and that these changes may not be possible without an effect on behaviour.[39] From the point of view of parent and teacher, the important thing is that they should do all they can to facilitate the adolescent's development and help him to reach maturity as early as possible. This means that adolescents must be treated as adults whenever possible and given as much responsibility as they can shoulder, whether in the

[36] Schofield, M., *op. cit.*
[37] For a description of how problems of sex appear to adolescents themselves see Jordan, G. W., and Fisher, E. M., *Self Portrait of Youth*. London: Heinemann, 1955, Ch. 6.
[38] The building up of sound values (see Chapter 14) in relation to sexual behaviour is a matter of the greatest importance to the well-being of society. Compare Hacker, E., *Telling the Teenagers*. London: Andre Deutsch, 1957.
[39] Tanner, J. M., *Physical Maturing and Behaviour at Adolescence*. London: National Children's Home, 1959.

home, or in the running of their affairs within the school. It also implies appropriate teaching techniques and suitable approaches to the subject matter being studied in the classroom.

Some will argue that the obstreperousness of youth is merely a sign of insufficient discipline. Barnes[40] counters this argument by pointing out that if modern youth is irresponsible, one of the main reasons is that the adult world gives it too few chances for shouldering responsibility. We have already noted that in some cultures, mostly different from our own, the adolescent period appears to pass with less stress if the individual is given status and responsibility early. Even in Great Britain traces of this can be seen, for, generally speaking, adolescents in the country do not have as many problems and difficulties as those who live in the cities. In the country everyone, whether adolescent or adult, is more likely to have a specific place in society, with a job and responsibilities suited to his particular circumstances. The adolescent thus tends to acquire his independence more easily and earlier, and because he is less frustrated, he is likely to have fewer problems.[41]

Physiological changes and Intellectual growth. We have already indicated that there is much individual variability in the age at which there are rapid changes (due mainly to heredity) in height, weight, and other physiological function, so that chronological age is a poor guide to physiological development at adolescence. According to Tanner[42] girls are always in advance of boys in the matter of *bone age*, and thus, it might be supposed, in general physiological development. The advancement begins before birth, and this may be the main reason why more boys than girls die at or around birth.

According to Tanner the menarcheal age has been getting earlier by some four months per decade, and the average ten-year-old today is the equal of the eleven-year-old, anatomically and physiologically, at the turn of the century. The causes of this trend are not yet clear, but it is likely to have educational consequences. It must also be added that it is likely that this trend to earlier puberty has now ceased.

Again, if intellectual maturity is related to developmental age rather than chronological age this could, as Tanner points out, have been an important issue when selecting children for different kinds of secondary education.[43] We may have selected for grammar schools some who are more physically mature and not always those who would ultimately possess

---

[40] Barnes, L. J., *Youth Service in an English County*. London: King George's Jubilee Trust, 1945.

[41] For further details concerning the psychology of Adolescence see: Hurlock, E. B., *Adolescent Development*. London: McGraw Hill, 3rd Edition, 1967. Gesell, A., Ilg, F. L., and Ames, L. B., *Youth*. London: Hamish Hamilton, 1956.

[42] Tanner, J. M., *Educational and Physical Growth*. London: University of London Press Ltd., 1961.

[43] For a discussion relevant to this point see Nisbet, J. D., and Entwistle, N. J., *Age of Transfer to Secondary Education*. London: University of London Press Ltd., 1966.

most ability. Long ago Dearborn and Rothney[44] pointed out the possibility that using percentage of growth, based on the estimated maximum growth of an individual or of an unselected group, we might get a better forecast of final mental level from present mental level, than from present IQ.

However, Nisbet[45] has produced evidence that early maturity does not affect performance in tests at 11+ to any marked degree. In a year group of 1,400 girls he found that early maturers (menarche before 12:3) had a slightly higher mean test score (103) than the others. But the early maturers maintained their same average superiority at 7, 9 and 13 as well as at 11. However, in a later paper, Nisbet et al.[46] suggest that the superiority of very early maturers on intelligence test scores at 13 is substantially reduced by 16, and late maturers make up much of their previous inferiority in average test scores. Douglas[47] in a longitudinal study of some 5,000 children, found that girls who reached puberty early were superior in behaviour and measured ability, but these advantages were not due to greater physical maturity but to the fact that a large proportion of them were only children or came from small families.

Boys who mature early are likely to be rated by their peers as more physically attractive, better dressed and more relaxed; and more often chosen as leaders in athletic and social activities. The late maturing boy, on the other hand, is more likely to feel inadequate, and dominated or rejected by others. In the case of girls, however, early maturation does not appear to have the same social significance.[48]

Language Structure and Social Class. Bernstein[49] has compared the *public language* of lower working class, with the *formal language* of middle class adolescents. The first-named language is characterised by a more *restricted code*, the second by a more *elaborate* one. Some of the characteristics of the public language are as follows: short, grammatically simple, often unfinished sentences; use of approximate nouns and verbs; simple repetitive use of conjunctions ('and', 'so'); rigid and limited use of adverbs and adjectives; statements are formulated as questions to set up a 'sympathetic circularity' ('It's only natural, isn't it?'); use of a fixed number of idiomatic

[44] Dearborn, W. F. and Rothney, J. W., *Predicting the Child's Development.* Cambridge, Mass.: *Sci-Art*, 1941, 286, 287.

[45] Nisbet, J. D. and Illsley, R., 'The Influence of Early Puberty on Test Performance at Age Eleven,' *Brit. J. Educ. Psychol.*, 1963, 33, 169–176.

[46] Nisbet, J. D., Illsley, R., Southerland, A. E. and Douse, M. J., 'Puberty and Test Performance: a Further Report,' *Brit. J. Educ. Psychol.*, 1964, 34, 202–203.

[47] Douglas, J. W. B., *The Home and the School.* London: MacGibbon and Kee, 1964.

[48] See Eichorn, D. H., 'Biological Correlates of Behaviour,' in *Child Psychology*: the Sixty-second Yearbook of the National Society for the Study of Education. Chicago: The University of Chicago Press, 1963, 32–52.

[49] Bernstein, B., 'Aspects of Language and Learning in the Genesis of the Social Process,' *J. Child Psychology and Psychiatry*, 1961, 1, 313–324. See also Brandis, W. and Henderson, D., *Social Class Language and Communication.* London: Routledge and Kegan Paul, 1970.

phrases; while reason and conclusion are often confounded to give a categoric statement ('Do as I tell you!'). This last point is very serious since the adult's reply to a child's question is frequently of the type, 'Because I told you so'.

These characteristics are not found as often in the language of middle class children. In Bernstein's view, these different language structures arise out of different modes of speech within the social strata which affect the child from the first year of life. These different modes of speech direct the child's attention to different aspects of the environment. In turn, children from lower working class homes tend to represent to themselves different aspects of the environment compared with children from middle class backgrounds. The former are less skilled, compared with the latter, in using language to handle spatial and temporal relationships and to deal with situations not immediately present. The middle class child uses language more frequently to handle the past and the future, to express spatial relationships (e.g. 'The small blue doll is behind the big clock on the sideboard') and generally make himself explicit even when the objects, persons or events are no longer in evidence. Once the linguistic structure has been learnt it is kept, for it is a way of eliciting and strengthening ways of thinking and feeling functionally related to the social group. It is not yet known if this is the complete explanation. It is possible that lower working class children who are culturally deprived, but who mix a great deal with middle class children, develop a language structure that is more akin to that of the latter and become 'bilingual'. Moreover, the somewhat greater mixing of the social classes due to contemporary life, and the greater varieties of language now available to all because of mass media, may well be doing something to bridge the gap between middle and lower working class children in respect of language. In any case, earlier workers such as Templin, while clearly finding small differences between the language of upper and lower socio-economic groups, did not find quite such great differences as Bernstein claims.

Language structure affects attitudes to, and performance at, school; e.g. at secondary school, public language may work against the development of Piaget's *formal thinking* where the logic of propositions is involved.

Chapter Eighteen

MALADJUSTED AND DELINQUENT CHILDREN

MALADJUSTMENT[1]

The Problem of Defining Normal Behaviour. No exact definition of normal behaviour can be given, but in general and somewhat loose terms, we may say that a person's behaviour is normal in so far as he can make his thoughts and behaviour conform to the major moral and social values of his cultural group. But note, carefully, the following:

(*a*) Normality is relative to the culture pattern. Some kinds of behaviour and thinking considered abnormal in one society may be thought normal in another. This also applies to sub-cultures within a wider culture pattern.

(*b*) Some forms of behaviour may be normal for one child or adult but abnormal for another. For example, an introverted child will find it less easy to make friends with other children than will an extravert.

(*c*) What may be normal behaviour at one age may be abnormal at another. In early adolescence many children have an intense interest in a member of their own sex. Later on the interest is normally in a member of the opposite sex.

(*d*) Our ideas of normality may change with time. A reformer in his own generation may be looked upon as a maladjusted and dangerous crank. In the next generation he may be looked upon as intelligent, progressive, and normal.

The report of the Ministry of Education on Maladjusted Children[2] suggests that maladjustment is a term describing an individual's relation at a particular time to the people or circumstances of his environment. It considers that a child is maladjusted if he is developing in ways which have a bad effect on himself or his fellows, ways which cannot be remedied by parent or teacher. There are, however, in the writer's view, degrees of maladjustment, and while we in this book are certainly interested in those whose maladjustment is severe enough for them to have to receive specialised help at, say, a Child Guidance Clinic, we are also concerned with those whose maladjustment is slight and who can be helped by parents and

[1] See also Chazan, M., 'Maladjusted Pupils: Trends in Post-War Theory and Practice,' *Educational Research*, 1963, **6**, 29–41. See also a series of five short papers, 'Symposium: Recent Research in Maladjustment,' *Brit. J. Educ. Psychol.*, 1968, **38**, 1–13.

[2] Ministry of Education, *Report of the Committee on Maladjusted Children.* London: H.M.S.O., 1955. For information regarding the likely incidence of maladjustment among children, see Appendix H of the report.

teachers alone. The report itself, and the definition of maladjustment, hardly allow for those less serious though far more numerous cases.

How Psychological Adjustment and Maladjustment Might Arise. Woodruff[3] has suggested, in effect, that healthy mental development depends upon the adequate reduction of personal needs. Primary and secondary needs bring about *striving* behaviour within the organism, which in turn brings about behaviour patterns directed towards the attainment of goals which will give need reduction. If the child reaches a large proportion of these goals, provided these goals are socially acceptable, then there will be healthy personal adjustment. But very often there are 'barriers'[4] resulting in the child's suffering frustration. If he is unable to make appropriate responses in these circumstances, and frequently obtains only partial success in reaching his goals, then he may become maladjusted. Further-more, if he repeatedly experiences no success whatever, he may eventually suffer mental breakdown. Note, however, that the selection of goals itself depends upon the psychological adjustment of the child (the maladjusted child more frequently attempts goals not acceptable to society); it also depends upon his sentiments, level of aspiration, the insight he has into his own condition and potentialities, and many other variables. Unfortun-ately, when a child becomes maladjusted, his parents and teachers frequent-ly put additional barriers between him and other goals which he might seek, and this often maintains the vicious circle of barrier, inappropriate response, partial success, maladjustment.

Every well-adjusted child cannot, of course, reach all his goals, but he attains a good proportion of goals which are acceptable in his culture pattern. Thus even the well-adjusted child suffers some frustration from time to time, but he seems to be able to handle it in a satisfactory manner, and to switch to fresh goals which are both likely to satisfy his needs and to be socially acceptable.

There are usually a number of circumstances or 'barriers' which cause maladjustment, although sometimes it is possible to pick out one which is more important than the others. Evidence now available strongly suggests that the tendency to maladjustment and eventual breakdown is, in part, genetically determined (Eysenck,[5] Mittler,[6] Shields[7]). That is to say, some children come into the world with, as it were, a more robust central nervous system than others, which enables them to handle frustrating

[3] Woodruff, A. D., *The Psychology of Teaching*. New York: Longmans, 1948.
[4] These barriers are usually in the external environment, but sometimes there are internal frustrations which are due to conflicting needs within the child. In the latter instance one psychological conflict may precipitate another.
[5] Eysenck, H. J., and Prell, D. B., 'The Inheritance of Neuroticism: An Experi-mental Study,' *J. Ment. Sci.*, 1951, **97**, 441–465.
[6] Mittler, P., *The Study of Twins*. Harmondsworth: Penguin, 1971.
[7] Shields, J., 'Personality Differences and Neurotic Traits in Normal Twin Schoolchildren,' *Eugenics Rev.*, 1954, **45**, 213–246. Also Shields, J., *Monozygotic Twins*. London: Oxford University Press, 1962.

situations more effectively. Such children are less liable to succumb to maladjustment when under psychological stress.[8] On the other hand, environmental conditions are of great importance, especially if the frustrating conditions persist over many years. Among the most important frustrating environmental conditions are defective parent-child relationships (both in the early years, and up to and including adolescence), in the sense that the parents fail to give the child the love, security, direction and acceptance that he needs[9, 10]; in consistency in the matter of praise and blame, rewards and punishments; and the failure to build up stable moral-social values. Major upheavals in the life of the community such as mass migration, unemployment, war; or the fact that the child has to live in daily contact with groups whose cultural and moral standards are very different from those of his own family, are also likely to precipitate maladjustment. Likewise, physical disabilities may give rise to maladjustment in a child since they limit his opportunities for reaching his goals, though they do not always do so. For example, a boy who cannot play games, or an older girl who cannot compete with other girls for the attention of young men, are likely to suffer frustration unless they can choose other goals.

It is possible that the proportion of maladjusted children is increasing. This may be due, among other causes, to the present rapid rate of social change, the fact that life is becoming very complex and less understandable to most children, the feeling that the family is often no longer part of an organic community, and to a real decline in moral values over the past sixty years.

Teachers are naturally concerned with the part which the school might play in causing maladjustment in children. It seems that heredity and family environment are more important in predisposing the child to maladjustment than are the stresses which he experiences during his school days. But the latter might act as precipitating factors. Periods which seem to be critical for a child during his school career are, his coming to school at 5 years of age; the period when he is learning to read, write and manipulate numbers; any period when undue pressure is put on the child to pass examinations; the period after he has been transferred to a new school (for whatever reason); and periods when he is unable to keep abreast with his school work. Other possible precipitating factors include a head or assistant teacher whose personal relationships with his pupils are poor, and the failure of the adolescent to secure within the school any sort of recognition, status, or security of personal relationships with other adolescents.[11]

[8] Everyone is likely to become maladjusted or to break down mentally if he suffers sufficient psychological stress over a sufficiently long period. The important thing to remember is that some succumb more easily than others.

[9] See Bowlby, J., *Maternal Care and Mental Health*. World Health Organization, Geneva, 1952.

[10] Stott, D. H., *Unsettled Children and their Families*. London: University of London Press Ltd., 1956.

[11] It is probable that equally often the school provides satisfaction that is absent in the home and this tends to reduce maladjustment.

Moore[12] studied children aged 6 and 11 years in schools of many different sizes, types, and philosophies. He found that about 80 per cent of the infant school pupils had difficulties in adjustment to the school situation, and in roughly one half of the instances the problems were moderate to severe in intensity. By 11 years of age, however, the incidence of adjustment difficulties had decreased somewhat. The commonest and most persistent problem was reluctance to go to school. In school itself, difficulties with teachers and work, dislike of school dinners and objections to toilets were all relatively frequent; but difficulties with other children and dislike of physical education were less often in evidence. Moore most usefully points out that conflict and maladjustment are inevitable concomitants of change, and the task of the teacher is to help pupils to overcome their difficulties and find solutions to their problems.

Possible Responses to Frustration. We have seen then that if a child is unable to vary his responses to a frustrating situation, so that his needs become satisfied in a socially acceptable manner, it is possible that he will become maladjusted to some extent. It must not be assumed that the individual's responses to frustration are always consciously thought out. As has been stressed earlier, many of our actions are determined by unconscious motivation. The number of responses to frustration are, of course, very large indeed, but for convenience we have grouped them under six main headings:

(a) *Aggression.* The child tries to attack, physically and/or verbally, the person(s) or object(s) linked with the frustrating situation. The aggression may be turned in upon himself, as in anxiety and guilt feelings, or directed towards a person or group distantly connected with the situation. The latter is well recognised as projection.

(b) *Psychosomatic disturbance.* Through developing some physical condition like asthma, diarrhoea, or even enuresis, the child is able to withdraw from the persistently frustrating situation with a rationalised excuse, that is, without 'loss of face'.

(c) *Compensation.* This can take many forms varying from compensatory day-dreaming to exhibitionism of many kinds.

(d) *Rationalisation.* The child puts the blame for his failure on to some person(s), or object(s), or else says that the goal is no longer worth attaining ('sour grapes').

(e) *Withdrawal.* The child withdraws physically from the situation and overtly becomes apathetic about the goal, or else withdraws from the situation psychologically through fantasy.

(f) *Regression.* The child reverts to a more infantile form of behaviour. Thus he may lose motor or language skills that have been acquired, or display tantrums.

[12] Moore, T., 'Difficulties of the Ordinary Child in Adjusting to the Primary School,' *J. Child Psychol. and Psychiat.*, 1966, 7, 17–38.

There is usually a good deal of overlap between these various types of responses. Moreover, although we have been speaking of children, all these signs can be observed in adults.

Some Symptoms of Maladjustment. Below are listed some symptoms which are usually indicative of maladjustment, particularly when a combination of two or three appears frequently and consistently. It is, however, important to remember that everyone shows some of these symptoms for a longer or shorter period. Very often the child goes through a phase and grows out of it. Thus, all children are stubborn at times, and all children like a certain amount of solitary play.

Destructive tendencies towards people and things.
Extreme restlessness.
Constant day-dreaming.
Feelings of inferiority.
Stubbornness.
Abnormal fears of the dark, animals, etc.
Oversensitivity to criticism and suggestion.
Inability to work hard at anything.
Inability to make decisions.
Tendency to bully other children.
Easily excited.
Frequent emotional upsets.
Feelings of 'differentness'.
Lying and cheating.
Marked solitariness.
Excessive sulking or pouting.
Achievement behind chronological age (other causes excluded).
Feelings of great importance.
Repeated truancy from home or school.
Bedwetting.
Thumb-sucking.
Fingernail biting.[13]
Facial tics and/or grimaces.
Frequent passing of urine (other causes excluded).
Obstinate constipation (other causes excluded).
Diarrhoea (other causes excluded).
Nervous finger movements and handwriting.
Talking to oneself.[14]

[13] Compare Birch, L. B., 'The Incidence of Nail Biting Among School Children,' *Brit. J. Educ. Psychol.*, 1955, **25**, 123–128.

[14] For some symptoms of maladjustment in children see Cummings, J. D., 'The Incidence of Emotional Symptoms in School Children,' *Brit. J. Educ. Psychol.*, 1944, **14**, 151–161. Cummings, J. D., 'A Follow-up Study of Emotional Symptoms in School Children,' *Brit. J. Educ. Psychol.*, 1946, **16**, 163–177. Compare also Maberly, A., 'Symposium on Personality II—Personality of the Problem Child,' *Brit. J. Educ. Psychol.*, 1946, **16**, 5–12.

Anxiety and Learning. Anxiety is likely to be linked with both introversion and neuroticism, and anxiety (as it is assessed by questionnaire) seems to be negatively correlated with attainment over certain IQ ranges at least. Thus Feldhusen and Klausmeier[15] produce evidence that anxiety is negatively correlated with scores on the WISC test, reading, arithmetic and language up to an IQ of 110 or so, but above an IQ of 120 the correlations are negligible. This is confirmed by Callard *et al.*[16] who studied over 3,500 English secondary school pupils. They found a negative correlation between intelligence and neuroticism only in the non-A forms of secondary modern, and grammar-technical schools. There are, however, great difficulties in defining and in measuring anxiety, and the field is in great need of clarification. Interested readers should study the papers of Hallworth,[17] Biggs,[18] Lynn,[19] and the further references that they give.[20]

The Role of the Teacher in the Treatment of Maladjusted Children. The ordinary teacher, as distinct from teachers in special schools for maladjusted children or in independent schools specialising in the teaching of such children, will be concerned with children who may be described as normal, with those whose degree of maladjustment is slight and who are not receiving special treatment, and with those whose condition is more serious and who are receiving treatment at a clinic. The following suggestions are, therefore, made for the class teacher:

(*a*) Get to know the characteristics of normal children and watch out for early signs of maladjustment. For example, the teacher should be on the look out for children who are excessively lazy, aggressive, anxious, living in fantasy, or without companions.

(*b*) Keep a close watch on pupil-teacher relationships. An aggressive attitude in the classroom is as unhelpful to children (they tend to react to aggression with aggression) as a weak, submissive attitude. An attempt should be made to combine firmness with friendliness and understanding. All children prefer order to disorder, for the former enables them to work and experience a sense of achievement; they also know what is expected of them and this lessens their mental conflicts. Some 'progressive' schools which indulge in completely 'free' discipline are likely to encourage maladjustment in children, since they no longer have the opportunity to develop habitual responses to deal with threatening situations.

[15] Feldhusen, J. F. and Klausmeier, H. J., *Child Developm.*, 1962, 33, 403–409.
[16] Callard, M. P. and Goodfellow, C. L., 'Neuroticism and Extraversion in Schoolboys as measured by the Junior M.P.I.,' *Brit. J. Educ. Psychol.*, 1962, 32, 241–250.
[17] Hallworth, H. J., *Brit. J. Educ. Psychol.*, 1961, 31, 281–291.
[18] Biggs, J. B., *Brit. J. Educ. Psychol.*, 1962, 188–195.
[19] Lynn, R., *Brit. J. Educ. Psychol.*, 1962, 196–199.
[20] For an extensive survey of research concerning the behaviour correlates of anxiety in children, see Ruebush, B. E., 'Anxiety,' in *Child Psychology*: the Sixty-second Yearbook of the National Society for the Study of Education. University of Chicago Press, 1963.

(c) Attempt to build up the morale of children. Arrange school work and extra-curricular activities in such a manner that poorly adjusted pupils get success in some field or other, and thus gain self confidence. Children who have been aggressive under excessive disapproval and failure, often 'blossom' and become cooperative under sincere social approval ond success.

(d) Remove obvious causes of irritation. Do not let dull or otherwise handicapped pupils feel neglected or unwanted.

(e) Do all that is possible to develop wider and more objective interests among children. Encourage them to play games, to take part in school societies and outside youth organisations, and to mix with other children.

(f) If the child's behaviour continues to cause concern, it might be helpful to have a consultation with the parents. If this is of no avail, then the child should be referred to the Child Guidance Clinic. Teachers should not attempt any form of psychotherapy as such.[21]

(g) The job of the teacher is to preserve mental health as far as possible by dealing with minor difficulties of children as soon as they arise.

It has already been indicated in Chapter 11 that there is a need for an increase in the number of persons available to give educational and vocational guidance in schools. But in a number of schools there is now a person also available for personal counselling. Such an individual should be fitted to help children to anticipate personal crises, and not merely to cope with them when they arise, although the latter is certainly part of his task. What has just been said does not imply that good teachers failed to act as personal counsellors and exercise pastoral care in so far as they were able, but rather it indicates that there are now persons who are trained, and given the time, to act in this capacity. Such persons have greater opportunities for visiting pupils' homes, and they are better informed in respect of the further services, such as Psychological, Medical and Welfare services, to which pupils in difficulty, or in danger of getting into difficulty, may have to be referred.[22]

The Modification of Racial, Religious, and Social Prejudice. There is evidence that racial and religious prejudices and attitudes are fairly well-developed by the time the child goes to school or soon after, and these reflect the values of the family and neighbourhood.[23] Thus Rowley[24] found

[21] When everything possible has been done some children will not improve. Others recover later for no particular reason as far as can be seen. In some instances symptoms come out in another form. For a full treatment of the relationship between school and mental health see Wall, W. D., *Education and Mental Health.* London: Harrap, 1955.

[22] See Lytton, H. and Craft, M., *Guidance and Counselling in British Schools.* Edward Arnold, 1969. Holden, A., *Teachers as Counsellors.* Constable, 1969. Holden, A., *Counselling in Secondary Schools.* London: Constable, 1971.

[23] Compare Frenkel-Brunswik, E., 'A Study of Prejudice in Children,' *Human Relat.,* 1948, I, 295–306. Radke, M., Trager, H. G., and Davis, H., 'Social Perceptions and Attitudes of Children,' *Genet. Psychol. Monogr.,* 1949, 40, 327–447.

[24] Rowley, K. G., 'Social Relationships between British and Immigrant Children,' *Educ. Res.,* 1968, 10, 145–148.

that British children of 7 years of age showed strong in-group tendencies, and that 90 per cent of British children at all ages from 7 to 15 years chose British rather than immigrant children as companions in each of three social situations. It is, of course, reasonable to suppose that if prejudice did not exist among adults it would rarely occur in children. Some well-meaning teachers and social scientists have suggested that if children of different racial and religious groups were brought together and lived in harmonious conditions for a while, the prejudices would tend to disappear. Unfortunately, experiment shows that this is not generally true. The work of Mussen,[25] Radke[26] et al., and others, has shown that when such children live together at, say, a camp, the attitudes of the children who are already psychologically secure can be changed through pleasant social experiences.[27] On the other hand, psychologically insecure children often use these situations to project their aggressive feelings, so that their prejudice may increase rather than diminish. Likewise Robb,[28] in a study of anti-Semitism among working class adults in Great Britain, has produced evidence strongly suggesting that anti-Semitism is not an isolated phenomenon but symptomatic of a more general condition of maladjustment. Thus it seems that whatever helps to improve a child's adjustment will help to remove prejudice.

Child Guidance Clinics and the School Psychological Service. Child Guidance Clinics are now provided by the Local Education Authorities or the regional hospital boards in almost all areas. Ideally they have on their staffs a psychiatric social worker, a psychologist, and a psychiatrist. The job of the social worker is to visit the home of the child who has been referred to the clinic, and find out as much about his earlier and present background as possible. The psychologist gets a report from the child's school, and also assesses his level of intelligence and attainments through the use of standardised tests. Similarly the psychiatrist will have a report from the School Medical Officer. At the clinic he may make a further physical examination, but his main function is to try to find out something of the child's emotional problems either through discussion or through the application of projective techniques.

After these investigations have been made, the staff pool their views and the treatment is decided upon. This may involve sending the child to a special school for maladjusted children, or to an independent school[29]

---

[25] Mussen, P. H., 'Some Personality and Social Factors related to Changes in Children's Attitudes towards Negroes,' *J. abnorm. soc. Psychol.*, 1950, 45, 423–441.

[26] Radke, M. *et al.*, *op. cit.* Sherif, M., 'Experiments in Group Conflict,' *Scientific American*, November, 1956, 54–58.

[27] Note that if the activities of the other groups are seen on rational grounds to be opposed to the 'perceived interests' of the child or adult, it is very difficult to dispel prejudice however well adjusted the individual may be.

[28] Robb, J. H., *Working Class Anti-Semite*. London: Tavistock Publications, 1954.

[29] Children are maintained at these schools by the L.E.A.

which specialises in dealing with this type of child. Alternatively, the child may visit the clinic about once a week for treatment, or simple advice may be given to the parents about the child's upbringing.[30]

Not all children referred to these clinics are maladjusted; some are merely dull and/or backward.

The psychologist often works only part-time at the clinic, the remainder of his time being spent in the more general psychological service to schools, which is not necessarily connected with maladjusted children at all. This service is primarily non-medical and is under the control of the Chief Education Officer. Outside the clinic the duties of the psychologist may include giving vocational guidance to school-leavers, advising the L.E.A. on the assessment of children, organising remedial classes for backward children, talking to parents and teachers about the development of normal children, and carrying out research for the L.E.A.

DELINQUENCY

In the preface to his classic work on the psychology of juvenile crime first published in 1925, Burt[31] considered delinquency to be 'an outstanding sample—dangerous perhaps and extreme, but none the less typical of common childish naughtiness'. The great amount of research carried out in this field since that time has produced no evidence that Burt's suggestion was incorrect. It is now realised that:

(a) The majority of delinquents are neither neurotic, mentally defective, nor completely devoid of moral standards, although their standards are sometimes low.

(b) There are no grounds, as yet, for suggesting that there are any clear-cut differences between all delinquents and so-called non-delinquents.

(c) Many children pass through a delinquent phase but are never caught.

(d) Delinquency is a relative term in that it depends upon breaking the laws of a particular country. A certain act could make a child delinquent in one country but not in another.

(e) Most children (and adults) will break the law if the personal need or the environmental stress are sufficiently strong. Some give way more easily than others. Many children show behaviour closely comparable to that of the delinquent which does not conflict with the law. In other words delinquency is part of the wider field of behaviour, including lying, breaking faith, and gross selfishness.

It must be realised, then, from the outset that the problem is a complex

[30] 'Symposium on Psychologists and Psychiatrists in the Child Guidance Service,' *Brit. J. Educ. Psychol.*, Vols. 21, 22, 23, 1951, 1952, 1953.
[31] Burt, C., *The Young Delinquent*. London: University of London Press Ltd., 1925.

one. We shall approach it from the point of view of the scientist,[32] bearing in mind its relevance to teachers.

A Survey of Some Relevant Investigations. Burt[33] studied 200 juvenile delinquents and carried out a parallel survey of 400 non-delinquents of the same age and social class, usually living in the same streets and attending the same schools. He found that among boys the most frequent offences were stealing and persistent truancy (either from home or school); and in girls, sexual misdemeanours, stealing, and being beyond control. Burt concluded that the following six[34] conditions, given in order of importance, were most frequently associated with delinquency:

(*a*) Defective home discipline. The discipline may be too strict, too lenient, or worst of all, alternating between strictness and leniency.

(*b*) Specific instincts (sex, acquisitiveness, wandering, self-assertion).

(*c*) General emotional instability.

(*d*) Mild morbid emotional conditions. For example, morbid self-assertion such as wish for power; antagonism to father.

(*e*) Family history of vice or crime.

(*f*) Intellectual dullness and backwardness in school subjects.[35]

He was, however, careful to point out that there is nearly always a number of contributing influences predisposing the child into committing crime, although often one factor seems to stand out as the most prominent.

In more recent years research in this field has followed two broad lines of approach. One has concentrated on the psychological make-up of the individual, especially as affected by the parent-child relationships, and the second has probed into the social and economic conditions within the environment of the offenders.

Bowlby,[36] after reviewing his own work and that of others, suggests that the extent to which an individual can make trusting, affectionate, and co-operative relationships with others depends to a large extent upon the relationships he has experienced in his early life. More specifically his thesis is that the persistent offender has been rejected or unkindly treated by his parents during the first five years of life, or else he has experienced prolonged separation from, or change in, the mother-figure during these years. A child who has undergone such treatment is likely to develop solitary habits, to be undemonstrative, to fail to respond to any kind of treatment, to show neither sympathy nor affection, and to be prone to

---

[32] For a review of recent approaches to delinquency see Burt, C., 'Recent Discussions of Juvenile Delinquency,' *Brit. J. Educ. Psychol.*, 1949, **19**, 32–43.

[33] Burt, C., *The Young Delinquent*. London: University of London Press Ltd., 1925.

[34] Burt, C., *op. cit.*, page 607 lists fifteen conditions altogether; we have mentioned only the six most important ones.

[35] The mean IQ of children in Approved Schools seems to be about 90. See Gittins, J., *Approved School Boys*. London: H.M.S.O., 1952.

[36] Compare Bowlby, J., *Maternal Care and Mental Health*. Geneva: World Health Organisation, 1952. See also Rutter, M., *op. cit.*

delinquency. Similarly, some American investigators conclude that families split by death, desertion, divorce, or prolonged absence; defective home discipline; mothers lacking in affection, and hostile fathers; are the primary influences predisposing a child to commit crime. They believe that social economic conditions, size of family, conflicts between ideas and standards of sub-culture patterns, are only secondary.

On the other hand there is much evidence from the work of Burt,[37] Carr-Saunders et al.,[38] also Mannheim,[39] that sociological conditions are related to the incidence of delinquency. Thus in an environment where there are over-crowding, poverty, unemployment, and low moral standards, delinquency is likely to be high. Again, the increase in the amount of delinquency immediately after a war, or when community life is unsettled, also points to the importance of sociological conditions.

Mays[40] suggests that the social surroundings are more important than family relationships in some cases.[41] He stresses that in under-privileged areas, characterised by a long history of low living standards, few children grow up without breaking the law. The average boy does not like to be thought different from the other members of his social group, and he succumbs temporarily to the temptations prevalent in his area. Mays usefully draws attention to the more or less normal boys who will be delinquent for a while, but who will later conform to the generally accepted standards of society because basically they are emotionally secure. He also points out that emotionally maladjusted boys are more likely to become persistent offenders, and follow the sequence of Approved School, Borstal, and Prison. These two groups will to some extent overlap.

Andry[42] has thrown some doubt on Bowlby's theory of 'maternal deprivation' in relation to delinquency (as has Naess in a study of Norwegian children) and has some evidence to show that the role of fathers is important. As compared with non-delinquents Andry showed that delinquents experience a more tense home atmosphere, less adequate parental training, and their deviant behaviour was less known to, and less adequately dealt with by their parents.

Much has been said about the relative parts played by heredity and environment in causing delinquency. We do not, of course, inherit delinquent actions; what we inherit is body-build, temperament, and the tendency to act in some ways rather than in others. Genetic and constitu-

[37] Burt, C., op. cit.

[38] Carr-Saunders, R. M., Mannheim, H., and Rhodes, E. C., Young Offenders: An Enquiry into Juvenile Delinquency. Cambridge: Cambridge University Press, 1942.

[39] Mannheim, H., Juvenile Delinquency in an English Middletown. London: Kegan Paul, 1948.

[40] Mays, J. B., Growing Up in the City. Liverpool: University of Liverpool Press, 1954.

[41] The importance of the sub-culture pattern is also stressed by Cohen. See Cohen, A. K., Delinquent Boys. London: Routledge & Kegan Paul, 1955.

[42] Andry, R., Delinquency and Parental Pathology. London: Methuen, 1960.

tional factors can certainly influence character formation (*see* Chapter 14) and predispose the individual to delinquent behaviour, given the appropriate environment. As both Friedlander[43] and S. and E. T. Glueck[44] have stressed, it is the point where social and biological forces interact that must be studied in delinquency. The Gluecks[45] have presented evidence that defective parent-child relationships or other environmental defects are much more likely to lead to delinquency in mesomorphic (*see* Chapter 4) than in other body types. Further, Stott[46] has surveyed much data which taken as a whole suggests that heredity, or adverse conditions during gestation or delivery, could impair both the physical development of some individuals and that part of the nervous system which controls behaviour. The latter might induce a greater delinquency proneness by reducing resistance to stress, and thus more frequent breakdowns under adverse environmental conditions.

A critical review of research and theory in relation to juvenile delinquency (as at 1962) was made by Wilkins[47] then of the Research Unit of the British Home Office. He concludes that it remains, in a way, true to say that the causes of delinquency remain unknown, and will continue unknown until research is carried out with more vigorous experimentation.

The Role of the School in Preventing Delinquency. There is considerable evidence that only some 10–20 per cent of juvenile offenders prolong their offences into adult years. While this is heartening, it is still important to detect potential delinquents early and to treat them before they come a problem to society. Naturally, parents and teachers cannot be solely responsible for the prevention of delinquency. The police, local authorities, the cinema, radio and television, newspapers and literature, also many social organisations, all have a part to play.[48] However, parents and teachers can help in many ways, some of which are now listed:

(*a*) Bear in mind that if the home and school do not give the child affection and security, and accept him as a person in his own right, then delinquency will offer one of the common ways of escape from an emotionally intolerable situation.[49]

[43] Friedlander, K., *The Psycho-Analytical Approach to Juvenile Delinquency.* London: Kegan Paul, 1947.

[44] Glueck, S., and Glueck, E. T., *Unravelling Juvenile Delinquency.* New York: Commonwealth Fund, 1950.

[45] Glueck, S. and Glueck, E. T., *Physique and Delinquency.* New York: Harper, 1956.

[46] Stott, D. H., 'Evidence for a Congenital Factor in Maladjustment and Delinquency,' *Amer. J. Psychiat.*, 1962, **118**, 781–794. Stott, D. H., *Studies of Troublesome Children.* London: Tavistock Pubs., 1966.

[47] Wilkins, L. T., 'Juvenile Delinquency: a Critical Review of Research and Theory,' *Educational Research*, 1962, **5**, 104–110.

[48] See Stott, D. H., *Saving Children from Delinquency.* London: University of London Press Ltd., 1952.

[49] Compare Stott, D. H., *Delinquency and Human Nature.* Carnegie United Kingdom Trust, 1950.

(*b*) Attempt to build up a stable system of moral-social values as indicated in Chapter 14. The ultimate aim in character formation is internalised motivation or self-discipline.

(*c*) Watch for signs of maladjustment. Early treatment may prevent the maladjustment from taking on a delinquent aspect.

(*d*) Try to get the child to direct his drives into socially acceptable channels. Thus, attempt to get him interested in football, cycling, swimming, camping, and other worth while outdoor and indoor games and hobbies. These activities give the child something else to think about, and make frustration less pressing. Games also often provide an opportunity for aggression to be worked off in an acceptable manner.

(*e*) Encourage the child to talk about, and admit, the existence of his anti-social tendencies. Do not condemn him for experiencing such drives, but show him that it would be wrong to give way to them. Point out the rival claims of, say, revenge on the one hand, and on the other hand of the need for self-esteem, the esteem of others, or the need to avoid punishment.

(*f*) When a child is known to be mixing with undesirable companions either within or without the school, have a frank talk with him and discuss the consequences likely to result from such an association. Likewise, when it appears that some emotional tension is mounting, do something to add to his security and feeling of acceptance.

(*g*) Minimise the chances of a child's going wrong by putting the smallest possible number of temptations in his way.

(*h*) Give a potential delinquent some post of special responsibility such as care of equipment, or the task of preventing other children from committing delinquent acts.

(*i*) If parent-child relationships are not normal, then try to arrange that the child is able to form a personal attachment to some adult. In the case of an actual delinquent the most suitable person might be the child care officer.

(*j*) Once a delinquent act has been detected, never pass it over. Make clear to the child that he has done wrong, and, if necessary, punish in an appropriate manner. But once any punishment has been given, accept the child again as a member of the community.

(*k*) Remember that each delinquent or potential delinquent is a unique individual with a number of influences acting on him specifically. Hence there must be an individual approach.

(*l*) Try not to be disappointed if your efforts fail. A few children seem to slip into delinquency and continue in crime whatever treatment they receive. Occasional failure must not blind us to the fact that we may be of great help to other children.

The personal counsellor mentioned earlier in the chapter will naturally have a role to play in preventing delinquent acts.

Predicting delinquency from non-delinquent behaviour. Workers in the U.S.A. have produced a number of scales for assessing psychological and sociological data about children from which it is said to be possible to predict delinquency from certain forms of earlier non-delinquent behaviour. In this country Stott[50] has brought forward evidence that the Bristol Social Adjustment Guides[51] might help to detect future offenders, the predictions being made between eight and ten years of age before delinquency, as such, was in evidence. In Stott's view behaviour disturbances manifest themselves prior to the onset of delinquency, and if a certain minimum maladjustment score attained on the Bristol Social Adjustment Guides is taken as a criterion, then a good proportion of potential delinquents would be detected. However, the available evidence suggests that great care should be exercised in attempting to forecast delinquent behaviour by this means.[52]

School Phobia and School Truancy. In recent years there has been increasing interest in children showing signs of school phobia, i.e. children who will not leave the house for school or who do so only after great pressure has been put on them by home and school. Hersov[53] has compared these children with school truants, i.e. children who leave home readily enough but who wander about or go elsewhere instead of going to school.

Hersov has shown that, compared with maladjusted children generally, pupils showing symptoms of school phobia more frequently have: a good standard of work at school; maternal overprotection; neurotic parents or other close relatives; eating disturbance; abdominal pain, nausea, vomiting; sleep disturbances; fears; anxiety reactions. In other words, school phobia is one manifestation of a psychoneurosis. On the other hand, school truants compared with maladjusted children generally more frequently have: a poor standard of work at school; absence of parents in earlier years; inconsistent home discipline; enuresis; persistent lying; stealing; juvenile court appearance. Thus school truancy is one aspect of a behaviour disorder. The parents and home are primarily responsible for these conditions, but the teacher can help these pupils by considering their individual needs.

The work of Chazan[54] generally supports that of Hersov, but the former makes the point that backwardness in school work may be a contributing factor in School Phobia in some children. Much of the literature on both school truants and school phobics has also been reviewed by Cooper.[55]

[50] Stott, D. H., 'The Prediction of Delinquency from Non-Delinquent Behaviour,' *Brit. J. Delinq.*, 1960, **10**, 195–210.
[51] Stott, D. H. and Sykes, E. G., *The Bristol Social Adjustment Guides.* London: University of London Press Ltd., 1956.
[52] See Marsh, R. W., 'The Validity of the Bristol Social Adjustment Guides in Delinquent Prediction,' *Brit. J. Educ. Psychol.*, 1969, **39**, 278–283.
[53] Hersov, L., 'Persistent Non-Attendance at School,' also 'Refusal to go to School,' *J. Child Psychology and Psychiatry*, 1960, **1**, 130–136, 137–145.
[54] Chazan, M., 'School Phobia,' *Brit. J. Educ. Psychol.*, 1962, **32**, 209–217.
[55] Cooper, M. G., 'School Refusal,' *Educ. Res.*, 1966, **8**, 115–127.

She concludes that while there is much evidence regarding the likely times when school phobia will arise (beginning of school, change of school or class, failure in school work, etc.) much research is needed both into the best ways of alleviating stress at these difficult times and into the structure of the psycho-social climate of the classes of the youngest pupils in primary and secondary schools. In a later paper Cooper also points out that in respect of the aetiology of both school phobia and truancy, the role of the school is minimal.[56] Tyerman,[57] too, has examined the differences between school phobia and truancy, and discussed the aetiology and treatment of both, drawing upon his own experience and on the relevant literature. One of his interesting findings is that the truant is frequently a fearful, unstable and friendless individual, with a tendency to withdraw from friends, parents, teachers and the world generally, and into himself.

[56] Cooper, M. G., 'School Refusal: An Inquiry into the part played by School and Home,' *Educ. Res.*, 1966, **8**, 223–229.
[57] Tyerman, M. J., *Truancy*. London: University of London Press Ltd., 1968.

Chapter Nineteen

SOME ASPECTS OF THE RELATIONSHIP
BETWEEN BODY AND MIND

THE relationship between body and mind has been a subject that has fascinated man for centuries. It is a problem of the greatest importance to an understanding of human thought and behaviour,[1] and is thus fundamental to the progress of psychology. Unfortunately we know very little about the topic even today.

There is not the slightest doubt, of course, that a connection exists between mental events, on the one hand, and brain structure and physiological conditions within the body, on the other. The brain is clearly affected by genetic influences, adverse uterine conditions, birth injuries, lesions, malnutrition, drugs, and other physical factors, and in these instances, mind is often affected too. Likewise, anxiety and other psychological conditions, acting through the brain, can lead to changes in the body in the form of psychosomatic disorders. It is quite sufficient for our purpose to accept the view that mental and physical events are in some way connected without fully understanding the vital link between them. We know now that all stimuli, whether from the external environment or from within our bodies, reach the brain in the form of electrical impulses, but we cannot suggest how the physical and chemical changes in the brain cells associated with the passage of these impulses can bring about 'mind'.[2] Neither can we say exactly how a thought will cause certain brain cells to become active but fail to affect others. Remembering, then, that our knowledge of the body-mind relationship is very limited, we turn to discuss in more detail what is known with some certainty.[3]

Relevant parts of the body. There are four main parts of the body which are of particular interest to psychologists:

(a) *The sense organs.* These include the eyes, ears, nose, tongue, and the vast number of sense organs embedded in the skin which are sensitive to pain, touch, and temperature.

---

[1] It must not be assumed, however, that the entire explanation of human personality is necessarily to be found in the dynamics of the nervous system.

[2] Some reconcile the apparent cleavage between body and mind by accepting various forms of philosophical doctrine which maintain that there is only one kind of being. Compare *Monism.*

[3] For a discussion of the brain-mind relationship, to which eminent scientists and philosophers contributed, see Laslett, P. (Editor), *The Physical Basis of Mind.* Oxford: Blackwell, 1950.

(b) *The central nervous system.* This consists of brain and spinal cord, together with the afferent nerve-fibres which convey the excitations from the sense organs to the central portion of the system, and efferent nerves which convey the impulse to the muscles causing them to contract.

(c) *The autonomic nervous system.* The nerves in this system run to the visceral organs, such as the stomach, intestines, lungs, heart, blood vessels, to the sweat-glands, and other glands. The system controls heart beat, rate of respiration, and activity of the stomach and intestines; it controls raising and lowering of blood pressure; and has other effects which play an important part in our emotions. It is closely linked with a part of the brain known as the hypothalamus (to be described later).

(d) *The Endocrine or ductless glands.* These glands make chemical substances (called hormones) which are poured directly into the blood stream, and which adjust the rate of activity of the body organs. Some of the best known endocrine glands are:

(i) *Thyroid.* This gland is in the neck in front of the larynx. It secretes a hormone called thyroxin[4] which seems to control the rate of metabolism. Over-activity results in the individual becoming tense, irritable, and restless. Defective activity from birth produces the cretin, who is both a dwarf and mentally subnormal (this condition can be relieved in some cases if thyroxin is given early enough), while under-activity in later life results in puffiness of skin and in the person's becoming mentally and physically sluggish.

(ii) *Adrenals.* These small glands are situated near the kidneys. Each gland consists of two parts, one secreting adrenalin, and the other cortisone. The function of adrenalin is to increase the activity of the body, and in particular to mobilise energy to meet a crisis. For example the heart beat is increased, and more sugar is passed into the blood stream as a source of increased energy. Cortisone influences certain aspects of body chemistry and in particular affects muscular and sexual activity.

(iii) *The gonads.* The ovaries and testes secrete hormones in addition to producing reproductive cells. These hormones influence the secondary physical sexual characteristics, as well as sexual outlook and interest. For example, in the female they control the menstrual cycle and breast-development, and in the male they affect stature, the breaking of the voice, and the growth of the beard.

(iv) *Pituitary.* This gland is situated in the brain and the hormones secreted by it affect the activity of the other endocrine glands; hence it is called the 'master gland'. The posterior lobe of this gland regulates many metabolic processes, while the anterior

[4] A simple explanation has been given here, but it is now known that in a single gland there is often multiple secretion rather than a single hormone.

lobe controls growth. Excess activity in the anterior lobe in childhood may produce giantism, and under-activity may bring about dwarfism.

Balance between the secretions of the endocrine glands is very important, and extreme under- or over-activity in any one of them can result in changes in the personality. Thus the ductless glands are among the fundamental biological factors that affect personality.[5] Something of their profound effects on behaviour has been known for a long time. Research is now showing how the external environment, acting through the central nervous system, affects the endocrine activity of the individual. For example, there is some evidence that psychological stress may influence endocrine function, mainly by affecting the output of the anterior pituitary.[6]

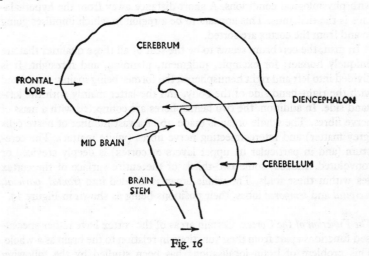

Fig. 16

The brain. To understand the more important parts of the brain, it will be necessary to refer to Fig. 16. If we follow the *spinal cord* upward it will be seen that at the top it enlarges into the *brain stem.* This is linked to the *diencephalon* by a short *mid brain,* while in front of the former the *cerebrum* spreads out, filling almost the whole of the skull. The outer layers of the cerebrum are known as the cortex. Part of the diencephalon is known as the *thalamus,* while its base is called the *hypothalamus.*

Nerve-fibres from all parts of the body enter into, and depart from, centres in the spinal cord and brain. Within the nervous system, signals received from the sense organs are sorted out and reordered into the impulses that give rise to responses. In the spinal cord, particularly, this

[5] See Mottram, V. H., *The Physical Basis of Personality.* Penguin Books, 1944.
[6] See 'Chemistry and Inter-Relationships of Endocrine Systems and their Psychological Effects,' *Nature,* March 21, 1953, 509–510.

re-ordering largely takes the form of elementary reflex actions. But re-actions that are routed through the brain are too complex to be termed simple reflexes. Thus the spinal cord is concerned with simple response reflexes like drawing away the hand from a hot poker; automatic reflexes operating through the brain stem control respiration and balance; while the *cerebellum* orders similar reflexes concerned with posture and balance. The hypothalamus and the cerebrum, however, are involved in the more complex responses of the individual.

The hypothalamus is a most important nerve centre. It is concerned with the fundamental aspects of body activity such as heart beat, respiration, body temperature, metabolism, and even the rhythm of sleeping and waking. But, and this is most interesting from the psychological viewpoint, it is intimately involved in emotional states which are, of course, linked with physiological conditions. A short distance away from the hypothalamus is the thalamus. This appears to be a region in which impulses going to and from the cortex are sorted.

In man, the cerebrum seems to be the seat of all those qualities that are uniquely human; for example, judgment, planning, and foresight. It is divided into left and right hemispheres, the former being mainly concerned with the right-hand side of the body, and the latter mainly with the left-hand side. In addition, the two hemispheres are connected with a mass of nerve fibres. The whole organ is made up of a vast number of nerve cells (grey matter) and interconnecting nerve fibres (white matter). The cerebrum (and in particular its upper layers or cortex) is deeply creviced or convoluted. Indeed, some two-thirds of the entire surface of the cortex lies within these folds. The whole organ is divided into *frontal*, *parietal*, *occipital* and *temporal* lobes, their positions being as shown in Figure 17.

The Function of the Cortex. Certain areas of the cortex have rather special-ised functions apart from their functions in relation to the brain as a whole. This problem of brain localisation[7] has been studied by the following methods:

(a) *Method of Extirpation.* Many experiments in which part of the brain has been removed have been conducted on animals, and the resulting loss of function noted. Similarly, in human beings, when part of the brain has been injured it is possible to study the handicaps which result.

(b) *Pathological method.* When a patient has suffered some loss of function, post-mortem examination has often revealed a fairly well-localised brain lesion.

(c) *Stimulation.* Weak electrical currents were applied to various parts of the exposed cortex when the patient was undergoing a surgical opera-tion, and the various body movements evoked were noted.

[7] The work of Head on *Aphasia* (speech defects) is very important for an under-standing of the way the brain functions. See Head, H., *Aphasia and Kindred Disorder of Speech*. Vol. I. Cambridge: Cambridge University Press, 1926.

(d) *Fibre Tracing.* Methods have been devised whereby it is possible to trace connections between certain parts of the cortex, through lower nerve-centres, to the ears or muscles, for example.

Thus we now know that signals from the eye are received by the visual areas (see Figure 17) and that this area is responsible for sight.[8] If this is damaged, irreparable blindness may result. Likewise, the auditory area of the cortex is concerned with hearing, the somaesthetic area with skin and

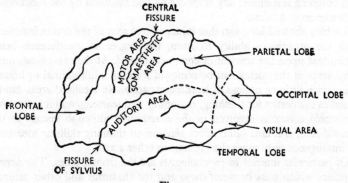

Fig. 17

muscle sense, and the motor area with movements of the feet, legs, trunk, arms, head, face, and so on. Damage to the motor area may result in partial or complete paralysis in some part of the body for a longer or shorter period. However, such areas concerned with the handling of specific incoming and outgoing signals are small in relation to the rest of the cortex. Moreover, there can be no rigid mapping out of the cortex into areas having specific functions, because sometimes, if one part of the cortex is destroyed, its functions seem to be taken over by another part of the brain. Indeed, Sholl[9] specifically reminds us that the relationship between certain regions of the cortex and activities in other parts of the body, is a very variable one.

The organism cannot adapt itself properly to its environment unless the cortex functions as a whole[10]; the main function of the cortex, then, appears to be that of co-ordination.[11] In addition to these primary sensory

---

[8] Some aspects of visual cognition depend upon centres outside the visual cortex proper.

[9] Sholl, D. A., *The Organisation of the Cerebral Cortex.* London: Methuen, 1956.

[10] Disturbance in behaviour as well as sensory disturbances follow destruction of the sensory areas. See Lashley, K. S., *Brain Mechanisms and Intelligence.* Chicago; University of Chicago Press, 1929. Lashley, K. S., 'Studies in Cerebral Function in Learning. XI. The Behaviour of the Rat in Latch Box Situations,' *Comp. Psychol. Monogr.*, 1935, **11**, No. 22, 1–42.

[11] Part of the brain stem (centrencephalic area) plays a vital role in integrating the functions of the cortical areas.

areas, there are also *association* areas. Their functions are not fully understood, but thought and behaviour are adversely affected if the fibres connecting the association areas and subcortical centres are cut. The number of nerve-fibres connecting the association areas, and concerned with co-ordination within the hemispheres of the cerebrum and brain stem, run into millions. It should now be clear why it is difficult to establish simple conditioned responses in human beings, since there is no 'straight through' connection, as it were, between the incoming signals and outgoing responses: any response will be modified by the functioning of the brain as a whole.

Lashley showed long ago that injury in any area of the cortex interferes with the organism's ability to learn, the degree of interference being dependent upon the amount of cortex destroyed. At the same time, quite large areas of the cortex can be removed from an adult animal or human being with little or no loss of learning capacity. No localised areas can be found in the cortex for thinking, reasoning, and learning, and it seems that the whole cortex is involved in these activities, although lesions in the parietal-temporal area often affect generalised thinking skills as measured by intelligence tests more than lesions in other areas.

Of particular interest to psychologists are the frontal lobes. The nerve-impulses which pass between these and the thalamus and other centres, somehow or other seem to be translated into feelings. In certain kinds of mental breakdown where there is, say, great anxiety, relief is sometimes given by cutting the nerve-fibres between the frontal lobes and the thalamus. This surgical operation is known in Great Britain as leucotomy. It takes various forms, and the nerve-fibres may be severed in different places. Sometimes the surgeon operates on the cells of the thalamus itself. Despite the frequent success of such operations it must be made clear that there is no real understanding of how they work. Scores on intelligence tests are not always affected significantly, but some leucotomised individuals become more extraverted and less neurotic.[12] At the same time they often show inability to plan ahead and manage their lives efficiently, and a certain indifference to social custom and lack of restraint in behaviour. Indeed, there appears to be a loss of ability in synthesising or combining the many signals being fed into the cortex, and in anticipating the effect of a given response, so that judgment and sense of responsibility are affected.

Some Aspects of the Problem of Thought and Behaviour. It is reckoned that there are about 10,000,000,000 nerve cells in the cortex, and these are connected with one another by an intricate network of nerve-fibres. A nerve-cell, then, rarely seems to be active without affecting its neighbours,

<hr />

[12] See Crown, S., 'Psychological Changes following Prefrontal Leucotomy; a Review,' *J. Ment. Sci.*, 1951, **97**, 49–83. Also, Petrie, A., *Personality and the Frontal Lobes*. London: Routledge and Kegan Paul, 1952.

the essence of this activity being a sudden change in the cell surface which permits a momentary escape of some of its molecules with accompanying electrical effects. This may happen up to fifty times a second, and each time an impulse passes out to a neighbouring cell, or to a more distant part of the central nervous system. To maintain this activity, the brain needs a plentiful blood supply, bringing it oxygen and foodstuffs (e.g. sugar) of exactly the right quality.

Research has suggested that consciousness and thought can only arise under certain physiological conditions within the brain. Eccles[13] after reviewing theses put forward by Sherrington[14] and Adrian[15] considers that:

(a) The liaison between brain and mind occurs primarily in the cerebral cortex, although other brain centres are also involved.

(b) Consciousness is only possible when there is a high level of activity in the cortex. Unconsciousness results when such activity is lowered, as in sleep, anaesthesia, or concussion.

(c) The uniqueness of each perception is due to a specific spatio-temporal pattern of nerve-cell activity in the cortex, resulting, of course, from some stimulation. In general, it may be said that any thought pattern (in the mind), has a corresponding, spatio-temporal pattern of nerve-cell activity (in the cortex).

More recently it has been shown that within the central core (or recticular formation) of the brain stem there are areas from which ascend a constantly fluctuating stream of impulses to the cortex.[16, 17] These impulses facilitate the efficient working of the cortex, and we are capable of our most complex waking achievements only when the ascending stream is at a high optimum level. Moreover, it is now recognised that different areas in the recticular formation have different functions in respect of consciousness; also that impulses fed back from the cortex control the degree of excitement in the recticular formation.

A most important question immediately arises out of our present discussion. What happens when we learn and experience, that subsequently tends to make us think and behave in certain ways rather than in others? To answer this we must go back once again to the problem of nerve-cell activity. When ordinary adults are sitting with eyes closed and not thinking about anything in particular, many of the nerve-cells seem to be linked

[13] Eccles, J. C., *Neurophysiological Basis of Mind*. Oxford: Oxford University Press, 1952. Eccles, J. C., 'Hypotheses Relating to the Brain-Mind Problem,' *Nature*, July 14, 1951, 53–57.

[14] Sherrington, C. S., *Man and his Nature*. Cambridge: Cambridge University Press, 1940.

[15] Adrian, E. D., *The Physical Background of Perception*. Oxford: Oxford University Press, 1947. Adrian, E. D., in *The Physical Basis of Mind*. (Editor) Laslett, P., *op. cit.*

[16] Magoun, H. W., *The Waking Brain*. Springfield, Illinois: Thomas, 1963, Second Edition.

[17] Oswald, I., 'The Experimental Study of Sleep,' *British Medical Bulletin*, 1964, **20**, 60–64.

together so that they are active and inactive at the same time. The electrical changes associated with such activity take place about ten times per second (in children the frequency is lower), thus yielding the well known *alpha rhythm* of the electroencephalograph. If these adults open their eyes, or think rather casually, the activity of the nerve-cells is not seriously disturbed, but should they begin to concentrate, the alpha rhythm tends to disappear.[18] In other words, the cells are no longer active in unison; some become more active, others less so. What we have to do is to try to find why some cells become more active, others less so, when a given signal or stimulus is fed into the brain.

There is now suggestive evidence that, when, as a result of stimulation, two nerve-fibres act together, there are likely to be physiological or chemical changes within them so that they tend to be active together again more easily. Furthermore, when nerve-cells act together repeatedly, changes are brought about so that these cells are more likely to be active together again.[19] In other words it has been proposed that the brain becomes modified or moulded through experience, so that certain spatio-temporal patterns of nerve-cell activity tend to arise, resulting in the individual's thinking and behaving in certain ways rather than in others. Hebb[20] has proposed a detailed although entirely speculative theory in this field. In his view, repeated stimulation due to say, observance of an object, results in the formation of assemblies of cells in the association areas acting together. Even when stimulation has ceased, an assembly of cells may act as a closed circuit, so that structural changes in the cells can go on for a further limited period. In a series of such cell-assemblies we get what Hebb calls a 'phase sequence', or larger pattern of cell-activity in the association areas. Thus these patterns of cell-activity, which are brought into being by the stimulus, are in part determined by previous experience (compare Piaget's and Bartlett's schemata) thus allowing for such psychological phenomena as expectancy and set.

We may suggest, then, that the resulting spatio-temporal patterns of cell-activity in the brain at a given instant (and therefore the resulting thought and behaviour patterns) will be determined by:

(a) The signals being received. These include stimulation from the external environment, signals from within the body, and signals 'fed back' from within the brain itself.[21]

---

[18] But see Walter, W. Grey, *The Living Brain*. London: Duckworth, 1953.

[19] Young, J. Z., *Doubt and Certainty in Science*. Oxford: Oxford University Press, 1951. See also Eccles, J. C., *op. cit.*

[20] Hebb, D. O., *The Organisation of Behaviour*. London: Chapman and Hall, 1949.

[21] The body has many controlling devices of the 'feed back' type (e.g. avoiding danger, or adjusting the temperature of the body to protect it against cold). In general, it means that behaviour is scanned for results, and the success or failure of the result modifies future behaviour. This 'feed back' mechanism makes the body responsive to environmental changes, and enables it to achieve some stability of behaviour.

(b) The structure and functioning of the nerve-cells, which depend both upon genetic effects and past usage.

(c) In addition, Eccles admits the importance of the 'field of extraneous influence'. This corresponds roughly to what we call 'mind' or 'will', or 'conscious attention'. Burt,[22] too, after reviewing later work, likewise concludes that while (a) and (b) are *necessary* for conscious activities they are not the *sole* and *sufficient* conditions, and argues a case for some psychical influence at work as well. How such a force operates, and causes some cells to be active and others inactive, is unknown.

We are now in a position to suggest that memory depends upon the development and continuation of a group of cells acting together.[23] Thus in the process of remembering, there is a particular predisposing or triggering cell-activity which results in a tendency for a given pattern of cell-activity to be brought into being. Hence, as the pattern of cell-activity takes place in the brain, the thought is 'remembered' in the mind. Of course, the reproduction will differ somewhat from the original as was explained in Chapter 9. But our neurophysiological hypothesis helps us to explain this. The patterns of cell-activity evoked by the original stimulus will be affected by the structure and functioning of the brain cells as a whole, which in turn reflect inherited and constitutional factors on the one hand, and expectancy, set, interest, attitude, customs, and so forth, on the other.[24]

We may also suggest following Bugelski, another definition of learning, which, while being entirely speculative, would be more acceptable to some psychologists. Learning may be defined as the process of forming relatively permanent circuits (spatio-temporal patterns) of nerve cells brought about by the simultaneous activity of cells which will form the future circuits. But it must be stressed that in spite of the suggestions made in the preceding paragraphs, the precise neural basis of learning remains unknown. Learning certainly involves altered responses to stimuli, and since the central nervous system is made of elements interconnected through synapses,[25] and synaptic transmission is chemically mediated in the mammal, a variety of chemical as well as structural alterations are likely to participate in neural changes during learning.[26] This study of the structural and chemical bases of learning is in its infancy. Young[27] in discussing possible synaptic changes during learning argues that learning takes place

---

[22] Burt, C., 'Brain and Consciousness,' *Brit. J. Psychol.*, 1968, 59, 55–70.

[23] Eccles, J. C., *op. cit.*

[24] It will now be realised that hypotheses involving 'traces' were too simple to explain memory.

[25] Synapses are the areas where the processes of two neurons come very close to one another and nerve impulses pass one to the other. The fibres of the two neurons are intermeshed, but there does not appear to be any direct continuity.

[26] Thompson, R. F., *Foundations of Physiological Psychology*. London: Harper and Row, 1967, Ch. 17.

[27] Young, J. Z., *The Memory System of the Brain*. London: Oxford University Press, 1966.

by the inhibition of an unwanted nerve pathway—or, to put it another way round, it takes place by lowering the threshold of the nerve path that has been used. He is, however, unable to go much further by way of explanantion.

It is, however, instructive to note, with Hebb, that there may be a difference between learning in infancy and learning in later childhood. In the former period, learning may consist in the slow build-up of phase cycles, and in the later period, of combining phase cycles to form new patterns and concepts. The second process is rapid for the older child learns many of his associations rapidly, perhaps in a few trials, or in no trial at all.

Over the last few paragraphs we have seen that patterns of cell-activity in the brain are in part determined by previous knowledge and experience, thus allowing for hypothesis, expectancy and set. The latter have a considerable effect on what is learned. Existing patterns of cell-activity interact with the incoming stimuli from the environment (or from within the body), and perception of thinking is affected by the strengthening or weakening of the hypothesis or expectancy already in being. Only those incoming stimuli which strengthen an existing hypothesis or expectancy tend to be perceived, and if there is no perception there is no learning. Much teaching can pass by our pupils unless the subject matter presented (external stimuli) fits into an existing body of knowledge (cf. page (130c)). Furthermore social psychology suggests that the assimilation of new knowledge into old, i.e. the development of new patterns of cell-activity, is aided by a social atmosphere which is acceptable to the learner.

Evidence of the selectivity of the central nervous system in handing incoming stimuli is provided by Broadbent.[28] From work on selective listening he has suggested that the system is of limited capacity. Some kind of filtering or selection goes on, especially when the stimuli are complex. The factors that determine the selection seem to be the nature of the incoming stimuli, the likelihood of their occurrence, and conditions within the individual such as expectancy and drives.

We may note that much has been said and written in recent years about the resemblance between electronic computing machines and the human brain. This important topic cannot be dealt with in this book and interested readers should refer to the books listed below.[29] Note, however, that Sholl points out that there is no evidence at least, as yet, of an analogy between the way these machines work and the way the brain works (Sholl, *op. cit.*, Chapter 6).

Newer developments in the theory of brain functioning. Pribram[30] says that recent developments in the theory of brain functioning have not interfered

[28] Broadbent, D. E., *Perception and Communication*. London: Pergamon, 1958.
[29] Wiener, N., *Cybernetics*. New York: Wiley, 1948. Wiener, N., *The Human Use of Human Beings*. London: Eyre and Spottiswoode, 1950. Walter W. Grey, *op. cit.*
[30] Pribram, K. H., 'A Review of Theory in Physiological Psychology,' *Ann. Rev. Psychol.*, 1960, 11, 1–40.

with the trend started by Hebb, but they have made the brain even more active. Pribram, following others, divides the brain, as it were, into the *intrinsic* and *extrinsic* systems. The former is connected with centres in the thalamus which receive no direct input from external organs, while the extrinsic system is connected with centres in the thalamus that relay signals from the ears, eyes and other sense organs. The intrinsic system could thus be looked upon as the analogue of the computor's memory where information and 'strategies' for processing information, built up largely out of past experience, are stored, while the extrinsic corresponds to the classical notion of the brain as an emitter of motor outputs.

The intrinsic system consists of two portions. The anterior portion includes the frontal cortex, and Pribram believes that it mediates intentions, i.e. how a sequence of actions is to be executed. The confusion of intention following frontal lobe operation, which has already been noted, seems to result from an inability to arrange and utilise the information coming from a task in the absence of persistent and detailed external instructions.

The posterior portion of the system consists of centres in the thalamus that have connections to the parietal, temporal and occipital lobes. Lesions or damage within the fibre tracts of this portion interfere with the identification of objects and the acquisition of learning sets. Connected with this system there are, presumably, the neuronal patterns of representation for objects and events that underlie object perception, discrimination and concept formation.

Pribram proposes that when the signals from the external environment arrive, a search is made among the store of representations either for action systems (anterior part of the intrinsic system), or for objects, events, processes, etc. (posterior portion) to find a model for the input. If incongruity exists between input and representation then presumably control is shifted to the extrinsic system. The latter will either operate on the receptor mechanisms (e.g. more intensive use of eyes, ears, etc.) or on the environment, or on both, until the incongruities are resolved and the individual 'recognises', (understands), and so on. One way of resolving the incongruities must, of course, be by learning.

Chapter Twenty

STATISTICS

STATISTICS is a branch of mathematics which deals with the analysis of complex numerical data, that is, data influenced by several causes. Thus in educational psychology, statistical methods are used for organising numerical results such as course and examination marks, test scores, experimental records, and so forth, in order to bring out their representatives and significance. Note, however, that since these methods merely arrange data so as to reveal their underlying regularities, it is of the greatest importance that all measurements, marks and assessments, should be made as accurately as possible in the first instance. Again, in planning any experiment, or educational-psychological investigation, great care is needed if clear-cut answers are to be obtained to the problems being studied. In this chapter it is hoped to cover statistical methods applicable to the kind of problems normally encountered by teachers in school situations.[1]

Tabulation. A pupil's mark of, say, 7/10 is meaningless unless we can relate it to the marks of a larger group. Thus, when we arrange a set of marks in order we are said to tabulate them. The best way to do this is as follows. Write down in the column every possible mark, in, say descending order, and beside it put another column indicating the number of persons who got that mark, that is Frequency or F column. Go through the mark list, taking each mark in turn and putting a tally at the appropriate place in the F column. When the fifth tally is reached, indicate by drawing a line through the first four tallies. Add up the latter to get the total in the F column, and see that the sum of the F column agrees with N, the number of persons.

Mark		F
5	||	2
4	††† ||	7
3	††† ††† ††† |	16
2	††† ||||	9
1	|	1
		35

[1] See McIntosh, D. M., *Statistics for the Teacher.* London: Pergamon, 1963. A more advanced book has been provided by Lewis, D. G., *Statistical Methods in Education.* London: University of London Press Ltd., 1967.

Class Intervals. When there is a difference of more than about 15 marks between the first and last candidates, it is better to group the marks into a series of classes, e.g. 0–4, 5–9, 10–14, etc., or by percentages, 0–9 per cent and so on. The number of persons whose marks fall within the class-intervals is then tabulated. It is usually convenient to have between ten and fifteen class-intervals. One first finds the total range of marks and then works out a suitable class-interval accordingly. If the class-interval contains an odd number of marks, say, 0–4, 5–9, etc., then we regard all the marks in the interval as lying at the mid-points, namely, 2 and 7 respectively. Similarly class-intervals of 0–5, 6–11, etc., have for their mid-points $2\frac{1}{2}$, $8\frac{1}{2}$, etc., respectively. Make sure that there is a clear statement of the exact range included in the interval. Thus we cannot have 0–10, 10–20, etc., but rather 0–9, 10–19, and so on. If half marks have been awarded, then the class-intervals would read 0–$9\frac{1}{2}$, 10–$19\frac{1}{2}$, 20–$29\frac{1}{2}$, etc.

The Graphical Representation of Marks. We can often display a table of marks more clearly by showing them graphically. This can be done either by drawing a Histogram or a Frequency Polygon.

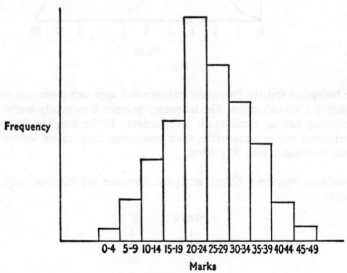

Fig. 18

Histogram. A series of rectangles or 'pillars' are drawn, side by side, standing on the horizontal axis, their width being equal to a mark or class-interval (Figure 18). The height of the rectangle along the vertical axis corresponds to the frequency, that is, the number of persons getting each mark, or the number within each class-interval.

Frequency Polygon. Frequencies on the vertical axis are plotted against marks (Figure 19), or mid-points of class-intervals on the horizontal axis, and the resultant points connected up by straight lines. As the class-intervals are made smaller, and the number of cases (N) gets larger, both

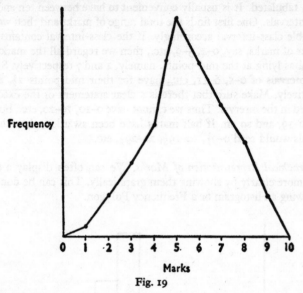

Fig. 19

the histogram and the frequency polygon will approach more and more closely to a smooth curve. The frequency polygon is especially useful for comparing two or more mark distributions. If the numbers in each distribution are not the same, then percentage frequencies instead of actual frequencies may be plotted.

Cumulative Frequency Graph or Ogive. Consider the following table of marks:

Marks	F
1	1
2	9
3	16
4	7
5	2
	35

Along the horizontal axis marks are again plotted, but along the vertical axis we have cumulative frequencies (Figure 20). Thus the first point is

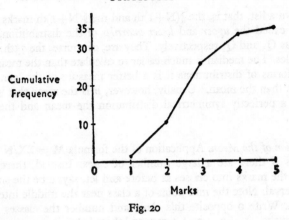

Fig. 20

plotted as mark 1, frequency 1; the second point is plotted as mark 2, cumulative frequency 10; the third point as mark 3, cumulative frequency 26; and so on. The vertical coordinate of the last point is 35. The uses of this cumulative frequency graph or ogive,[2] are brought out later in this chapter.

Frequency Distribution Curves. Graphical distributions of some of the measurements made in education tend to approximate to the normal curve or normal frequency distribution. This was discussed in Chapter 3, as were some of the asymmetrical or skewed types of distributions, which we sometimes deliberately set out to obtain. School examination marks, however, often show very irregular or skewed distributions. A certain amount of departure from a normal curve must be expected from a class of 30–40 pupils or less, but larger irregularities usually indicate that the questions set were too easy or too difficult for the class, or that the marking system was inefficient.

Averages and Other Measures of 'Central Tendency'. There are two forms of the average that we commonly use in statistics in educational psychology, the *mean* and the *median*. If X is my mark or score, and N the number of subjects, the mean mark is $\Sigma X/N$, where ΣX stands for the sum of all the X's. The median, which is usually a close approximation to the mean, may be defined as the middle point, or central value of the variable, when the scores are ranged in order of merit; it is in effect, the mark half-way down the list. When N is an odd number, say, 51, the median is the 26th highest mark since it has 25 marks above and below it. Thus the median is the $(N+1)/2$th mark. The marks one-quarter and three-quarters of the

---

[2] Note that when the origin is not zero on the horizontal scale, it should be placed at the mid-point of the class-interval next below the lowest interval in which there are any scores.

way down a list, that is, the $\frac{1}{4}(N+1)$th and the $\frac{3}{4}(N+1)$th marks from the top, are called the *upper* and *lower quartiles* of the distribution, and are written as Q_3 and Q_1 respectively. They are, of course, the 75th and 25th percentiles. The median is much easier to calculate than the mean, and in certain forms of distributions it is a better measure of the 'general run' of scores than the mean.[3] Usually, however, it is the mean that we calculate. In a perfectly symmetrical distribution the mean and the median coincide.

Calculation of the Mean. Application of the formula $M = \Sigma X/N$ becomes laborious if there are a large number of cases. Instead, therefore, we tabulate the marks into classes as before and let, say, c be the size of the class-interval. Note the mid-point of a class near the middle interval and call it A. Write 0 opposite this class, and number the classes above it consecutively $+1, +2, +3, +4$, etc., and those below it $-1, -2, -3, -4$, etc., as shown:

Mark	F	x	Fx	Fx²
20–19	2	+4	8	32
18–17	4	+3	12	36
16–15	4	+2	8	16
14–13	5	+1	5	5
			33	
12–11	7	0	0	0
10–9	6	−1	−6	6
8–7	3	−2	−6	12
6–5	4	−3	−12	36
4–3	4	−4	−16	64
2–1	1	−5	−5	25
	40		−45	232

This gives the column headed x. Now work out the value of Fx in each case and sum. Then:

$$\text{Mean (M)} = \frac{c\Sigma Fx}{N} + A$$

$$= 2 \times \frac{(-12)}{40} + 11 \cdot 5 = -0 \cdot 6 + 11 \cdot 5$$

$$= 10 \cdot 9$$

[3] See Yule, G. U., and Kendall, M. G., *An Introduction to the Theory of Statistics.* London: Griffin, 1948, Ch. 7.

Measures of Dispersion. The significance of a mark cannot be judged until we know not only the mean or median, but also the scatter, spread, dispersion, or range of marks. The total range of marks is not a good measure of scatter as it depends merely on the highest and lowest marks, and not on the spread of marks among the majority of the candidates. A better measure is the distance between the quartiles (Q_3 and Q_1), for it shows the range of marks obtained by the middle half of the group. Half of this is called the *semi-interquartile range*, and is denoted by Q, the value of Q being about one-eighth the total range of marks.

The most commonly used measure of spread (still assuming an approximately normal distribution of marks) is the *Standard Deviation*. This is defined as the square root of the mean of all the squares of all deviations, these deviations being measured from the means of the marks or observations. The standard deviation is always denoted by σ.

$$\sigma = \sqrt{\frac{\Sigma(M-X)^2}{N}}$$

where X is any mark and M the mean of the marks. In practice we tabulate the marks as before, and assume once again an arbitrary mean. Then:

$$\sigma = c\sqrt{\frac{\Sigma(Fx)^2}{N} - \left(\frac{\Sigma Fx}{N}\right)^2}$$

Thus in our example where we calculated the mean:

$$\sigma = 2\sqrt{\frac{232}{40} - \left(\frac{-12}{40}\right)^2}$$
$$= 2\sqrt{5 \cdot 8 - \cdot 09} = 4 \cdot 78$$

Significance of the Standard Deviation. A normal distribution has a certain algebraic formulation which connects F, the frequency of the mark, with X the mark. In this formula σ is a constant, so that if we know σ, we can obtain the proportion of pupils who obtain a definite mark. For example, $2 \cdot 5$ per cent have marks which are $1 \cdot 96\sigma$ units above the mean, and another $2 \cdot 5$ per cent have marks $1 \cdot 96\sigma$ below. Similarly, about $\frac{1}{2}$ per cent have scores $2 \cdot 58\sigma$ units above the mean, and $\frac{1}{2}$ per cent have scores $2 \cdot 58\sigma$ below. Indeed, almost all scores fall within the total range of 3σ to -3σ.

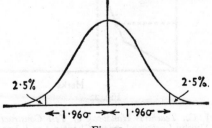

$2 \cdot 5\%$ $2 \cdot 5\%$.

← $1 \cdot 96\sigma$ →←$1 \cdot 96\sigma$ →

Fig. 21

From 'normal probability integral tables' which are given in most text books on statistics, we can obtain the percentages or proportions with other levels of scores (see Figure 21).

The Conversion of Marks. It often happens that tests with known means and standard deviations are not available, and we have to use tests or examinations which we devise ourselves. When this is so, we cannot directly compare the marks on, say, a problem arithmetic test, with marks obtained on a test of mechanical arithmetic, unless both have been devised to yield the same mean and the same standard deviation—which is very unlikely. Thus we cannot say if 70 per cent on the problem arithmetic is as good as, say, 85 per cent on the mechanical paper. In order to overcome this difficulty, we convert the raw marks obtained on the tests into two sets of scores which do have the same mean and standard deviation. The simplest way of doing this, if our two sets of marks are normally distributed, is to assume first some arbitrary mean of, say, 50, and an arbitrary standard deviation of, say, 15. The new scores are then given by:

$$\frac{(\text{Raw Score} - \text{Mean of Raw Scores})}{\text{Standard Deviation of Raw Scores}} \times 15 + 50$$

Thus each of our marks on the problem arithmetic test is converted in terms of a scale which ranges from about 10 up to 90, and which has a mean of 50. We can then do the same with the marks on the mechanical arithmetic test so that we finish with two sets of marks which are directly comparable. If we wish, we can choose an arbitrary mean of 100 and a standard deviation of 15; indeed, we can convert both sets of raw scores into any scales we select.[4]

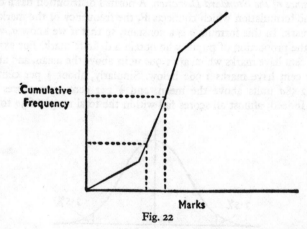

Fig. 22

[4] See Daniels, J. C., *Teachers' Handbook of Test Construction, Marking and Records*. London: Crosby Lockwood, 1949, Chapter 5 and Appendix 3.

When the distribution of raw scores does not approximate to a normal curve, we may proceed as follows. Suppose we wish to compare marks obtained in Arithmetic and English. First, draw a cumulative frequency curve for the arithmetic marks. Draw horizontal lines through the points on the vertical scale representing 1, 10, 25, 50, 75, 90 and 99 per cent of N, to cut the curve. Thus the marks corresponding to the 1st, 10th, 25th, 50th, 75th, 90th, and 99th percentiles are obtained (Figure 22).

Secondly, having obtained the marks corresponding to the above percentiles in Arithmetic and English, plot these marks on another graph and join up the points by means of a straight line or smoothed curve. Then,

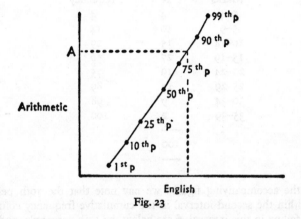

Fig. 23

to find the English mark corresponding to any Arithmetic mark A, draw through A a horizontal line to cut the curve, and from this point of intersection drop a vertical line to the horizontal axis (Figure 23).

Either method may, of course, be extended so that we can compare the raw marks obtained in three or any number of tests.

Addition of Marks. From what has been said in the previous section it is obvious that marks in different subjects should not be added to yield a sum if the means and standard deviations of the raw scores differ widely. If, for example, it is required to add together marks in ten subjects to get a 'class position', then, provided each set of marks is more or less normally distributed, we ought first to convert each set of marks before the scores are added to get totals. Teachers do not do this, nor can they be expected to do so on account of the labour involved. Nevertheless, they should realise that a wrong answer is obtained by adding raw scores together unless the means and standard deviations for the tests are roughly the same. In many important public examinations, marks are converted to a common scale before they are added.

Calculation of Percentiles. It was seen in Chapter 3 that when percentiles are used, a set of marks is divided up into hundredths. Thus the 60th percentile is the mark obtained by the person who is better than 60 per cent of the group, and equal to, or poorer than, the mark obtained by 40 per cent of the group. It is the $\frac{6}{10}(N+1)$th mark from the bottom. We can read off the mark corresponding to a given percentile from a cumulative frequency graph, or else calculate it by interpolation, as follows:

Marks	N	Cumulative Frequency
0–4	4	4
5–9	10	14
10–14	15	29
15–19	27	56
20–24	19	75
25–29	14	89
30–34	9	98
35–39	2	100
	100	

From the accompanying figures we nay note that the 10th percentile falls within the second interval in the cumulative frequency column. Of the 10 falling in this interval, 6 are below the 10th percentile, and 4 at or above the percentile. Thus:

Mark falling at the 10th percentile: $5 + \left(\frac{6}{10} \times 5\right) = 8 \cdot 0$

Mark falling at the 20th percentile: $10 + \left(\frac{6}{15} \times 5\right) = 12 \cdot 0$

Similarly, any other mark corresponding to a given percentile may be calculated.

Correlation Coefficient. The meaning of the term correlation coefficient has already been discussed in Chapter 1. Two of the methods commonly used for calculating it are now described.

Spearman Rank Correlation Coefficient. Suppose that pupils are arranged in order of merit either by means of marks, or some other form of assessment, the first number being 1, the second number 2, and so on. They are then said to be *ranked*. In the accompanying example we have ranked six pupils for order of merit in two subjects, with a view to calculating the Spearman Rank Correlation Coefficient between the subjects.

Pupil	Order of Merit in Subject 1	Order of Merit in Subject 2	Difference in rank (d)	Difference in rank squared (d²)
a	1	3	−2	4
b	2	1	1	1
c	3	4	−1	1
d	4	6	−2	4
e	5	2	3	9
f	6	5	1	1
				20

Then the rank correlation coefficient is given by:

$$\rho = 1 - \frac{6\Sigma d^2}{N(N^2-1)} = 1 - \frac{6\times 20}{6\times 35} = \cdot 43$$

If, when making out the rank order of merit, we fill, say, the 6th place, but find that the next two pupils are of equal merit (that is they have equal marks or assessments), we rank each of the latter as $7\frac{1}{2}$ and the next pupil as 9. If, after filling the 6th place we had found three pupils of equal merit, then each of these is ranked as 8 and the next as 10. The rank correlation coefficient is easy to calculate and does not take much time. It is suitable for most school purposes, but in a more thorough investigation it is preferable to calculate the product moment correlation.

Product Moment Correlation Coefficient. Suppose that we have the scores obtained by 40 pupils on Test A and Test B. By 'tallying' the scores into cells in Table 2 we obtain a *scatter diagram* for these pairs of scores. The column f to the right of the table is the frequency distribution of Test B, and the usual procedure for calculating the mean and standard deviation is followed. Similarly the row f at the bottom of the table gives the frequency distribution of Test A, together with the calculations of its mean and standard deviation. The xy value for each cell is now calculated and inserted in each cell and a ring placed around it. Care must be exercised over the signs. Some values of x and y are negative, so that the value of xy may be positive, negative, or zero. These xy values are then multiplied by the frequency (the number of tallies) within the cell, and summed. The product moment correlation coefficient, indicated by r, is then calculated as follows:

Table 2

Test A

Test B	10	9	8	7	6	5	4	3	2	1	0	f	y	fy	fy²
20 – 19	'(20)	'(16)		'(8)								3	+4	12	48
18 – 17			"(18)		'(3)							3	+3	9	27
16 – 15					'(2)	III						4	+2	8	16
14 – 13				'(2)			"(-2)	"(-4)				5	+1	5	5
12 – 11				"		IIII	I	"				9	0	0	0
10 – 9						II	'(2)		"(12)			6	-1	-6	6
8 – 7						I	"(8)	'(6)				4	-2	-8	16
6 – 5								"(18)	"(24)			4	-3	-12	36
4 – 3										"(40)		2	-4	-8	32
f	1	1	2	4	2	10	3	7	3	5	2	40			
x	+5	+4	+3	+2	+1	0	-1	-2	-3	-4	-5				
fx	5	4	6	8	2	0	-3	-14	-9	-20	-10				
fx²	25	16	18	16	2	0	3	28	27	80	50				

1. $\Sigma fx = -31$ $\qquad\qquad$ $\Sigma fy = 0$
$\Sigma fx^2 = 265$ $\qquad\qquad$ $\Sigma fy^2 = 186$

2. $\dfrac{\Sigma fx}{N} = \dfrac{-31}{40} = -\cdot775$ $\qquad\qquad$ $\dfrac{\Sigma fy}{N} = \dfrac{0}{40} = 0$

3. $\left(\dfrac{\Sigma fx}{N}\right)^2 = (-\cdot775)^2 = \cdot601$ $\qquad\qquad$ $\left(\dfrac{\Sigma fy}{N}\right)^2 = 0$

4. $\left(\dfrac{\Sigma fx}{N}\right)\left(\dfrac{\Sigma fy}{N}\right) = 0$

5. $\Sigma xy = 173$

6. $\sigma_x = \sqrt{\dfrac{\Sigma fx^2}{N} - \left(\dfrac{\Sigma fx}{N}\right)^2}$ $\qquad\qquad$ $\sigma_y = \sqrt{\dfrac{\Sigma fy^2}{N} - \left(\dfrac{\Sigma fy}{N}\right)^2}$

$= \sqrt{\dfrac{265}{40} - \cdot601}$ $\qquad\qquad$ $= \sqrt{\dfrac{186}{40} - 0}$

$= 2\cdot455$ $\qquad\qquad\qquad$ $= 2\cdot156$

7. $r = \dfrac{\dfrac{\Sigma xy}{N} - \left(\dfrac{\Sigma fx}{N}\right)\left(\dfrac{\Sigma fy}{N}\right)}{\sigma_x \times \sigma_y}$ $\qquad = \dfrac{\dfrac{173}{40} - 0}{2\cdot455 \times 2\cdot156} = \cdot817$

The Interpretation of a Correlation Coefficient. It is necessary to repeat a warning, given in Chapter 1, that great care must be exercised in interpreting a correlation coefficient. Because two variables, say performance at Latin and Greek, correlate highly, it does not mean that one causes the other. There is certainly a connection between the variables but it might be that a third agent, high intelligence, is causing a high level of performance in both subjects. When significant correlation coefficients are found, there is no doubt that the variables are causally related, but it is not possible to tell the actual form of the connection from the correlation coefficient alone.

Standard Error. If we wished to find the mean height of all 10-year-old boys in the British Isles it would be impossible to measure all such children, but we could measure, say, 100 groups each containing 30 such boys. The means so obtained would vary somewhat, and would cluster around the *true mean* (obtainable only if the whole population is measured) and be distributed normally. Thus every measurement we make (mean, standard deviation, correlation coefficient, involving height, intelligence, or any other characteristic) which is based on a random sample, is likely to be in error to a greater or lesser extent. Though we cannot determine the true mean, nor the amount of error from measurements of a sample—or several samples—of the population, we can assess the probable limits of error by calculating what is called the Standard Error of the Measurement.

Standard Error (S.E.) of a Mean. Let the mean of a set of marks obtained by N pupils be M, and let their standard deviation be σ. Then the S.E. of the mean is given by $\sigma/\sqrt{N}$. Thus, almost all values of the mean obtained from samples of similar children will lie between the limits $M \pm 3\sigma/\sqrt{N}$, and so it is almost certain that the true mean will fall between these limits. Further, there are 95 chances out of 100 that the true mean will fall between $M \pm 1 \cdot 96\sigma/\sqrt{N}$, and 99 chances out of 100 that the mean will fall between $M \pm 2 \cdot 58\sigma/\sqrt{N}$. The limits equal to $1 \cdot 96$ and $2 \cdot 58$ times the S.E. on either side of the mean are called the *confidence* or *fiducial* limits, since they show the amount of confidence we can place in our mean.

Example. A random sample of 100 children took a test and their scores yielded a mean of 50 and a Standard Deviation of 10.

$$S.E. = 10/\sqrt{100} = 1 \cdot 0$$

There are thus 95 chances in 100 that the true mean for all similar samples will fall between $48 \cdot 04$ and $51 \cdot 96$.

Standard Error of a Correlation Coefficient. The Standard Error of a product moment correlation coefficient is given by,[5] $S.E. = \dfrac{1-r^2}{\sqrt{N}}$.

In a normal distribution of sample correlation coefficients, $2\frac{1}{2}$ per cent of the sample would exceed 1·96 times the standard error, and $\frac{1}{2}$ per cent would exceed 2·58 times the standard error. In other words, if our value of r is 1·96 or 2·58 times its standard error, then the likelihood of r of this size occurring by chance is 1 in 20, and 1 in 100 respectively.[6] That is, our value of r would be *significant* at the 5 per cent and 1 per cent level respectively. If, however, our value of r is less than 1·96 times the standard error, it could have occurred more often than 5 times in 100 by chance, and we usually reject it in our experiments in educational psycholology. Thus to test the significance of r, we divide it by its standard error.

Example. In a random sample of 100 children a correlation coefficient of 0·2 was obtained. Is this value of r significant?

$$S.E. = \frac{1-\cdot04}{10} = \cdot096$$

Thus the value of r is significant at the 5 per cent level but not at the 1 per cent level, since ·2/·096 = 2·08 approximately.

The Standard Error of the Spearman Rank Correlation Coefficient is given approximately by, $S.E. = \dfrac{1\cdot05(1-\rho^2)}{\sqrt{N}}$.

A correlation coefficient should always be quoted together with its standard error, in order to see whether the coefficient is significant, or whether a correlation of that size could have arisen more than 5 times in 100 by chance.

The Reliability of the Difference Between Means. Consider two groups, the first of which obtained a mean mark of M_1, and a standard deviation of σ_1, on some test or examination, and the second group obtained a mean mark of M_2, and a standard deviation of σ_2 on the same test. In order to find whether the difference between the means is significant, we first find the S.E. of the difference between the means. If N_1+N_2 is greater than 30 this is given by:

$$S.E._{\text{diff.}} = \sqrt{\frac{\sigma_1{}^2}{N_1} + \frac{\sigma_2{}^2}{N_2}}$$

[5] This formula is suitable only for moderate values of r and for a large population. If r is large or N is small, readers should consult a statistical textbook. In the following pages when we deal with the significance of differences it is assumed that the numbers involved are fairly large. If this is not so the readers should again consult a standard textbook.

[6] Compare Figure 22. Five per cent of the coefficients would lie outside the limits $\pm 1\cdot96 \times S.E.$, and one per cent outside the limits $\pm 2\cdot58 \times S.E.$

where N_1 is the number of cases in the first group and N_2 the number in the second. If, now, the difference between the means (i.e. $M_1 - M_2$) is divided by the S.E.$_{\text{diff.}}$, we can interpret the ratio by reference to the normal probability integral tables and see if the ratio is significant.

If the means are in some way correlated, as when the same group takes tests in Arithmetic and English, or takes the same test before and after coaching, the S.E.$_{\text{diff.}}$ is given by:

$$\sqrt{\frac{1}{N}\left(\sigma_1{}^2 + \sigma_2{}^2 - 2r\sigma_1\sigma_2\right)}$$

where r is the correlation between the test results. The difference between the means is then divided by the S.E.$_{\text{diff.}}$ as before in order to assess its significance.

Standard Error of a Percentage and of the Difference between Percentages. If, instead of the actual numbers of pupils, or marks, we are given percentages, the standard error of a percentage, p, is $\sqrt{\dfrac{pq}{N}}$, where $q = 100 - p$, provided N is greater than 100, and neither p nor q less than 10.

Example. In a school of 320 pupils, 20 per cent come to shool on bicycles. Is this a reliable percentage for all similar pupils?

$$\text{S.E.} = \sqrt{\frac{20 \times 80}{320}} = 2 \cdot 2$$

Thus the true percentage for all similar pupils will lie between $20 \pm (3 \times 2 \cdot 2)$ per cent, that is between $26 \cdot 6$ and $13 \cdot 4$ per cent. The standard error of a difference between two percentages obtained from two unrelated groups is given by:

$$\sqrt{\frac{p_1 q_1}{N_1} + \frac{p_2 q_2}{N_2}}$$

The Construction of an Attitude Test. The method referred to in Chapter 4, which will now be described, is much the same as that of Thurstone.[7] Other techniques jave been devised by Likert,[8] also Eysenck and Crown,[9] but Thurstone's method is the easiest for a beginner and generally yields equally good results. Suppose we wish to devise an attitude test which will assess the attitude of our pupils to some school-subject. At least sixty statements, for and against the issue, are collected from pupils' own written or oral opinions, or made up. These should be short and unambiguous,

[7] Thurstone, L. L., and Chave, E., *The Measurement of Attitude.* Chicago: University of Chicago Press, 1929.

[8] Likert, R., 'A Technique for the Measurement of Attitudes,' *Arch. Psychol.*, 1932, 22, No. 140.

[9] Eysenck, H. J., and Crown, S., 'An Experimental Study in Opinion-Attitude Methodology,' *Int. J. Opinion Attitude Research*, 1949, 3, 47–86.

varied in content, should deal with the whole range of points of view and should describe concrete behaviour towards the subject as far as possible. Each statement is then written on a separate postcard.

About twenty judges are asked to sort these cards independently. They are placed, first, into three piles, and then into nine. Their own attitude to the subject does not matter. Those statements which, in a judge's view, reflect strong disapproval of the subject (regardless of his own personal attitude to the subject), are put in his pile 9, while pile 1 receives statements which represent strong approval.

A cumulative frequency graph is drawn for each statement (Figure 24). For example, suppose a certain statement is sorted as follows:

Pile	Number of judges putting into given pile.
9	
8	2
7	3
6	7
5	5
4	2
3	1
2	
1	

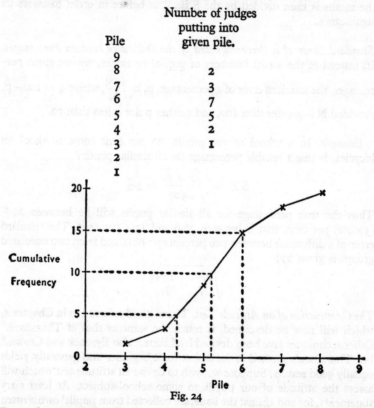

Fig. 24

From the cumulative frequency graph the pile values corresponding to the 5th, 10th, and 15th judges are 4·3, 5·2, 6·0. The *scale value* is then 5·2, and Q, the quartile range (a measure of disagreement among the judges), is 1·7.

Twenty to thirty statements are selected for the final attitude scale which appear varied in content, have small Q's and whose scale values cover the whole range from about 1·3 to 8·7 as evenly as possible. These statements are arranged in random order. Pupils tick the statements with which they agree, and the mean scale value of those they have ticked is their score for the attitude. The reliability of the test can be obtained by giving it a second time, say a week later. Worth while results from attitude tests can hardly be expected from children until they have reached a mental and educational age of about 12 years. It is essential, too, that the topic should be one about which they have definite ideas, and one which is of interest and significance to the testees.

More recently Adams[10] has given suggestions for a simple, uncomplicated, and effective way of measuring attitudes, that might prove useful in the classroom.

Standardised Scores on Intelligence and other Tests.[11] In Chapter 3 we stated a person's standing on a test is now often expressed in terms of standard scores. Raw scores are first obtained for a specific group in a truly representative population as described on page 42. Percentiles are then obtained from raw scores as indicated on page 45. Thus we may find that on a certain test a raw score of 69 falls at the 84th percentile. The percentiles are then converted into standard scores on a scale having $M = 100$, $\sigma = 15$. From 'normal probability integral tables' we know that a mark at the 84th percentile will correspond to a standard score of 115 (assuming the scale to have $M = 100$, $\sigma = 15$). Thus a raw score of 69 is converted into a scaled score of 115. Similarly for any other raw score.

The standard score obtained from an intelligence test is broadly the equivalent of a Binet IQ, and indeed is termed the person's IQ, yet it is not obtained from a prior calculation of mental age. It is often termed a 'deviation IQ' and this prevents confusion.

In the new revision of the Binet Scale (p. 38) a deviation is employed. In neither W.A.I.S. nor W.I.S.C. (p. 38) is IQ calculated from mental age. Both scales consist of a number of Verbal and Performance subtests. In W.I.S.C., raw scores on each subtest are first converted into scaled scores within the child's own age group; tables of such scaled scores being provided for four-monthly intervals. The conversion was carried out by the method given on p. 296, when the tables were drawn up, and the scaled scores yield $M = 10$, S.D. $= 3$. Scaled scores are then added and the total converted into a deviation IQ. Almost exactly the same procedure is followed in W.A.I.S. In either scale one can get a Verbal IQ and a Performance IQ by considering scores from the Verbal and Performance subtests separately, and a Full Scale IQ from the Verbal and Performance IQ.

[10] Adams, R. S., 'A Further Approach to Attitude Sealing,' *Brit. J. Educ. Psychol.*, 1962, 32, 201–208.
[11] See Pidgeon, D. A., 'The Design, Construction and Use of Standardized Tests—Part I,' *Educational Research*, 1961, 3, 89–99.

LIST OF SELECTED BOOKS

THE short bibliography given below is in addition to the many books and articles listed in the footnotes. Readers should note that new editions of the books listed below will become available from time to time, and they should consult the latest edition when possible.

ANASTASI, A. *Psychological Testing*. New York: Macmillan. 3rd Ed., 1968.

ANTHONY, E. J. Jean Piaget and Child Psychiatry. *Brit J. Med. Psychol.*, 1956, 29, 20–34.

BELL, J. E. *Projective Techniques*. London: Longmans, Green, 1949.

BOWLEY, A. H. *Modern Child Psychology*. London: Hutchinson's University Library, 1948.

BREARLEY, M. and HITCHFIELD, E. *A Teacher's Guide to Reading Piaget*. London: Routledge and Kegan Paul, 1966.

BURT, C. *Mental and Scholastic Tests*. London: Staples Press. Revised Ed., 1947.

BURT, C. *The Causes and Treatment of Backwardness*. London: University of London Press Ltd. 4th Ed., 1963.

BURT, C. The Evidence for the Concept of Intelligence. *Brit. J. Educ. Psychol.*, 1955, 25, 158–177.

CATTELL, R. B. *An Introduction to Personality Study*. London: Hutchinson's University Library, 1950.

CATTELL, R. B. *The Scientific Analysis of Personality*. London: Penguin Books, 1965.

CONNELL, R. W. *The Child's Construction of Politics*. Melbourne: Melbourne University Press, 1971.

CRONBACH, L. J. *Essentials of Psychological Testing*. New York: Harper Row. 2nd Ed., 1960.

DALE, R. R. *Mixed or Single-Sex Schools*. London: Routledge and Kegan Paul, 1969.

DANIELS, J. C. *Statistical Methods in Educational Research*. University of Nottingham Institute of Education, 1953.

ERICKSON, E. H. *Identity: Youth and Crisis*. London: Faber, 1968.

EYSENCK, H. J. and EYSENCK, S. B. G. *Personality Structure and Measurements*. London: Routledge and Kegan Paul, 1969.

FENTON, N. *Mental Hygiene in School Practice*. Oxford: University Press, 1949.

FERGUSON, T. *The Young Delinquent in his Social Setting*. London: Oxford University Press, 1952.

FLEMING, C. M. *Adolescence*. London: Routledge and Kegan Paul, 1948.

FURTH, H. G., *Piaget and Knowledge*. London: Prentice-Hall, 1969.

GARRETT, H. E. *Statistics in Psychology and Education*. London: Longmans, Green. 4th Ed., 1953.

GUILFORD, J. P. *Psychometric Methods*. London: McGraw-Hill. 2nd Ed., 1954.

HEBB, D. O. *A Textbook of Psychology*. London: Saunders, 1958.

HEIM, A. W. *The Appraisal of Intelligence*. London: Methuen, 1954.

ISAACS, S. *Intellectual Growth in Young Children*. London: Routledge, 1930.

ISAACS, S. *Social Development in Young Children*. London: Routledge, 1933.

JERSILD, A. T. *Child Psychology*. London: Staples Press. 6th Ed., 1969.

JERSILD, A. T. *The Psychology of Adolescence*. London: Collier-Macmillan. 2nd Ed. 1963.

KNIGHT, R. *Intelligence and Intelligence Tests*. London: Methuen. 4th Ed., 1949.

KNIGHT, R. and KNIGHT, M. *A Modern Introduction to Psychology*. London: University Tutorial Press. 3rd Ed., 1952.

MCINTOSH, D. M. & ASSOCIATES. *The Scaling of Teachers' Marks and Estimates*. London: Oliver and Boyd, 1949.

MATHER, D. R., FRANCE, N. and SARE, G. T. *The Certificate of Secondary Education: A Handbook for Moderators*. London: Collins, 1965.

MUNN, N. L. *The Evolution and Growth of Human Behaviour*. London: Harrap. 2nd Ed., 1965.

MUSGROVE, F. *Youth and the Social Order*. London: Routledge and Kegan Paul, 1964.

MUSSEN, P. H., CONGER, J. J. and KAGAN, J. *Child Development and Personality*. London: Harper Row. 2nd Ed., 1963.

PEEL, E. A. *The Psychological Basis of Education*. London: Oliver and Boyd, 1956.

PIAGET, J. *The Language and Thought of the Child*. London: Kegan Paul, Trench, Trübner, 1926.

PIAGET, J. *The Child's Conception of the World*. London: Kegan Paul, Trench, Trübner, 1929.

PIAGET, J. *The Psychology of Intelligence*. London: Routledge and Kegan Paul, 1950.

SODDY, K. (Editor). *Mental Health and Infant Development*. London: Routledge and Kegan Paul, 1955.

SUMNER, W. L. *Statistics in School*. Oxford: Basil Blackwell. 2nd Ed., 1950.

THOMSON, G. H. *How to Calculate Correlations*. London: Harrap. Revised Ed., 1947.

THOMSON, G. H. *The Factorial Analysis of Human Ability*. London: University of London Press Ltd. 5th Ed., 1951.

THYNE, J. M. *The Psychology of Learning and Techniques of Teaching*. London: University of London Press Ltd., 1963.

VALENTINE, C. W. *The Difficult Child and the Problem of Discipline.* London: Methuen. 4th Ed., 1947.

VALENTINE, C. W. *Intelligence Tests for Children.* London: Methuen. 6th Ed., 1958.

VALENTINE, C. W. *Introduction to Experimental Psychology.* London: University Tutorial Press. 5th Ed., 1953.

WALL, W. D. *The Adolescent Child.* London: Methuen, 1948.

WOODWORTH, R. S. *Contemporary Schools of Psychology.* London: Methuen. 8th Ed., 1949.

INDEX TO NAMES

INDEX TO SUBJECTS